A CHRONOLOGY OF MAJOR LEAGUE BASEBALL RECORDS

12/91

To: Freddie

May you enjoy fruitful
hours of baseball "Trivia"!

Love,
the baseball freaks
from Boston

Also by John A. Mercurio

**A CHRONOLOGY OF
BOSTON RED SOX RECORDS**

**A CHRONOLOGY OF
NEW YORK YANKEE RECORDS**

A CHRONOLOGY OF
MAJOR
LEAGUE
BASEBALL
RECORDS

JOHN A. MERCURIO

PERENNIAL LIBRARY

HARPER & ROW, PUBLISHERS, NEW YORK

Cambridge, Philadelphia, San Francisco
London, Mexico City, São Paulo, Singapore, Sydney

The photographs on pp. 7, 18, 19, 28, 29, 35, 39, 45, 52, 85, 103, 109, 116, 139, 148, 149, 158, 162, and 163 appear courtesy of the National Baseball Hall of Fame and Museum, Inc., Cooperstown, N.Y.

FIRST EDITION

Designer: Joan Greenfield

LIBRARY OF CONGRESS CATALOG CARD NUMBER: 88-45627

ISBN: 0-06-096243-7

89 90 91 92 93 DT/MPC 10 9 8 7 6 5 4 3 2 1

DEDICATION

To my parents, John and Celia Mercurio, immigrants from Italy, who taught me the meaning of hard work and determination.

To my wife, Jean, who put up with my typing, seven days a week for the last eight years.

To my sons and daughter, Michael, Andrew and Donna, of whom I am so very proud.

To my most beautiful grandchildren Christopher and Johnathan, whom I love dearly.

To my Aunt ZiZi, who was crippled at birth yet never lost her smile.

To my sisters and brothers, Ann, Connie, Tess, Angelo, and Joe. They were a constant source of encouragement.

To Tom and Mildred Miggins, the dearest and most loving in-laws I have ever known.

And to all of my friends and relatives. They told me this day would come.

CONTENTS

PROLOGUE

The main objective of this book is to preserve baseball records. Typical record books eliminate old records when new ones are created. In direct contrast, this book includes every season and career record starting in the first year of organized baseball, 1876, and adds each new record with the date it was established. Thus a complete history of records is now, for the first time, preserved in batting, pitching and fielding. Rookie and manager records are also included.

All records are in chronological order, making it easy to see who broke whose record, how long each mark lasted before it was broken, and which records have never been broken. The resulting lists represent a complete history of each record category.

Moreover, the number of records established by each player can be determined, and this never before available information is presented as a listed summary of Top Record Producers. Now you can see how many records Babe Ruth, Ty Cobb, and any other player have established.

The second objective of this book is to fill a void. Baseball still does not have an "official" record book even though our national pastime has been played for more than 100 years. What other book could be more qualified to be called "official" than this one, which includes every season and career record ever created?

Anything you ever wanted to know about baseball records is now at your fingertips.

HOW TO USE THIS BOOK

UNDERSTANDING THE CHRONOLOGY LISTS

The following is an example of the Major League season home run record.

Most Home Runs

1876	George Hall, Phi, NL	5
1879	Charley Jones, Bos, NL	9
1883	Harry Stovey, Phi, AA	14
1884	Ned Williamson, Chi, NL	27
1919	Babe Ruth, Bos, AL	29
1920	Babe Ruth, NY, AL	54
1921	Babe Ruth, NY, AL	59
1927	Babe Ruth, NY, AL	60
1961	**Roger Maris, NY, AL**	**61**

The above represents the complete history of the Major League season home run record. The first home run champion was George Hall, who played for Philadelphia in the National League. Because of the dead ball used in his era, not many home runs were hit and Hall's five round-trippers was the most in the first year of baseball.

Three years later, Charley Jones became the new home run king by hitting nine home runs, and his mark stood until 1883 when Harry Stovey of Philadelphia in the American Association (also a Major League) became the first player to hit double figures in home runs. But Stovey's record only lasted one year as Ned Williamson astounded the baseball world by blasting 27 home runs (and this still the dead ball era!).

Williamson's achievement was so great it lasted 35 years and took a fellow by the name of Babe Ruth to break it. The Babe dominated the record book and broke his own marks several times until Roger Maris took the title in 1961. The last player in the chronology list is always the present record holder.

TEAMS PLAYERS ARE LISTED WITH

In the lists of career records, the team name following each player represents the club with which the record setter played the most games. For season records, the team shown following the player is the team with which the record was set.

SUMMARIES

At the conclusion of each division grouping, summaries are made in the form of two lists. One shows the players with the greatest number of records set. The other represents the most outstanding record producers by showing a combined total of the number of years their records have lasted.

As one might imagine, players who were active in the earliest years of baseball record keeping often have a disproportionate number of records produced. For this reason, the Most Outstanding Producers list is in most cases the more meaningful of the two summaries, since it reflects the truly great record setters based on the *longevity* of their records. All records are calculated through the 1988 season.

THE MAJOR LEAGUE COLUMN

In some cases, the figures shown in the National and American League columns will not be the same as the figure seen as a Major League record. This is due to the fact that some players have split time between the two leagues, or played in other major leagues such as the American Association, the Players League or the Federal League, and those stats must be included as part of a Major League record.

BASES ON BALLS

The National and Major League records for bases on balls earned and bases on balls allowed should be interpreted in light of the following rule changes between 1876 and 1889: From 1876 through 1879 it took nine balls for a batter to earn a base on balls; from 1880 through 1883 it took eight balls to earn (or allow) a walk; in 1884 and 1885 the rule was six balls; in 1886, seven balls; and in 1887 and 1888, five balls. In 1889 batters were allowed to walk on four balls, and the rule has not changed since.

DOUBLE PLAY RECORDS

The figures seen for double play records indicate the number of double plays a player has participated in. They do not represent assists, putouts or unassisted double plays.

HOME RUN PERCENTAGE

The figures shown in the home run percentage columns represent the percentage of times a player hits a home run per at bat. A player with a 9.3 home run percentage hits a home run 9.3 percent of the time he comes to bat.

CAREER QUALIFICATION

Career fielding records begin with players who have a minimum of a five-year career. Batting and pitching records are based on a minimum of two years.

TEAM AND LEAGUE ABBREVIATIONS

Team and league identifications in the record lists are abbreviated as follows:

Alt—Altoona*, UL
Atl—Atlanta Braves, NL
Bal—Baltimore Orioles, AL
Bkn—Brooklyn Dodgers, NL
Bos—Boston Braves, NL
Bos—Boston Red Sox, AL
Buf—Buffalo, NL
Cal—California Angels, AL
Chi—Chicago Cubs, NL
Chi—Chicago White Sox, AL
Cin—Cincinnati Reds, NL
Cle—Cleveland Indians, AL
Col—Columbus, NL
C-P—Chicago-Pittsburgh, NL
Det—Detroit Tigers, AL
Har—Hartford, NL
Hou—Houston Astros, NL
Hou—Houston Colt .45's, NL
Ind—Indianapolis, NL
KC—Kansas City Athletics, AL
KC—Kansas City Royals, AL
LA—Los Angeles Angels, AL
LA—Los Angeles Dodgers, NL
Lou—Louisville, NL
Mil—Milwaukee Braves, NL
Mil—Milwaukee Brewers, AL
Min—Minnesota Twins, AL
Mon—Montreal Expos, NL
Nwk—Newark Bears, NL
NYG—New York Giants, NL
NYM—New York Mets, NL
NYY—New York Yankees, AL
Oak—Oakland Athletics, AL

Phi—Philadelphia Athletics, AL
Phi—Philadelphia Phillies, NL
Pit—Pittsburgh Pirates, NL
Pro—Providence, NL
Ric—Richmond, NL
Roc—Rochester, NL
SD—San Diego Padres, NL
Sea—Seattle Mariners, AL
Sea—Seattle Pilots, AL
SF—San Francisco Giants, NL
StL—St. Louis Browns, AL
StL—St. Louis Cardinals, NL
STP—St. Paul, NL
Syr—Syracuse, NL
Tex—Texas Rangers, AL
Tol—Toledo, NL
Tor—Toronto Blue Jays, AL
Tro—Troy, NL
Was—Washington Senators, AL
Wil—Wilmington, NL
Wor—Worcester, NL

(All the above teams have had Major League status)

* Many of the early teams did not have official team names.

LEAGUES

AA—American Association
AL—American League
FL—Federal League
ML—Major League
NL—National League
PL—Players League
UL—Union League

(All the above leagues have had Major League status)

ACKNOWLEDGMENTS

This book would never have been possible were it not for the many fine people who gave me their help and support.

For the use of their equipment, I would like to thank my sisters Connie and Tess and my neighbors, Dr. John and Betty Diamond.

Extra-special thanks goes to four of my very best friends, Mike Rotundo, Roger Dunham, Tony Boffa, and Scotty Krol, for the use of their offices and equipment and for their very sound advice.

I especially want to thank Mike Rotundo for the countless hours he spent with me during these last eight years. We have shared many hours of joy, and his support deserves this special thanks.

Thanks also to the National Baseball Hall of Fame and the many Major League teams and players who have provided photographs.

My final thanks go to my friend Daniel Bial of Harper & Row, who went to bat for me and hit a grand slam.

A CHRONOLOGY OF MAJOR LEAGUE BASEBALL RECORDS

CHAPTER 1

SEASON BATTING RECORDS

NATIONAL LEAGUE QUIZ

1. Who was the first player to come to bat more than 600 times in one season?
2. Two outstanding hitters are tied for most hits at 254. Can you name them?
3. The doubles record has not been broken in 50 years. Do you know who holds it?
4. The triples record is now 76 years old and still stands at 36. Who is the Pirate player who is the proud owner?
5. This Cub Hall of Famer has three unbroken records, each of which have not been broken in 58 years. Name him.

AMERICAN LEAGUE QUIZ

1. There have been four home run champions since the American League began play in 1901. How many can you name?
2. How many unbroken season batting records does Babe Ruth still have?
3. This Hall of Famer is one of the few players who was

able to break Babe Ruth's records and he presently is the RBI king. Who is he?
4. Only one player has ever belted more than 100 extra base hits in a season. Name him.
5. Name the two players who share the strikeout record.

MAJOR LEAGUE QUIZ

1. The modern stolen base record started with 59 in 1898 and had reached 130 in 1982. Who was the first player to steal 100 bases in one season?
2. There were only three batting average record holders before 1900. Can you name each of them and the averages they had?
3. The slugging average record is now 68 years old. Can you name the slugger who holds it?
4. Seven pinch hitters have come to bat more than 70 times. How many can you name?
5. The first pinch hit record was 2 in 1893; it has since risen to 25 in 1976. Who is the all-time pinch hit champion?

NATIONAL LEAGUE	AMERICAN LEAGUE	MAJOR LEAGUE

Most At Bats

NATIONAL LEAGUE			AMERICAN LEAGUE			MAJOR LEAGUE		
1876	George Wright, Bos	335	1901	Tommy Dowd, Bos	594	1876	George Wright, Bos, NL	335
1879	Paul Hines, Pro	409	1904	Pat Dougherty, Bos	647	1879	Paul Hines, Pro, NL	409
1883	Joe Hornung, Bos	446	1921	Jack Tobin, StL	671	1883	Jud Birchall, Phi, AA	449
1884	Abner Dalrymple, Chi	521	1953	Harvey Kuenn, Det	679	1886	George Pinchney, Bkn, AA	597
1886	Hardy Richardson, Buf	538	1963	Bobby Richardson, NL	692	1887	Arlie Latham, StL, AA	627
1887	Sam Thompson, Phi	545	**1980**	**Willie Wilson, KC**	**705**	1892	Tom Brown, Lou, NL	660
1887	Monte Ward, NY	545				1921	Jack Tobin, StL, AL	671
1888	Dick Johnston, Bos	585				1922	Rabbit Maranville, Pit, NL	672
1891	Ed McKean, Cle	603				1931	Lloyd Waner, Pit, NL	681
1892	Tom Brown, Lou	660				1935	Joe Moore, NY, NL	681
1922	Rabbit Maranville, Pit	672				1936	Woody Jensen, Pit, NL	696
1931	Lloyd Waner, Pit	681				1969	Matty Alou, Phi, NL	698
1935	Joe Moore, NY	681				1975	Dave Cash, Phi, NL	699
1936	Woody Jensen, Pit	696				**1980**	**Willie Wilson, KC, AL**	**705**
1969	Matty Alou, Pit	698						
1975	Dave Cash, Phi	699						
1984	**Juan Samuel, Phi**	**701**						

DID YOU KNOW . . . *That prior to 1902 in the NL and 1903 in the AL, a foul ball did not count as a strike?*

Most Hits

NATIONAL LEAGUE			AMERICAN LEAGUE			MAJOR LEAGUE		
1876	Ross Barnes, Chi	138	1901	Nap Lajoie, Phi	229	1876	Ross Barnes, Chi, NL	138
1879	Paul Hines, Pro	146	1911	Ty Cobb, Det	248	1879	Paul Hines, Pro, NL	146
1883	Dan Brouthers, Buf	159	**1920**	**George Sisler, StL**	**257**	1883	Dan Brouthers, Buf, NL	159
1884	Jim O'Rourke, NY	162				1884	Fred Dunlap, StL, UL	185
1885	Roger Connor, NY	169				1886	Dave Orr, NY, AA	193
1886	Hardy Richardson, Buf	189				1887	Tip O'Neill, StL, AA	225
1887	Sam Thompson, Phi	203				1894	Hugh Duffy, Bos, NL	236
1889	Jack Glasscock, Cle	205				1896	Jesse Burkett, Cle, NL	240
1893	Sam Thompson, Phi	222				1897	Willie Keeler, Bal, NL	243
1894	Hugh Duffy, Bos	236				1911	Ty Cobb, Det, AL	248
1896	Jesse Burkett, Cle	240				**1920**	**George Sisler, StL, AL**	**257**
1897	Willie Keeler, Bal	243						
1922	Rogers Hornsby, StL	250						
1929	**Lefty O'Doul, Phi**	**254**						
1930	**Bill Terry, StL**	**254**						

Most Singles

NATIONAL LEAGUE			AMERICAN LEAGUE			MAJOR LEAGUE		
1876	Ross Barnes, Chi	102	1901	Nap Lajoie, Phi	154	1876	Ross Barnes, Chi, NL	102
1879	Paul Hines, Pro	109	1903	Pat Dougherty, Chi	160	1879	Paul Hines, Pro, NL	109
1884	Roger Connor, NY	115	1904	Willie Keeler, NY	162	1883	Ed Swartwood, Bkn, AA	112
1885	Roger Connor, NY	130	1906	Willie Keeler, NY	167	1884	Harry Moore, Was, UL	126
1886	Hardy Richardson, Buf	140	1911	Ty Cobb, Det	169	1885	Roger Connor, NY, NL	130
1887	Monte Ward, NY	162	1920	George Sisler, StL	171	1886	Arlie Latham, StL, AA	142
1893	Hugh Duffy, Bos	167	1923	Charlie Jamieson, Cle	172	1887	Monte Ward, NY, NL	162
1894	Billy Hamilton, Phi	179	1925	Sam Rice, Was	182	1887	Pete Browning, Lou, AA	162
1896	Jesse Burkett, Cle	191	1980	Willie Wilson, KC	184	1890	Monte Ward, NY, PL	176
1897	Willie Keeler, Bal	196	**1985**	**Wade Boggs, Bos**	**187**	1894	Billy Hamilton, Phi, NL	179
1898	**Willie Keeler, Bal**	**201**				1896	Jesse Burkett, Cle, NL	191
						1897	Willie Keeler, Bal, NL	196
						1898	**Willie Keeler, Bal, NL**	**201**

Most Singles after 1900

NATIONAL LEAGUE			MAJOR LEAGUE		
1900	Willie Keeler, NY	179	1900	Willie Keeler, Bkn, NL	179
1901	Jessie Burkett, Cle	180	1901	Jesse Burkett, StL, NL	180
1927	Lloyd Waner, Pit	198	1927	Lloyd Waner, Pit, NL	198

NATIONAL LEAGUE		
Most Doubles		
1876	Ross Barnes, Chi	21
1876	Dick Higham, Har	21
1876	Paul Hines, Chi	21
1878	Dick Higham, Pro	22
1879	Charlie Eden, Cle	31
1882	King Kelly, Chi	37
1883	Ned Williamson, Chi	49
1895	Ed Delahanty, Phi	49
1899	Ed Delahanty, Phi	56
1930	Chuck Klein, Phi	59
1932	Paul Waner, Pit	62
1936	**Joe Medwick, StL**	**64**
Most Triples		
1876	Ross Barnes, Chi	14
1879	Buttercup Dickerson, Cin	14
1880	Harry Stovey, Wor	14
1882	Roger Connor, Tro	18
1884	Buck Ewing, NY	20
1886	Roger Connor, NY	20
1887	Sam Thompson, Phi	23
1890	Long John Reilly, Cin	26
1893	Perry Werden, StL	33
1912	**Owen Wilson, Pit**	**36**
Most Home Runs		
1876	George Hall, Phi	5
1879	Charley Jones, Bos	9
1883	Buck Ewing, NY	10
1884	Ned Williamson, Chi	27
1922	Rogers Hornsby, StL	42
1929	Chuck Klein, Pit	43
1930	**Hack Wilson, Chi**	**56**
Highest Home Run Percentage		
1876	George Hall, Phi	1.9
1879	Charley Jones, Bos	2.5
1881	Dan Brouthers, Buf	3.0
1884	Ned Williamson, Chi	6.5
1922	Rogers Hornsby, StL	6.7
1923	Cy Williams, Phi	7.7
1925	Rogers Hornsby, StL	7.7
1929	Mel Ott, NY	7.7
1930	**Hack Wilson, Chi**	**9.6**
Most Runs Scored		
1876	Ross Barnes, Chi	126
1886	King Kelly, Chi	155
1894	**Billy Hamilton, Phi**	**196**
Most Runs Scored after 1900		
1900	Roy Thomas, Phi	134
1901	Jesse Burkett, StL	139
1922	Rogers Hornsby, StL	141
1925	Kiki Cuyler, Chi	144
1929	Rogers Hornsby, StL	156
1930	**Chuck Klein, Phi**	**158**

AMERICAN LEAGUE		
Most Doubles		
1901	Nap Lajoie, Phi	48
1904	Nap Lajoie, Cle	50
1910	Nap Lajoie, Cle	51
1912	Tris Speaker, Cle	53
1923	Tris Speaker, Cle	59
1926	George Burns, Cle	64
1931	**Earl Webb, Bos**	**67**
Most Triples		
1901	Bill Keister, Bal	21
1901	Jimmy Williams, Bal	21
1902	Jimmy Williams, Bal	21
1903	Sam Crawford, Det	25
1912	**Joe Jackson, Cle**	**26**
1914	**Sam Crawford, Det**	**26**
Most Home Runs		
1901	Nap Lajoie, Phi	14
1902	Socks Seybold, Phi	16
1919	Babe Ruth, Bos	29
1920	Babe Ruth, NY	54
1921	Babe Ruth, NY	59
1927	Babe Ruth, NY	60
1961	**Roger Maris, NY**	**61**
Highest Home Run Percentage		
1901	Nap Lajoie, Phi	2.6
1901	Mike Grady, Bal	2.6
1902	Socks Seybold, Phi	3.1
1918	Babe Ruth, Bos	3.5
1919	Babe Ruth, Bos	6.7
1920	**Babe Ruth, NY**	**11.8**
Most Runs Scored		
1901	Nap Lajoie, Phi	145
1911	Ty Cobb, Det	147
1920	Babe Ruth, NY	158
1921	**Babe Ruth, NY**	**177**

DID YOU KNOW . . . *That in 1894 when Billy Hamilton scored his amazing total of 196 runs he did it in a 128-game schedule? This averages out to 1½ runs per game!*

MAJOR LEAGUE		
Most Doubles		
1876	Ross Barnes, Chi, NL	21
1876	Dick Higham, Har, NL	21
1876	Paul Hines, Chi, NL	21
1878	Dick Higham, Pro, NL	22
1879	Charlie Eden, Cle, NL	31
1882	King Kelly, Chi, NL	37
1883	Ned Williamson, Chi, NL	49
1887	Tip O'Neill, StL, AA	52
1899	Ed Delahanty, Phi, NL	56
1923	Tris Speaker, Cle, AL	59
1930	Chuck Klein, Phi, NL	59
1931	**Earl Webb, Bos, AL**	**67**
Most Triples		
1876	Ross Barnes, Chi, NL	14
1879	Buttercup Dickerson, Cin, NL	14
1880	Harry Stovey, Wor, NL	14
1882	Roger Connor, Tro, NL	18
1884	Harry Stovey, Phi, AA	25
1886	Dave Orr, NY, AA	31
1893	Perry Werden, StL, NL	33
1912	**Owen Wilson, Pit, NL**	**36**
Most Home Runs		
1876	George Hall, Phi, NL	5
1879	Charley Jones, Bos, NL	9
1883	Harry Stovey, Phi, AA	14
1884	Ned Williamson, Chi, NL	27
1919	Babe Ruth, Bos, AL	29
1920	Babe Ruth, NY, AL	54
1921	Babe Ruth, NY, AL	59
1927	Babe Ruth, NY, AL	60
1961	**Roger Maris, NY, AL**	**61**
Highest Home Run Percentage		
1876	George Hall, Phi, NL	1.9
1879	Charley Jones, Bos, NL	2.5
1881	Dan Brouthers, Buf, NL	3.0
1883	Harry Stovey, Phi, AA	3.3
1884	Ned Williamson, Chi, NL	6.5
1919	Babe Ruth, Bos, AL	6.7
1920	**Babe Ruth, NY, AL**	**11.8**
Most Runs Scored		
1876	Ross Barnes, Chi, NL	126
1884	Fred Dunlap, StL, UL	160
1887	Tip O'Neill, StL, AA	167
1891	Tom Brown, Bos, AA	177
1894	**Billy Hamilton, Phi, NL**	**196**
Most Runs after 1900		
1900	Roy Thomas, Phi, NL	134
1901	Nap Lajoie, Phi, AL	145
1911	Ty Cobb, Det, AL	147
1920	Babe Ruth, NY, AL	158
1921	**Babe Ruth, NY, AL**	**177**

NATIONAL LEAGUE			AMERICAN LEAGUE			MAJOR LEAGUE		
Most RBIs			*Most RBIs*			*Most RBIs*		
1876	Deacon White, Chi	60	1901	Nap Lajoie, Phi	125	1876	Deacon White, Chi, NL	60
1879	Charley Jones, Bos	62	1911	Ty Cobb, Det	144	1879	Charley Jones, Bos, NL	62
1879	John O'Rourke, Bos	62	1921	Babe Ruth, NY	171	1879	John O'Rourke, Bos, NL	62
1880	Cap Anson, Chi	74	1927	Lou Gehrig, NY	175	1880	Cap Anson, Chi, NL	74
1881	Cap Anson, Chi	82	**1931**	**Lou Gehrig, NY**	**184**	1881	Cap Anson, Chi, NL	82
1882	Cap Anson, Chi	83				1882	Cap Anson, Chi, NL	83
1885	Cap Anson, Chi	114				1885	Cap Anson, Chi, NL	114
1886	Cap Anson, Chi	147				1886	Cap Anson, Chi, NL	147
1887	Sam Thompson, Phi	166				1887	Sam Thompson, Phi, NL	166
1930	**Hack Wilson, Chi**	**190**				1921	Babe Ruth, NY, AL	171
						1927	Lou Gehrig, NY, AL	175
						1930	**Hack Wilson, Chi, NL**	**190**
Most Extra Base Hits			*Most Extra Base Hits*			*Most Extra Base Hits*		
1876	Ross Barnes, Chi	36	1901	Nap Lajoie, Phi	75	1876	Ross Barnes, Chi, NL	36
1879	Charlie Eden, Cle	41	1911	Ty Cobb, Det	79	1879	Charlie Eden, Cle, NL	41
1879	Charley Jones, Bos	41	1920	Babe Ruth, NY	99	1879	Charley Jones, Bos, NL	41
1880	Harry Stovey, Wor	41	**1921**	**Babe Ruth, NY**	**119**	1880	Harry Stovey, Wor, NL	41
1882	Roger Connor, Tro	44				1882	Roger Connor, Tro, NL	44
1883	Dan Brouthers, Buf	61				1883	Dan Brouthers, Buf, NL	61
1886	Dan Brouthers, Buf	66				1884	Harry Stovey, Phi, AA	61
1887	Dan Brouthers, Buf	68				1886	Dan Brouthers, Buf, NL	66
1893	Ed Delahanty, Phi	72				1887	Tip O'Neill, StL, AA	85
1894	Hugh Duffy, Bos	81				1920	Babe Ruth, NY, AL	99
1895	Sam Thompson, Phi	84				**1921**	**Babe Ruth, NY, AL**	**119**
1922	Rogers Hornsby, StL	102						
1930	**Chuck Klein, Phi**	**107**						
Most Total Bases			*Most Total Bases*			*Most Total Bases*		
1876	Ross Barnes, Chi	190	1901	Nap Lajoie, Phi	345	1876	Ross Barnes, Chi, NL	190
1879	Paul Hines, Pro	197	1911	Ty Cobb, Det	367	1879	Paul Hines, Pro, NL	197
1883	Dan Brouthers, Buf	243	1920	George Sisler, StL	399	1883	Dan Brouthers, Buf, NL	243
1884	Abner Dalrymple, Chi	263	**1921**	**Babe Ruth, NY**	**457**	1884	Harry Stovey, Phi, AA	287
1886	Dan Brouthers, Buf	284				1886	Dave Orr, NY, AA	301
1887	Sam Thompson, Phi	311				1887	Tip O'Neill, StL, AA	357
1893	Ed Delahanty, Phi	347				1894	Hugh Duffy, Bos, NL	366
1894	Hugh Duffy, Bos	366				1920	George Sisler, StL, AL	399
1921	Rogers Hornsby, StL	378				**1921**	**Babe Ruth, NY, AL**	**457**
1922	**Rogers Hornsby, StL**	**450**						
Most Bases on Balls			*Most Bases on Balls*			*Most Bases on Balls*		
1876	Ross Barnes, Chi	20	1901	Dummy Hoy, Chi	86	1876	Ross Barnes, Chi, NL	20
1877	Jim O'Rourke, NY	20	1902	Topsy Hartsel, Phi	87	1877	Jim O'Rourke, NY, NL	20
1879	Charley Jones, Bos	29	1905	Topsy Hartsel, Phi	121	1879	Charley Jones, Bos, NL	29
1881	John Clapp, Cle	35	1920	Babe Ruth, NY	148	1881	John Clapp, Cle, NL	35
1883	Tom York, Pro	37	**1923**	**Babe Ruth, NY**	**170**	1883	Tom York, Pro, NL	37
1884	George Gore, Chi	61				1884	Candy Nelson, NY, AA	74
1885	Ned Williamson, Chi	75				1885	Ned Williamson, Chi, NL	75
1886	George Gore, Chi	102				1886	George Gore, Chi, NL	102
1890	Cap Anson, Chi	113				1887	Paul Radford, NY, AA	106
1892	John Crooks, StL	136				1888	Yank Robinson, StL, AA	116
1911	Jimmy Sheckard, Chi	147				1889	Yank Robinson, StL, AA	118
1945	**Eddie Stanky, Bkn**	**148**				1890	Bill Joyce, Bkn, PL	123
1969	**Jimmy Wynn, Hou**	**148**				1892	John Crooks, StL, NL	136
						1911	Jimmy Sheckard, Chi, NL	147
						1920	Babe Ruth, NY, AL	148
						1923	**Babe Ruth, NY, AL**	**170**

DID YOU KNOW ... *That 1889 was the first year that it took only four balls for a batter to earn a walk? The earliest rule, in 1876, allowed a pitcher nine balls before he gave up a base on balls.*

NATIONAL LEAGUE

Most Strikeouts
1876	Lew Brown, Bos	22
1877	Lew Brown, Bos	33
1878	Lew Brown, Pro	37
1879	Pud Galvin, Buf	56
1880	Pud Galvin, Buf	57
1881	Pud Galvin, Buf	70
1883	Pud Galvin, Buf	79
1884	Sam Wise, Bos	104
1935	Dolf Camilli, Bkn	113
1938	Vince DiMaggio, Pit	134
1960	Pancho Herrara, Phi	136
1963	Donn Clendenon, Pit	136
1968	Donn Clendenon, Pit	163
1969	Bobby Bonds, SF	187
1970	**Bobby Bonds, SF**	**189**

Most Stolen Bases (old rule)*
1876–1886	Records not kept	
1887	Monte Ward, NY	111
1889	**Billy Hamilton, Phi**	**117**

Most Stolen Bases (modern rule)
1898	Billy Hamilton, Phi	59
1899	Jimmy Sheckard, Chi	77
1911	Bob Bescher, Cin	81
1962	Maury Wills, LA	104
1974	**Lou Brock, StL**	**118**

Highest Batting Average
1876	Ross Barnes, Chi	.429
1894	**Hugh Duffy, Bos**	**.438**

Highest Batting Average after 1900
1900	Honus Wagner, Pit	.381
1901	Jesse Burkett, StL	.382
1921	Rogers Hornsby, StL	.397
1922	Rogers Hornsby, StL	.401
1924	**Rogers Hornsby, StL**	**.424**

* The Baseball Rules Committee acknowledges only one set of records, with no separation as to before or after 1900. One exception is the category of stolen bases. From 1876 to 1897, a runner was given credit for a stolen base when he advanced a base on a ground or fly ball, or went from first to third on a single. That was considered the old rule. The stolen base rule as we know it today began in 1898.

AMERICAN LEAGUE

Most Strikeouts
1901–1912	Records not kept	
1913	Danny Moeller, Was	103
1914	Gus Williams, StL	120
1953	Larry Doby, Cle	121
1956	Jim Lemon, Det	138
1961	Jake Wood, Det	141
1962	Harmon Killebrew, Min	142
1963	**Dave Nicholson, Chi**	**175**
1979	**Gorman Thomas, Mil**	**175**

DID YOU KNOW... *That Pud Galvin was the first pitcher in baseball to give pitchers the reputation that pitchers could not hit? He set four consecutive strikeout records.*

Most Stolen Bases
1901	Frank Isbell, Chi	52
1909	Ty Cobb, Det	76
1910	Eddie Collins, Phi	81
1911	Ty Cobb, Det	83
1912	Clyde Milan, Was	88
1915	Ty Cobb, Det	96
1980	Rickey Henderson, Oak	100
1982	**Rickey Henderson, Oak**	**130**

DID YOU KNOW... *That prior to 1898, a runner was given credit for a stolen base if he advanced from first to third on a single, or advanced a base on a ground or fly ball?*

Highest Batting Average
1901	Nap Lajoie, Phi	.422

DID YOU KNOW... *That strikeouts were few during the early years of baseball because foul balls did not count as strikes, it took four strikes for a strike-out when the last strike was called, and batters were allowed to call for high or low pitches according to their liking? A high pitch was from the belt to the shoulders, a low pitch from the knees to the belt. If the pitcher failed to place the ball as requested, it was called a ball.*

MAJOR LEAGUE

Most Strikeouts
1876	Lew Brown, Bos, NL	22
1877	Lew Brown, Bos, NL	33
1878	Lew Brown, Bos, NL	37
1879	Pud Galvin, Buf, NL	56
1880	Pud Galvin, Buf, NL	57
1881	Pud Galvin, Buf, NL	70
1883	Pud Galvin, Buf, NL	79
1884	Sam Wise, Bos, NL	104
1914	Gus Williams, StL, AL	120
1938	Vince DiMaggio, Pit, NL	134
1956	Jim Lemon, Det, AL	138
1961	Jake Wood, Det, AL	141
1962	Harmon Killebrew, Min, AL	142
1963	Dave Nicholson, Chi, AL	175
1969	Bobby Bonds, SF, NL	187
1970	**Bobby Bonds, SF, NL**	**189**

Most Stolen Bases (old rule)
1887	Hugh Nichol, Cin, NL	138

Most Stolen Bases (modern rule)
1898	Bill Hamilton, Phi, NL	59
1899	Jimmy Sheckard, Chi, NL	77
1910	Eddie Collins, Phi, AL	81
1911	Ty Cobb, Det, AL	83
1912	Clyde Milan, Was, AL	88
1915	Ty Cobb, Det, AL	96
1962	Maury Wills, LA, NL	104
1974	Lou Brock, StL, NL	118
1982	**Rickey Henderson, Oak, AL**	**130**

Highest Batting Average
1876	Ross Barnes, Chi, NL	.429
1887	Tip O'Neill, StL, AA	.435
1894	**Hugh Duffy, Bos, NL**	**.438**

Highest Batting Average after 1900
1900	Honus Wagner, Pit, NL	.381
1901	Nap Lajoie, Phi, AL	.422
1924	**Rogers Hornsby, StL, NL**	**.424**

NATIONAL LEAGUE	AMERICAN LEAGUE	MAJOR LEAGUE

The .400 Hitters of the National League

1876	Ross Barnes, Chi	.429
1894	Hugh Duffy, Bos	.438
	Terry Turner, Phi	.416
	Sam Thompson, Phi	.404
	Ed Delahanty, Phi	.400
1895	Jessie Burkett, Cle	.423
1896	Jessie Burkett, Cle	.410
1897	Willie Keeler, Bal	.432
	Fred Clarke, Lou	.406
1899	Ed Delahanty, Phi	.408
	Jessie Burkett, StL	.402
1922	Rogers Hornsby, StL	.401
1924	Rogers Hornsby, StL	.424
1925	Rogers Hornsby, StL	.403
1930	Bill Terry, NYG	.401

Highest Slugging Average

1876	Ross Barnes, Chi	.590
1894	Hugh Duffy, Bos	.679
1922	Rogers Hornsby, StL	.722
1925	**Rogers Hornsby, StL**	**.756**

Most Pinch At Bats (min. 6 at bats)

1876–1892	None	
1893	Jake Stenzel, Pit	6
1896	Duke Farrell, NY	10
1897	Duke Farrell, NY	14
1905	Sammy Strang, NY	14
1907	Sammy Strang, NY	19
1909	Ham Hyatt, Pit	37
1910	Ward Miller, Cin	40
1913	Doc Miller, Phi	56
1931	Red Lucas, Cin	60
1932	Sam Leslie, NY	72
1962	Red Schoendienst, StL	72
1970	Vic Davalillo, StL	73
1976	Jose Morales, Mon	78
1983	**Rusty Staub, NY**	**81**

Most Pinch Hits

1893	John Sharrott, Phi	2
1894	Tom Parrott, Cin	2
1894	Mike Grady, Phi	2
1895	Win Mercer, Was	2
1895	Tuck Turner, Phi	2
1896	Doggie Miller, Lou	6
1897	Duke Farrell, NY	8
1905	Sammy Strang, NY	8
1909	Ham Hyatt, Pit	9
1910	Ward Miller, Cin	11
1913	Doc Miller, Phi	20
1932	Sam Leslie, NY	22
1953	Peanuts Lowrey, StL	22
1970	Vic Davalillo, StL	24
1976	**Jose Morales, Mon**	**25**

The .400 Hitters of the American League

1901	Nap Lajoie, Phi	.422
1911	Ty Cobb, Det	.420
1911	Joe Jackson, Chi	.408
1912	Ty Cobb, Det	.412
1920	George Sisler, StL	.407
1922	George Sisler, StL	.420
1941	Ted Williams, Bos	.406

Highest Slugging Average

1901	Nap Lajoie, Phi	.635
1919	Babe Ruth, Bos	.657
1920	**Babe Ruth, NY**	**.847**

Most Pinch At Bats (min. 10 at bats)

1901	Nixey Callahan, Chi	10
1903	Jake Stahl, Bos	11
1906	Joe Yeager, NY	18
1907	Piano Legs Hickman, Was	22
1908	Dode Criss, StL	41
1910	Dode Criss, StL	44
1917	Bill Rumler, StL	71
1961	**Elmer Valo, Phi**	**72**
1961	**Dave Philley, Bal**	**72**

Most Pinch Hits

1901	Nixey Callahan, Chi	3
1903	Jake Stahl, Bos	5
1906	Howard Wakefield, Was	9
1908	Dode Criss, StL	12
1912	Ted Easterly, Cle	13
1917	Bill Rumler, StL	16
1929	Bob Fothergill, Det	19
1936	Ed Coleman, StL	20
1961	**Dave Philley, Bal**	**24**

Other .400 Hitters of the Major Leagues

1884	Fred Dunlap, StL, UA	.412
	Harry Stovey, Phi, AA	.404
1887	Tip O'Neill, StL, AA	.435
	Pete Browning, Lou, AA	.402

DID YOU KNOW ... *That when Hugh Duffy set the highest single season batting average of .438 in 1894, foul tips did not count as strikes?*

Highest Slugging Average

1876	Ross Barnes, Chi, NL	.590
1884	Harry Stovey, Phi, AA	.641
1887	Tip O'Neill, StL, AA	.691
1920	**Babe Ruth, NY, AL**	**.847**

Most Pinch At Bats

1893	Jake Stenzel, Pit, NL	6
1896	Duke Farrell, NY, NL	10
1897	Duke Farrell, NY, NL	14
1905	Sammy Strang, NY, NL	14
1906	Joe Yeager, NY, AL	18
1907	Piano Legs Hickman, Was, AL	22
1908	Dode Criss, StL, AL	41
1913	Doc Miller, Phi, NL	56
1917	Bill Rumler, StL, AL	71
1932	Sam Leslie, NY, NL	72
1961	Elmer Valo, Phi, AL	72
1961	Dave Philley, Bal, AL	72
1970	Vic Davalillo, StL, NL	73
1976	Jose Morales, Mon, NL	78
1983	**Rusty Staub, NY, NL**	**81**

Most Pinch Hits

1893	John Sharrott, Phi, NL	2
1894	Tom Parrott, Cin, NL	2
1894	Mike Grady, Phi, NL	2
1895	Win Mercer, Was, NL	2
1895	Tuck Turner, Phi, NL	2
1896	Doggie Miller, Lou, NL	6
1897	Duke Farrell, NY, NL	8
1905	Sammy Strang, NY, NL	8
1906	Howard Wakefield, Was, AL	9
1908	Dode Criss, StL, AL	12
1912	Ted Easterly, Cle, AL	13
1913	Doc Miller, Phi, NL	20
1932	Sam Leslie, NY, NL	22
1953	Peanuts Lowrey, StL, NL	22
1961	Dave Philley, Bal, AL	24
1976	**Jose Morales, Mon, NL**	**25**

NATIONAL LEAGUE

Highest Pinch Batting Average
(min. 30 at bats)

1909	Ham Hyatt, Pit	.243
1910	Ward Miller, Cin	.275
1913	Doc Miller, Phi	.357
1938	Frenchy Bordagaray, StL	.465
1974	**Ed Kranepool, NY**	**.486**

AMERICAN LEAGUE

Highest Pinch Batting Average
(min. 30 at bats)

1908	Dode Criss, StL	.292
1912	Ted Easterly, Cle	.433
1931	**Smead Jolley, Chi**	**.467**

MAJOR LEAGUE

Highest Pinch Batting Average
(min. 30 at bats)

1908	Dode Criss, StL, AL	.292
1912	Ted Easterly, Cle, AL	.433
1931	**Smead Jolley, Chi, AL**	**.467**
1974	**Ed Kranepool, NY, NL**	**.486**

NATIONAL LEAGUE SUMMARY

Top Record Producers

1	Rogers Hornsby, StL	11
2	Ross Barnes, Chi	10
3	Dan Brouthers, Buf	7
4	Sam Thompson, Phi	6
4	Hugh Duffy, Bos	6
4	Roger Connor, NY	6
7	Cap Anson, Chi	5
7	Charley Jones, Cin	5
7	Paul Hines, Pro	5

AMERICAN LEAGUE SUMMARY

Top Record Producers

1	Babe Ruth, NY	17
2	Nap Lajoie, Cle	13
3	Ty Cobb, Det	9
4	George Sisler, StL	3
4	Dode Criss, StL	3

MAJOR LEAGUE SUMMARY

Top Record Producers

1	Babe Ruth, NY, AL	13
2	Ross Barnes, Chi, NL	10
3	Harry Stovey, Phi, AA	8
4	Tip O'Neill, StL, AA	7
5	Cap Anson, Chi, NL	5
5	Paul Hines, Pro, NL	5
5	Dan Brouthers, Buf, NL	5
5	Charley Jones, Bos, NL	5

Most Outstanding Record Producers

Hack Wilson, Chi	3 for 174 years
Rogers Hornsby, StL	11 for 166 years
Willie Keeler, Bal	3 for 116 years
Billy Hamilton, Phi	3 for 97 years
Sam Thompson, Det	6 for 80 years

Most Outstanding Record Producers

Babe Ruth, NY	17 for 458 years
Nap Lajoie, Cle	13 for 172 years
Ty Cobb, Det	9 for 122 years
Sam Crawford, Det	2 for 83 years
Joe Jackson, Cle	1 for 76 years

Most Outstanding Record Producers

Babe Ruth, NY, AL	13 for 390 years
Hugh Duffy, Bos, NL	3 for 122 years
Willie Keeler, Bal, NL	3 for 105 years
Billy Hamilton, Phi, NL	3 for 95 years
Ned Williamson, Chi, NL	3 for 71 years

In 1876, all records were up for grabs and Ross Barnes took most of them. Barnes was baseball's first great little man. He stood only 5' 8½" and weighed a paltry 145 pounds. Yet he outhit and outslugged every player in the league. He was baseball's first .400 hitter, and although he had only one home run, he still slugged for .590 to lead the league.

Probably the most underrated and overlooked player in baseball is Harry Stovey, who played part of his career in the American Association and part in the National League. He was one of the first great power hitters. His eight Major League records place him third next to Babe Ruth and Ross Barnes. Yet he is still overlooked by those who do the voting for the Hall of Fame. Tip O'Neill and Paul Hines are two other pioneer players who deserve Hall of Fame recognition.

Willie "Hit 'Em Where They Ain't" Keeler will always be known as baseball's greatest singles hitter, and his three records have been in the books for 116 years.

Rogers Hornsby looms as the greatest of all National League players, as his 11 records are far more valuable than are the 10 marks of Ross Barnes. Hack Wilson has produced the records which have lasted the greatest number of years in the National League. His 3 records have faced the test of time for 174 years, while Hornsby's 11 marks have been good for 166 years.

It is interesting to note that of Hornsby's 11 records, none were good enough to become Major League marks. This is due to the fact that he was unable to surpass many of the records of Babe Ruth. This was a hurdle for many other great players as well.

The Babe, of course, was the dominating slugger in the American League, and his greatness can easily be seen by his massive total of 17 records, which have lasted a sum of 458 years! Nap Lajoie is the closest rival to Ruth, with 13 marks lasting 172 years. Lajoie is another example of a great player with many records but none of them good enough to become a Major League mark.

Roger Maris did what most experts thought was impossible when he broke Babe Ruth's 1927 record of 60 home runs. Many considered Maris' record tainted because he had a longer season, and it is true that he played in 161 games and had 590 at bats to the Babe's 151 games and 540 at bats. However, in 1927 pitchers "held" opposing batters to a composite .285 batting average, while in 1961 the league batting average was only .256—indicating that Maris was faced with much tougher pitching in general and relief pitching in particular. Moreover, when the Babe hit his 60 home runs there was no pressure on him, since he already owned the home run record of 59. Maris had to overcome the extreme pressure of Ruth's legend, and he did it on the last day of the season to boot!

Finally, it is important to note that in 1927 what we now know as ground-rule doubles were counted as home runs, though experts say none of the balls Ruth hit bounced into the stands.

Hack Wilson was the first real threat to Ruth's home run record when he smashed 56 round-trippers in 1930. Hack had a tremendous season in 1930. In addition to his great home run explosion, his 9.6 home run percentage and amazing total of 190 RBIs have never been broken by any player in all of baseball!

Little Ross Barnes also deserves a little more ink because in his days of 1876, little was written about his great accomplishments. Of the 15 categories of positive records, Barnes led the league (and thus set the first set of records) in ten categories. No other player can boast of this achievement, and he would easily have won the MVP award if one had existed. He led the Chicago White Stockings (as they were then called) to baseball's first pennant. (This team later became known as the Cubs.)

Barnes was a master at the fair-foul bunt play, which at that time allowed the batter to bunt the ball so that it would land in fair territory and then go foul and away from the basemen. By this time, Barnes—who possessed fine speed—was safely on first base.

ROGERS HORNSBY
Many consider the "Rajah" the greatest righthanded hitter ever. From 1921 to 1925 he averaged .402. He was the first player to win the Triple Crown twice.

BABE RUTH

The Babe set many records for hitting—not only home runs, but also RBIs, walks, runs scored, extra base hits, and strikeouts. Besides also being a fine pitcher, he set several fielding records in left field.

CHAPTER 2

CAREER BATTING RECORDS

NATIONAL LEAGUE QUIZ

1. This Hall of Famer was the first NL player to play in 3,000 games. Do you know him?
2. This exceptional player was the first Major Leaguer to bat more than 10,000 times. His record lasted 46 years before it was broken. Name him.
3. Only one player has ever come to bat more than 13,000 times. Do you know him?
4. This Hall of Famer was the first player to get 2,000 and 3,000 hits. Who is he?
5. Can you name the only two NL players with more than 700 doubles?

AMERICAN LEAGUE QUIZ

1. The doubles record has not been broken in 60 years. Do you know who holds it?
2. This great player slugged 297 triples, and his 60-year-old record remains unbroken. Who is he?
3. Can you name the first AL player to slam 100 home runs?

4. Before Babe Ruth took over the AL lead in home runs, who was the slugger with the most homers?
5. This outstanding second baseman was the first to score 1,000 runs. Do you remember him?

MAJOR LEAGUE QUIZ

1. The most runs driven in by any Major Leaguer is 2,297. Do you know this superstar?
2. Can you name the first player to stroke more than 1,000 extra base hits?
3. This Hall of Famer had more total bases than Ty Cobb. His record lasted 34 years before Hank Aaron broke it in 1962. Name him.
4. If an average of 500 at bats makes a full season, and if this special player received all his bases on balls in succession, he would have played four years without making an out. Who has the most bases on balls in baseball history?
5. Can you name three Hall of Famers, one who has over 700 stolen bases, the second who has more than 800 steals and the third with more than 900 thefts?

NATIONAL LEAGUE		AMERICAN LEAGUE		MAJOR LEAGUE		

Most Games Played

NATIONAL LEAGUE			AMERICAN LEAGUE			MAJOR LEAGUE		
1876–77	George Hall, Lou	121	1901–05	Candy LaChance, Bos	581	1876–77	George Hall, Lou, NL	121
1876–79	Cal McVey, Cin	265	1901–06	Chick Stahl, Bos	781	1876–79	Cal McVey, Cin, NL	265
1876–80	Charley Jones, Cin	331	1901–07	Lave Cross, Phi	847	1876–84	Lew Brown, Bos, AA	378
1876–83	Tom York, Pro	585	1901–08	Fielder Jones, Chi	1158	1876–85	Tom York, Pro, NL	690
1876–86	Joe Start, Pro	798	1901–09	Hobe Ferris, Bos	1286	1876–86	Joe Start, Pro, NL	788
1878–88	Abner Dalrymple, Chi	919	1901–11	Freddy Parent, Bos	1325	1876–88	Charley Jones, Cin, AA	882
1876–89	John Morrill, Bos	1263	1902–13	Danny Murphy, Phi	1411	1876–90	Deacon White, Buf, NL	1299
1876–90	Paul Hines, Pro	1427	1901–16	Nap Lajoie, Cle	1989	1876–91	Paul Hines, Pro, NL	1481
1878–94	Monte Ward, NY	1697	1903–17	Sam Crawford, Det	2114	1880–93	Harry Stovey, Phi, AA	1488
1879–95	Jack Glasscock, Cle	1698	1905–28	Ty Cobb, Det	3034	1878–94	Monte Ward, NY, NL	1825
1876–97	Cap Anson, Chi	2276	**1961–83**	**Carl Yastrzemski, Bos**	**3308**	1876–97	Cap Anson, Chi, NL	2276
1891–11	Billy Dahlen, Chi	2443				1888–07	Jake Beckley, Pit, NL	2386
1897–17	Honus Wagner, Pit	2786				1890–11	Billy Dahlen, Chi, NL	2443
1941–63	Stan Musial, StL	3026				1896–16	Nap Lajoie, Cle, AL	2475
1954–74	Hank Aaron, Atl	3076				1897–17	Honus Wagner, Pit, NL	2786
1961–86	**Pete Rose, Cin**	**3562**				1905–28	Ty Cobb, Det, AL	3034
						1954–76	Hank Aaron, Atl, NL	3298
						1961–83	Carl Yastrzemski, AL	3308
						1961–86	**Pete Rose, Cin, NL**	**3562**

DID YOU KNOW . . . *That Stan Musial was the first National Leaguer to play in more than 3,000 games?*

Most At Bats

NATIONAL LEAGUE			AMERICAN LEAGUE			MAJOR LEAGUE		
1876–77	George Hall, Lou	537	1901–05	Candy LaChance, Bos	2225	1876–77	George Hall, Lou, NL	537
1876–79	Cal McVey, Cin	1199	1901–06	Chick Stahl, Bos	3004	1876–79	Cal McVey, Cin, NL	1199
1876–80	Charley Jones, Cin	1412	1901–07	Lave Cross, Phi	3383	1876–84	Lew Brown, Bos, AA	1531
1876–83	Tom York, Pro	2332	1901–08	Fielder Jones, Chi	4299	1876–85	Tom York, Pro, NL	2733
1876–86	Joe Start, Pro	3433	1901–09	Hobe Ferris, Bos	4800	1876–86	Joe Start, Pro, NL	3433
1878–88	Abner Dalrymple, Chi	4037	1901–11	Freddy Parent, Bos	4976	1876–88	Charley Jones, Cin, AA	3687
1876–89	John Morrill, Bos	4905	1902–13	Danny Murphy, Phi	5134	1876–90	Deacon White, Buf, NL	5335
1876–90	Paul Hines, Pro	6047	1901–16	Nap Lajoie, Cle	7501	1876–91	Paul Hines, Pro, NL	6253
1878–94	Monte Ward, NY	7086	1903–17	Sam Crawford, Det	7994	1878–94	Monte Ward, NY, NL	7647
1876–97	Cap Anson, Chi	9108	1905–28	Ty Cobb, Det	11,429	1876–97	Cap Anson, Chi, NL	9108
1897–17	Honus Wagner, Pit	10,427	**1961–83**	**Carl Yastrzemski, Bos**	**11,988**	1888–07	Jake Beckley, Pit, NL	9527
1941–63	Stan Musial, StL	10,972				1896–16	Nap Lajoie, Cle, AL	9589
1954–74	Hank Aaron, Atl	11,628				1897–17	Honus Wagner, Pit, NL	10,427
1961–86	**Pete Rose, Cin**	**14,053**				1905–28	Ty Cobb, Det, AL	11,429
						1954–76	Hank Aaron, Atl, NL	12,364
						1961–86	**Pete Rose, Cin, NL**	**14,053**

DID YOU KNOW . . . *That Honus Wagner was the first Major Leaguer to come to bat more than 10,000 times?*

Most Hits

NATIONAL LEAGUE			AMERICAN LEAGUE			MAJOR LEAGUE		
1876–77	George Hall, Lou	185	1901–05	Candy LaChance, Bos	587	1876–77	George Hall, Lou, NL	185
1876–79	Cal McVey, Cin	393	1901–06	Chick Stahl, Bos	877	1876–79	Cal McVey, Cin, NL	393
1876–80	Charley Jones, Cin	431	1901–07	Lave Cross, Phi	986	1876–85	Tom York, Pro, NL	741
1876–83	Tom York, Pro	648	1901–08	Fielder Jones, Chi	1155	1876–86	Joe Start, Pro, NL	1031
1876–86	Joe Start, Pro	1031	1901–09	Jimmy Williams, NY	1178	1876–88	Charley Jones, Cin, AA	1101
1878–88	Abner Dalrymple, Chi	1160	1901–10	Bill Bradley, Cle	1266	1876–90	Deacon White, Buf, NL	1619
1876–89	Deacon White, Buf	1505	1901–11	Freddy Parent, Bos	1305	1876–91	Paul Hines, Pro, NL	1881
1876–90	Paul Hines, Pro	1823	1902–13	Danny Murphy, Phi	1488	1878–94	Monte Ward, NY, NL	2123
1878–94	Monte Ward, NY	1916	1901–16	Nap Lajoie, Cle	2523	1876–97	Cap Anson, Chi, NL	3041
1879–95	Jack Glasscock, Cle	1980	**1905–28**	**Ty Cobb, Det**	**4191**	1896–16	Nap Lajoie, Cle, AL	3251
1876–97	Cap Anson, Chi	3041				1897–17	Honus Wagner, Pit, NL	3430
1897–17	Honus Wagner, Pit	3430				1905–28	Ty Cobb, Det, AL	4191
1941–63	Stan Musial, StL	3630				**1961–86**	**Pete Rose, Cin, NL**	**4256**
1961–86	**Pete Rose, Cin**	**4256**						

DID YOU KNOW . . . *That Cap Anson was baseball's first player to collect 3,000 base hits?*

NATIONAL LEAGUE

Most Singles

1876–77	George Hall, Lou	137
1876–79	Cal McVey, Cin	321
1876–83	Tom York, Pro	435
1876–86	Joe Start, Pro	862
1876–89	Deacon White, Buf	1214
1876–90	Paul Hines, Pro	1327
1878–94	Monte Ward, NY	1592
1879–95	Jack Glasscock, Cle	1595
1876–97	Cap Anson, Chi	2289
1897–17	Honus Wagner, Pit	2426
1961–86	**Pete Rose, Cin**	**3310**

Most Doubles

1876–77	George Hall, Lou	22
1876–79	Cal McVey, Cin	52
1876–80	Charley Jones, Cin	77
1876–83	Tom York, Pro	156
1878–88	Abner Dalrymple, Chi	210
1876–89	John Morrill, Bos	239
1876–90	Paul Hines, Pro	361
1876–97	Cap Anson, Chi	532
1897–17	Honus Wagner, Pit	651
1941–63	Stan Musial, StL	725
1961–86	**Pete Rose, Cin**	**746**

Most Triples

1876–77	George Hall, Lou	21
1876–80	Charley Jones, Cin	34
1876–83	Tom York, Pro	48
1876–86	Joe Start, Pro	55
1878–88	Abner Dalrymple, Chi	76
1876–89	John Morrill, Bos	80
1879–92	Hardy Richardson, Buf	106
1880–97	Roger Connor, NY	218
1888–07	Jake Beckley, Pit	244
1897–17	**Honus Wagner, Pit**	**252**

Most Home Runs

1876–77	George Hall, Lou	5
1876–80	Charley Jones, Cin	23
1878–88	Abner Dalrymple, Chi	42
1878–89	Ned Williamson, Chi	62
1878–93	King Kelly, Chi	63
1880–97	Roger Connor, NY	123
1885–98	Sam Thompson, Phi	128
1909–26	Zack Wheat, Bkn	131
1915–37	Rogers Hornsby, StL	297
1926–47	Mel Ott, NY	511
1951–73	Willie Mays, NY	660
1954–74	**Hank Aaron, Atl**	**733**

AMERICAN LEAGUE

Most Singles

1901–05	Candy LaChance, Bos	477
1901–06	Chick Stahl, Bos	676
1901–07	Lave Cross, Phi	764
1901–08	Fielder Jones, Chi	970
1902–11	Patsy Dougherty, Chi	1061
1902–13	Danny Murphy, Phi	1068
1901–16	Nap Lajoie, Cle	1862
1905–28	**Ty Cobb, Det**	**3052**

Most Doubles

1901–05	Dave Fultz, NY	79
1901–06	Chick Stahl, Bos	122
1901–07	Lave Cross, Phi	171
1901–08	John Anderson, StL	214
1901–10	Bill Bradley, Cle	236
1902–13	Danny Murphy, Phi	279
1901–16	Nap Lajoie, Cle	511
1907–28	**Tris Speaker, Cle**	**793**

Most Triples

1902–05	Danny Green, Chi	34
1901–06	Chick Stahl, Bos	62
1901–07	Buck Freeman, Bos	90
1901–09	Jimmy Williams, NY	100
1902–10	Elmer Flick, Cle	109
1903–17	Sam Crawford, Det	250
1905–28	**Ty Cobb, Det**	**297**

DID YOU KNOW . . . *That "Wahoo" Sam Crawford is the only player in history to have over 300 triples?*

Most Home Runs

1902–03	Ed Delahanty, Was	11
1901–06	Chick Stahl, Bos	17
1901–07	Buck Freeman, Bos	48
1901–08	Socks Seybold, Phi	51
1901–16	Nap Lajoie, Cle	51
1903–17	Sam Crawford, Det	70
1908–22	Frank Baker, Phi	96
1908–23	Tilly Walker, Phi	118
1905–28	Ty Cobb, Det	118
1918–29	Ken Williams, StL	196
1914–34	**Babe Ruth, NY**	**708**

DID YOU KNOW . . . *That for the first 14 years of Babe Ruth's career, ground rule doubles were counted as home runs?*

MAJOR LEAGUE

Most Singles

1876–77	George Hall, Lou, NL	137
1876–79	Cal McVey, Cin, NL	321
1876–85	Tom York, Pro, NL	500
1876–86	Joe Start, Pro, NL	862
1876–90	Deacon White, Buf, NL	1311
1876–91	Paul Hines, Pro, NL	1373
1878–94	Monte Ward, NY, NL	1768
1876–97	Cap Anson, Chi, NL	2289
1892–10	Willie Keeler, NY, AL	2536
1905–28	Ty Cobb, Det, AL	3052
1961–86	**Pete Rose, Cin, NL**	**3310**

DID YOU KNOW . . . *That in addition to breaking Ty Cobb's hit record, Pete Rose has also broken his singles mark?*

Most Doubles

1876–77	George Hall, Lou, NL	22
1876–79	Cal McVey, Cin, NL	52
1876–84	Lew Brown, Bos, AA	83
1876–85	Tom York, Pro, NL	174
1876–90	John Morrill, NL	239
1876–91	Paul Hines, Pro, NL	368
1876–97	Cap Anson, Chi, NL	532
1896–16	Nap Lajoie, Cle, AL	648
1897–17	Honus Wagner, Pit, NL	651
1907–28	**Tris Speaker, Cle, AL**	**793**

Most Triples

1876–77	George Hall, Lou, NL	21
1876–84	Lew Brown, Bos, AA	31
1876–85	Tom York, Pro, NL	57
1876–88	Charley Jones, Cin, AA	98
1880–91	John Reilly, Cin, AA	139
1880–93	Harry Stovey, Phi, AA	185
1880–97	Roger Connor, NY, NL	233
1888–07	Jake Beckley, Pit, NL	244
1899–17	**Sam Crawford, Det, AL**	**312**

Most Home Runs

1876–77	George Hall, Lou, NL	5
1876–84	Lew Brown, Bos, AA	10
1876–85	Tom York, Pro, NL	10
1876–88	Charley Jones, Cin, AA	55
1878–90	Ned Williamson, Chi, NL	63
1880–91	John Reilly, Cin, AA	67
1879–92	Hardy Richardson, Buf, NL	73
1880–93	Harry Stovey, Phi, AA	120
1880–97	Roger Connor, NY, NL	136
1915–29	Ken Williams, StL, AL	196
1914–35	Babe Ruth, NY, AL	714
1954–76	**Hank Aaron, Atl**	**755**

NATIONAL LEAGUE

Highest Home Run Percentage

1876–77	George Hall, Lou	0.9
1876–80	Charley Jones, Cin	1.5
1880–97	Roger Connor, NY	1.7
1892–98	Bill Joyce, Was	2.6
1912–20	Gavvy Cravath, Phi	3.2
1915–37	Rogers Hornsby, StL	3.7
1926–47	Mel Ott, NY	5.4
1946–54	**Ralph Kiner, Pit**	**7.1**

Most Runs Scored

1876–77	George Hall, Lou	104
1876–79	Cal McVey, Cin	227
1876–80	Charley Jones, Cin	272
1876–83	Tom York, Pro	397
1876–86	Joe Start, Pro	590
1878–88	Abner Dalrymple, Chi	782
1876–89	John Morrill, Bos	820
1876–90	Paul Hines, Pro	1058
1879–92	George Gore, Chi	1195
1878–93	King Kelly, Chi	1209
1878–94	Monte Ward, NY	1274
1876–97	Cap Anson, Chi	1719
1897–17	Honus Wagner, Pit	1740
1926–47	Mel Ott, NY	1859
1941–63	Stan Musial, StL	1949
1951–73	Willie Mays, NY	2062
1954–74	Hank Aaron, Atl	2107
1961–86	**Pete Rose, Cin**	**2165**

DID YOU KNOW . . . *That Willie Mays was the first National Leaguer to score more than 2,000 runs?*

Most RBIs

1876–77	George Hall, Lou	71
1876–91	Cal McVey, Cin	172
1876–80	Charley Jones, Cin	214
1876–83	Tom York, Pro	217
1876–86	Joe Start, Pro	220
1878–88	Abner Dalrymple, Chi	276
1876–89	John Morrill, Bos	580
1876–90	Paul Hines, Pro	600
1878–93	King Kelly, Chi	665
1879–95	Jack Glasscock, Cle	730
1876–97	Cap Anson, Chi	1715
1897–17	Honus Wagner, Pit	1732
1926–47	Mel Ott, NY	1860
1941–63	Stan Musial, StL	1951
1954–74	**Hank Aaron, Atl**	**2202**

AMERICAN LEAGUE

Highest Home Run Percentage

1902–03	Ed Delahanty, Was	1.3
1901–07	Buck Freeman, Bos	1.5
1908–22	Frank Baker, Phi	1.6
1911–23	Tilly Walker, Phi	2.3
1918–29	Ken Williams, StL	4.0
1914–34	**Babe Ruth, NY**	**8.5**

Most Runs Scored

1901–05	Dave Fultz, NY	331
1901–06	Chick Stahl, Bos	465
1901–08	Fielder Jones, Chi	695
1901–16	Nap Lajoie, Cle	1082
1903–17	Sam Crawford, Det	1115
1905–28	**Ty Cobb, Det**	**2245**

Most RBIs

1901–05	Candy LaChance, Bos	236
1901–06	Chick Stahl, Bos	339
1901–07	Buck Freeman, Bos	504
1901–08	John Anderson, NY	557
1901–09	Jimmy Williams, NY	610
1902–13	Danny Murphy, Phi	664
1901–16	Nap Lajoie, Cle	1141
1903–17	Sam Crawford, Det	1264
1905–28	Ty Cobb, Det	1961
1914–34	**Babe Ruth, NY**	**2199**

MAJOR LEAGUE

Highest Home Run Percentage

1876–77	George Hall, Lou, NL	0.9
1876–88	Charley Jones, Cin, AA	1.5
1880–93	Harry Stovey, Phi, AA	2.0
1884–98	Bill Joyce, Was, NL	2.1
1885–06	Sam Thompson, Phi, NL	2.1
1908–20	Gavvy Cravath, Phi, NL	3.0
1915–29	Ken Williams, StL, AL	4.0
1914–35	**Babe Ruth, NY, AL**	**8.5**

Most Runs Scored

1876–77	George Hall, Lou, NL	104
1876–79	Cal McVey, Cin, NL	227
1876–85	Tom York, Pro, NL	467
1876–86	Joe Start, Pro, NL	590
1876–88	Charley Jones, Cin, AA	728
1876–90	Deacon White, Buf, NL	849
1876–91	Paul Hines, Pro, NL	1083
1879–92	George Gore, Chi, NL	1327
1880–93	Harry Stovey, Phi, AA	1494
1876–97	Cap Anson, Chi, NL	1719
1892–10	Willie Keeler, NY, AL	1722
1897–17	Honus Wagner, Pit, NL	1740
1905–28	**Ty Cobb, Det, AL**	**2245**

DID YOU KNOW . . . *That Ty Cobb's runs scored record has not been broken in 58 years, though Pete Rose came close to breaking it (Cobb 2245, Rose 2165)?*

Most RBIs

1876–77	George Hall, Lou, NL		71
1876–79	Cal McVey, Cin, NL		172
1876–85	Tom York, Pro, NL		217
1876–86	Joe Start, Pro, NL		220
1876–90	Deacon White, Buf, NL		602
1876–91	Paul Hines, Pro, NL		631
1879–92	Hardy Richardson, Buf, NL		645
1878–93	King Kelly, Chi, NL		794
1876–97	Cap Anson, Chi, NL		1715
1897–17	Honus Wagner, Pit, NL		1732
1905–28	Ty Cobb, Det, AL		1961
1914–35	Babe Ruth, NY, AL		2211
1954–76	**Hank Aaron, Atl, NL**		**2297**

NATIONAL LEAGUE

Most Extra Base Hits

1876–77	George Hall, Lou	48
1876–79	Cal McVey, Cin	72
1876–80	Charley Jones, Cin	134
1876–83	Tom York, Pro	213
1878–88	Abner Dalrymple, Chi	328
1878–89	Ned Williamson, Chi	365
1876–90	Paul Hines, Pro	496
1880–97	Roger Connor, NY	758
1897–17	Honus Wagner, Pit	1004
1926–47	Mel Ott, NY	1071
1941–63	Stan Musial, StL	1377
1954–74	**Hank Aaron, Atl**	**1453**

Most Total Bases

1876–77	George Hall, Lou	264
1876–79	Cal McVey, Cin	488
1876–80	Charley Jones, Cin	645
1876–83	Tom York, Pro	827
1876–86	Joe Start, Pro	1269
1876–88	Abner Dalrymple, Chi	1648
1876–89	John Morrill, Bos	1802
1876–90	Paul Hines, Pro	2510
1879–95	Jack Glasscock, Cle	2517
1876–97	Cap Anson, Chi	4109
1897–17	Honus Wagner, Pit	4888
1926–47	Mel Ott, NY	5041
1941–63	Stan Musial, StL	6134
1954–74	**Hank Aaron, Atl**	**6587**

Most Bases on Balls

1876–77	George Hall, Lou	20
1876–79	Cal McVey, Cin	23
1876–80	Charley Jones, Cin	66
1876–83	Tom York, Pro	133
1876–86	Joe Start, Pro	150
1876–88	Abner Dalrymple, Chi	197
1878–89	Ned Williamson, Chi	470
1879–92	George Gore, Chi	640
1880–97	Roger Connor, NY	1002
1890–01	Billy Hamilton, Phi	1096
1897–13	Jimmy Sheckard, Chi	1135
1926–47	Mel Ott, NY	1708
1963–83	**Joe Morgan, Cin**	**1799**

AMERICAN LEAGUE

Most Extra Base Hits

1901–05	Danny Green, Chi	113
1901–06	Chick Stahl, Bos	201
1901–07	Buck Freeman, Bos	296
1901–08	Socks Seybold, Phi	316
1901–09	Jimmy Williams, NY	334
1901–10	Bill Bradley, Cle	336
1902–13	Danny Murphy, Phi	420
1901–16	Nap Lajoie, Cle	661
1903–17	Sam Crawford, Det	723
1905–28	Ty Cobb, Det	1139
1914–34	**Babe Ruth, NY**	**1350**

Most Total Bases

1901–05	Candy LaChance, Bos	739
1901–06	Chick Stahl, Bos	1174
1901–07	Buck Freeman, Bos	1264
1901–08	Socks Seybold, Phi	1536
1901–09	Jimmy Williams, NY	1682
1901–10	Bill Bradley, Cle	1728
1902–13	Danny Murphy, Phi	2089
1901–16	Nap Lajoie, Cle	3385
1903–17	Sam Crawford, Det	3579
1905–28	**Ty Cobb, Det**	**5860**

Most Bases on Balls

1902–05	Danny Green, Chi	216
1901–06	Chick Stahl, Bos	280
1901–08	Fielder Jones, Chi	551
1902–11	Topsy Hartsel, Phi	733
1907–28	Tris Speaker, Cle	1381
1906–30	Eddie Collins, Phi	1503
1914–34	**Babe Ruth, NY**	**2036**

MAJOR LEAGUE

Most Extra Base Hits

1876–77	George Hall, Lou, NL	48
1876–79	Cal McVey, Cin, NL	72
1876–84	Lew Brown, Bos, AA	124
1876–85	Tom York, Pro, NL	241
1876–88	Charley Jones, Cin, AA	323
1878–90	Ned Williamson, Chi, NL	377
1876–91	Paul Hines, Pro, NL	508
1880–93	Harry Stovey, Phi, AA	653
1880–97	Roger Connor, NY, NL	811
1896–16	Nap Lajoie, Cle, AL	893
1897–17	Honus Wagner, Pit, NL	1004
1905–28	Ty Cobb, Det, AL	1139
1914–35	Babe Ruth, NY, AL	1356
1941–63	Stan Musial, StL, NL	1377
1954–76	**Hank Aaron, Atl, NL**	**1477**

Most Total Bases

1876–77	George Hall, Lou, NL	264
1876–79	Cal McVey, Cin, NL	488
1876–88	Charley Jones, Cin, AA	645
1876–85	Tom York, Pro, NL & AA	1058
1876–86	Joe Start, Pro, NL	1269
1876–88	Charley Jones, Cin, AA	1632
1876–90	Deacon White, Buf, NL	2036
1876–91	Paul Hines, Pro, NL	2585
1880–93	Harry Stovey, Phi, AA	3022
1876–97	Cap Anson, Chi, NL	4109
1888–07	Jake Beckley, Pit, NL	4158
1896–16	Nap Lajoie, Cle, AL	4471
1897–17	Honus Wagner, Pit, NL	4888
1905–28	Ty Cobb, Det, AL	5863
1941–63	Stan Musial, StL, NL	6134
1954–76	**Hank Aaron, Atl, NL**	**6856**

Most Bases on Balls

1876–77	George Hall, Lou, NL	20
1876–79	Cal McVey, Cin, NL	23
1876–81	Ross Barnes, Chi, NL	59
1876–85	Tom York, Pro, NL & AA	175
1876–88	Charley Jones, Cin, AA	237
1878–90	Ned Williamson, Chi, NL	506
1879–92	George Gore, Chi, NL	717
1880–97	Roger Connor, NY, NL	1002
1888–01	Billy Hamilton, Phi, NL	1187
1907–28	Tris Speaker, Cle, AL	1381
1906–30	Eddie Collins, Phi, AL	1503
1914–35	**Babe Ruth, NY, AL**	**2056**

NATIONAL LEAGUE

Most Strikeouts

1876–77	George Hall, Lou	23
1876–79	Cal McVey, Cin	38
1876–80	Charley Jones, Cin	124
1876–81	Lew Brown, Bos	155
1876–83	Tom York, Pro	186
1878–88	Abner Dalrymple, Chi	341
1876–89	John Morrill, Bos	655
1910–29	Max Carey, Pit	695
1912–30	Cy Williams, Phi	721
1921–38	Kiki Cuyler, Chi	752
1937–46	Vince DiMaggio, Pit	837
1926–47	Met Ott, NY	896
1947–64	Duke Snider, Bkn	1237
1952–67	Eddie Mathews, Mil	1463
1951–73	Willie Mays, SF	1526
1961–79	Lou Brock, StL	1730
1962–82	**Willie Stargell, Pit**	**1936**

Most Stolen Bases (modern rule)

1898–01	Billy Hamilton, Phi	126
1898–11	Billy Dahlen, Chi	289
1898–13	Jimmy Sheckard, Chi	460
1898–17	Honus Wagner, Pit	703
1910–29	Max Carey, Pit	738
1961–79	**Lou Brock, StL**	**938**

Highest Batting Average
(min. 4 years)

1876–79	Cal McVey, Cin	.328
1876–97	Cap Anson, Chi	.334
1896–00	Nap Lajoie, Phi	.349
1890–01	Jesse Burkett, Cle	.355
1892–02	**Willie Keeler, Bal**	**.372**

Highest Slugging Average

1876–79	Cal McVey, Cin	.407
1876–80	Charley Jones, Cin	.455
1880–97	Roger Connor, NY	.487
1879–04	Dan Brouthers, Buf	.519
1915–37	**Rogers Hornsby, StL**	**.577**

AMERICAN LEAGUE

Most Strikeouts

1901–12	Records not kept	
1913–16	Nap Lajoie, Cle	74
1913–17	Sam Crawford, Det	104
1913–20	Joe Jackson, Chi	158
1907–22	Clyde Milan, Was	197
1911–23	Tilly Walker, Phi	511
1910–27	Roger Peckinpaugh, NY	609
1914–34	Babe Ruth, NY	1306
1951–68	Mickey Mantle, NY	1710
1967–87	**Reggie Jackson, Oak**	**2597**

DID YOU KNOW . . . *That in 1887 it took four strikes for a strikeout when the first third called strike did not count? This rule was changed to three strikes in 1888.*

Most Stolen Bases

1901–05	Dave Fultz, NY	170
1901–08	Fielder Jones, Chi	206
1901–09	Frank Isbell, Chi	250
1902–11	Pat Dougherty, Chi	261
1901–16	Nap Lajoie, Cle	295
1903–17	Sam Crawford, Det	317
1907–22	Clyde Milan, Was	495
1905–28	**Ty Cobb, Det**	**892**

Highest Batting Average
(min. 4 years)

1902–05	Danny Green, Chi	.282
1901–06	Chick Stahl, Bos	.290
1901–07	Lave Cross, Phi	.292
1901–08	Socks Seybold, Phi	.295
1902–10	Elmer Flick, Cle	.318
1901–16	Nap Lajoie, Cle	.334
1908–20	Joe Jackson, Chi	.356
1905–28	**Ty Cobb, Det**	**.367**

Highest Slugging Average

1902–05	Danny Green, Chi	.367
1901–06	Chick Stahl, Bos	.389
1901–07	Buck Freeman, Bos	.436
1901–16	Nap Lajoie, Cle	.448
1903–17	Sam Crawford, Det	.448
1908–20	Joe Jackson, Chi	.518
1918–29	Ken Williams, StL	.531
1914–34	**Babe Ruth, NY**	**.690**

MAJOR LEAGUE

Most Strikeouts

1876–77	George Hall, Lou, NL	23
1876–79	Cal McVey, Cin, NL	38
1876–81	Ross Barnes, Chi, NL	53
1876–84	Lew Brown, Bos, NL & AA	155
1876–85	Tom York, Pro, NL & AA	186
1876–90	John Morrill, Bos, NL	656
1910–29	Max Carey, Pit, NL	695
1912–30	Cy Williams, Phi, NL	721
1914–35	Babe Ruth, NY, AL	1330
1951–68	Mickey Mantle, NY, AL	1710
1961–79	Lou Brock, StL, NL	1730
1962–82	Willie Stargell, Pit, NL	1936
1967–87	**Reggie Jackson, Oak, AL**	**2597**

Most Stolen Bases (modern rule)

1898–01	Billy Hamilton, Phi, NL	126
1898–10	Willie Keeler, NY, AL	275
1898–11	Billy Dahlen, Chi, NL	289
1898–13	Jimmy Sheckard, Chi, NL	460
1898–17	Honus Wagner, Pit, NL	703
1905–28	Ty Cobb, Det, AL	892
1961–79	**Lou Brock, StL, NL**	**938**

Highest Batting Average

1876–79	Cal McVey, Cin, NL	.328
1882–94	Pete Browning, Lou, AA	.343
1888–01	Billy Hamilton, Phi, NL	.344
1880–03	Ed Delahanty, Phi, NL	.345
1892–10	Willie Keeler, NY, AL	.345
1908–20	Joe Jackson, Chi, AL	.356
1905–28	**Ty Cobb, Det, AL**	**.367**

Highest Slugging Average

1876–79	Cal McVey, Cin, NL	.407
1876–88	Charley Jones, Cin, AA	.443
1880–93	Harry Stovey, Phi, AA	.476
1880–97	Roger Conner, NY, NL	.487
1888–03	Ed Delahanty, Phi, NL	.504
1879–04	Dan Brouthers, Buf, NL	.520
1915–29	Ken Williams, StL, AL	.531
1914–35	**Babe Ruth, NY, AL**	**.690**

DID YOU KNOW . . . *That Hall Of Famer Ed Delahanty was the first player to retire with a slugging average over .500? Not bad for a fellow playing his entire career in the dead ball era!*

NATIONAL LEAGUE

Most Pinch At Bats
(min. 147 at bats)

1909–15	Ham Hyatt, Pit	219
1923–38	Red Lucas, Cin	437
1954–66	Jerry Lynch, Pit	447
1962–82	**Manny Mota, LA**	**505**

Most Pinch Hits

1888–02	Duke Farrell, NY	22
1910–14	Doc Miller, Phi	39
1909–15	Ham Hyatt, Pit	53
1923–38	Red Lucas, Cin	114
1954–66	Jerry Lynch, Pit	116
1962–82	**Manny Mota, LA**	**150**

Highest Pinch Batting Average
(min. 147 at bats)

1909–15	Ham Hyatt, Pit	.242
1923–38	Red Lucas, Cin	.260
1934–45	**Frenchy Bordagaray, Bkn**	**.312**

AMERICAN LEAGUE

Most Pinch At Bats
(min. 147 at bats)

1908–11	Dode Criss, StL	147
1910–21	Ray Caldwell, NY	154
1922–33	Bob Fothergill, Det	253
1941–62	Dave Philley, Bal	311
1963–75	**Gates Brown, Det**	**414**

Most Pinch Hits

1901–03	Harry Gleason, Bos	3
1901–05	Dave Fultz, NY	3
1901–07	Buck Freeman, Bos	6
1902–08	Piano Legs Hickman, Cle	9
1902–10	Harry Bemis, Cle	18
1908–11	Dode Criss, StL	35
1909–13	Ted Easterly, Cle	37
1922–33	Bob Fothergill, Det	76
1941–62	Dave Philley, Bal	93
1963–75	**Gates Brown, Det**	**107**

Highest Pinch Batting Average
(min. 147 at bats)

1908–11	Dode Criss, StL	.238
1909–13	Ted Easterly, Cle	.296
1922–33	**Bob Fothergill, Det**	**.300**

MAJOR LEAGUE

Most Pinch At Bats
(min. 147 at bats)

1908–11	Dode Criss, StL, AL	147
1909–18	Ham Hyatt, Pit, NL	240
1922–33	Bob Fothergill, Det, AL	253
1923–38	Red Lucas, Cin, NL	437
1949–67	**Smokey Burgess, Pit, NL**	**507**

Most Pinch Hits

1888–05	Duke Farrell, NY, NL	23
1908–11	Dode Criss, StL, AL	35
1909–13	Ted Easterly, Cle, AL	37
1910–14	Doc Miller, Phi, NL	39
1909–18	Ham Hyatt, Pit, NL	57
1922–33	Bob Fothergill, Det, AL	76
1923–38	Red Lucas, Cin, NL	114
1949–67	Smokey Burgess, Pit, NL	145
1962–82	**Manny Mota, LA, NL**	**150**

Highest Pinch Batting Average
(min. 147 at bats)

1908–11	Dode Criss, StL, AL	.238
1909–13	Ted Easterly, Cle, AL	.296
1922–33	Bob Fothergill, Det, AL	.300
1934–45	Frenchy Bordagaray, Bkn, NL	.312
1959–76	**Tommy Davis, LA, NL**	**.320**

NATIONAL LEAGUE SUMMARY

Top Record Producers

1	George Hall, Lou	13
1	Charley Jones, Cin	13
3	Cal McVey, Cin	12
4	Tom York, Pro	11
4	Abner Dalrymple, Chi	11
4	Honus Wagner, Pit	11
7	Cap Anson, Chi	9
7	Joe Start, Pro	9
7	Paul Hines, Pro	9
10	Stan Musial, StL	8

Most Outstanding Record Producers

Honus Wagner, Pit	11 for 454 years
Cap Anson, Chi	9 for 157 years
Mel Ott, NY	7 for 133 years
Stan Musial, StL	8 for 107 years
Hank Aaron, Atl	7 for 88 years

AMERICAN LEAGUE SUMMARY

Top Record Producers

1	Chick Stahl, Bos	14
2	Nap Lajoie, Cle	13
3	Ty Cobb, Det	12
4	Sam Crawford, Det	10
5	Danny Murphy, Phi	8

Most Outstanding Record Producers

Ty Cobb, Det	12 for 543 years
Babe Ruth, NY	6 for 324 years
Sam Crawford, Det	10 for 90 years
Tris Speaker, Cle	2 for 62 years
Nap Lajoie, Cle	13 for 49 years

MAJOR LEAGUE SUMMARY

Top Record Producers

1	George Hall, Lou, NL	13
2	Cal McVey, Cin, NL	12
3	Tom York, Pro, NL & AA	11
3	Charley Jones, Cin, AA	11
5	Ty Cobb, Det, AL	10
6	Nap Lajoie, Cle, AL	9
6	Paul Hines, Pro, NL	9
6	Honus Wagner, Pit, NL	9

Most Outstanding Record Producers

Ty Cobb, Det, AL	10 for 426 years
Babe Ruth, NY, AL	6 for 269 years
Cap Anson, Chi, NL	8 for 114 years
Honus Wagner, Pit, NL	9 for 99 years
Cal McVey, Cin, NL	12 for 75 years

The most recent record setters in each of the career batting categories are truly among the game's greatest players, while the top four on the record producers list show the advantage that the pioneer players had at the starting points.

The ability of a player to create records does not necessarily guarantee his degree of greatness. A perfect case in point is Rogers Hornsby. He established only three National League career records and no Major League marks, yet most experts would place him as one of the top five players of all time.

A major factor in the creation of career records is longevity. A player's ability to remain uninjured and in good health provides an advantage over similarly talented players who have shorter careers.

A second major factor in establishing career records is being in the right place at the right time. Had Hornsby played before Honus Wagner he would have

HANK AARON

Hank Aaron set numerous career batting records, although of course he is best remembered for hitting 755 home runs.

HONUS WAGNER
"The Flying Dutchman" set many records, including most hits, most extra base hits, and most stolen bases.

had a bushel of records, and the same can be said of many players who had the misfortune of playing after Ty Cobb and Babe Ruth.

Modern-day players have noticeably few records in part due to the "two-platoon" system used today. Only players with superstar potential are given the opportunity to play against lefty and righty pitchers, and those players who are platooned have absolutely no chance at setting career records.

Even the modern-day superstar has a long row to hoe if, for example, he wants to break Hank Aaron's home run record. All he would have to do is average better than 32.7 home runs for 23 years! When one looks at those astronomical numbers and reflects for a moment, one realizes just how great Hank Aaron really was. And to think that Aaron accomplished his tremendous feat during one of the most difficult times for a hitter. Aaron's era saw some of the most difficult pitching ever. Relief pitching was in full swing, and in many games Hammering Hank would see three or four different pitchers, all with strong, rested arms, right-hand pitchers going against right-hand batters, and so forth. Aaron also had to create his monstrous home run record while playing day games after night games and fighting jet lag after traveling across time zones. Finally, let us not overlook the tremendous pressure the new home run king was under. Taking Babe Ruth down from the number one position seemed to be against national honor and many a baseball fan did not want the Babe's record to be broken.

Of course the Sultan of Swat will always be our hero. He is *the* player who brought the fans out to the ball-parks, and he will always be considered baseball's greatest player. In a later chapter Ruth's greatness will be discussed in detail, especially in terms of his 69 batting titles—more than any player in baseball history.

Pete Rose has now announced his official retirement as a player and his career totals can now be calculated. The stats that Rose posted show that "Charlie Hustle" is a guaranteed Hall of Famer. Charlie Hustle has played more games, had more at bats and more hits than any human being who ever put on a pair of spikes. And he accomplished this feat without having the pure talent of a Babe Ruth, Ty Cobb or Hank Aaron. Pete had to hustle, scratch and claw his way to fame.

A chapter on career records would be amiss if the name of Ty Cobb was not discussed. He is the closest to Ruth in greatness, and one would have to be great to score more runs than any other player in baseball. He would have to be great to compile a lifetime batting average of .367. Did you know that Cobb batted over .300 for 23 consecutive years? And that most of the time his averages were closer to .400 than .300?

CHAPTER 3

SEASON PITCHING RECORDS

NATIONAL LEAGUE QUIZ

1. Only one pitcher has ever appeared in 106 games in one season. Do you know him?
2. This outstanding pitcher started 75 games and, believe it or not, completed all 75 games. Do you know this remarkable performer?
3. Can you name the only pitcher in baseball who has won 60 games in one season?
4. The highest winning percentage ever registered in the NL is .889. Do you remember this pitcher?
5. One of the most amazing pitching records is 16 shutouts, tossed by two spectacular pitchers: one pitcher did this in the very first year of baseball in 1876; the other accomplished the feat in 1916. Can you name these two pitchers?

AMERCIAN LEAGUE QUIZ

1. The shutouts record began with 5 in 1901 and stands at 13 in 1910. Five different pitchers hold shutout records. How many can you name?
2. This Hall of Famer set three consecutive strikeout records from 1902 through 1904. Do you remember him?
3. Can you name the last two pitchers who worked over 450 innings in one season?
4. One of the AL's greatest strikeout pitchers also allowed the most bases on balls. Who is he?
5. Who was the first AL relief pitcher to appear in more than 80 games?

MAJOR LEAGUE QUIZ

1. From 1909 through 1913, this fantastic relief pitcher set five consecutive appearance records. Name him.
2. Can you name the first relief pitcher to appear in 70 games?
3. Only one relief pitcher has won as many as 18 games. He only lost one game and his winning percentage of .947 is the highest in baseball history. Name him.
4. The most losses ever suffered by a relief pitcher is 16. Do you know this hard-luck pitcher?
5. For the first time in baseball history, a relief pitcher recently saved 46 games. Who is this modern phenom?

NATIONAL LEAGUE

Most Total Games
1876	Jim Devlin, Lou	68
1879	Will White, Cin	76
1883	Pud Galvin, Buf	76
1883	Hoss Radbourn, Pro	76
1965	Ted Abernathy, Chi	84
1969	Wayne Granger, Cin	90
1973	Mike Marshall, Mon	92
1974	**Mike Marshall, LA**	**106**

Most Starts
1876	Jim Devlin, Lou	68
1879	**Will White, Cin**	**75**

Most Starts after 1900
1900	Pink Hawley, NY	38
1901	Dummy Taylor, NY	43
1902	Vic Willis, Bos	46
1903	**Joe McGinnity, NY**	**48**

Most Games Completed
1876	Jim Devlin, Lou	66
1879	**Will White, Cin**	**75**

Most Games Completed after 1900
1900	Pink Hawley, NY	34
1901	Noodles Hahn, Cin	41
1902	**Vic Willis, Bos**	**45**

Most Wins
1876	Al Spalding, Chi	47
1879	Monte Ward, Pro	47
1883	Hoss Radbourn, Pro	49
1884	**Hoss Radbourn, Pro**	**60**

Most Wins after 1900
1900	Joe McGinnity, Bkn	29
1903	Joe McGinnity, NY	31
1904	Joe McGinnity, NY	35
1908	**Christy Mathewson, NY**	**37**

Most Losses
1876	Jim Devlin, Lou	35
1879	Jim McCormick, Cle	40
1879	George Bradley, Tro	40
1880	Will White, Cin	42
1883	**John Coleman, Phi**	**48**

Most Losses after 1900
1900	Bill Carrick, NY	22
1901	Dummy Taylor, NY	27
1905	**Vic Willis, Bos**	**29**

AMERICAN LEAGUE

Most Total Games
1901	Joe McGinnity, Bal	48
1904	Jack Chesbro, NY	55
1907	Ed Walsh, Chi	56
1908	Ed Walsh, Chi	66
1955	Ellis Kinder, Bos	69
1964	John Wyatt, KC	81
1965	Eddie Fisher, Chi	82
1968	Wilbur Wood, Chi	88
1979	**Mike Marshall, Min**	**90**

Most Starts
1901	Joe McGinnity, Bal	43
1902	Cy Young, Bos	43
1904	**Jack Chesbro, NY**	**51**

Most Games Completed
1901	Joe McGinnity, Bal	39
1902	Cy Young, Bos	41
1904	**Jack Chesbro, NY**	**48**

Most Wins
1901	Cy Young, Bos	33
1904	**Jack Chesbro, NY**	**41**

Most Losses
1901	Pete Dowling, Cle	26
1909	Bob Groom, Was	26

MAJOR LEAGUE

Most Total Games
1876	Jim Devlin, Lou, NL	68
1879	Will White, Cin, NL	76
1883	Pud Galvin, Buf, NL	76
1883	Hoss Radbourn, Pro, NL	76
1884	Guy Hecker, Lou, AA	76
1964	John Wyatt, KC, AL	81
1965	Ted Abernathy, Chi, NL	84
1968	Wilbur Wood, Chi, AL	88
1969	Wayne Granger, Cin, NL	90
1973	Mike Marshall, Mon, NL	92
1974	**Mike Marshall, LA, NL**	**106**

Most Starts
1876	Jim Devlin, Lou, NL	68
1879	**Will White, Cin, NL**	**75**

Most Starts after 1900
1900	Pink Hawley, NY, NL	38
1901	Dummy Taylor, NY, NL	43
1901	Joe McGinnity, Bal, AL	43
1902	Vic Willis, Bos, NL	46
1903	Joe McGinnity, NY, NL	48
1904	**Jack Chesbro, NY, AL**	**51**

Most Games Completed
1876	Jim Devlin, Lou, NL	66
1879	**Will White, Cin, NL**	**75**

Most Games Completed after 1900
1900	Pink Hawley, NY, NL	38
1901	Noodles Hahn, Cin, NL	41
1902	Vic Willis, Bos, NL	45
1904	**Jack Chesbro, NY, AL**	**48**

Most Wins
1876	Al Spalding, Chi, NL	47
1879	Monte Ward, Pro, NL	47
1883	Hoss Radbourn, Pro, NL	49
1884	**Hoss Radbourn, Pro, NL**	**60**

Most Wins after 1900
1900	Joe McGinnity, Bkn, NL	29
1901	Cy Young, Bos, AL	33
1904	**Jack Chesbro, NY, AL**	**41**

Most Losses
1876	Jim Devlin, Lou, NL	35
1879	Jim McCormick, Cle, NL	40
1879	George Bradley, Tro, NL	40
1880	Will White, Cin, NL	42
1883	**John Coleman, Phi, NL**	**48**

Most Losses after 1900
1900	Bill Carrick, NY, NL	22
1901	Dummy Taylor, NY, NL	27
1905	**Vic Willis, Bos, NL**	**29**

NATIONAL LEAGUE

Highest Winning Percentage,
Starters
1876	Al Spalding, Chi	.783
	(47–13)	
1876	Jack Manning, Bos	.783
	(18–5)	
1880	Fred Goldsmith, Chi	.875
	(21–3)	
1940	**Freddie Fitzsimmons, Bkn**	**.889**
	(16–2)	

Lowest ERA
1876	George Bradley, StL	1.23
1906	**Three Finger Brown, Chi**	**1.04**

Most Innings Pitched
1876	Jim Devlin, Lou	622
1879	**Will White, Cin**	**680**

Most Innings Pitched after 1900
1900	Joe McGinnity, Bkn	347
1901	Noodles Hahn, Cin	375
1902	Vic Willis, Bos	410
1903	**Joe McGinnity, NY**	**434**

Most Hits Allowed
1876	Bob Mathews, NY	693
1883	**John Coleman, Phi**	**772**

Most Hits Allowed after 1900
1900	Bill Carrick, NY	415

Most Bases on Balls Allowed
1876	Joe Bordon, Bos	51
1877	Tricky Nichols, StL	53
1877	Terry Larkin, Har	53
1878	The Only Nolan, Ind	56
1879	Jim McCormick, Cle	74
1880	Larry Corcoran, Chi	99
1882	Jim McCormick, Cle	103
1884	Mickey Welch, NY	146
1886	Mickey Welch, NY	163
1890	**Amos Rusie, NY**	**289**

Most Bases on Balls Allowed
after 1900
1900	Joe McGinnity, Bkn	113
1901	Wild Bill Donovan, Bkn	152
1911	Bob Harmon, StL	181
1955	**Sam Jones, Chi**	**185**

AMERICAN LEAGUE

Highest Winning Percentage
1901	Clark Griffith, Chi	.774
	(24–7)	
1902	Bill Bernhard, Cle	.783
	(17–5)	
1907	Bill Donovan, Det	.862
	(25–4)	
1912	Joe Wood, Bos	.872
	(34–5)	
1931	Lefty Grove, Phi	.886
	(31–4)	
1937	**Johnny Allen, Cle**	**.938**
	(15–1)	

Lowest ERA
1901	Cy Young, Bos	1.62
1904	Addie Joss, Cle	1.59
1905	Rube Waddell, Phi	1.48
1908	Addie Joss, Cle	1.16
1913	Walter Johnson, Was	1.09
1914	**Dutch Leonard, Bos**	**1.01**

Most Innings Pitched
1901	Joe McGinnity, Bal	382
1902	Cy Young, Bos	385
1904	Jack Chesbro, NY	455
1908	**Ed Walsh, Chi**	**464**

Most Hits Allowed
1901	Joe McGinnity, Bal	412

Most Bases on Balls Allowed
1901	Chick Fraser, Phi	132
1905	George Mullin, Det	138
1938	**Bob Feller, Cle**	**208**

DID YOU KNOW . . . *That the bases on balls allowed record zoomed from 51 in 1876 (when it took nine balls for a walk) to 289 in 1890 (when it took four balls for a base on balls)?*

DID YOU KNOW . . . *That a pioneer pitcher would be charged with an error when he issued a base on balls? This rule was changed in 1887.*

MAJOR LEAGUE

Highest Winning Percentage
1876	Al Spalding, Chi, NL	.783
1876	Jack Manning, Bos, NL	.783
1880	Fred Goldsmith, Chi, NL	.875
1931	Lefty Grove, Phi, AL	.886
1940	**Fred Fitzsimmons, Bkn,**	
	NL	**.889**

DID YOU KNOW . . . *That home plate used to be a 12-inch square (1876–1899), and it was changed to a 17-inch five-sided figure in 1900?*

Lowest ERA
1876	George Bradley, StL, NL	1.23
1906	Three Finger Brown, Chi,	
	NL	1.04
1914	**Dutch Leonard, Bos, AL**	**1.01**

Most Innings Pitched
1876	Jim Devlin, Lou, NL	622
1879	**Will White, Cin, NL**	**680**

Most Innings Pitched after 1900
1900	Joe McGinnity, Bkn, NL	347
1901	Joe McGinnity, Bal, AL	382
1902	Vic Willis, Bos, NL	410
1903	Joe McGinnity, NY, NL	434
1904	Jack Chesbro, NY, AL	455
1908	**Ed Walsh, Chi, AL**	**464**

Most Hits Allowed
1876	Bob Mathews, NY, NL	693
1883	**John Coleman, Phi, NL**	**772**

Most Hits Allowed after 1900
1900	Bill Carrick, NY, NL	415

Most Bases on Balls Allowed
1876	Joe Bordon, Bos, NL	51
1877	Tricky Nichols, StL, NL	53
1877	Terry Larkin, Har, NL	53
1878	The Only Nolan, Ind, NL	56
1879	Jim McCormick, Cle, NL	74
1880	Larry Corcoran, Chi, NL	99
1882	Jim McCormick, Cle, NL	103
1884	Mickey Welch, NY, NL	146
1886	Toad Ramsey, Lou, AA	207
1889	Mark Baldwin, Col, AA	274
1890	**Amos Rusie, NY, NL**	**289**

Most Bases on Balls Allowed
after 1900
1900	Joe McGinnity, Bkn, NL	113
1901	Wild Bill Donovan, Bkn, NL	152
1911	Bob Harmon, StL, NL	181
1938	**Bob Feller, Cle, AL**	**208**

NATIONAL LEAGUE		AMERICAN LEAGUE		MAJOR LEAGUE	

Most Strikeouts

National League		American League		Major League	
1876 Jim Devlin, Lou	122	1901 Cy Young, Bos	158	1876 Jim Devlin, Lou, NL	122
1877 Tommy Bond, Bos	170	1902 Rube Waddell, Phi	210	1877 Tommy Bond, Bos, NL	170
1878 Tommy Bond, Bos	182	1903 Rube Waddell, Phi	302	1878 Tommy Bond, Bos, NL	182
1879 Monte Ward, Pro	239	1904 Rube Waddell, Phi	349	1879 Monte Ward, Pro, NL	239
1880 Larry Corcoran, Chi	268	1973 Nolan Ryan, Cal	383	1880 Larry Corcoran, Chi, NL	268
1883 Jim Whitney, Bos	345			1883 Tim Keefe, NY, AA	361
1884 Hoss Radbourn, Pro	**441**			1884 One Arm Dailey, C-P, UL	483
				1886 Matt Kilroy, Bal, AA	**513**

DID YOU KNOW...*That a foul ball caught on one bounce was once an out (1876–1883)?*

Most Strikeouts after 1900

National League				Major League	
1900 Rube Waddell, Pit	130			1900 Rube Waddell, Pit, NL	130
1901 Noodles Hahn, Cin	239			1901 Noodles Hahn, Cin, NL	239
1903 Christy Mathewson, NY	267			1903 Rube Waddell, Phi, AL	302
1961 Sandy Koufax, LA	269			1904 Rube Waddell, Phi, AL	349
1963 Sandy Koufax, LA	306			1965 Sandy Koufax, LA, NL	382
1965 Sandy Koufax, LA	**382**			1973 Nolan Ryan, Cal, AL	383

Most Shutouts

National League		American League		Major League	
1876 George Bradley, StL	16	1901 Cy Young, Bos	5	1876 George Bradley, StL, NL	16
1916 Grover Alexander, Phi	16	1901 Clark Griffith, Chi	5	1916 Grover Alexander, Phi, NL	16
		1902 Addie Joss, Cle	5		
		1903 Cy Young, Bos	7		
		1904 Cy Young, Bos	10		
		1906 Ed Walsh, Chi	10		
		1908 Ed Walsh, Chi	11		
		1910 Jack Coombs, Phi	**13**		

Most Relief Appearances

National League		American League		Major League	
1876 Jack Manning, Bos	14	1901 Pete Dowling, Cle	9	1876 Jack Manning, Bos, NL	14
1906 George Ferguson, NY	21	1904 Ed Walsh, Chi	10	1905 Clark Griffith, NY, AL	18
1909 Doc Crandall, NY	23	1905 Clark Griffith, NY	18	1906 George Ferguson, NY, NL	21
1910 Doc Crandall, NY	24	1908 Rube Vickers, Phi	20	1909 Doc Crandall, NY, NL	23
1911 Doc Crandall, NY	26	1912 Ed Walsh, Chi	21	1910 Doc Crandall, NY, NL	24
1911 Three Finger Brown, Chi	26	1913 Bert Gallia, Was	27	1911 Doc Crandall, NY, NL	26
1912 Doc Crandall, NY	27	1915 Sam Jones, Cle	39	1911 Three Finger Brown, Chi, NL	26
1913 Doc Crandall, NY	32	1917 Dan Danforth, Chi	41	1912 Doc Crandall, NY, NL	27
1928 Bob McGraw, Phi	36	1923 Allan Russell, Was	46	1913 Doc Crandall, NY, NL	32
1929 Bob McGraw, Phi	37	1925 Firpo Marberry, Was	55	1915 Sam Jones, Cle, AL	39
1931 Jack Quinn, Bkn	38	1926 Firpo Marberry, Was	59	1917 Dan Danforth, Chi, AL	41
1932 Jack Quinn, Bkn	42	1950 Joe Page, NY	60	1923 Allan Russell, Was, AL	46
1937 Mace Brown, Pit	48	1951 Ellis Kinder, Bos	61	1925 Firpo Marberry, Was, AL	55
1938 Mace Brown, Pit	49	1953 Ellis Kinder, Bos	69	1926 Firpo Marberry, Was, AL	59
1942 Ace Adams, NY	61	1964 John Wyatt, KC	81	1942 Ace Adams, NY, NL	61
1943 Ace Adams, NY	70	1965 Eddie Fisher, Chi	82	1943 Ace Adams, NY, NL	70
1950 Jim Konstanty, Phi	74	1968 Wilbur Wood, Chi	86	1950 Jim Konstanty, Phi, NL	74
1965 Ted Abernathy, Chi	84	**1979 Mike Marshall, Min**	**89**	1964 John Wyatt, KC, AL	81
1969 Wayne Granger, Cin	90			1965 Ted Abernathy, Chi, NL	84
1973 Mike Marshall, Mon	92			1969 Wayne Granger, Cin, NL	90
1974 Mike Marshall, LA	**106**			1973 Mike Marshall, Mon, NL	92
				1974 Mike Marshall, LA, NL	**106**

DID YOU KNOW...*That for many years the bat did not have to be round? Some bats were flat on one side and round on the other. The rule for a completely round bat did not come into effect until 1893.*

NATIONAL LEAGUE

Most Relief Wins

1876	Jack Manning, Bos	4
1879	Monte Ward, Pro	5
1891	Bill Hutchinson, Chi	7
1894	Nig Cuppy, Cle	8
1929	Johnny Morrison, Bkn	10
1932	Ben Cantwell, Bos	12
1938	Mace Brown, Pit	15
1950	Jim Konstanty, Phi	16
1959	**Elroy Face, Pit**	**18**

Most Relief Losses

1876–82	Many tied with one	
1883	Hoss Radbourn, Pro	2
1887	Mike Tiernan, NY	2
1888	George VanHaltren, Chi	2
1889	Kid Gleason, Phi	2
1891	Cy Young, Cle	3
1892	Frank Killen, Was	3
1893	Ted Breitenstein, StL	3
1894	Pink Hawley, StL	5
1899	Sam Leever, Pit	5
1909	Forrest More, StL	5
1911	Frank Smith, Cin	5
1912	Doc Crandall, NY	5
1913	Bob Harmon, StL	6
1922	Tony Kaufmann, Chi	6
1928	Bob McGraw, Phi	8
1932	Ben Cantwell, Bos	8
1938	Mace Brown, Pit	8
1944	Ace Adams, NY	9
1945	Ace Adams, NY	9
1947	Harry Gumpert, Cin	10
1949	Nels Potter, Bos	11
1956	Elroy Face, Pit	12
1961	Elroy Face, Pit	12
1974	Mike Marshall, LA	12
1975	Mike Marshall, LA	14
1979	**Gene Garber, Atl**	**16**

AMERICAN LEAGUE

Most Relief Wins

1901	Clark Griffith, Chi	3
1904	Jack Chesbro, NY	3
1905	Chief Bender, Phi	7
1911	Ed Walsh, Chi	7
1913	Byron Houch, Phi	8
1923	Allan Russell, Was	9
1925	Elam Vangilder, StL	11
1927	Wilcy Moore, NY	13
1946	Earl Caldwell, Chi	13
1947	Joe Page, NY	14
1961	Luis Arroyo, NY	15
1963	Dick Radatz, Bos	15
1964	Dick Radatz, Bos	16
1974	**John Hiller, Det**	**17**
1976	**Bill Campbell, Min**	**17**

Most Relief Losses

1901	Pete Dowling, Cle	4
1911	Ed Walsh, Chi	5
1913	Chief Bender, Phi	5
1917	Dan Danforth, Chi	6
1918	George Mogridge, NY	7
1921	Jim Middleton, Det	8
1928	Firpo Marberry, Was	9
1933	Chief Hogsett, Det	9
1940	Al Benton, Det	10
1961	Frank Funk, Cle	11
1965	Dick Radatz, Bos	11
1970	**Darold Knowles, Was**	**14**
1974	**John Hiller, Det**	**14**
1979	**Mike Marshall, Min**	**14**

DID YOU KNOW . . . *That the early rule regarding a pitcher's delivery was that his arm must dip below his waist? We know this as a submarine pitch. The rule was changed to a shoulder-high delivery in 1884.*

DID YOU KNOW . . . *That the spitball was a legal pitch until 1920? The outlawing of the spitball, plus a new livelier ball, began a new and exciting home run era.*

MAJOR LEAGUE

Most Relief Wins

1876	Jack Manning, Bos, NL	4
1879	Monte Ward, Pro, NL	5
1891	Bill Hutchinson, Chi, NL	7
1891	Clark Griffith, StL, NL	7
1894	Nig Cuppy, Cle, NL	8
1913	Byron Houch, Phi, AL	8
1925	Elam Vangilder, StL, AL	11
1927	Wilcy Moore, NY, AL	13
1938	Mace Brown, Pit, NL	15
1950	Jim Konstanty, Phi, NL	16
1959	**Elroy Face, Pit, NL**	**18**

Most Relief Losses

1885	Pop Corkhill, Cin, AA	3
1891	Cy Young, Cle, NL	3
1892	Frank Killen, Was, NL	3
1893	Ted Breitenstein, StL, NL	3
1894	Pink Hawley, StL, NL	5
1899	Sam Leever, Pit, NL	5
1909	Forrest More, Bos, NL	5
1911	Frank Smith, Cin, NL	5
1911	Ed Walsh, Chi, AL	5
1912	Doc Crandall, NY, NL	5
1913	Bob Harmon, StL, NL	6
1917	Dan Danforth, Chi, Al	6
1918	George Mogridge, NY, AL	7
1921	Jim Middleton, Det, AL	8
1928	Firpo Marberry, Was, AL	9
1933	Chief Hogsett, Det, AL	9
1940	Al Benton, Det, AL	10
1949	Nels Potter, Bos, NL	11
1956	Elroy Face, Pit, NL	12
1961	Elroy Face, Pit, NL	12
1970	Darold Knowles, Was, AL	14
1974	John Hiller, Det, AL	14
1975	Mike Marshall, LA, NL	14
1979	**Gene Garber, Atl, NL**	**16**

NATIONAL LEAGUE		
Most Saves		
1876	Jack Manning, Bos	5
1904	Joe McGinnity, NY	5
1905	Claude Elliott, NY	6
1906	George Ferguson, NY	6
1909	Three Finger Brown, Chi	7
1910	Three Finger Brown, Chi	7
1911	Three Finger Brown, Chi	13
1931	Jack Quinn, Bkn	15
1945	Andy Karl, Phi	15
1947	Hugh Casey, Bkn	18
1950	Jim Konstanty, Phi	22
1954	Jim Hughes, Bkn	24
1960	Lindy McDaniel, StL	26
1962	Elroy Face, Pit	28
1965	Ted Abernathy, Chi	31
1970	Wayne Granger, Cin	35
1972	Clay Carroll, Cin	37
1978	Rollie Fingers, SD	37
1979	Bruce Sutter, Chi	37
1984	**Bruce Sutter, StL**	**45**

Most Relief Wins and Saves		
1876	Jack Manning, Bos	9
1908	Three Finger Brown, Chi	9
1910	Doc Crandall, NY	11
1911	Three Finger Brown, Chi	18
1929	Johnny Morrison, Bkn	18
1931	Jack Quinn, Bkn	20
1938	Mace Brown, Pit	20
1945	Ace Adams, NY	26
1947	Hugh Casey, Bkn	28
1950	Jim Konstanty, Phi	38
1960	Lindy McDaniel, StL	38
1970	Wayne Granger, Cin	41
1972	Clay Carroll, Cin	43
1973	Mike Marshall, Mon	45
1982	Bruce Sutter, StL	45
1984	**Bruce Sutter, StL**	**50**

Most Relief Wins without a Loss		
1876	Jack Manning, Bos	4
1891	Bill Hutchinson, Chi	7
1894	**Nig Cuppy, Cle**	**8**
1937	**Charlie Root, Chi**	**8**
1946	**Emil Kush, Chi**	**8**
1953	**Lew Burdette, Mil**	**8**

AMERICAN LEAGUE		
Most Saves		
1901	Bill Hoffer, Cle	3
1906	Chief Bender, Phi	3
1907	Ed Walsh, Chi	4
1908	Ed Walsh, Chi	6
1909	Frank Arellanes, Bos	8
1912	Ed Walsh, Chi	10
1924	Firpo Marberry, Was	15
1925	Firpo Marberry, Was	15
1926	Firpo Marberry, Was	22
1949	Joe Page, NY	27
1953	Ellis Kinder, Bos	27
1961	Luis Arroyo, NY	29
1964	Dick Radatz, Bos	29
1966	Jack Aker, KC	32
1970	Ron Perranoski, Min	34
1972	Sparky Lyle, NY	35
1973	John Hiller, Det	38
1983	Dan Quisenberry, KC	45
1986	**Dave Righetti, NY**	**46**

Most Relief Wins and Saves		
1901	Clark Griffith, Chi	4
1902	Rube Waddell, Phi	5
1905	Rube Waddell, Phi	8
1908	Ed Walsh, Chi	11
1909	Frank Arellanes, Bos	11
1911	Ed Walsh, Chi	11
1912	Ed Walsh, Chi	14
1917	Dan Danforth, Chi	17
1923	Allan Russell, Was	18
1924	Firpo Marberry, Was	21
1925	Firpo Marberry, Was	23
1926	Firpo Marberry, Was	31
1947	Joe Page, NY	31
1949	Joe Page, NY	40
1961	Luis Arroyo, NY	44
1964	Dick Radatz, Bos	45
1973	John Hiller, Det	48
1983	Dan Quisenberry, KC	50
1984	Dan Quisenberry, KC	50
1986	**Dave Righetti, NY**	**54**

Most Relief Wins without a Loss		
1901	Clark Griffith, Chi	3
1902	Rube Waddell, Phi	5
1905	Rube Waddell, Phi	8
1926	**Joe Pate, Phi**	**9**

MAJOR LEAGUE		
Most Saves		
1876	Jack Manning, Bos, NL	5
1889	Tony Mullane, Cin, AA	5
1904	Joe McGinnity, NY, NL	5
1905	Claude Elliott, NY, NL	6
1906	George Ferguson, NY, NL	6
1908	Ed Walsh, Chi, AL	6
1909	Frank Arellanes, Bos, AL	8
1911	Three Finger Brown, Chi, NL	13
1924	Firpo Marberry, Was, AL	15
1925	Firpo Marberry, Was, AL	15
1926	Firpo Marberry, Was, AL	22
1949	Joe Page, NY, AL	27
1953	Ellis Kinder, Bos, AL	27
1961	Luis Arroyo, NY, AL	29
1964	Dick Radatz, Bos, AL	29
1965	Ted Abernathy, Chi, NL	31
1966	Jack Aker, KC, AL	32
1970	Wayne Granger, Cin, NL	35
1972	Clay Carroll, Cin, NL	37
1973	John Hiller, Det, AL	38
1983	Dan Quisenberry, KC, AL	45
1984	Bruce Sutter, StL, NL	45
1986	**Dave Righetti, NY, AL**	**46**

Most Relief Wins and Saves		
1876	Jack Manning, Bos, NL	9
1908	Ed Walsh, Chi, AL	11
1909	Frank Arellanes, Bos, AL	11
1910	Doc Crandall, NY, NL	11
1911	Three Finger Brown, Chi, NL	18
1923	Allan Russell, Was, AL	18
1924	Firpo Marberry, Was, AL	21
1925	Firpo Marberry, Was, AL	23
1926	Firpo Marberry, Was, AL	31
1947	Joe Page, NY, AL	31
1949	Joe Page, NY, AL	40
1961	Luis Arroyo, NY, AL	44
1964	Dick Radatz, Bos, AL	45
1973	John Hiller, Det, AL	48
1983	Dan Quisenberry, KC, AL	50
1984	Dan Quisenberry, KC, AL	50
1984	Bruce Sutter, StL, NL	50
1986	**Dave Righetti, NY, AL**	**54**

Most Relief Wins without a Loss		
1876	Jack Manning, Bos, NL	4
1886	Tony Mullane, Cin, AA	4
1889	Bob Caruthers, Bkn, AA	4
1891	Clark Griffith, StL, NL	7
1891	Bill Hutchinson, Chi, NL	7
1894	Nig Cuppy, Cle, NL	8
1905	Rube Waddell, Phi, AL	8
1914	George Mullin, Ind, FL	8
1926	**Joe Pate, Phi, AL**	**9**

NATIONAL LEAGUE SUMMARY

Top Record Producers before 1900:
Starters

1	Jim Devlin, Lou	5
2	Will White, Cin	4
2	Hoss Radbourn, Pro	4
4	Al Spalding, Chi	2
4	Monte Ward, Pro	2
4	George Bradley, StL	2
4	Tommy Bond, Bos	2

Top Record Producers after 1900:
Starters

1	Joe McGinnity, NY	6
2	Noodles Hahn, Cin	3
2	Sandy Koufax, LA	3
2	Vic Willis, Bos	3
5	Christy Mathewson, NY	2
5	Pink Hawley, NY	2

Top Record Producers after 1900:
in Relief

1	Doc Crandall, NY	6
2	Three Finger Brown, Chi	5
3	Jack Quinn, Bkn	4
3	Mace Brown, Pit	4
3	Jim Konstanty, Phi	4
3	Bruce Sutter, StL	4

Most Outstanding Record Producers:
Starters before 1900

Will White, Cin	4 for 331 years
Hoss Radbourn, Pro	4 for 293 years
George Bradley, StL	2 for 142 years

Most Outstanding Record Producers:
Starters after 1900

Joe McGinnity, NY	6 for 176 years
Christy Mathewson, NY	2 for 138 years
Vic Willis, Pit	3 for 90 years
Three Finger Brown, Chi	1 for 82 years
Grover Alexander, Phi	1 for 72 years

Most Outstanding Record Producers:
Relievers after 1900

Jim Konstanty, Phi	4 for 48 years
Three Finger Brown, Chi	5 for 43 years
Elroy Face, Pit	2 for 32 years
Jack Quinn, Bkn	4 for 27 years
Mace Brown, Pit	4 for 24 years
Mike Marshall, LA	3 for 24 years
Doc Crandall, NY	6 for 20 years

AMERICAN LEAGUE SUMMARY

Top Record Producers: Starters

1	Cy Young, Bos	9
2	Jack Chesbro, NY	5
2	Ed Walsh, Chi	5
4	Rube Waddell, Phi	4
5	Addie Joss, Cle	3

Top Record Producers: in Relief

1	Ed Walsh, Chi	8
1	Firpo Marberry, Was	8
3	Joe Page, NY	5
4	Dick Radatz, Bos	4
4	Clark Griffith, NY	4
4	Rube Waddell, Phi	4
7	Allan Russell, Was	3
7	Ellis Kinder, Bos	3

Most Outstanding Record Producers:
Starters

Jack Chesbro, NY	5 for 259 years
Ed Walsh, Chi	5 for 132 years
Jack Coombs, Phi	1 for 78 years
Rube Waddell, Phi	4 for 76 years
Dutch Leonard, Bos	1 for 74 years

Most Outstanding Record Producers:
in Relief

Firpo Marberry, Was	8 for 73 years
Joe Pate, NY	1 for 62 years
Joe Page, NY	5 for 31 years
Rube Waddell, Phi	4 for 27 years
Ed Walsh, Chi	8 for 23 years
Dick Radatz, Bos	4 for 22 years
John Hiller, Det	2 for 20 years

MAJOR LEAGUE SUMMARY

Top Record Producers before 1900:
Starters

1	Jim Devlin, Lou, NL	5
2	Will White, Cin, NL	4
3	Hoss Radbourn, Pro, NL	3

Top Record Producers after 1900:
Starters

1	Joe McGinnity, NY, NL	5
2	Jack Chesbro, NY, AL	4
3	Vic Willis, Bos, NL	3
3	Rube Waddell, Phi, AL	3

Top Record Producers after 1900:
in Relief

1	Firpo Marberry, Was, AL	8
2	Doc Crandall, NY, NL	6
3	Three Finger Brown, Chi, NL	3
3	Joe Page, NY, AL	3
3	Dan Quisenberry, KC, AL	3

Most Outstanding Record Producers:
Starters before 1900

Will White, Cin, AA	4 for 331 years
Hoss Radbourn, Pro, NL	4 for 293 years
George Bradley, StL, NL	2 for 142 years

Most Outstanding Record Producers:
Starters after 1900

Jack Chesbro, NY, AL	5 for 259 years
Joe McGinnity, NY, NL	6 for 172 years
Christy Mathewson, NY, NL	2 for 136 years
Ed Walsh, Chi, AL	5 for 132 years
Vic Willis, Pit, NL	3 for 88 years

Most Outstanding Record Producers:
in Relief after 1900

Firpo Marberry, Was, AL	8 for 73 years
Joe Pate, Phi, AL	1 for 62 years
Jim Konstanty, Phi, NL	4 for 48 years
Three Finger Brown, Chi, NL	5 for 43 years
Joe Page, NY, AL	5 for 31 years

There is no way of comparing pioneer pitchers with our modern pitchers, due to their different methods and theories of pitching. This is another example of why the rules committee decision that baseball is to have only one set of records serves an injustice upon the modern-day player.

With the pitching methods of today, it is inconceivable that anyone will ever break Will White's records of 75 starts, 75 completions and 680 innings pitched in 1879. In those early days, the limitations of pitchers were not known, and since they used the "under the hip" delivery and only had to toss the ball 45 and then 50 feet, it certainly isn't fair to expect pitchers with overhand deliveries and a 60′6″ pitching distance to do

ED WALSH
Ed Walsh was both a star starter and reliever, racking up records in both capacities.

GROVER ALEXANDER

*In 1916, Alexander the Great started 45 games, completed 38, and tossed
16 shutouts. He won 30 or more games 3 times and also had 6 seasons
of 20 wins or more. He led the league in various pitching departments
44 times.*

the same things the pioneer pitcher did. All that needs
to be done to correct the situation is to start a new set
of records that begin when the mound was moved to
60′6″.

It is reasonable to assume that the great early pitchers
would also have been outstanding if they played in
modern times, since their arms would have been much
better protected and rested.

Old Hoss Radbourn was an early-day wonder and his
two records may last forever. Presumably, no one will
ever again win 60 games in one season or strike out
441 batters. Radbourn's 441 strikeouts are only a National League record because Matt Kilroy, while playing
in the American Association, struck out an unbelievable
513 batters in 1886. Certainly this mark will never be

broken. Kilroy "was there," accomplishing this feat as a
20-year-old rookie! But even with his great strikeout
ability, Kilroy was unable to keep his team out of last
place. Saddled with a weak hitting and fielding team,
Kilroy won 29 of the team's 48 games.

George Bradley was another outstanding pitcher in
the first year of baseball. In 1876, he won 45 and lost
19, and his record of 16 shutouts still stands, though it
has been tied by Grover Alexander. But Bradley's arm
could not take the punishment of his 573 innings
pitched. Over the remainder of his ten-year career, he
had a winning percentage of less than .500. In fact,
during his last two years he didn't pitch at all but merely
came to bat 51 times and made four hits.

Al Spalding, Monte Ward and Tommy Bond were

other superb pitchers in those interesting early years.

The highlight achievements after 1900 were created by "Iron Man" Joe McGinnity of the Giants. He was a throwback to the pioneer pitchers, and was such a hardworking pitcher that his records may also never be matched by modern pitchers. In 1900, 1903 and 1904, McGinnity won 29, 31, and 35 games from a distance of 60'6" but none of these fine efforts have found their way into the National League records books, due to the ruling that records set at shorter distances also be included in the record book.

Christy Mathewson certainly would have many more records if a modern ruling were put into effect, as he has won the most games after 1900. No National League hurler has ever threatened his 37 victories of 1908, and his 267 strikeouts in 1903 were not improved upon for 58 years, until Sandy Koufax whiffed 269 batters in 1961. Koufax then went on to strike out 306 in 1963 and 382 in 1965. But due to the present ruling, Koufax's great achievements will never enter the record book either.

Three Finger Brown's ERA of 1.04 set in 1906 is a record that still stands in the National League, and the ERA category tells a lot about a pitcher's talent. There is no doubt that Brown, who had only three fingers on his pitching hand, was one of the game's greatest pitchers. It has been said that having two less fingers on his pitching hand actually helped him throw the curve ball. Brown later became a valuable pitcher coming out of the bullpen.

Speaking of outstanding National League relief pitchers, Doc Crandall of the Giants has the most records, but Jim Konstanty of the Phils has records which have best stood the test of time. Konstanty's 74 appearances in 1950 was a milestone that stood for 15 years before Ted Abernathy appeared in 84 games in 1965. Konstanty's 16 wins was good enough for 9 years, his 22 saves lasted for 4 years and his combination of wins and saves (38) stood for 20 years before Wayne Granger posted 41 in 1970.

One of the greatest seasons enjoyed by a reliever was that of Elroy Face in 1959, when he won 18 and lost only 1. This represents a winning percentage of .947, the highest of any pitcher in baseball history.

In the American League, Jack Chesbro of the Yankees has produced the records most difficult to break. His five marks have lasted 259 years and continue to grow, as it is doubtful whether any modern pitcher will start 51 games, complete 48 of them and win 41, as did Chesbro in 1904.

Another superstar hurler was Big Ed Walsh of the White Sox. When he wasn't starting a game he was effective as a relief pitcher. He was another of the Iron Horse–type pitchers, and his record of 464 innings worked in 1908 still stands. But Walsh gained his fame by having the lowest career ERA in baseball history.

Jack Coombs won 31 games in 1910 and is famous for his 13 shutouts, a mark which has never been duplicated or surpassed by any American Leaguer.

Rube Waddell was one of the American League's first great strikeout pitchers. His 349 strikeouts in 1904 lasted until Nolan Ryan sent 383 batters dragging their bats back to the dugout in 1973.

The stingiest pitcher for a single season was Dutch Leonard, who posted a sizzling 1.01 ERA in 1914, which is another long-standing record that is likely to remain intact.

The American League has had many exciting relief pitchers, the first of whom was Firpo Marberry of the Senators. His marks have lasted more years than any other reliever, yet he is not in the Hall of Fame. Marberry was the first reliever to appear in more than 50 games in a season, and his 59 relief jobs of 1926 lasted 24 years, before Joe Page of the Yankees became the new champion fireman.

Page was the first reliever to appear in an amazing 60 games and strike out 100 batters. Rube Waddell and Ed Walsh did some fine relief work in the early part of the century, while Yankees Wilcy Moore and Johnny Murphy were very successful in the years before Joe Page entered the scene. Dick Radatz, John Hiller, Rollie Fingers and Dan Quisenberry, to name but a few, are some of the modern greats.

CHAPTER 4

CAREER PITCHING RECORDS

NATIONAL LEAGUE QUIZ

1. Who were the first pitchers to have appeared in 600, 700, and 800 games?
2. The most starts ever made by an NL pitcher is 665. Who is he?
3. Can you name the first NL pitcher to win 300 games?
4. The oldest career pitching record is in the category of ERA and is now over 100 years old. Name the oldtimer who holds it.
5. This sensational pitcher has pitched the most innings of any NL pitcher. Do you know him?

AMERICAN LEAGUE QUIZ

1. Can you name the first AL pitcher to pitch more than 5000 innings?
2. Can you name the first AL pitcher to strike out 1000 batters? 2000 batters? 3000 batters?
3. This Hall of Famer has tossed 110 shutouts in his remarkable career. This is the most in Major League history. Name him.
4. Who was the first AL pitcher to appear in 300 relief games? 500 games?
5. Only one AL relief pitcher has won as many as 87 games. Do you know him?

MAJOR LEAGUE QUIZ

1. There has only been one relief pitcher to earn Hall of Fame honors. Who is he?
2. The relief pitcher to appear in 100 games was known for a physical imperfection. His real first name was Mordecai. Name him.
3. Who is the famous pitcher who has completed 751 games, the most in baseball history?
4. The highest winning percentage by any pitcher with more than 200 wins is .692. This record has not been broken in 94 years! Do you know this pitcher? He had 218 wins and 97 losses.
5. This Hall of Famer had a career ERA of 1.82, the best in baseball history. This achievement has not been broken in 72 years. Can you name him?

NATIONAL LEAGUE

Most Total Games

1876–77	Jim Devlin, Lou	129
1877–81	Will White, Cin	195
1876–82	Tommy Bond, Bos	294
1881–87	Jim McCormick, Cle	468
1880–91	Hoss Radbourn, Pro	487
1879–92	Pud Galvin, Buf	616
1890–06	Kid Nichols, Bos	621
1900–16	Christy Mathewson, NY	636
1911–30	Grover Alexander, Phi	696
1942–65	Warren Spahn, Mil	750
1953–69	Elroy Face, Pit	846
1974–88	**Kent Tekulve, Pit**	**1,013**

Most Starts

1876–77	Jim Devlin, Lou	129
1877–81	Will White, Cin	194
1876–82	Tommy Bond, Bos	288
1878–87	Jim McCormick, Cle	462
1880–91	Hoss Radbourn, Pro	465
1879–92	Pud Galvin, Buf	602
1942–65	**Warren Spahn, Mil**	**665**

Most Games Completed

1876–77	Jim Devlin, Lou	127
1877–81	Will White, Cin	190
1876–82	Tommy Bond, Bos	270
1878–87	Jim McCormick, Cle	445
1880–91	Hoss Radbourn, Pro	453
1879–92	**Pud Galvin, Buf**	**609**

Most Wins

1876–77	Jim Devlin, Lou	65
1877–81	Will White, Cin	93
1876–82	Tommy Bond, Bos	180
1878–87	Jim McCormick, Cle	243
1880–91	Hoss Radbourn, Pro	281
1879–92	Pud Galvin, Buf	317
1882–94	John Clarkson, Bos	326
1890–06	Kid Nichols, Bos	360
1900–16	**Christy Mathewson, NY**	**373**
1911–30	**Grover Alexander, Phi**	**373**

Most Losses

1876–77	Jim Devlin, Lou	60
1876–81	Will White, Cin	97
1876–82	George Bradley, StL	105
1878–87	John McCormick, Cle	211
1879–92	**Pud Galvin, Buf**	**269**

Most Losses after 1900

1912–33	Eppa Rixey, Cin	251

AMERICAN LEAGUE

Most Total Games

1902–06	Red Donahue, Cle	150
1901–07	Roy Patterson, Chi	184
1901–08	Casey Patten, Was	270
1903–09	Jack Chesbro, NY	270
1902–10	Rube Waddell, Phi	335
1901–11	Cy Young, Bos	390
1902–13	George Mullin, Det	447
1901–17	Eddie Plank, Phi	580
1907–27	Walter Johnson, Was	802
1967–82	**Sparky Lyle, NY**	**807**

Most Starts

1902–06	Red Donahue, Cle	142
1901–07	Bill Bernard, Cle	161
1901–08	Casey Patten, Was	239
1902–10	Rube Waddell, Phi	278
1901–11	Cy Young, Bos	353
1902–13	George Mullin, Det	404
1901–17	Eddie Plank, Phi	496
1907–27	**Walter Johnson, Was**	**666**

Most Games Completed

1902–06	Red Donahue, Cle	130
1901–07	Bill Bernhard, Phi	145
1901–08	Casey Patten, Was	206
1902–10	Addie Joss, Cle	234
1901–11	Cy Young, Bos	321
1902–13	George Mullin, Det	339
1901–17	Eddie Plank, Phi	389
1907–27	**Walter Johnson, Was**	**531**

Most Wins

1902–06	Red Donahue, Cle	76
1901–07	Bill Bernhard, Phi	95
1901–08	Casey Patten, Was	105
1903–09	Jack Chesbro, NY	129
1902–10	Rube Waddell, Phi	163
1901–11	Cy Young, Bos	222
1901–17	Eddie Plank, Phi	306
1907–27	**Walter Johnson, Was**	**416**

Most Losses

1902–06	Jack Townsend, Was	76
1901–08	Casey Patten, Was	127
1901–10	Harry Howell, StL	133
1901–11	Cy Young, Bos	141
1902–12	Jake Powell, StL	174
1902–13	George Mullin, Det	184
1907–27	**Walter Johnson, Was**	**279**

MAJOR LEAGUE

Most Total Games

1876–77	Jim Devlin, Lou, NL	129
1876–84	Tommy Bond, Bos, NL	322
1877–86	Will White, Cin, NL	403
1878–87	Jim McCormick, Cle, NL	494
1880–91	Hoss Radbourn, Pro, NL	528
1879–92	Pud Galvin, Buf, NL	697
1890–11	Cy Young, Cle, NL	906
1952–72	**Hoyt Wilhelm, Chi, AL**	**1070**

Most Starts

1876–77	Jim Devlin, Lou, NL	129
1876–84	Tommy Bond, Bos, NL	314
1877–86	Will White, Cin, NL	401
1878–87	Jim McCormick, Cle, NL	488
1880–91	Hoss Radbourn, Pro, NL	503
1879–92	Pud Galvin, Buf, NL	682
1890–11	**Cy Young, Cle, NL**	**815**

Most Games Completed

1876–77	Jim Devlin, Lou, NL	127
1876–84	Tommy Bond, Bos, NL	294
1877–86	Will White, Cin, NL	394
1878–87	Jim McCormick, Cle, NL	466
1880–91	Hoss Radbourn, Pro, NL	489
1879–92	Pud Galvin, Buf, NL	639
1890–11	**Cy Young, Cle, NL**	**751**

Most Wins

1876–77	Jim Devlin, Lou, NL	65
1876–84	Tommy Bond, Bos, NL	193
1877–86	Will White, Cin, NL	229
1878–87	Jim McCormick, Cle, NL	264
1880–91	Hoss Radbourn, Pro, NL	308
1879–92	Pud Galvin, Buf, NL	361
1890–11	**Cy Young, Cle, NL**	**511**

DID YOU KNOW ... *That a starting pitcher can get credit for a win by pitching only four innings? This can happen when a game is called after only five innings.*

Most Losses

1876–77	Jim Devlin, Lou, NL	60
1876–84	Tommy Bond, Bos, NL	115
1877–86	Will White, Cin, NL	166
1878–87	Jim McCormick, Cle, NL	214
1879–92	Pud Galvin, Buf, NL	310
1890–11	**Cy Young, Cle, NL**	**313**

NATIONAL LEAGUE

Highest Winning Percentage

1876–77	Jim Devlin, Lou	.520
1876–82	Tommy Bond, Bos	.640
1880–87	Larry Corcoran, Chi	.663
1900–16	**Christy Mathewson, NY**	**.665**

DID YOU KNOW . . . *That one year after the spitball was abolished, another vote was taken which allowed eight NL and nine AL spitball pitchers to use it for the rest of their careers?*

Lowest ERA (min. 5 years)

1877–81	Will White, Cin	2.78
1876–82	Tommy Bond, Bos	2.73
1876–82	George Bradley, StL	2.73
1878–84	**Monte Ward, Pro**	**2.10**

Lowest ERA after 1900

1900–16	Christy Mathewson, NY	2.13

Most Innings Pitched

1876–77	Jim Devlin, Lou	1181
1877–81	Will White, Cin	1710
1876–82	Tommy Bond, Bos	2548
1878–87	Jim McCormick, Cle	4042
1880–91	Hoss Radbourn, Pro	4192
1879–92	Pud Galvin, Buf	5179
1911–30	Grover Alexander, Phi	5189
1942–65	**Warren Spahn, Mil**	**5244**

Most Hits Allowed

1876–77	Jim Devlin, Lou	1183
1877–81	Will White, Cin	1754
1876–82	Tommy Bond, Bos	2610
1878–87	Jim McCormick, Cle	3858
1880–91	Hoss Radbourn, Pro	3983
1879–92	**Pud Galvin, Buf**	**5419**

Most Hits Allowed after 1900

1900–06	Kid Nichols, Bos	999
1900–08	Joe McGinnity, NY	2365
1900–10	Vic Willis, Bos	3080
1900–16	Christy Mathewson, NY	4216
1911–30	**Grover Alexander, Phi**	**4868**

AMERICAN LEAGUE

Highest Winning Percentage

1902–06	Red Donahue, Cle	.529
1901–07	Bill Bernhard, Phi	.590
1902–10	Addie Joss, Cle	.623
1905–14	Chief Bender, Phi	.649
1925–41	Lefty Grove, Phi	.680
1950–67	**Whitey Ford, NY**	**.690**

Lowest ERA (min. 5 years)

1902–06	Red Donahue, Cle	2.77
1901–07	Roy Patterson, Chi	2.75
1901–08	Ed Siever, Det	2.60
1901–09	Frank Owen, Chi	2.55
1902–10	Addie Joss, Cle	1.88
1904–16	**Eddie Walsh, Chi**	**1.82**

Most Innings Pitched

1902–06	Red Donahue, Cle	1240
1901–07	Bill Bernhard, Phi	1441
1901–08	Casey Patten, Was	2062
1902–10	Rube Waddell, Phi	2408
1901–11	Cy Young, Bos	3236
1902–13	George Mullin, Det	3452
1901–17	Eddie Plank, Phi	4237
1907–27	**Walter Johnson, Was**	**5924**

Most Hits Allowed

1902–06	Red Donahue, Cle	1282
1901–07	Bill Bernhard, Phi	1456
1901–08	Casey Patten, Was	2154
1901–11	Cy Young, Bos	2823
1902–13	George Mullin, Det	3275
1901–17	Eddie Plank, Phi	3744
1907–27	**Walter Johnson, Was**	**4925**

MAJOR LEAGUE

Highest Winning Percentage

1876–77	Jim Devlin, Lou, NL	.520
1876–84	Tommy Bond, Bos, NL	.627
1880–87	Larry Corcoran, Chi, NL	.663
1884–92	**Bob Caruthers, StL, AA**	**.692**
	(He won 218 and lost 97.)	

Highest Winning Percentage after 1900

1900–16	Christy Mathewson, NY, NL	.665
1946–55	Vic Raschi, NY, AL	.667
1949–67	**Whitey Ford, NY, AL**	**.690**

DID YOU KNOW . . . *That Bob Caruthers, the pitcher with the highest winning percentage in baseball history, had four seasons with winning percentages over .700? In six consecutive seasons, he had 40, 30, 29, 29, 40 and 23 wins!*

Lowest ERA

1878–84	Monte Ward, Pro, NL	2.10
1902–10	Addie Joss, Cle, AL	1.88
1904–17	**Eddie Walsh, Chi, AL**	**1.82**

Most Innings Pitched

1876–77	Jim Devlin, Lou, NL	1181
1876–84	Tommy Bond, Bos, NL	2780
1877–86	Will White, Cin, NL	3543
1878–87	Jim McCormick, Cle, NL	4276
1880–91	Hoss Radbourn, Pro, NL	4535
1879–92	Pud Galvin, Buf, NL	5941
1890–11	**Cy Young, Cle, NL**	**7356**

Most Hits Allowed

1876–77	Jim Devlin, Lou, NL	1183
1876–84	Tommy Bond, Bos, NL	2857
1877–86	Will White, Cin, NL	3440
1878–87	Jim McCormick, Cle, NL	4092
1880–91	Hoss Radbourn, Pro, NL	4335
1879–92	Pud Galvin, Buf, NL	6352
1890–11	**Cy Young, Cle, NL**	**7092**

NATIONAL LEAGUE

Most Bases on Balls Allowed

1876–77	Jim Devlin, Lou	78
1877–81	Will White, Cin	172
1879–83	Lee Richmond, Wor	258
1878–87	Jim McCormick, Cle	691
1880–91	Hoss Radbourn, Pro	775
1880–92	Mickey Welch, NY	1297
1889–01	**Amos Rusie, NY**	**1716**

Most Bases on Balls Allowed after 1900

1900–06	Kid Nichols, Bos	272
1900–08	Joe McGinnity, NY	588
1900–09	Chick Fraser, Phi	704
1900–10	Vic Willis, Bos	947
1911–30	Grover Alexander, Phi	953
1912–33	Eppa Rixey, Cin	1082
1916–34	Burleigh Grimes, Bkn	1295
1942–65	Warren Spahn, Mil	1434
1964–83	Phil Niekro, Atl	1452
1965–88	**Steve Carlton, Phi**	**1608**

Most Strikeouts

1876–77	Jim Devlin, Lou	263
1877–81	Will White, Cin	574
1876–82	Tommy Bond, Bos	712
1878–84	Monte Ward, Pro	920
1878–87	Jim McCormick, Cle	1571
1880–91	Hoss Radbourn, Pro	1750
1880–92	Mickey Welch, NY	1850
1882–94	John Clarkson, Bos	2015
1900–16	Christy Mathewson, NY	2502
1942–65	Warren Spahn, Mil	2583
1959–75	Bob Gibson, StL	3117
1965–85	**Steve Carlton, Phi**	**3910**

Most Shutouts

1876–77	Jim Devlin, Lou	9
1877–81	Will White, Cin	13
1876–82	Tommy Bond, Bos	36
1879–92	Pud Galvin, Buf	54
1900–16	Christy Mathewson, NY	80
1911–30	**Grover Alexander, Phi**	**90**

AMERICAN LEAGUE

Most Bases on Balls Allowed

1902–06	Jack Townsend, Was	352
1901–08	Casey Patten, Was	557
1902–10	Rube Waddell, Phi	653
1902–13	George Mullin, Det	1131
1907–27	Walter Johnson, Was	1405
1924–47	Red Ruffing, NY	1541
1934–53	Bobo Newsom, Was	1631
1936–56	Bob Feller, Cle	1764
1939–63	**Early Wynn, Cle**	**1775**

Most Strikeouts

1902–06	Red Donahue, Cle	413
1901–07	Bill Bernhard, Phi	473
1901–08	Casey Patten, Was	757
1903–09	Jack Chesbro, NY	916
1902–10	Rube Waddell, Phi	1965
1901–17	Eddie Plank, Phi	2099
1907–27	**Walter Johnson, Was**	**3508**

Most Shutouts

1902–06	Red Donahue, Cle	16
1901–07	Roy Patterson, Chi	17
1902–09	Bill Dinneen, Bos	23
1902–10	Rube Waddell, Phi	47
1904–16	Eddie Walsh, Chi	57
1901–17	Eddie Plank, Phi	63
1907–27	**Walter Johnson, Was**	**110**

MAJOR LEAGUE

Most Bases on Balls Allowed

1876–77	Jim Devlin, Lou, NL	78
1878–84	Monte Ward, Pro, NL	253
1877–86	Will White, Cin, NL	496
1878–87	Jim McCormick, Cle, NL	749
1880–91	Hoss Radbourn, Pro, NL	875
1880–92	Mickey Welch, NY, NL	1297
1881–94	Tony Mullane, Cin, AA	1409
1889–01	Amos Rusie, NY, AL	1716
1929–53	Bobo Newsom, Was, AL	1732
1936–56	Bob Feller, Cle, AL	1764
1939–63	Early Wynn, Cle, AL	1775
1966–88	**Nolan Ryan, Cal, AL**	***2442**

DID YOU KNOW . . . *That in 1887 a base on balls was counted as a base hit?*

Most Strikeouts

1876–77	Jim Devlin, Lou, NL	263
1878–84	Monte Ward, Pro, NL	920
1877–86	Will White, Cin, NL	1041
1878–87	Jim McCormick, Cle, NL	1704
1880–91	Hoss Radbourne, Pro, NL	1830
1880–92	Mickey Welch, NY, NL	1850
1880–93	Tim Keefe, NY, AA	2533
1890–11	Cy Young, Cle, NL	2799
1907–27	Walter Johnson, Was, AL	3508
1966–88	**Nolan Ryan, Hou, NL**	***4775**

Most Shutouts

1876–77	Jim Devlin, Lou, NL	9
1876–84	Tommy Bond, Bos, NL	36
1877–86	Will White, Cin, NL	36
1879–92	Pud Galvin, Buf, NL	57
1890–11	Cy Young, Cle, NL	76
1900–16	Christy Mathewson, NY, NL	80
1907–27	**Walter Johnson, Was, AL**	**110**

* Still active.

NATIONAL LEAGUE

Most Relief Appearances, NL

1876–78	Jack Manning, Bos	22
1878–84	Monte Ward, Pro	30
1888–95	Kid Gleason, Phi	33
1892–00	Nig Cuppy, Cle	38
1890–06	Kid Nichols, Bos	59
1899–08	Joe McGinnity, NY	75
1898–10	Sam Leever, Pit	89
1903–16	Three Finger Brown, Chi	130
1908–18	Doc Crandall, NY	142
1927–37	Ben Cantwell, Bos	153
1935–41	Mace Brown. Pit	230
1923–45	Guy Bush, Chi	234
1941–46	Ace Adams, NY	295
1935–49	Clyde Shoun, StL	353
1950–62	Clem Labine, Bkn	461
1955–68	Lindy McDaniel, StL	578
1953–69	Elroy Face, Pit	819
1974–88	**Kent Tekulve, Pit**	**1,013**

Most Relief Wins

1876–78	Jack Manning, Bos	4
1878–84	Monte Ward, Pro	11
1892–00	Nig Cuppy, Cle	15
1890–06	Kid Nichols, Bos	15
1899–08	Joe McGinnity, NY	19
1898–10	Sam Leever, Pit	19
1903–16	Three Finger Brown, Chi	28
1908–18	Doc Crandall, NY	30
1927–37	Ben Cantwell, Bos	31
1926–41	Charlie Root, Chi	42
1923–45	Guy Bush, Chi	43
1935–49	Hugh Casey, Bkn	50
1955–68	Lindy McDaniel, StL	76
1953–69	**Elroy Face, Pit**	**96**

DID YOU KNOW . . . *That in 1950 the strike zone was lowered from the shoulders to the armpits and from the bottom of the knee to the top of the knee?*

AMERICAN LEAGUE

Most Relief Appearances

1901	Pete Dowling, Cle	15
1902–06	Jack Townsend, Was	25
1901–07	Clark Griffith, NY	52
1902–10	Rube Waddell, Phi	57
1903–14	Chief Bender, Phi	96
1904–16	Ed Walsh, Chi	114
1915–25	Allan Russell, Was	233
1920–32	Ed Rommel, Phi	251
1923–36	Firpo Marberry, Was	363
1932–47	Johnny Murphy, NY	375
1958–69	Hoyt Wilhelm, Chi	570
1967–82	**Sparky Lyle, NY**	**807**

Most Relief Wins

1902–06	Willie Sudhoff, StL	7
1901–07	Clark Griffith, NY	14
1902–10	Rube Waddell, Phi	22
1903–14	Chief Bender, Phi	23
1901–17	Eddie Plank, Phi	25
1915–25	Allan Russell, Was	34
1912–26	Hooks Dauss, Det	40
1907–27	Walter Johnson, Was	40
1920–32	Ed Rommel, Phi	51
1923–36	Firpo Marberry, Was	53
1932–47	Johnny Murphy, NY	73
1967–82	**Sparky Lyle, NY**	**87**

MAJOR LEAGUE

Most Relief Appearances

1876–78	Jack Manning, Bos, NL	22
1878–84	Monte Ward, Pro, NL	30
1884–92	Bob Caruthers, StL, AA	30
1881–94	Tony Mullane, Cin, AA	51
1890–06	Kid Nichols, Bos, NL	59
1899–08	Joe McGinnity, NY, NL	85
1898–10	Sam Leever, Pit, NL	89
1890–11	Cy Young, Cle, NL	91
1903–16	Three Finger Brown, Chi, NL	149
1908–18	Doc Crandall, NY, NL	168
1915–25	Allan Russell, Was, AL	233
1920–32	Ed Rommel, Phi, AL	251
1923–36	Firpo Marberry, Was, AL	364
1930–45	Joe Heving, Cle, AL	390
1944–56	Jim Konstanty, Phi, NL	397
1947–61	Gerry Staley, StL, NL	454
1950–62	Clem Labine, Bkn, NL	475
1950–67	John Klippstein, Chi, NL	549
1952–68	Stu Miller, SF, NL	611
1953–69	Elroy Face, Pit, NL	821
1952–72	**Hoyt Wilhelm, Chi, AL**	**1018**

Most Relief Wins

1876–78	Jack Manning, Bos, NL	4
1879–83	Curry Foley, Bos, NL	5
1878–84	Monte Ward, Pro, NL	11
1884–92	Bob Caruthers, StL, AA	11
1881–94	Tony Mullane, Cin, AA	15
1892–01	Nig Cuppy, Cle, NL	15
1890–06	Kid Nichols, Bos, NL	15
1899–08	Joe McGinnity, NY, NL	21
1897–10	Rube Waddell, Phi, AL	22
1890–11	Cy Young, Cle, NL	30
1908–18	Doc Crandall, NY, NL	37
1912–26	Hooks Dauss, Det, AL	40
1907–27	Walter Johnson, Was, AL	40
1920–32	Ed Rommel, Phi, AL	51
1923–36	Firpo Marberry, Was, AL	53
1930–45	Joe Heving, Cle, AL	60
1932–47	Johnny Murphy, NY, AL	73
1952–68	Stu Miller, SF, NL	79
1953–69	Elroy Face, Pit, NL	96
1952–72	**Hoyt Wilhelm, Chi, AL**	**123**

NATIONAL LEAGUE		AMERICAN LEAGUE		MAJOR LEAGUE	
Most Relief Losses		*Most Relief Losses*		*Most Relief Losses*	
1876–82 Tommy Bond, Bos	2	1901 Pete Dowling, Cle	4	1876–82 Tommy Bond, Bos, NL	2
1878–84 Monte Ward, Pro	5	1901–07 Roy Patterson, Chi	5	1878–84 Monte Ward, Pro, NL	5
1888–95 Kid Gleason, Phi	7	1901–07 Clark Griffith, NY	5	1880–91 Hoss Radbourn, Pro, NL	5
1889–01 Amos Rusie, NY	7	1901–08 Casey Patten, Was	8	1881–94 Tony Mullane, Cin, AA	5
1890–06 Kid Nichols, Bos	9	1903–12 Barney Pelty, StL	11	1888–95 Kid Gleason, Phi, NL	7
1899–08 Joe McGinnity, NY	12	1903–14 Chief Bender, Phi	14	1889–01 Amos Rusie, NY, NL	7
1899–10 Sam Leever, Pit	12	1915–25 Allan Russell, Was	21	1890–06 Kid Nichols, Bos, NL	9
1890–11 Cy Young, Cle	15	1912–26 Hooks Dauss, Det	23	1899–08 Joe McGinnity, NY, NL	13
1903–16 Three Finger Brown, Chi	15	1907–27 Walter Johnson, Was	30	1890–11 Cy Young, Cle, NL	18
1927–37 Ben Cantwell, Bos	19	1923–36 Firpo Marberry, Was	37	1903–16 Three Finger Brown,	
1926–41 Charlie Root, Chi	24	1932–47 Johnny Murphy, NY	42	Chi, NL	19
1941–46 Ace Adams, NY	31	1957–69 Hoyt Wilhelm, Chi	66	1915–25 Allan Russell, Was, AL	21
1944–56 Jim Konstanty, Phi	32	**1967–82 Sparky Lyle, NY**	**67**	1912–26 Hooks Dauss, Det, AL	23
1950–62 Clem Labine, Bkn	42			1907–27 Walter Johnson, Was, AL	30
1955–68 Lindy McDaniel, StL	58			1923–36 Firpo Marberry, Was, AL	37
1953–69 Elroy Face, Pit	**82**			1950–62 Clem Labine, Bkn, NL	45
				1952–68 Stu Miller, SF, NL	67
				1953–69 Elroy Face, Pit, NL	82
				1952–72 Hoyt Wilhelm, Chi, AL	**102**
Most Saves		*Most Saves*		*Most Saves*	
1876–78 Jack Manning, Bos	6	1901–07 Clark Griffith, NY	4	1876–78 Jack Manning, Bos, NL	6
1888–95 Kid Gleason, Phi	6	1901–08 Casey Patten, Was	5	1881–94 Tony Mullane, Cin, AA	15
1890–06 Kid Nichols, Bos	16	1902–09 Bill Dinneen, Bos	7	1890–06 Kid Nichols, Bos, NL	16
1899–08 Joe McGinnity, NY	22	1901–11 Cy Young, Bos	8	1899–08 Joe McGinnity, NY, NL	23
1903–16 Three Finger Brown, Chi	45	1902–12 Jake Powell, StL	12	1903–16 Three Finger Brown,	
1941–46 Ace Adams, NY	49	1903–14 Chief Bender, Phi	18	Chi, NL	48
1935–49 Hugh Casey, Bkn	52	1904–16 Ed Walsh, Chi	34	1927–33 Wilcy Moore, NY, AL	49
1943–54 Al Brazle, StL	60	1915–25 Allan Russell, Was	42	1923–36 Firpo Marberry, Was, AL	101
1950–62 Clem Labine, Bkn	90	1927–33 Wilcy Moore, NY	49	1932–47 Johnny Murphy, NY, AL	107
1955–68 Lindy McDaniel, StL	112	1923–36 Firpo Marberry, Was	101	1952–68 Stu Miller, SF, NL	154
1953–69 Elroy Face, Pit	**193**	1932–47 Johnny Murphy, NY	107	1953–69 Elroy Face, Pit, NL	193
		1957–69 Hoyt Wilhelm, Chi	157	1952–72 Hoyt Wilhelm, Chi, AL	227
		1967–82 Sparky Lyle, NY	**232**	**1968–84 Rollie Fingers, Oak, AL**	**324**
Most Relief Wins and Saves		*Most Relief Wins and Saves*		*Most Relief Wins and Saves*	
1876–78 Jack Manning, Bos	10	1902–06 Willie Sudhoff, StL	7	1876–78 Jack Manning, Bos, NL	10
1878–84 Monte Ward, Pro	14	1901–07 Clark Griffith, NY	18	1878–84 Monte Ward, Pro, NL	14
1892–00 Nig Cuppy, Cle	20	1902–10 Rube Waddell, Phi	26	1884–92 Bob Caruthers, StL, AA	14
1890–06 Kid Nichols, Bos	31	1903–14 Chief Bender, Phi	41	1881–94 Tony Mullane, Cin, AA	30
1899–08 Joe McGinnity, NY	41	1904–16 Ed Walsh, Chi	56	1890–06 Kid Nichols, Bos, NL	31
1903–16 Three Finger Brown, Chi	70	1915–25 Allan Russell, Was	76	1899–08 Joe McGinnity, NY, NL	44
1926–41 Charlie Root, Chi	82	1912–26 Hooks Dauss, Det	80	1890–11 Cy Young, Cle, NL	46
1941–46 Ace Adams, NY	86	1920–32 Ed Rommell, Phi	80	1903–16 Three Finger Brown,	
1935–49 Hugh Casey, Bkn	102	1923–36 Firpo Marberry, Was	154	Chi, NL	77
1950–62 Clem Labine, Bkn	153	1932–47 Johnny Murphy, NY	180	1912–26 Hooks Dauss, Det, AL	80
1955–68 Lindy McDaniel, StL	188	1957–69 Hoyt Wilhelm, Chi	229	1920–32 Ed Rommel, Phi, AL	80
1953–69 Elroy Face, Pit	**289**	**1967–82 Sparky Lyle, NY**	**319**	1927–33 Wilcy Moore, NY, AL	88
				1923–36 Firpo Marberry, Was, AL	154
				1932–47 Johnny Murphy, NY, AL	180
				1952–68 Stu Miller, SF, NL	233
				1953–69 Elroy Face, Pit, NL	289
				1952–72 Hoyt Wilhelm, Chi, AL	350
				1968–84 Rollie Fingers, Oak, AL	**430**

NATIONAL LEAGUE SUMMARY

Top Record Producers: Starters

1	Tommy Bond, Bos	9
2	Jim Devlin, Lou	8
3	Will White, Cin	8
4	Jim McCormick, Cle	6
4	Hoss Radbourn, Pro	6
4	Pud Galvin, Buf	6

Top Record Producers: in Relief

1	Elroy Face, Pit	5
2	Joe McGinnity, NY	4
2	Kid Nichols, Bos	4
2	Jack Manning, Bos	4
2	Lindy McDaniel, StL	4

Most Outstanding Record Producers: Starters

Pud Galvin, Buf	6 for 251 years
Christy Mathewson, NY	5 for 221 years
Grover Alexander, Phi	4 for 188 years
Monte Ward, Pro	2 for 107 years
Warren Spahn, Mil	4 for 60 years

Most Outstanding Record Producers: in Relief

Elroy Face, Pit	5 for 93 years
Three Finger Brown, Chi	3 for 57 years
Jack Manning, Bos	4 for 46 years
Hugh Casey, Bkn	3 for 37 years

AMERICAN LEAGUE SUMMARY

Top Record Producers: Starters

1	Cy Young, Bos	9
2	Jack Chesbro, NY	5
2	Ed Walsh, Chi	5
3	Rube Waddell, Phi	4
4	Addie Joss, Cle	3

Top Record Producers: in Relief

1	Sparky Lyle, NY	5
1	Clark Griffith, NY	5
3	Roy Patterson, Chi	4
3	Chief Bender, Phi	4
3	Allan Russell, Was	4
3	Firpo Marberry, Was	4
3	Johnny Murphy, NY	4

Most Outstanding Record Producers: Starters

Jack Chesbro, NY	5 for 253 years
Ed Walsh, Chi	5 for 130 years
Jack Coombs, Phi	1 for 76 years
Rube Waddell, Phi	4 for 74 years
Dutch Leonard, Bos	1 for 72 years

Most Outstanding Record Producers: in Relief

1	Johnny Murphy, NY	4 for 101 years
2	Firpo Marberry, Was	4 for 44 years
3	Hoyt Wilhelm, Chi	3 for 39 years
4	Sparky Lyle, NY	6 for 36 years
5	Eddie Walsh, Chi	3 for 29 years

MAJOR LEAGUE SUMMARY

Top Record Producers: Starters

1	Cy Young, Cle, AL	9
2	Jim Devlin, Lou, NL	8
3	Tommy Bond, Bos, NL	7
3	Will White, Cin, NL	7
5	Jim McCormick, Cle, NL	6
5	Pud Galvin, Buf, NL	6
5	Hoss Radbourn, Pro, NL	6

Top Record Producers: in Relief

1	Hoyt Wilhelm, Chi, AL	4
1	Jack Manning, Bos, NL	4
1	Tony Mullane, Cin, AA	4
1	Kid Nichols, Bos, NL	4
1	Joe McGinnity, NY, NL	4
1	Firpo Marberry, Was, AL	4
1	Stu Miller, SF, NL	4

Most Outstanding Record Producers: Starters

Cy Young, Cle, AL	9 for 550 years
Walter Johnson, Was, AL	2 for 118 years
Pud Galvin, Buf, NL	6 for 114 years
Bob Caruthers, StL, AA	1 for 96 years
Eddie Walsh, Chi, AL	1 for 72 years

Most Outstanding Record Producers: in Relief

Hoyt Wilhelm, Chi, AL	5 for 72 years
Johnny Murphy, NY, AL	3 for 63 years
Tony Mullane, Cin, AA	4 for 43 years
Firpo Marberry, Was, AL	4 for 40 years
Jack Manning, Bos, NL	4 for 33 years

Pud Galvin probably was not as great a pitcher as Christy Mathewson, Grover Alexander or Warren Spahn, but he has produced the records which have lasted the most years due to the pitching methods of his day.

There is no doubt that Christy Mathewson and Grover Alexander were two of the National League's greatest pitchers. Each share the record for most wins at 373, each appeared in more than 600 games, Mathewson has the highest winning percentage and Alexander has the most shutouts. Alexander was a cunning pitcher who bore down when he had to, while pacing himself when blessed with a big lead. Alexander gave up the most hits of any National League pitcher after 1900, and yet tossed the most shutouts: when the game was on the line, he knew how to get the batters out.

Hall of Famer Monte Ward shows up fourth, with two records lasting a total of 107 years. Monte split his career between pitching and the infield and was sensational at both. He worked from the mound for the first seven years, winning 161 and dropping 101. During that time he posted a tough 2.10 ERA, the lowest in National League history. Monte played shortstop and second base for the next ten years and averaged 50.4 stolen

bases per year while batting .278, collecting 2,123 hits. He was voted into the Hall of Fame in 1964.

Warren Spahn, whose 23-year career ended in 1965, fits the mold of the old pioneer pitchers. In 1963, when he won 23 and lost 7—at the age of 42!—he became the oldest pitcher in baseball to win more than 20 games. On the All-Time pitchers record list, which includes All-Star and World Series records, Spahnny ranks 13th, with 26 total records—of which 11 have never been broken! His 11 unbroken records place him 7th in that category. Spahn was one of the most successful pitchers of his era; he won league-leading titles 34 times. In this category he ranks 5th. In the category of most 20-win seasons, he is tied for 2nd with 13 (Mathewson also has 13 seasons of 20 or more wins). Six of Spahn's 20-win seasons came in succession.

The most outstanding records produced by a National League relief pitcher belong to Elroy Face of the Pirates. Face has a very unusual distinction in that he is one of the few pitchers who holds records who has never had one broken!

Three Finger Brown sneaks into second place in the relief department with three fine records indicating he was a relief pitcher far ahead of his time. He was the first National League pitcher to relieve in more than 100 games. So ahead of his time was Brown that his saves mark lasted 30 years before being broken, and his combination of wins and saves mark lasted a quarter of a century.

Going back to the first year of baseball, 1876, Jack Manning of Boston became the first outstanding relief pitcher. A more appropriate name for the relief pitchers of his day would be "emergency pitchers," for they usually appeared only when a pitcher was injured. The concept of replacing a pitcher because he was tired or losing his stuff didn't come about until many, many years later. Manning's records set in relief, like Brown's, were a quarter of a century ahead of his time.

The highest winning percentage of any National League relief pitcher belongs to Brooklyn's Hugh Casey. His 51 wins against 20 losses represents a whopping .717 winning percentage. This is also a Major League mark.

In the American League, Donahue, Patten and Bernhard were the early record setters, but Walter Johnson, Eddie Plank and Rube Waddell were, by far, the most outstanding pitchers of their time.

Walter Johnson's records were so difficult to break that his seven marks have lasted a total of 409 years! This count is sure to continue to rise, as six of Johnson's seven records remain unbroken, and most likely will never be surpassed. "The Big Train," as he was called, produced 85 records during his incredible career. This total includes records set in World Series games as well as the American League and Major League categories. His 85 records place him second to Cy Young on the All-Time composite records list. Johnson stands alone in the number one position for pitchers with the most league-leading titles. His 53 league-leading titles is 9

WALTER JOHNSON
"Big Train" is the only pitcher to toss more than 100 shutouts. Even though he pitched for the usually terrible Washington Senators, he led the league in various pitching departments an amazing 52 times!

CY YOUNG

*Cy Young owns many of the most important pitching career records
(including most wins, complete games, and innings pitched). He also set
many single-season and league-leader records.*

more than the great Grover Alexander, who chalked up 44. On the All-Time list of pitchers who have won 20 or more games in a season, Johnson ranks third with 12. Ten of those seasons he won 20 or more games in a row. Probably the stat which best reveals his greatness, however, is that Johnson won 137 more games than he lost even though he played on a losing team most of his career! His 137 games over the .500 level places him in the 8th position in that category.

Eddie Walsh was another superstar hurler in the American League. He posted one of the most cherished records of them all: his career ERA of 1.82 is the lowest in Major League history and this mark still stands.

On the composite record list, Walsh stands in fourth place with 55 outstanding records. Seven of these marks remain unbroken and that has earned Walsh an 11th place finish in that department. Walsh also won 34

league-leading titles, an achievement which earns him the fifth spot along with Warren Spahn.

Eddie "Gettysburg" Plank of the Athletics had seven fine marks which lasted ten years each before they were broken by Walter Johnson. Plank had a marvelous 17-year career, winning 327 games, the ninth best in baseball. His 69 shutouts ranks fifth, he won 20 or more games in eight seasons and he finished his career with a super ERA of 2.34.

Of the American League relief pitchers, Johnny "The Fireman" Murphy put together four records which have lasted a total of 101 years, and that is good enough to give him the number one position in records of longevity. Firpo Marberry, the first reliever to appear in 300 games while saving 100, is in second place with four marks for 44 years.

Hoyt Wilhelm, who is the only relief pitcher to have

entered the Hall of Fame, ranks third in the American League with 3 records lasting 39 years. His career was split between the National and American league and his records will fare better in the Major League category.

Sparky Lyle has the most current records of any American League relief pitcher. His records have lasted only a few years thus far because he retired so recently. His marks are sure to last many more years before any reliever passes him. As of this date, all of Sparky's records remain unbroken.

In the Major League records category, the early pioneer pitchers continue to get the top numbers, but this time Cy Young receives his due as one of baseball's all-time greatest pitchers. He has not been heard much of to this point because he split his career between the National and American leagues. Under those circumstances it is most difficult to establish career records in either league. But in the Major League category, Cy Young shows why so many experts rate him the greatest pitcher of all time. Surely no pitcher will ever win 511 games or come close to Cy's career marks. His nine records have already lasted 550 years and those numbers may climb forever.

Cy Young has the most Major League records of any pitcher in the game. His 33 marks are 11 more than second-place Walter Johnson's. Cy's nine unbroken Major League records are also the most of any pitcher in baseball. Sandy Koufax is second in this category with seven. Young was a league leader 31 times and is tied for sixth place with Robin Roberts in this area. Perhaps the most impressive of Cy Young's credentials is his 16 seasons of winning 20 or more games, doing it 14 years in succession! Both of those feats place him in first place in those categories. And finally, the bottom line, as they say, on Cy Young is that he won 198 more games than he lost, which also puts him at the top of the list among pitchers who are above the .500 winning percentage level.

In a much shorter career, Bob Caruthers has posted the highest winning percentage of all hurlers. In his nine-year career he won 218 while losing only 97. He was a 40-game winner twice, won 30 as a third high, then won 29 twice and 23 to round out his short but spectacular career.

In the relief department, Hoyt Wilhelm shows why he has been selected for the Hall of Fame. His five marks have lasted more years than any other reliever and will continue to rise, as very few pitchers are closing in on the career numbers of the great knuckleballer. Johnny Murphy was also outstanding as the New York Yankees' Fireman #1. Joe Page later replaced him as the second Yankee Fireman.

Of the pioneer pitchers, Tony Mullane deserves mention as a fine reliever; his achievements lasted for 43 years.

CHAPTER 5

SEASON FIELDING RECORDS

NATIONAL LEAGUE QUIZ

1. The most putouts ever made by a first baseman is 1,759. This record has not been broken in 68 years. Do you know who holds it?
2. This exceptional first baseman established five assists records, four of them in succession. Can you name him?
3. Do you know the first baseman who has made the most errors since 1900?
4. The double play record by a first baseman is 182 and is held by a Pirate. Do you know him?
5. Can you name the only first baseman who has gone through a full season without making an error?

AMERICAN LEAGUE QUIZ

1. The longest unbroken putouts record for a second baseman is 52 years. This record was set in 1922. Can you name this player, who later went on to manage the New York Yankees?
2. The present record for putouts by a second baseman is 484. This mark is now 14 years old. Can you name this player?

3. The assists record for second basemen is now 59 years old and was created by a player with the St. Louis Browns in 1930. Do you know him?
4. This exceptional second baseman set three consecutive double play records, the only player ever to accomplish this feat at his position. Who is he?
5. Can you name the Hall of Famer who registered the most total chances of any second baseman?

MAJOR LEAGUE QUIZ

1. The oldest unbroken double play record is 22 years old. Can you name the second baseman who holds this mark?
2. Two outstanding shortstops share the record for most putouts. Do you know them?
3. The highest fielding average ever had by a third baseman is .989. Name this player.
4. Can you name the first catcher to field 1.000?
5. Can you name the outfielder who has made more putouts in a season than any other in baseball history?

FIRST BASE

NATIONAL LEAGUE

Most Putouts

1876	Herman Dehlman, StL	750
1879	Oscar Walker, Buf	828
1880	Joe Start, Pro	954
1883	Dan Brouthers, Buf	1040
1884	Cap Anson, Chi	1211
1885	Cap Anson, Chi	1253
1886	Mike McQuery, KC ,	1295
1887	Roger Connor, NY	1325
1888	John Morrill, Bos	1398
1889	Cap Anson, Chi	1409
1891	Joe Virtue, Cle	1465
1892	Jake Beckley, Pit	1523
1904	Jake Beckley, StL	1526
1905	Fred Tenney, Bos	1556
1906	Joe Nealon, Pit	1592
1908	Fred Tenney, NY	1634
1911	Ed Konetchy, StL	1652
1920	**George Kelly, NY**	**1759**

Most Assists

1876	Joe Gerhardt, Lou	13
1877	Juice Latham, Lou	24
1879	Oscar Walker, Buf	30
1881	Cap Anson, Chi	43
1884	Cap Anson, Chi	58
1886	Cap Anson, Chi	66
1887	Cap Anson, Chi	70
1888	John Morrill, Bos	72
1889	Cap Anson, Chi	79
1891	Jake Beckley, Pit	87
1892	Jake Beckley, Pit	132
1905	Fred Tenney Bos	152
1982	Bill Buckner, Chi	159
1983	**Bill Buckner, Chi**	**161**

Most Errors

1876	Tim Murnane, Bos	55
1884	**Cap Anson, Chi**	**58**

Most Errors after 1900

1900	Jack Doyle, NY	41

AMERICAN LEAGUE

Most Putouts

1901	Frank Isbell, Chi	1387
1902	Candy LaChance, Bos	1544
1904	Candy LaChance, Bos	1691
1906	Jiggs Donahue, Chi	1697
1907	**Jiggs Donahue, Chi**	**1846**

DID YOU KNOW... *That it was Alexander Cartwright who created the rule of throwing to the base ahead of the runner to register an out? Prior to this, the runner could be hit with the ball and retired.*

Most Assists

1901	Frank Isbell, Chi	101
1905	Jiggs Donahue, Chi	114
1906	Jiggs Donahue, Chi	118
1907	Jiggs Donahue, Chi	140
1914	Chick Gandil, Was	143
1942	Rudy York, Det	146
1943	Rudy York, Det	149
1949	**Mickey Vernon, Was**	**155**

Most Errors

1901	Buck Freeman, Bos	36
1902	Piano Legs Hickman, Cle	40
1903	Piano Legs Hickman, Cle	40
1908	Jerry Freeman, Was	41

MAJOR LEAGUE

Most Putouts

1876	Herman Dehlman, StL, NL	750
1879	Oscar Walker, Buf, NL	828
1880	Joe Start, Pro, NL	954
1883	Charley Comiskey, StL, AA	1085
1884	Cap Anson, Chi, NL	1211
1885	Cap Anson, Chi, NL	1253
1886	Dave Orr, NY, AA	1445
1888	Bill Phillips, KC, AA	1476
1892	Jake Beckley, Pit, NL	1523
1902	Candy LaChance, Bos, AL	1544
1904	Candy LaChance, Bos, AL	1691
1906	Jiggs Donahue, Chi, AL	1697
1907	**Jiggs Donahue, Chi, AL**	**1846**

Most Assists

1876	Joe Gerhardt, Lou, NL	13
1877	Juice Latham, Lou, NL	24
1879	Oscar Walker, Buf, NL	30
1881	Cap Anson, Chi, NL	43
1884	Cap Anson, Chi, NL	58
1886	Cap Anson, Chi, NL	66
1887	Cap Anson, Chi, NL	70
1888	John Morrill, Bos, NL	72
1889	Cap Anson, Chi, NL	79
1890	Roger Connor, NY, PL	80
1891	Jake Beckley, Pit, NL	87
1892	Jake Beckley, Pit, NL	132
1905	Fred Tenney, Bos, NL	152
1949	Mickey Vernon, Was, AL	155
1982	Bill Buckner, Chi, NL	159
1983	**Bill Buckner, Chi, NL**	**161**

Most Errors

1876	Tim Murnane, Bos, NL	55
1883	Dan Stearns, Bal, AA	57
1884	**Jack Quinn, StL, AA**	**62**

Most Errors after 1900

1900	Jack Doyle, NY, NL	41
1908	Jerry Freeman, Was, AL	41

FIRST BASE

NATIONAL LEAGUE			AMERICAN LEAGUE			MAJOR LEAGUE		
Most Double Plays			*Most Double Plays*			*Most Double Plays*		
1876	Tim Murnane, Bos	30	1901	John Anderson, Mil	81	1876	Tim Murnane, Bos, NL	30
1878	John Morrill, Bos	36	1902	Frank Isbell, Chi	97	1878	John Morrill, Bos, NL	36
1879	Oscar Walker, Buf	52	1918	George Burns, Phi	109	1879	Oscar Walker, Buf, NL	52
1882	Bill Phillips, Cle	55	1921	Earl Sheely, Chi	121	1882	Bill Phillips, Cle, NL	55
1883	Martin Powell, Det	62	1922	Joe Judge, Was	131	1883	Martin Powell, Det, NL	62
1884	Cap Anson, Chi	86	1924	Joe Hauser, Phi	131	1884	Cap Anson, Chi, NL	86
1891	Cap Anson, Chi	86	1925	Earl Sheely, Chi	136	1891	Mike Lehane, Col, AA	98
1892	Charley Comiskey, Cin	103	1926	George Sisler, StL	141	1892	Charlie Comiskey, Cin, NL	103
1898	Bill Everett, Chi	123	1929	Lew Fronseca, Cle	141	1898	Bill Everett, Chi, NL	123
1921	George Kelly, NY	132	1934	Hal Trosky, Cle	145	1921	George Kelly, NY, NL	132
1923	Stuffy McInnis, Bos	136	1935	Joe Kuhel, Was	150	1923	Stuffy McInnis, Bos, NL	136
1924	Charlie Grimm, Pit	139	1936	Zeke Bonura, Chi	150	1924	Charlie Grimm, Pit, NL	139
1926	Wally Pipp, Cin	140	1938	Lou Gehrig, NY	157	1926	George Sisler, StL, AL	141
1927	Jim Bottomley, StL	149	1940	George McQuinn, StL	157	1927	Jim Bottomley, StL, NL	149
1933	Gus Suhr, Pit	151	1944	Rudy York, Det	163	1933	Gus Suhr, Pit, NL	151
1939	Frank McCormick, Cin	153	**1949**	**Ferris Fain, Phi**	**194**	1938	Lou Gehrig, NY, AL	157
1950	Gil Hodges, Bkn	159				1940	George McQuinn, StL, AL	157
1951	Gil Hodges, Bkn	171				1944	Rudy York, Det, AL	163
1966	**Donn Clendenon, Pit**	**182**				**1949**	**Ferris Fain, Phi, AL**	**194**
Most Total Chances			*Most Total Chances*			*Most Total Chances*		
1876	Herman Dehlman, StL	791	1901	Frank Isbell, Chi	1519	1876	Harry Dehlman, StL, NL	791
1879	Oscar Walker, Buf	907	1902	Candy LaChance, Bos	1617	1879	Oscar Walker, Buf, NL	907
1880	Joe Start, Pro	993	1904	Candy LaChance, Bos	1764	1880	Joe Start, Pro, NL	993
1883	Dan Brouthers, Buf	1119	1905	Jiggs Donahue, Chi	1780	1883	Charley Comiskey, StL, AA	1148
1884	Cap Anson, Chi	1309	1906	Jiggs Donahue, Chi	1837	1884	Cap Anson, Chi, NL	1309
1885	Cap Anson, Chi	1349	**1907**	**Jiggs Donahue, Chi**	**1998**	1885	Cap Anson, Chi, NL	1349
1886	Mike McQuery, KC	1388				1886	Dave Orr, NY, AA	1507
1888	John Morrill, Bos	1501				1888	Bill Phillips, KC, AA	1563
1889	Cap Anson, Chi	1515				1892	Jake Beckley, Pit, NL	1693
1891	Joe Virtue, Cle	1553				1904	Candy LaChance, Bos, AL	1764
1892	Jake Beckley, Pit	1693				1905	Jiggs Donahue, Chi, AL	1780
1905	Fred Tenney, Bos	1740				1906	Jiggs Donahue, Chi, AL	1837
1908	Fred Tenney, NY	1769				**1907**	**Jiggs Donahue, Chi, AL**	**1998**
1920	**George Kelly, NY**	**1873**						
Highest Fielding Average			*Highest Fielding Average*			*Highest Fielding Average*		
1876	Joe Start, NY	.964	1901	John Anderson, Mil	.982	1876	Joe Start, NY, NL	.964
1877	Joe Start, Har	.964	1902	Scoops Carey, Was	.989	1877	Joe Start, Har, NL	.964
1878	Chub Sullivan, Cin	.975	1904	Candy LaChance, Bos	.992	1878	Chub Sullivan, Cin, NL	.975
1879	Cap Anson, Chi	.975	1907	Jiggs Donahue, Chi	.994	1879	Cap Anson, Chi, NL	.975
1880	Cap Anson, Chi	.977	1909	Frank Isbell, Chi	.994	1880	Cap Anson, Chi, NL	.977
1884	Joe Start, Pro	.980	1914	Stuffy McInnis, Phi	.995	1884	Joe Start, Pro, NL	.980
1886	Sid Farrar, Phi	.980	1916	Chick Gandil, Cle	.995	1886	Dave Orr, NY, AA	.981
1887	Roger Connor, NY	.993	1917	Chick Gandil, Chi	.995	1887	Roger Connor, NY, NL	.993
1897	Patsy Tebeau, Cle	.994	1919	Chick Gandil, Chi	.997	1897	Patsy Tebeau, Cle, NL	.994
1906	Dan McGann, NY	.995	**1921**	**Stuffy McInnis, Bos**	**.999**	1906	Dan McGann, NY, NL	.995
1913	Ed Konetchy, StL	.995	**1981**	**Eddie Murray, Bal**	**.999**	1913	Ed Konetchy, StL, NL	.995
1914	Ed Konetchy, Pit	.995				1914	Ed Konetchy, Pit, NL	.995
1915	Fritz Mollwitz, Cin	.996				1914	Stuffy McInnis, Phi, AL	.995
1921	Walter Holke, Bos	.997				1915	Fritz Mollwitz, Cin, NL	.996
1946	Frank McCormick, Cin	.999				1919	Chick Gandil, Chi, AL	.997
1968	Wes Parker, LA	.999				1921	Stuffy McInnis, Bos, AL	.999
1981	Steve Garvey, LA	.999				1946	Frank McCormick, Cin, NL	.999
1984	**Steve Garvey, SD**	**1.000**				1968	Wes Parker, LA, NL	.999
						1981	Steve Garvey, LA, NL	.999
						1981	Eddie Murray, Bal, AL	.999
						1984	**Steve Garvey, SD, NL**	**1.000**

FIRST BASE

NATIONAL LEAGUE SUMMARY

Top Record Producers

1	Cap Anson, Chi	16
2	Jake Beckley, Pit	5
2	Fred Tenney, Bos	5
2	Joe Start, Pro	5
5	Oscar Walker, Buf	4

Most Outstanding Record Producers

George Kelly, NY	3 for	138 years
Fred Tenney, Bos	5 for	96 years
Jake Beckley, Pit	5 for	40 years
Frank McCormick, Cin	1 for	38 years
Cap Anson, Chi	16 for	30 years

AMERICAN LEAGUE SUMMARY

Top Record Producers

1	Jiggs Donahue, Chi	9
2	Candy LaChance, Bos	5
2	Frank Isbell, Chi	5
4	Chick Gandil, Chi	4
5	Rudy York, Det	3

Most Outstanding Record Producers

Jiggs Donahue, Chi	9 for	175 years
Stuffy McInnis, Phi	2 for	72 years
Mickey Vernon, Was	1 for	39 years
Ferris Fain, Phi	1 for	39 years
Chick Gandil, Chi	4 for	33 years

MAJOR LEAGUE SUMMARY

Top Record Producers

1	Cap Anson, Chi, NL	12
2	Joe Start, Pro, NL	5
2	Jiggs Donahue, Chi, AL	5
4	Jake Beckley, Pit, NL	4
4	Oscar Walker, Buf, NL	4

Most Outstanding Record Producers

Jiggs Donahue, Chi, AL	5 for	166 years
Stuffy McInnis, Bos, AL	3 for	65 years
Fred Tenney, Bos, NL	1 for	44 years
Ferris Fain, Phi, AL	1 for	39 years
Frank McCormick, Cin, NL	1 for	38 years

GEORGE SISLER
Not only was George Sisler a tremendous hitter, he set a double play record for first basemen in 1926.

FIRST BASE

Cap Anson has proven to be the most successful record-producing first baseman, having gathered 16 National League and 12 Major League marks. He has five assists records in the National League, which are Major League records as well. What is most impressive about Anson's five assists records is that four of them were done in succession and no other first baseman has ever equalled or bettered this achievement. The big negative on Anson's slate is his 58 errors committed in 1884, a record that remains unbroken after 105 years! There were many errors committed in the early days of baseball due to the fact that it was a bare-handed game when they started and decent gloves were not invented for almost a quarter of a century. Even though Anson committed the most errors of any first baseman, he was also one of the best, as evidenced by his two fielding average records, which were both National and Major League records at the time.

Another argument for keeping separate records prior to and after 1900 is the tremendous difference in gloves. Why should an early-day player be saddled with the most errors records when he used a glove offering little protection compared to the bushel baskets of today or played without any glove at all? To leave the impression that these pioneer players were unable to catch a ground or fly ball is absurd. Instead of tabbing them with the most errors records, these pioneer brutes should be touted for the bravery with which they faced down "daisy cutters," as hard-hit grounders were called in their day, without gloves or with gloves with very little padding.

George Kelly, Jake Beckley and Fred Tenney were other excellent National League first basemen. Bill Buckner will now be best known for the ball that rolled through his legs in the 1986 World Series and enabled the Mets to win, but few know that he is the all-time leader in assists with his 161 in 1983. Donn Clendenon has participated in the most double plays, while Steve Garvey is the only first baseman ever to go through a full season without making a single error.

In the American League, Candy LaChance, Frank Isbell and Chick Gandil were excellent first basemen, but the man with the big records is Jiggs Donahue who has nine brilliant marks. He set back-to-back putout records in 1906 and 1907, three consecutive records in assists (1905–1907), and was the first to reach the .994 fielding average plateau. Donahue's putout and total chance records still stand today.

Another outstanding first baseman was Stuffy McInnis, who played in both the American and National leagues. Mac was the first to have an almost-perfect fielding year, in 1921 when he made only one error for a .999 fielding average. This is truly remarkable when one considers the still poorly made gloves of those days. McInnis' feat was so sensational that it took 60 years before another American League first baseman could equal his mark. Eddie Murray of the Baltimore Orioles turned the trick in 1981. In the National League, Frank McCormick fielded .999 in 1946 and Wes Parker of the Dodgers equalled this mark in 1968. Steve Garvey was the next to field .999, in 1981, and then in 1984 Garvey accomplished perfection. He did not commit a miscue for the entire season, and remains the only first baseman ever to field 1.000.

Back in the American League, two other first basemen who deserve mention are Mickey Vernon and Ferris Fain. Vernon is the assists king, while Fain has participated in more double plays than any first baseman in baseball history.

SECOND BASE

NATIONAL LEAGUE			AMERICAN LEAGUE			MAJOR LEAGUE		

NATIONAL LEAGUE

Most Putouts

1876	Jack Burdock, Har	211
1878	Jack Burdock, Bos	245
1879	Jack Burdock, Bos	303
1880	Jack Burdock, Bos	328
1884	Fred Pfeffer, Chi	395
1888	Fred Pfeffer, Chi	421
1889	Fred Pfeffer, Chi	452
1912	Bill Sweeney, Bos	459
1933	**Billy Herman, Chi**	**466**

Most Assists

1876	Ed Somerville, Lou	251
1879	Joe Quest, Chi	331
1883	Jack Farrell, Pro	365
1884	Fred Pfeffer, Chi	442
1887	Charley Bassett, Ind	444
1888	Fred Pfeffer, Chi	457
1889	Fred Pfeffer, Chi	483
1891	Bid McPhee, Cin	492
1892	Lou Bierbauer, Pit	555
1922	Frank Parkinson, Phi	562
1924	Rabbit Maranville, Pit	568
1926	Hughie Critz, Cin	588
1927	**Frankie Frisch, StL**	**641**

Most Errors

1876	Ed Somerville, Lou	69
1880	**Pop Smith, Cin**	89

Most Errors after 1900

1900	**Cupid Childs, Chi**	52

AMERICAN LEAGUE

Most Putouts

1901	Nap Lajoie, Phi	395
1905	Germany Schaefer, Det	403
1907	Hobe Ferris, Bos	424
1908	Nap Lajoie, Cle	450
1922	Bucky Harris, Was	479
1974	**Bobby Grich, Bal**	**484**

DID YOU KNOW ... *That since 1920 a stolen base is not credited to the runner if no attempt is made at putting him out?*

Most Assists

1901	Kid Gleason, Det	457
1902	Hobe Ferris, Bos	461
1904	Jimmy Williams, NY	465
1908	Nap Lajoie, Cle	538
1930	**Oscar Melillo, StL**	**572**

Most Errors

1901	Kid Gleason, Det	64

DID YOU KNOW ... *That in 1876 the infielders played very close to the base they were in charge of? This left large holes in the infield.*

MAJOR LEAGUE

Most Putouts

1876	Jack Burdock, Har, NL	211
1878	Jack Burdock, Bos, NL	245
1879	Jack Burdock, Bos, NL	303
1880	Jack Burdock, Bos, NL	328
1884	Bid McPhee, Cin, AA	415
1886	**Bid McPhee, Cin, AA**	**529**

Most Putouts after 1900

1900	Bobby Lowe, Bos, NL	323
1901	Nap Lajoie, Phi, AL	395
1905	Germany Schaefer, Det, AL	403
1907	Hobe Ferris, Bos, AL	424
1908	Nap Lajoie, Cle, AL	450
1912	Bill Sweeney, Bos, NL	459
1922	Bucky Harris, Was, AL	479
1974	**Bobby Grich, Bal, AL**	**484**

Most Assists

1876	Ed Somerville, Lou, NL	251
1879	Joe Quest, Chi, NL	331
1883	Jack Farrell, Pro, NL	365
1884	Fred Pfeffer, Chi, NL	442
1886	Bid McPhee, Chi, AA	464
1889	Fred Pfeffer, Chi, NL	483
1891	Bid McPhee, Chi, NL	492
1892	Lou Bierbauer, Pit, NL	555
1922	Frank Parkinson, Phi, NL	562
1924	Rabbit Maranville, Pit, NL	568
1926	Hughie Critz, Cin, NL	588
1927	**Frankie Frisch, StL, NL**	**641**

Most Errors

1876	Ed Somerville, Lou, NL	69
1880	Pop Smith, Cin, NL	89
1883	Cub Stricker, Phi, AA	93
1884	Tom Evers, Was, AA	94
1886	Yank Robinson, StL, AA	95
1887	**Bill McClellan, Bkn, AA**	**105**

Most Errors after 1900

1900	Cupid Childs, Chi, NL	52
1901	**Kid Gleason, Det, AL**	**64**

SECOND BASE

Most Double Plays			*Most Double Plays*			*Most Double Plays*		
1876	Charlie Sweasy, Cin	30	1901	Hobe Ferris, Bos	68	1876	Charlie Sweasy, Cin, NL	30
1877	Joe Gerhardt, Lou	30	1902	Tom Daly, Chi	70	1877	Joe Gerhardt, Lou, NL	30
1878	Jack Burdock, Bos	34	1906	Nap Lajoie, Cle	76	1878	Jack Burdock, Bos, NL	34
1879	Chick Fulmer, Buf	46	1907	Nap Lajoie, Cle	86	1879	Chick Fulmer, Buf, NL	46
1882	Fred Dunlap, Cle	62	1921	Bucky Harris, Was	91	1882	Fred Dunlap, Cle, NL	62
1884	Fred Pfeffer, Chi	85	1922	Bucky Harris, Was	116	1884	Fred Pfeffer, Chi, NL	85
1892	Bid McPhee, Cin	86	1923	Bucky Harris, Was	120	1886	Bid McPhee, Cin, AA	90
1893	Bid McPhee, Cin	101	1935	Buddy Myer, Was	138	1893	Bid McPhee, Cin, NL	101
1924	Rabbit Maranville, Pit	109	**1950**	**Gerry Priddy, Det**	**150**	1922	Bucky Harris, Was, AL	116
1928	Freddie Maguire, Chi	126				1923	Bucky Harris, Was, AL	120
1931	Tony Cuccinello, Cin	128				1935	Buddy Myer, Was, AL	138
1936	Tony Cuccinello, Bos	128				1950	Gerry Priddy, Det, AL	150
1950	Jackie Robinson, Bkn	133				**1966**	**Bill Mazeroski, Pit, NL**	**161**
1951	Jackie Robinson, Bkn	137						
1954	Red Schoendienst, StL	137						
1961	Bill Mazeroski, Pit	144						
1966	**Bill Mazeroski, Pit**	**161**						

Most Total Chances			*Most Total Chances*			*Most Total Chances*		
1876	Ed Somerville, Lou	530	1901	Hobe Ferris, Bos	870	1876	Ed Somerville, Lou, NL	530
1879	Jack Burdock, Bos	662	1907	Hobe Ferris, Bos	913	1879	Jack Burdock, Bos, NL	662
1883	Jack Farrell, Pro	674	**1908**	**Nap Lajoie, Cle**	**1025**	1883	Jack Farrell, Pro, NL	674
1884	Fred Pfeffer, Chi	905				1884	Fred Pfeffer, Chi, NL	905
1888	Fred Pfeffer, Chi	943				1888	Fred Pfeffer, Chi, NL	943
1889	Fred Pfeffer, Chi	991				1889	Fred Pfeffer, Chi, NL	991
1927	**Frankie Frisch, StL**	**1059**				1908	Nap Lajoie, Cle, AL	1025
						1927	**Frankie Frisch, StL, NL**	**1059**

Highest Fielding Average			*Highest Fielding Average*			*Highest Fielding Average*		
1876	Ross Barnes, Chi	.910	1901	Nap Lajoie, Phi	.960	1876	Ross Barnes, Chi, NL	.910
1878	Jack Burdock, Bos	.918	1904	Gus Dundon, Chi	.973	1878	Jack Burdock, Bos, NL	.918
1879	Joe Quest, Chi	.925	1905	Gus Dundon, Chi	.978	1879	Joe Quest, Chi, NL	.925
1880	Dave Force, Buf	.939	1923	Aaron Ward, NY	.980	1880	Dave Force, Buf, NL	.939
1886	Charlie Bastian, Phi	.945	1931	Buddy Myer, Was	.984	1886	Charley Bastian, Phi, NL	.945
1889	Fred Dunlap, Pit	.950	1932	Max Bishop, Phi	.988	1889	Fred Dunlap, Pit, NL	.950
1890	Charley Bassett, NY	.952	1933	Oscar Melillo, StL	.991	1890	Charlie Bassett, NY, NL	.952
1891	Bid McPhee, Cin	.954	1948	George Stirnweiss, NY	.993	1891	John Crooks, Col, AA	.957
1893	Lou Bierbauer, Pit	.959	1948	Bobby Doerr, Bos	.993	1893	Lou Bierbauer, Pit, NL	.959
1894	Heinie Reitz, Bal	.968	1964	Jerry Adair, Bal	.994	1894	Heinie Reitz, Bal, NL	.968
1896	Bid McPhee, Cin	.978	1970	Tim Collen, Was	.994	1896	Bid McPhee, Cin, NL	.978
1919	George Cutshaw, Pit	.980	**1973**	**Bobby Grich, Bal**	**.995**	1905	Gus Dundon, Chi, AL	.978
1925	Sparky Adams, Chi	.983	**1980**	**Rob Wilfong, Min**	**.995**	1915	Baldy Louden, Buf, FL	.978
1943	Lonnie Frey, Cin	.985				1919	George Cutshaw, Pit, NL	.980
1947	Eddie Stanky, Bkn	.985				1923	Aaron Ward, NY, AL	.980
1949	Red Schoendienst, StL	.987				1925	Sparky Adams, Chi, NL	.983
1951	Jackie Robinson, Bkn	.992				1931	Buddy Myer, Was, AL	.984
1973	**Tito Fuentes, SF**	**.993**				1932	Max Bishop, Phi, AL	.988
1977	**Joe Morgan, Cin**	**.993**				1933	Oscar Melillo, StL, AL	.991
						1948	George Stirnweiss, NY, AL	.993
						1948	Bobby Doerr, Bos, AL	.993
						1964	Jerry Adair, Bal, AL	.994
						1970	Tim Cullen, Was, AL	.994
						1973	**Bobby Grich, Bal, AL**	**.995**
						1980	**Rob Wilfong, Min, AL**	**.995**

SECOND BASE

NATIONAL LEAGUE SUMMARY

Top Record Producers

1	Fred Pfeffer, Chi	10
2	Jack Burdock, Bos	7
3	Bid McPhee, Cin	5
4	Jackie Robinson, Bkn	3

Most Outstanding Record Producers

Frankie Frisch, StL	2 for 122 years
Fred Pfeffer, Chi	10 for 75 years
Bid McPhee, Cin	5 for 58 years
Billy Herman, Chi	1 for 55 years
Bill Mazeroski, Pit	2 for 27 years

AMERICAN LEAGUE SUMMARY

Top Record Producers

1	Nap Lajoie, Phi	7
2	Hobe Ferris, Bos	5
3	Bucky Harris, Was	4

Most Outstanding Record Producers

Nap Lajoie, Phi	7 for 124 years
Oscar Mellilio, StL	2 for 73 years
Bucky Harris, Was	4 for 66 years
Gerry Priddy, Det	1 for 38 years
Gus Dundon, Chi	2 for 19 years

MAJOR LEAGUE SUMMARY

Top Record Producers

1	Bid McPhee, Cin, AA	8
2	Jack Burdock, Bos, NL	7
3	Fred Pfeffer, Chi, NL	4

Most Outstanding Record Producers

Bid McPhee, Cin, AA	8 for 208 years
Frankie Frisch, StL, NL	2 for 122 years
Bill Mazeroski, Pit, NL	1 for 22 years

Jack Burdock, Fred Pfeffer and Bid McPhee were the three most outstanding second basemen prior to 1900. McPhee split his career between the National League and American Association and broke most of Burdock's and Pfeffer's records.

McPhee established a Major League record in 1886 that still stands today. His 529 putouts have never been matched or bettered by any second baseman in baseball history.

Billy Herman is the National League champion in putouts with 466, a record he set in 1933. The putouts champion in the American League is Bobby Grich, who sent 484 runners back to their dugouts in 1974.

Frankie Frisch and Bill Mazeroski are two of the National League's finest and busiest second basemen. Frisch's 641 assists and 1,059 total chances are both National and Major League marks which have remained unbroken since 1927.

Bill Mazeroski set back-to-back double play records in 1961 and 1966. He stands out as the best second baseman to turn the double play; his 161 DPs in 1966 remains both the National and Major League record.

Although Jackie Robinson started off at first base, he will go down in baseball history as one of the game's best-fielding second basemen. He was the first in the National League to field over .990, and his .992 mark in 1951 stood for 22 years before it was broken. Tito Fuentes and Joe Morgan share the fielding average record at .993.

The dominant American League second baseman is Bobby Grich, who has two unbroken records and is tied with Rob Wilfong for the highest fielding average with a .995. Oscar Melillo is the assist king, and Gerry Priddy takes honors for participating in the most double plays. Hall of Famer Nap Lajoie proved he was as good with the glove as he was with the bat when he set the oldest unbroken record, 1,025 total chances in 1908.

SHORTSTOP

NATIONAL LEAGUE	AMERICAN LEAGUE	MAJOR LEAGUE

NATIONAL LEAGUE

Most Putouts

1876	Dave Force, Phi	108
1877	Johnny Peters, Chi	124
1882	Fred Pfeffer, Tro	161
1883	Saddie Houck, Det	162
1884	Bill McClellan, Phi	165
1885	Monte Ward, NY	167
1887	Monte Ward, NY	226
1889	Jack Glasscock, Ind	246
1890	Bob Allen, Phi	337
1891	Herman Long, Bos	345
1895	**Hugh Jennings, Bal**	**425**

Most Putouts after 1900

1900	Monte Cross, Phi	339
1901	Monte Cross, Phi	343
1903	Rudy Hulswitt, Phi	354
1904	Charlie Babb, Bkn	370
1905	Ed Abbaticchio, Bos	386
1906	Mickey Doolan, Phi	395
1914	**Rabbit Maranville, Pit**	**407**

Most Assists

1876	George Wright, Bos	251
1879	George Wright, Pro	319
1880	Arthur Irwin, Wor	339
1885	Jack Glasscock, StL	397
1887	Jack Glasscock, Ind	493
1890	Bob Allen, Phi	500
1891	Germany Smith, Cin	507
1892	Germany Smith, Cin	561
1898	Tommy Corcoran, Cin	561
1908	Joe Tinker, Chi	570
1914	Rabbit Maranville, Bos	574
1920	Dave Bancroft, NY	598
1924	Glen Wright, Pit	601
1980	**Ozzie Smith, SD**	**621**

Most Errors

1876	Jimmy Hallihan, NY	67
1879	Johnny Peters, Chi	71
1882	Fred Pfeffer, Tro	73
1883	Sammy Wise, Bos	88
1885	Tom Burns, Chi	96
1892	**Herman Long, Bos**	**99**
1892	**Frank Shugart, Pit**	**99**

Most Errors after 1900

1900	Monte Cross, Phi	62
1901	Bobby Wallace, StL	66
1902	Joe Tinker, Chi	72
1903	**Rudy Hulswitt, Phi**	**81**

AMERICAN LEAGUE

Most Putouts

1901	Kid Elberfeld, Det	332
1902	Monte Cross, Phi	373
1905	Bobby Wallace, StL	385
1913	Buck Weaver, Chi	392
1914	**Donnie Bush, Det**	**425**

Most Assists

1901	Billy Clingman, Was	462
1902	Freddy Parent, Bos	496
1904	George Davis, Chi	514
1905	John Cassidy, Was	520
1906	Tuck Turner, Cle	570
1969	Leo Cardenas, Min	570
1979	**Roy Smalley, Min**	**572**

Most Errors

1901	Bill Keister, Bal	97
1903	**Johnny Gochnaur, Cle**	**98**

MAJOR LEAGUE

Most Putouts

1876	Dave Force, Phi, NL	108
1877	Johnny Peters, Chi, NL	124
1882	Fred Pfeffer, Tro, NL	161
1883	Saddie Houck, Det, NL	162
1884	Billy Geer, Bkn, AA	176
1887	Monte Ward, NY, NL	226
1889	Herman Long, KC, AA	335
1890	Bob Allen, Phi, NL	337
1891	Herman Long, Bos, NL	345
1895	**Hugh Jennings, Bal, NL**	**425**
1914	**Donnie Bush, Det, AL**	**425**

Most Assists

1876	George Wright, Bos, NL	251
1879	George Wright, Pro, NL	319
1880	Arthur Irwin, Wor, NL	339
1884	Saddie Houck, Phi, AA	379
1885	Germany Smith, Bkn, AA	455
1886	Frank Fennelly, Cin, AA	485
1887	Jack Glasscock, Ind, NL	493
1889	Ollie Beard, Cin, AA	537
1892	Germany Smith, Cin, NL	561
1898	Tommy Corcoran, Cin, NL	561
1906	Tuck Turner, Cle, AL	570
1908	Joe Tinker, Chi, NL	570
1914	Rabbit Maranville, Bos, NL	574
1920	Dave Bancroft, NY, NL	598
1924	Glen Wright, Pit, NL	601
1980	**Ozzie Smith, SD, NL**	**621**

Most Errors

1876	Jimmy Hallihan, NY, NL	67
1879	Johnny Peters, Chi, NL	71
1882	Bill Gleason, StL, AA	85
1883	Sammy Wise, Bos, NL	88
1885	Tom Burns, Chi, NL	96
1886	Frank Fennelly, Cin, AA	117
1890	**Bill Shindle, Phi, PL**	**119**

Most Errors after 1900

1900	Monte Cross, Phi, NL	62
1901	Bill Keister, Bal, AL	97
1903	**Johnny Gochnaur, Cle, AL**	**98**

SHORTSTOP

NATIONAL LEAGUE	AMERICAN LEAGUE	MAJOR LEAGUE

Most Double Plays

NATIONAL LEAGUE			AMERICAN LEAGUE			MAJOR LEAGUE		
1876	Johnny Peters, Chi	16	1901	Kid Elberfeld, Det	62	1876	Johnny Peters, Chi, NL	16
1876	George Wright, Bos	16	1902	George Davis, Chi	72	1876	George Wright, Bos, NL	16
1877	Johnny Peters, Chi	23	1902	Billy Gilbert, Bal	72	1877	Johnny Peters, Chi, NL	23
1878	George Wright, Bos	24	1913	Buck Weaver, Chi	73	1878	George Wright, Bos, NL	24
1879	Dave Force, Buf	26	1915	Doc Lavan, StL	81	1879	Dave Force, Buf, NL	26
1880	Arthur Irwin, Wor	27	1917	Roger Peckinpaugh, NY	84	1880	Arthur Irwin, Wor, NL	27
1881	Saddie Houck, Det	40	1922	Wally Gerber, StL	93	1881	Saddie Houck, Det, NL	40
1882	Jack Glasscock, Cle	40	1922	Roger Peckinpaugh, Was	93	1882	Jack Glasscock, Cle, NL	40
1886	Jack Glasscock, StL	43	1923	Roger Peckinpaugh, Was	105	1886	Frank Fennelly, Cin, AA	54
1887	Jack Glasscock, Ind	58	1933	Billy Rogell, Det	116	1887	Jack Glasscock, Ind, NL	58
1889	Jack Glasscock, Ind	60	1938	Frank Crosetti, NY	120	1889	Ollie Beard, Cin, AA	63
1890	Bob Allen, Phi	68	1943	Lou Boudreau, Cle	122	1890	Bob Allen, Phi, NL	68
1894	Germany Smith, Cin	75	1944	Lou Boudreau, Cle	134	1894	Germany Smith, Cin, NL	75
1898	Bill Dahlen, Chi	77	1979	Roy Smalley, Min	144	1898	Bill Dahlen, Chi, NL	77
1900	George Davis, NY	94	**1980**	**Rick Burleson, Bos**	**147**	1900	George Davis, NY, NL	94
1921	Dave Bancroft, NY	105				1921	Dave Bancroft, NY, NL	105
1925	Glen Wright, Pit	109				1923	Roger Peckinpaugh, Was, AL	105
1928	Hod Ford, Cin	128				1925	Glen Wright, Pit, NL	109
1954	Roy McMillan, Cin	129				1928	Hod Ford, Cin, NL	128
1970	**Bobby Wine, Mon**	**137**				1944	Lou Boudreau, Cle, AL	134
						1970	Bobby Wine, Phi, NL	137
						1979	Roy Smalley, Min, AL	144
						1980	**Rick Burleson, Bos, AL**	**147**

Most Total Chances

NATIONAL LEAGUE			AMERICAN LEAGUE			MAJOR LEAGUE		
1876	Dave Force, Phi	384	1901	Kid Elberfeld, Det	819	1876	Dave Force, Phi, NL	384
1877	Johnny Peters, Chi	384	1902	Monte Cross, Phi	905	1877	Johnny Peters, Chi, NL	384
1879	George Wright, Pro	449	1904	George Davis, Chi	909	1879	George Wright, Pro, NL	449
1880	Arthur Irwin, Wor	485	1905	Bobby Wallace, StL	953	1880	Arthur Irwin, Wor, NL	485
1882	Fred Pfeffer, Tro	510	1908	Heinie Wagner, Bos	1003	1882	Bill Gleason, StL, AA	510
1883	Saddie Houck, Det	575	1911	Donnie Bush, Det	1003	1882	Fred Pfeffer, Tro, NL	510
1885	Jack Glasscock, StL	603	**1914**	**Donnie Bush, Det**	**1027**	1883	Saddie Houck, Det, NL	575
1886	Jack Glasscock, StL	605				1884	Billy Geer, Bkn, AA	617
1887	Jack Glasscock, Ind	777				1885	Germany Smith, Bkn, AA	697
1889	Jack Glasscock, Ind	791				1886	Frank Fennelly, Cin, AA	771
1890	Bob Allen, Phi	906				1887	Jack Glasscock, Ind, NL	777
1892	Hugh Jennings, Lou	970				1889	Herman Long, KC, AA	931
1898	Monte Cross, Phi	1003				1892	Hugh Jennings, Lou, NL	970
1914	**Rabbit Maranville, Bos**	**1046**				1898	Monte Cross, Phi, NL	1003
1922	**Dave Bancroft, NY**	**1046**				1908	Heinie Wagner, Bos, AL	1003
						1911	Donnie Bush, Det, AL	1003
						1914	**Rabbit Maranville, Bos, NL**	**1046**
						1922	**Dave Bancroft, NY, NL**	**1046**

Highest Fielding Average

NATIONAL LEAGUE			AMERICAN LEAGUE			MAJOR LEAGUE		
1876	Johnny Peters, Chi	.932	1901	Billy Clingman, Was	.932	1876	Johnny Peters, Chi, NL	.932
1878	George Wright, Bos	.947	1902	George Davis, Chi	.951	1878	George Wright, Bos, NL	.947
1903	Bill Dahlen, Bkn	.948	1906	Tuck Turner, Cle	.960	1903	Bill Dahlen, Bkn, NL	.948
1905	Tommy Corcoran, Cin	.952	1910	Tuck Turner, Cle	.973	1905	Tommy Corcoran, Cin, NL	.952
1908	Joe Tinker, Chi	.958	1918	Everett Scott, Bos	.976	1906	Tuck Turner, Cle, AL	.960
1912	Honus Wagner, Pit	.962	1919	Everett Scott, Bos	.976	1910	Tuck Turner, Cle, AL	.973
1913	Joe Tinker, Chi	.968	1944	Lou Boudreau, Cle	.978	1918	Everett Scott, Bos, AL	.976
1926	Johnny Cooney, Chi	.972	1947	Lou Boudreau, Cle	.982	1919	Everett Scott, Bos, AL	.976
1928	Hod Ford, Cin	.972	1950	Phil Rizzuto, NY	.982	1942	Eddie Miller, Bos, NL	.983
1937	Billy Jurges, Chi	.975	1963	Luis Aparicio, Bal	.983	1959	Ernie Banks, Chi, NL	.985
1942	Eddie Miller, Bos	.983	1971	Leo Cardenas, Min	.985	1971	Larry Bowa, Phi, NL	.986
1959	Ernie Banks, Chi	.985	**1972**	**Eddie Brinkman, Det**	**.990**	1972	Eddie Brinkman, Det, AL	.990
1971	Larry Bowa, Phi	.986				**1979**	**Larry Bowa, Phi, NL**	**.991**
1972	Larry Bowa, Phi	.987						
1979	**Larry Bowa, Phi**	**.991**						

SHORTSTOP

NATIONAL LEAGUE SUMMARY		
Top Record Producers		
1 Jack Glasscock, Ind		11
2 George Wright, Bos		6
3 Johnny Peters, Chi		5
4 Bob Allen, Phi		4
Most Outstanding Record Producers		
Hugh Jennings, Bal	2 for 99 years	
Rabbit Maranville, Bos	2 for 80 years	
Dave Bancroft, NY	3 for 74 years	
Glen Wright, Pit	2 for 59 years	
Hod Ford, Cin	2 for 35 years	

AMERICAN LEAGUE SUMMARY		
Top Record Producers		
1 Lou Boudreau, Cle		4
1 George Davis, Chi		4
3 Kid Elberfeld, Det		3
3 Donnie Bush, Det		3
3 Tuck Turner, Cle		3
Most Outstanding Record Producers		
Donnie Bush, Det	3 for 151 years	
Tuck Turner, Cle	3 for 85 years	
Lou Boudreau, Cle	4 for 55 years	
Everett Scott, Bos	2 for 25 years	
George Davis, Chi	4 for 17 years	

MAJOR LEAGUE SUMMARY		
Top Record Producers		
1 George Wright, Bos, NL		6
2 Johnny Peters, Chi, NL		5
3 Saddie Houck, Det, NL		4
3 Germany Smith, Bkn, AA		4
3 Jack Glasscock, Ind, NL		4
Most Outstanding Record Producers		
Hugh Jennings, Bal, NL	2 for 99 years	
Rabbitt Maranville, Bos, NL	2 for 80 years	
Donnie Bush, Det, AL	2 for 77 years	
Dave Bancroft, NY, NL	3 for 74 years	
Glen Wright, Pit, NL	2 for 59 years	

Johnny Peters, George Wright and Davy Force were the three outstanding pioneer shortstops who set the early records for others to approach and surpass. Jack Glasscock, Bob Allen and Hugh "Ee-Yah" Jennings were others who starred prior to 1900. Jennings is the only one of this group to have made the Hall of Fame. His record of 425 putouts in 1895 is still standing. This mark was tied by Donnie Bush of the Tigers in 1914.

Ozzie Smith of the Cardinals has fielded the most ground balls in one season, and his assists record, set in 1980, stands at 621. Ozzie is easily the most acrobatic shortstop in baseball history, and many say he is the most gifted ever to play the position.

Bobby Wine of the Expos has turned the most double plays in the National League, while Rick Burleson of the Red Sox has that honor in the American League. Roy Smalley is the American League assists champion, and Donnie Bush is the all-time most active shortstop with 1,027 total chances set back in 1914. His records have lasted more years than any other shortstop.

RABBIT MARANVILLE
Rabbit Maranville set fielding records as both a second baseman and as a shortstop.

SHORTSTOP

Monte Cross in 1898 was the first shortstop to come up with more than 1,000 total chances in a season. Cross had 1,003 total chances and was then tied by Heinie Wagner in 1908 and Donnie Bush in 1911. What are the odds against that happening again?

The Major League record for total chances was set by two Hall of Fame inductees, Rabbit Maranville and Dave Bancroft. Maranville tallied 1,046 in 1914 and, as strange as it seems, Bancroft also had 1,046 in 1922. Larry Bowa is the shortstop with the highest fielding average. Starring for the Phils, Bowa set three consecutive marks and sits atop the list with a sparkling .991 fielding average. Eddie Brinkman of Detroit is the American League fielding average champion at .990.

THIRD BASE

NATIONAL LEAGUE		
Most Putouts		
1876	Cap Anson, Chi	135
1881	Frank Hankinson, Tro	151
1883	Jerry Denny, Pro	178
1886	Jerry Denny, StL	182
1887	Billy Nash, Bos	207
1889	Tom Burns, Chi	225
1898	Jimmy Collins, Bos	243
1899	**Jimmy Williams, Pit**	**251**
1900	Jimmy Collins, Bos	251

Most Assists		
1876	Cap Anson, Chi	147
1878	Bill Hague, Pro	177
1879	Ned Williamson, Chi	193
1881	Ned Williamson, Chi	194
1882	Ned Williamson, Chi	210
1883	Ned Williamson, Chi	252
1885	Ned Williamson, Chi	258
1886	Jerry Denny, StL	270
1887	Jim Donnelly, Was	275
1889	Tom Burns, Chi	301
1890	Will Smalley, Cle	327
1891	Arlie Latham, Cin	370
1892	Bill Shindle, Bal	382
1966	Ron Santo, Chi	391
1967	Ron Santo, Chi	393
1974	**Mike Schmidt, Phi**	**404**

Most Errors		
1876	Al Nichols, NY	73
1883	**Ned Williamson, Chi**	**87**

Most Errors after 1900		
1900	Piano Legs Hickman, NY	86

AMERICAN LEAGUE		
Most Putouts		
1901	Bill Coughlin, Det	232
1913	Frank Baker, Phi	233
1927	Willie Kamm, Chi	236
1928	**Willie Kamm, Chi**	**243**

Most Assists		
1901	Jimmy Collins, Bos	328
1902	Sammy Strang, Chi	334
1904	Lee Tannehill, Chi	369
1916	Ossie Vitt, Det	385
1937	Harlond Clift, StL	405
1971	**Graig Nettles, Cle**	**412**

Most Errors		
1901	Doc Casey, Det	58
1902	Sammy Strang, Chi	62

DID YOU KNOW . . . *That in 1876 there was free substitution for the first four innings but thereafter substitutions were only for the sick or injured?*

MAJOR LEAGUE		
Most Putouts		
1876	Cap Anson, Chi, NL	135
1881	Frank Hankinson, Tro, NL	151
1883	Jerry Denny, Pro, NL	178
1886	George Pinckney, Bkn, AA	184
1887	**Denny Lyons, Phi, AA**	**255**

Most Putouts after 1900		
1900	Jimmy Collins, Bos, NL	251

Most Assists		
1876	Cap Anson, Chi, NL	147
1878	Bill Hague, Pro, NL	177
1879	Ned Williamson, Chi, NL	193
1881	Ned Williamson, Chi, NL	194
1882	Ned Williamson, Chi, NL	210
1883	Joe Battin, Pit, AA	258
1884	Arlie Latham, StL, AA	302
1886	Frank Hankinson, NY, AA	316
1888	Bill Shindle, Bal, AA	340
1890	Charlie Reilly, Col, AA	354
1891	Arlie Latham, Cin, NL	370
1892	Bill Shindle, Bal, NL	382
1916	Ossie Vitt, Det, AL	385
1937	Harlond Clift, StL, AL	405
1971	**Graig Nettles, Cle, AL**	**412**

Most Errors		
1876	Al Nichols, NY, NL	73
1882	Jack Gleason, StL, NL	83
1883	Ned Williamson, Chi, NL	87
1884	John Irwin, Bos, AA	87
1886	Arlie Latham, StL, AA	88
1887	Joe Werrick, Lou, AA	89
1888	Jumbo Davis, KC, AA	91
1890	**Bill Joyce, Bkn, AA**	**107**

Most Errors after 1900		
1900	Piano Legs Hickman, NY, NL	86

THIRD BASE

NATIONAL LEAGUE		AMERICAN LEAGUE		MAJOR LEAGUE	
Most Double Plays		*Most Double Plays*		*Most Double Plays*	
1876 Cap Anson, Chi	8	1901 Doc Casey, Det	25	1876 Cap Anson, Chi, NL	8
1877 Cap Anson, Chi	9	1902 Barry McCormick, StL	26	1877 Cap Anson, Chi, NL	9
1877 Curry Foley, Cin	9	1908 Hobe Ferris, StL	27	1877 Curry Foley, Cin, NL	9
1879 Ned Williamson, Chi	13	1910 Frank Baker, Phi	35	1879 Ned Williamson, Chi, NL	13
1881 Frank Hankinson, Tro	21	1921 Hank Shanks, Was	35	1881 Frank Hankinson, Tro, NL	21
1884 Ned Williamson, Chi	25	1925 Gene Robertson, StL	41	1884 Ned Williamson, Chi, NL	25
1889 Tom Burns, Chi	30	1927 Sammy Hale, Phi	46	1886 Frank Hankinson, NY, AA	26
1898 Barry McCormick, Chi	31	1937 Harlond Clift, StL	50	1887 Denny Lyons, Phi, AA	29
1915 Heinie Groh, Cin	34	1971 Graig Nettles, Cle	54	1889 Tom Burns, Chi, NL	30
1918 Heinie Groh, Cin	37	**1977 Butch Hobson, Bos**	**57**	1891 Pete Gilbert, Bal, AA	34
1925 Pie Traynor, Pit	41			1910 Frank Baker, Phi, AL	35
1950 Hank Thompson, NY	43			1918 Heinie Groh, Cin, NL	37
1974 Darrell Evans, Atl	**45**			1925 Pie Traynor, Pit, NL	41
				1925 Gene Robertson, StL, AL	41
				1927 Sammy Hale, Phi, AL	46
				1937 Harlond Clift, StL, AL	50
				1971 Graig Nettles, Cle, AL	54
				1977 Butch Hobson, Bos, AL	**57**
Most Total Chances		*Most Total Chances*		*Most Total Chances*	
1876 Cap Anson, Chi	332	1901 Jimmy Collins, Bos	581	1876 Cap Anson, Chi, NL	332
1881 Frank Hankinson, Tro	353	1911 Jimmy Austin, StL	607	1881 Frank Hankinson, Tro, NL	353
1882 Jerry Denny, Pro	397	1916 Ossie Vitt, Det	615	1882 Jerry Denny, Pro, NL	397
1883 Ned Williamson, Chi	450	**1937 Harlond Clift, StL**	**637**	1883 Joe Battin, Pit, AA	459
1886 Jerry Denny, StL	505			1884 Arlie Latham, StL, AA	514
1887 Billy Nash, Bos	508			1886 Frank Hankinson, NY, AA	569
1888 Tom Burns, Chi	516			1888 Bill Shindle, Bal, AA	605
1889 Tom Burns, Chi	598			1889 Bill Shindle, Bal, AA	636
1890 Will Smalley, Cle	612			1892 Bill Shindle, Bal, NL	660
1891 Arlie Latham, Cin	622			**1899 Jimmy Williams, Pit, NL**	**671**
1892 Bill Shindle, Bal	660				
1899 Jimmy Williams, Pit	**671**				
Most Total Chances after 1900				*Most Total Chances after 1900*	
1900 Jimmy Collins, Bos	620			1900 Jimmy Collins, Bos, NL	620
1904 Tommy Leach, Pit	**643**			**1904 Tommy Leach, Pit, NL**	**643**
Highest Fielding Average		*Highest Fielding Average*		*Highest Fielding Average*	
1876 Joe Battin, StL	.867	1901 Bill Bradley, Cle	.930	1876 Joe Battin, StL, NL	.867
1877 Cap Anson, Chi	.883	1902 Jimmy Collins, Bos	.954	1877 Cap Anson, Chi, NL	.883
1878 Bill Hague, Pro	.925	1904 Bill Bradley, Cle	.955	1878 Bill Hague, Pro, NL	.925
1890 Chippy McGarr, Bos	.933	1914 Terry Turner, Cle	.963	1890 Chippy McGarr, Bos, NL	.933
1894 Billy Nash, Bos	.933	1915 Ossie Vitt, Det	.964	1894 Billy Nash, Bos, NL	.933
1895 Lave Cross, Phi	.940	1916 Ossie Vitt, Det	.964	1895 Lave Cross, Phi, NL	.940
1897 Bill Clingman, Lou	.947	1918 Frank Baker, NY	.972	1897 Bill Clingman, Lou, NL	.947
1899 Lave Cross, StL	.940	1920 Larry Gardner, Cle	.976	1899 Lave Cross, StL, NL	.960
1907 Harry Steinfeldt, Chi	.967	1926 Willie Kamm, Chi	.978	1907 Harry Steinfeldt, Chi, NL	.967
1913 Hans Lobert, Phi	.974	1929 Willie Kamm, Chi	.978	1913 Hans Lobert, Phi, NL	.974
1923 Heinie Groh, NY	.975	1932 Jimmy Dykes, Phi	.980	1920 Larry Gardner, Cle, AL	.976
1924 Heinie Groh, NY	**.983**	1933 Willie Kamm, Cle	.984	1924 Heinie Groh, NY, NL	.983
		1946 George Kell, Det	.984	1933 Willie Kamm, Cle, AL	.984
		1947 Hank Majeski, Phi	.988	1946 George Kell, Det, AL	.984
		1974 Don Money, Mil	**.989**	1947 Hank Majeski, Phi, AL	.988
				1974 Don Money, Mil, NL	**.989**

THIRD BASE

NATIONAL LEAGUE SUMMARY		AMERICAN LEAGUE SUMMARY		MAJOR LEAGUE SUMMARY	

Top Record Producers

NATIONAL LEAGUE		AMERICAN LEAGUE		MAJOR LEAGUE	
1 Ned Williamson, Chi	9	1 Willie Kamm, Cle	5	1 Ned Williamson, Chi, NL	6
2 Cap Anson, Chi	6	2 Ossie Vitt, Det	4	1 Cap Anson, Chi, NL	6
3 Jerry Denny, Pro	5	3 Harlond Clift, StL	3	1 Frank Hankinson, NY, AA	6
3 Tom Burns, Chi	5	3 Jimmy Collins, Bos	3	4 Bill Shindle, Bal, AA	5
5 Heinie Groh, NY	4	3 Frank Baker, NY	3	5 Arlie Latham, StL, AA	4

Most Outstanding Record Producers

NATIONAL LEAGUE		AMERICAN LEAGUE		MAJOR LEAGUE	
Jimmy Williams, Pit	2 for 178 years	Harlond Clift, StL	3 for 119 years	Denny Lyons, Phi, AA	2 for 103 years
Jimmy Collins, Bos	2 for 89 years	Willie Kamm, Cle	5 for 81 years	Jimmy Williams, Pit, NL	1 for 89 years
Heinie Groh, NY	4 for 75 years	Ossie Vitt, Det	4 for 45 years	Harlond Clift, StL, AL	2 for 68 years
Hank Thompson, NY	1 for 24 years	Frank Baker, NY	3 for 31 years	Hank Majeski, Phi, AL	1 for 27 years
Tom Burns, Chi	5 for 21 years	Hank Majeski, Phi	1 for 27 years	Bill Shindle, Bal, AA	5 for 27 years

Cap Anson, Jerry Denny and Ned Williamson were three of the early superstar third basemen. They sacrificed their bodies in the attempt at stopping balls at the hot corner, without aid of a glove, or with a glove which had little padding.

Williamson accomplished the rare feat of setting five consecutive assists records from 1879 through 1885. No other third baseman (with or without gloves!) has ever duplicated this feat.

As the nineteenth century was coming to a close, Arlie Latham, George Burns, Billy Shindle, Jimmy Collins and Jimmy Williams were the most outstanding and most courageous players at the hot corner, but only Collins is in the Hall of Fame. (Cap Anson is in the Hall of Fame but earned his honor as a first baseman.)

Billy Shindle was exceptionally busy; he established three consecutive total chance marks from 1888 through 1892. And, believe it or not, Jimmy Collins and Jimmy Williams put out an identical 251 runners to share the National League record. As the season schedules grew longer, the number of putouts and assists likewise increased. Mike Schmidt of the Phils became the only third baseman to register more than 400 putouts in one season.

Darrell Evans of the Braves stands alone at the top of the National League double play record with 45 in 1974. Jimmy Williams' 671 total chances is both a National and Major League record, which has stood since 1899!

Willie Kamm was the American League star during the late 1920s and he holds the number one position in putouts with 243. Graig Nettles is the all-time leader in assists with 412, which is also a Major League record. Harlond Clift starred during the 1930s for the St. Louis Browns and was the first to register 50 double plays. Nettles broke that record with 54 double plays, only to have Butch Hobson of the Red Sox replace him with 57 in 1977 to set the current mark. Harlond Clift remains the total chance champion with 637, a mark that has lasted half a century.

The fielding average records have risen dramatically, as would be expected, with the progressive development of the modern glove. The fielding average record at third base started at .867 in 1876, and had improved to .989 in 1974. Joe Battin is credited with the initial record in 1876. Don Money, who set the current mark in 1974, surpassed Battin's early record by more than 100 points. Fielding averages have also improved because of smoother playing surfaces. Baseball fields in the early years weren't much more than cow pastures, with potholes and bumps everywhere. There were few true hops in those days.

Another factor that has helped the players over the years is that games are now played either in broad daylight or in well-lighted stadiums at night. In the early years of baseball, most games started at 3 o'clock, so that fans could see most of the game after work. But since umpires did not get paid for an incomplete game, many contests were concluded in total darkness. This certainly did not help the fielders any, and it was a dangerous situation for batters as well. There is a story told about one rightfielder who took an orange out to his position and saved it for the right time. With two outs in the last inning, the opposing team down by three runs and the bases loaded, a long drive was hit over the rightfielder's head. As he raced into the darkness he took out the orange with his bare hand, deftly placed it in his glove and made one of the most sensational "catches" ever seen, or, perhaps, not seen. He trotted back to the infield, where his manager and the other players slapped him on the back and congratulated him as the umpire shouted "This game is over!" The manager then asked for the ball, since balls were precious commodities in those days. To the surprise of the manager and the other players, the rightfielder presented them with his orange. The next day, the ball was found deep in the high grass of the outfield.

In trying to determine the most outstanding fielder among third basemen, the best clue we have is a look

THIRD BASE

at the records that have lasted the longest. Bill Hague's .925 fielding average of 1878 lasted 12 years before being broken, the longest-standing record prior to 1900. Willie Kamm's .984 mark in 1933 lasted 14 years before Hank Majeski set a new mark of .988 in 1947. Majeski's record may have been the greatest fielding feat by a third baseman, since it lasted 27 years and was beaten only by one point when Don Money turned in his Major League record .989 in 1974.

The most outstanding mark in the National League was set by Heinie Groh when he fielded .983 way back in 1924. This record still stands and represents the longest-lasting third base record. The question now is whether Majeski's .988 in 1947 is considered greater than Groh's .983 in 1924. Do you think the improvements in gloves from 1924 to 1947 are a greater advantage than the five points which separate these records?

CATCHING

NATIONAL LEAGUE		
Most Putouts		
1876	John Clapp, StL	333
1877	Lew Brown, Bos	360
1879	Pop Snyder, Bos	398
1880	Emil Gross, Pro	429
1882	Charlie Bennett, Det	446
1884	Barney Gilligan, Pro	605
1908	Roger Bresnahan, NY	657
1911	Chief Meyers, NY	729
1953	Roy Campanella, Bkn	807
1959	John Roseboro, LA	848
1961	John Roseboro, LA	877
1963	Johnny Edwards, Cin	1008
1969	**Johnny Edwards, Cin**	**1135**

Most Assists		
1876	Pop Snyder, Lou	86
1878	Silver Flint, Ind	102
1879	Pop Snyder, Bos	142
1887	Tom Daly, Chi	148
1888	Connie Mack, Was	152
1890	Chief Zimmer, Cle	188
1903	**Pat Moran, Bos**	**214**

Most Errors		
1876	Nate Hicks, NY	94

Most Errors after 1900		
1900	Frank Bowerman, NY	28
1904	Red Dooin, Phi	37
1909	**Red Dooin, Phi**	**40**

Most Double Plays		
1876	John Clapp, StL	5
1877	Pop Snyder, Lou	8
1879	Pop Snyder, Bos	10
1881	Doc Bushong, Wor	10
1882	Bill Holbert, Tro	13
1885	Barney Gilligan, Pro	13
1886	Charlie Bennett, Det	13
1887	Connie Mack, Was	15
1897	Jack Warner, NY	17
1903	Pat Moran, Bos	17
1908	Red Dooin, Phi	17
1909	Bill Bergen, Bkn	18
1910	Larry McLean, Cin	18
1912	Johnny Kling, Bos	20
1922	Bob O'Farrell, Chi	22
1968	**Tom Haller, LA**	**23**

AMERICAN LEAGUE		
Most Putouts		
1901	Mike Powers, Phi	400
1903	Ossee Schreckengost, Phi	514
1904	Ossee Schreckengost, Phi	589
1905	Ossee Schreckengost, Phi	790
1961	Earl Battey, Min	812
1962	Earl Battey, Min	872
1964	Elston Howard, NY	939
1967	Bill Freehan, Det	950
1968	**Bill Freehan, Det**	**971**

DID YOU KNOW . . . *That in 1876, home plate was made of white marble or stone?*

Most Assists		
1901	Mike Powers, Phi	137
1903	Lou Criger, Bos	156
1908	Boss Schmidt, Det	184
1909	Gabby Street, Was	210
1911	**Oscar Stanage, Det**	**212**

Most Errors		
1901	Ossee Schreckengost, Bos	30
1907	Boss Schmidt, Det	34
1908	Boss Schmidt, Det	37
1911	**Oscar Stanage, Det**	**41**

Most Double Plays		
1901	Billy Sullivan, Chi	13
1907	Boss Schmidt, Det	14
1908	Gabby Street, Was	14
1909	Gabby Street, Was	18
1910	Jim Stephens, StL	18
1914	Steve O'Neill, Cle	22
1915	John Lapp, Phi	23
1916	**Steve O'Neill, Cle**	**36**

DID YOU KNOW . . . *That in 1876, an illegal pitch was called a foul balk? If three foul balks were committed in one inning, that team would lose by forfeit.*

DID YOU KNOW . . . *That prior to 1880 a catcher was not required to catch the third strike on the fly in order to retire a batter on a strikeout?*

MAJOR LEAGUE		
Most Putouts		
1876	John Clapp, StL, NL	333
1877	Lew Brown, Bos, NL	360
1879	Pop Snyder, Bos, NL	398
1880	Emil Gross, Pro, NL	429
1882	Charlie Bennett, Det, NL	446
1883	Bill Holbert, NY, AA	527
1884	Barney Gilligan, Pro, NL	605
1886	Doc Bushong, StL, AA	647
1905	Ossee Schreckengost, Phi, AL	790
1953	Roy Campanella, Bkn, NL	807
1959	John Roseboro, LA, NL	848
1961	John Roseboro, LA, NL	877
1963	Johnny Edwards, Cin, NL	1008
1969	**Johnny Edwards, Cin, NL**	**1135**

Most Assists		
1876	Pop Snyder, Lou, NL	86
1878	Silver Flint, Ind, NL	102
1879	Pop Snyder, Bos, NL	142
1884	Bill Holbert, NY, AA	142
1886	John Kerins, Lou, AA	157
1890	Chief Zimmer, Cle, NL	188
1903	Pat Moran, Bos, NL	214
1914	Bill Rariden, Ind, FL	215
1915	**Bill Rariden, Nwk, FL**	**238**

Most Errors		
1876	Nate Hicks, NY, NL	94

Most Errors after 1900		
1900	Frank Bowerman, NY, NL	28
1904	Red Dooin, Phi, NL	37
1908	Boss Schmidt, Det, AL	37
1909	Red Dooin, Phi, NL	40
1911	**Oscar Stanage, Det, AL**	**41**

Most Double Plays		
1876	John Clapp, StL, NL	5
1877	Pop Snyder, Lou, NL	8
1879	Pop Snyder, Bos, NL	10
1881	Doc Bushong, Wor, NL	10
1882	Bill Holbert, Tro, NL	13
1885	Barney Gilligan, Pro, NL	13
1886	Doc Bushong, StL, AA	14
1887	Connie Mack, Was, NL	15
1897	Jack Warner, NY, NL	17
1903	Pat Moran, Bos, NL	17
1908	Red Dooin, Phi, NL	17
1909	Bill Bergen, Bkn, NL	18
1909	Gabby Street, Was, AL	18
1910	Larry McLean, Cin, NL	18
1912	Johnny Kling, Bos, NL	20
1914	Steve O'Neill, Cle, AL	22
1915	Jack Lapp, Phi, AL	23
1916	**Steve O'Neill, Cle, AL**	**36**

CATCHING

NATIONAL LEAGUE	AMERICAN LEAGUE	MAJOR LEAGUE

Most Total Chances

NATIONAL LEAGUE		AMERICAN LEAGUE		MAJOR LEAGUE	
1876 John Clapp, StL	445	1901 Mike Powers, Phi	564	1876 John Clapp, StL, NL	445
1877 Lew Brown, Bos	476	1903 Lou Criger, Bos	661	1877 Lew Brown, Bos, NL	476
1879 Pop Snyder, Bos	584	1904 Ossee Schreckengost, Phi	679	1879 Pop Snyder, Bos, NL	584
1880 Emil Gross, Pro	641	1905 Ossee Schreckengost, Phi	919	1880 Emil Gross, Pro, NL	641
1884 Barney Gilligan, Pro	753	1909 Gabby Street, Was	942	1883 Bill Holbert, NY, AA	723
1903 Johnny Kling, Chi	778	1962 Earl Battey, Min	963	1884 Barney Gilligan, Pro, NL	753
1908 Roger Bresnahan, NY	809	1964 Elston Howard, NY	1008	1886 Doc Bushong, StL, AA	829
1909 George Gibson, Pit	862	1967 Bill Freehan, Det	1021	1905 Ossee Schreckengost,	
1953 Roy Campanella, Bkn	874	**1968 Bill Freehan, Det**	**1050**	Phi, AL	919
1959 John Roseboro, LA	910			1909 Gabby Street, Was, AL	942
1961 John Roseboro, LA	946			1914 Bill Rariden, Ind, FL	947
1963 Johnny Edwards, Cin	1101			1915 Bill Rariden, Nwk, FL	968
1969 Johnny Edwards, Cin	**1221**			1963 Johnny Edwards, Cin, NL	1101
				1969 Johnny Edwards, Cin, NL	**1221**

Highest Fielding Average

NATIONAL LEAGUE		AMERICAN LEAGUE		MAJOR LEAGUE	
1876 Doug Allison, Har	.881	1901 Billy Sullivan, Chi	.967	1876 Doug Allison, Har, NL	.881
1877 Pop Snyder, Lou	.910	1903 Harry Bemis, Cle	.988	1877 Pop Snyder, Lou, NL	.910
1878 Pop Snyder, Bos	.912	1904 Joe Sugden, StL	.989	1878 Pop Snyder, Bos, NL	.912
1879 Pop Snyder, Bos	.925	1922 Ray Schalk, Chi	.989	1879 Pop Snyder, Bos, NL	.925
1880 Silver Flint, Chi	.932	1923 Hank Severeid, StL	.993	1880 Silver Flint, Chi, NL	.932
1881 Charlie Bennett, Det	.962	1930 Mickey Cochrane, Phi	.993	1881 Charlie Bennett, Det, NL	.962
1888 Charlie Bennett, Det	.966	1931 Bill Dickey, NY	.996	1888 Charlie Bennett, Det, NL	.966
1893 Farmer Vaughn, Cin	.969	**1946 Buddy Rosar, Phi**	**1.000**	1893 Farmer Vaughn, Cin, NL	.969
1895 Wilbert Robinson, Bal	.979	**1957 Pete Daley, Bos**	**1.000**	1895 Wilbert Robinson, Bal, NL	.979
1897 Heinie Peitz, Cin	.979	**1957 Lous Berberet, Was**	**1.000**	1897 Heinie Peitz, Cin, NL	.979
1899 Chief Zimmer, Lou	.985	**1958 Yogi Berra, NY**	**1.000**	1899 Chief Zimmer, Lou, NL	.985
1903 Jack Warner, NY	.986			1903 Harry Bemis, Cle, AL	.988
1905 Pat Moran, Bos	.986			1904 Joe Sugden, StL, AL	.989
1907 Johnny Kling, Chi	.987			1908 Bill Bergen, Bkn, NL	.989
1908 Bill Bergen, Bkn	.989			1912 George Gibson, Pit, NL	.990
1912 George Gibson, Pit	.990			1923 Hank Severeid, StL, AL	.993
1923 Frank Snyder, NY	.990			1930 Mickey Cochrane, Phi, AL	.993
1931 Shanty Hogan, NY	.996			1931 Bill Dickey, NY, AL	.996
1932 Earl Grace, Pit	.998			1931 Shanty Hogan, NY, NL	.996
1950 Wes Westrum, NY	**.999**			1932 Earl Grace, Pit, NL	.998
				1946 Buddy Rosar, Phi, AL	**1.000**
				1957 Pete Daley, Bos, AL	**1.000**
				1957 Lou Berberet, Was, AL	**1.000**
				1958 Yogi Berra, NY, AL	**1.000**

DID YOU KNOW . . . *That prior to 1920, a catcher had to appear in 50 percent of scheduled games to qualify for a fielding title? After 1920, 90 games were required for qualification.*

CATCHING

NATIONAL LEAGUE SUMMARY			AMERICAN LEAGUE SUMMARY			MAJOR LEAGUE SUMMARY		

Top Record Producers

National			American			Major		
1	Pop Snyder, Box	9	1	Ossee Schreckengost, Phi	6	1	Pop Snyder, Bos, NL	9
2	Charlie Bennett, Det	4	2	Gabby Street, Was	4	2	Doc Bushong, StL, AA	4
2	John Roseboro, LA	4	2	Bill Freehan, Det	4	2	Bill Rariden, Ind, FL	4
2	Johnny Edwards, Cin	4	4	Earl Battey, Min	3	2	Johnny Edwards, Cin, NL	4
5	Pat Moran, Bos	3				2	Bill Holbert, NY, AA	4
5	Barney Gilligan, Pro	3						

Most Outstanding Record Producers

National		American		Major	
Pat Moran, Bos	3 for 92 years	Oscar Stanage, Det	1 for 77 years	Bill Rariden, Ind, FL	4 for 123 years
George Gibson, Pit	2 for 61 years	Steve O'Neill, Cle	2 for 74 years	Steve O'Neill, Cle, AL	2 for 73 years
Johnny Edwards, Cin	4 for 50 years	Ossee Schreckengost, Phi	6 for 63 years	Johnny Edwards, Cin, NL	4 for 50 years
Bob O'Farrell, Chi	1 for 46 years	Gabby Street, Was	4 for 57 years	Buddy Rosar, Phi, AL	1 for 42 years
Barney Gilligan, Pro	3 for 44 years	Bill Freehan, Det	4 for 42 years	Lou Berberet, Was, AL	1 for 31 years

Pop Snyder was the most effective catcher during the early years of baseball. He had the courage to work behind the plate for 15 years without the aid of shin guards or a chest protector. Masks were not used until 1877, and they were so flimsy that balls would often go right through them, causing great injury. It was said that catchers in those days possessed either a high degree of courage or a low degree of intelligence.

The catcher's mitts were not much more than a leather covering on the hand. For many years, catchers would play back and take the ball on the first bounce. This was easier on the hands but tough on the shins; many balls would short hop the catcher and bounce off his already aching and bleeding legs.

Charlie Bennett had the best catching ability of the pioneer catchers. His fielding average record lasted 12 years. In 1932, Earl Grace made only one error and fielded a marvelous .998, a mark which stood for 14 years until Buddy Rosar of the Philadelphia Athletics became the first catcher to go through a season without making an error. Rosar accomplished this feat in 1946 and it wasn't done again until 1957, when Pete Daley and Lou Berberet were both perfect. Yogi Berra was the last to do it, in 1958.

Of the catchers who had 1.000 fielding averages, Rosar had the most chances to handle with 605; Daley had only 309 chances, Berberet had 397 and Berra had 550.

Johnny Edwards is the busiest catcher in history. His 1,135 putouts and 1,221 total chances in 1969 are National and Major League records that still stand. Pat Moran turned in 214 assists back in 1903, and this is an unbroken National League record as well. Bill Rariden has the Major League assists mark of 238 set in 1915.

Tom Haller is the double play champion in the National League, while Steve O'Neill is the American and Major League champion with 36 in 1916. Prior to the fine work of Johnny Edwards, Roy Campanella and John Roseboro of the Dodgers put their names in the record book many times.

In the American League, Mike Powers was the catcher who set the standards for others to shoot for. Ossee Schreckengost of the Athletics was a hard-working catcher who set three consecutive putout marks from 1903 through 1905. Gabby Street and Steve O'Neill were also standout receivers.

Elston Howard of the Yankees was the first AL catcher to register more than 1,000 total chances. He was followed by Bill Freehan of the Tigers, who has been the most active catcher in American League history. His putouts and total chance records are the current league marks.

In the National League, Wes Westrum deserves recognition for his fine season in 1950, when he handled 680 chances while making only one error. This represents the greatest catching performance in National League history. Many would argue that when Earl Grace of the Pirates fielded .998 with one error and 413 total chances in 1932 it was just as impressive a feat as Westrum's, due to the fact that Grace did not have the advantage of a modern catcher's mitt.

The catching position was responsible for the creation of the rule that a substitution cannot be made until the ball is dead. Back in the early 1880s, the most colorful character in the game was King Kelly. One day he was sitting on the bench while his team was on the field. A foul pop-up was coming his way, so he stood up and called, "Kelly in for the catcher!" and proceeded to catch the ball. This caused a furor, of course, and the result was the new rule. There were many occurrences during games in the early years that baseball did not yet have a rule to cover. New rules were added as the game presented the need for them.

LEFT FIELD

NATIONAL LEAGUE		AMERICAN LEAGUE		MAJOR LEAGUE	
Most Putouts		*Most Putouts*		*Most Putouts*	
1876 Fred Treacey, NY	202	1901 Tommy Dowd, Bos	288	1876 Fred Treacey, NY, NL	202
1879 Mike Mansell, Syr	204	1902 Jesse Burkett, StL	300	1879 Mike Mansell, Syr, NL	204
1883 George Wood, Det	226	1904 Matty McIntyre, Det	334	1883 George Wood, Det, NL	226
1888 Walt Wilmot, Was	260	1916 Burt Shotton, StL	357	1886 Tip O'Neill, StL, AA	279
1890 Cliff Carroll, Chi	265	1920 Bobby Veach, Det	357	1889 Harry Stovey, Phi, AA	287
1891 Billy Hamilton, Phi	287	1921 Bobby Veach, Det	384	1891 Billy Hamilton, Phi, NL	287
1892 Billy Hamilton, Phi	291	1925 Goose Goslin, Was	385	1892 Billy Hamilton, Phi, NL	291
1893 Ed Delahanty, Phi	318	1932 Joe Vosmik, Cle	432	1893 Ed Delahanty, Phi, NL	318
1895 Fred Clarke, Lou	344	**1980 Willie Wilson, KC**	**482**	1895 Fred Clarke, Lou, NL	344
1898 Fred Clarke, Lou	344			1898 Fred Clarke, Lou, NL	344
1899 Kip Selbach, Cin	355			1899 Kip Selbach, Cin, NL	355
1909 Fred Clarke, Pit	362			1909 Fred Clarke, Pit, NL	362
1912 Max Carey, Pit	369			1912 Max Carey, Pit, NL	369
1921 Austin McHenry, StL	371			1921 Bobby Veach, Det, AL	384
1926 Eddie Brown, Bos	**401**			1925 Goose Goslin, Was, AL	385
				1926 Eddie Brown, Bos, NL	401
				1932 Joe Vosmik, Cle, AL	432
				1980 Willie Wilson, KC, AL	**482**
Most Assists		*Most Assists*		*Most Assists*	
1876 Fred Treacey, NY	9	1901 Doc Nance, Det	20	1876 Fred Treacey, NY, NL	9
1877 Charley Jones, Cin	11	1902 Sam Mertes, Chi	26	1877 Charley Jones, Cin, NL	11
1878 Tom York, Pro	14	1910 Duffy Lewis, Bos	28	1878 Tom York, Pro, NL	14
1879 Charley Jones, Bos	20	1913 Duffy Lewis, Bos	29	1879 Charley Jones, Bos, NL	20
1881 Buttercup Dickerson, Wor	28	1914 Tilly Walker, StL	30	1881 Buttercup Dickerson,	
1886 Jim Lillie, KC	30	**1917 Ping Bodie, Phi**	**32**	Wor, NL	28
1893 Ed Delahanty, Phi	31			**1883 Tom Dolan, StL, AA**	**51**
1903 Jimmy Sheckard, Bkn	**36**				
				Most Assists after 1900	
				1900 Kip Selbach, NY, NL	25
				1902 Sam Mertes, Chi, AL	26
				1903 Jimmy Sheckard, Bkn, NL	**36**
Most Errors		*Most Errors*		*Most Errors*	
1876 Fred Treacey, NY	39	1901 Tommy Dowd, Bos	20	1876 Fred Treacey, NY, NL	39
1876 George Hall, Phi	39	1902 Jesse Burkett, StL	26	1876 George Hall, Phi, NL	39
1888 Walt Wilmont, Was	41	1921 Ken Williams, StL	26	1883 Jud Birchall, Phi, AA	45
1893 Jesse Burkett, Cle	46	**1929 Roy Johnson, Det**	**31**	**1890 Ed Beecher, Buf, PL**	**55**
1895 Fred Clarke, Lou	**49**				
				Most Errors after 1900	
Most Errors after 1900				1900 Jimmy Slagle, Phi, NL	29
1900 Jimmy Slagle, Phi	29			1901 Dick Harley, Cin, NL	30
1901 Dick Harley, Cin	**30**			**1929 Roy Johnson, Det, AL**	**31**

LEFT FIELD

NATIONAL LEAGUE			AMERICAN LEAGUE			MAJOR LEAGUE		
Most Double Plays			*Most Double Plays*			*Most Double Plays*		
1876	George Hall, Phi	3	1901	Doc Nance, Det	6	1876	George Hall, Phi, NL	3
1877	Mike Dorgan, StL	3	1905	Matty McIntyre, Det	6	1877	Mike Dorgan, StL, NL	3
1878	Abner Dalrymple, Mil	3	1906	Matty McIntyre, Det	8	1878	Abner Dalrymple, Mil, NL	3
1878	Tom York, Pro	3	1910	Duffy Lewis, Bos	9	1878	Tom York, Pro, NL	3
1880	Mike Mansell, Cin	5	1919	**Jack Tobin, StL**	15	1880	Mike Mansell, Cin, NL	5
1880	Pete Gillespie, Tro	5				1880	Pete Gillespie, Tro, NL	5
1881	Pete Gillespie, Tro	5				1881	Pete Gillespie, Tro, NL	5
1881	Joe Hornung, Bos	5				1881	Joe Hornung, Bos, NL	5
1882	George Wood, Det	8				1882	George Wood, Det, NL	8
1892	Charlie Duffee, Was	8				1889	Joe Hornung, Bal, AA	10
1893	Ed Delahanty, Phi	8				1891	George Wood, Phi, AA	10
1894	Tom McCarthy, Bos	10				1894	Tom McCarthy, Bos, NL	10
1899	Kip Selbach, Cin	10				1899	Kip Selbach, Cin, NL	10
1911	**Jimmy Sheckard, Chi**	12				1911	Jimmy Sheckard, Chi, NL	12
						1919	**Jack Tobin, StL, AL**	15
Most Total Chances			*Most Total Chances*			*Most Total Chances*		
1876	Fred Treacey, NY	250	1901	Tommy Dowd, Bos	319	1876	Fred Treacey, NY, NL	250
1883	George Wood, Det	275	1902	Jesse Burkett, StL	343	1883	Tom Dolan, StL, AA	277
1887	Emmett Seery, Ind	275	1904	Matty McIntyre, Det	365	1886	Henry Larkin, Phi, AA	329
1888	Walt Wilmot, Was	320	1916	Burt Shotton, StL	402	1889	Harry Stovey, Phi, AA	362
1891	Billy Hamilton, Phi	335	1921	Bobby Veach, Det	416	1893	Ed Delahanty, Phi, NL	368
1892	Billy Hamilton, Phi	345	1925	Goose Goslin, Was	421	1895	Fred Clarke, Lou, NL	413
1893	Ed Delahanty, Phi	368	1929	Roy Johnson, Det	433	1921	Bobby Veach, Det, AL	416
1895	Fred Clarke, Lou	413	1932	Joe Vosmik, Cle	449	1925	Goose Goslin, Was, AL	421
1926	**Eddie Brown, Bos**	426	1980	**Willie Wilson, KC**	497	1926	Eddie Brown, Bos, NL	426
						1929	Roy Johnson, Det, AL	433
						1932	Joe Vosmik, Cle, AL	449
						1980	**Willie Wilson, KC, AL**	497
Highest Fielding Average			*Highest Fielding Average*			*Highest Fielding Average*		
1876	Andy Leonard, Bos	.925	1901	Herm McFarland, Chi	.946	1876	Andy Leonard, Bos, NL	.925
1879	Charley Jones, Bos	.933	1902	Ed Delahanty, Was	.961	1879	Charley Jones, Bos, NL	.933
1880	Tom York, Pro	.934	1903	Topsy Hartsel, Phi	.968	1880	Tom York, Pro, NL	.934
1881	Joe Hornung, Bos	.948	1904	Nixey Callahan, Chi	.977	1881	Joe Hornung, Bos, NL	.948
1886	Abner Dalrymple, Chi	.953	1906	Matty McIntyre, Det	.982	1883	Tom Dolan, StL, AA	.957
1888	Jim O'Rourke, NY	.960	1912	Amos Strunk, Phi	.990	1888	Jim O'Rourke, NY, NL	.960
1897	Hugh Duffy, Bkn	.975	1919	Babe Ruth, Bos	.992	1897	Hugh Duffy, Bkn, NL	.975
1899	Joe Kelley, Bkn	.977	1943	Charlie Keller, NY	.994	1899	Joe Kelley, Bkn, NL	.977
1905	Spike Shannon, StL	.984	1949	Dale Mitchell, Cle	.994	1905	Spike Shannon, StL, NL	.984
1906	Jimmy Sheckard, Chi	.986	1949	Hoot Evers, Det	.994	1906	Jimmy Sheckard, Chi, NL	.986
1907	Fred Clarke, Pit	.987	1950	Hoot Evers, Det	.997	1907	Fred Clarke, Pit, NL	.987
1909	Fred Clarke, Pit	.987	1957	Charlie Maxwell, Det	.997	1909	Fred Clarke, Pit, NL	.987
1919	George Burns, NY	.990	1968	Roy White, NY	.997	1912	Amos Strunk, Phi, AL	.990
1922	Zack Wheat, Bkn	.991	1969	Ted Uhlaender, Min	.997	1919	Babe Ruth, Bos, AL	.992
1923	Pat Duncan, Cin	.993	1971	**Roy White, NY**	1.000	1923	Pat Duncan, Cin, NL	.993
1930	Rube Bressler, Bkn	.995	1977	**Carl Yastrzemski, Bos**	1.000	1930	Rube Bressler, Bkn, NL	.995
1942	**Danny Litwhiler, Phi**	1.000	1980	**Gary Roenicke, Bal**	1.000	1942	Danny Litwhiler, Phi, NL	1.000
			1982	**Brian Downing, Cal**	1.000	1971	Roy White, NY, AL	1.000
			1982	**John Lowenstein, Bal**	1.000	1977	Carl Yastrzemski, Bos, AL	1.000
			1984	**Brian Downing, Cal**	1.000	1980	Gary Reonicke, Bal, AL	1.000
						1982	Brian Downing, Cal, AL	1.000
						1982	John Lowenstein, Bal, AL	1.000
						1984	Brian Downing, Cal, AL	1.000

LEFT FIELD

NATIONAL LEAGUE SUMMARY		AMERICAN LEAGUE SUMMARY		MAJOR LEAGUE SUMMARY	
Top Record Producers		*Top Record Producers*		*Top Record Producers*	
1 Fred Clarke, Pit	7	1 Matty McIntyre, Det	5	1 Fred Clarke, Pit, NL	6
2 Ed Delahanty, Phi	4	2 Duffy Lewis, Bos	3	2 Charley Jones, Bos, NL	3
2 Billy Hamilton, Phi	4	2 Bobby Veach, Det	3	2 George Wood, Det, NL	3
2 Fred Treacey, NY	4			2 Tom York, Pro, NL	3
				2 Joe Hornung, Bos, NL	3
				2 Tom Dolan, StL, AA	3

NATIONAL LEAGUE SUMMARY		AMERICAN LEAGUE SUMMARY		MAJOR LEAGUE SUMMARY	
Most Outstanding Record Producers		*Most Outstanding Record Producers*		*Most Outstanding Record Producers*	
Jimmy Sheckard, Chi	3 for 163 years	Joe Vosmik, Cle	2 for 96 years	Tom Dolan, StL, AA	3 for 113 years
Eddie Brown, Bos	2 for 124 years	Ping Bodie, Phi	1 for 71 years	Joe Vosmik, Cle, AL	2 for 96 years
Fred Clarke, Pit	5 for 50 years	Jack Tobin, StL	1 for 69 years	Jack Tobin, StL, AL	1 for 69 years
Danny Litwhiler, Phi	1 for 46 years	Matty McIntyre, Det	5 for 35 years	Danny Litwhiler,	
George Wood, Det	3 for 22 years	Babe Ruth, Bos	1 for 24 years	Phi, NL	1 for 46 years
Kip Selbach, Cin	2 for 22 years			Fred Clarke, Pit, NL	6 for 38 years

Billy Hamilton was the first National League player to set back-to-back records in putouts and total chances, a feat he accomplished in 1891 and 1892. Fred Clarke had three putout records and was the first to gather more than 400 total chances. But the most active of all National League leftfielders was Eddie Brown of Boston, whose 401 putouts and 426 total chances are records that still stand.

It is important to note that many of the pioneer players hold putout, assist and total chance records, due to the fact that they played in ballparks where the fences were 250 to 300 feet from home plate. The dead ball used during their era did not travel much farther than that; consequently, outfielders at the time had smaller areas to cover. They also had much shorter distances to throw to, which is why they have more assists than modern players. Since the bases were exactly the same, the early players had an advantage over our modern players who, in order to gain an assist, must throw from 300 to 400 feet to home plate. This is yet another reason why the rules committee should consider separate records before and after 1900.

Jimmy Sheckard is both the National and Major League leader in assists, as his 36 assists in 1903 has never been duplicated. Sheckard also holds the double play record in the National League with 12.

Fred Clarke, Rube Bressler and Danny Litwhiler are the three outstanding fielding average leaders. Clarke's .987 average in 1907 lasted 12 years, Bressler's .995 in 1930 was also good for 12 years, and in 1942 Litwhiler of the Phils became the first outfielder in baseball history to go a season without making a single error. To this date, he stands as the only leftfielder in the National League to have this distinction.

In the American League, speedy Willie Wilson of Kansas City has been the most active, with two unbroken records in putouts and total chances established in 1980. These are also the Major League marks.

Bobby Veach had back-to-back records in putouts, Duffy Lewis also had them in assists and Matty McIntyre was a back-to-back champion in double plays, to name a few outstanding American League leftfielders.

In 1917, Ping Bodie produced 32 assists to claim an American League record that still stands, while Jack Tobin of the St. Louis Browns has been the double play king ever since his 15 was tops in 1919.

The American League's fielding averages have increased from Herm McFarland's .946 in 1901 to 1.000 shared by five players. Brian Downing of the Angels is the only leftfielder to do it twice.

An unusual assists record was set in 1883 by Tom Dolan, who was playing for St. Louis in the American Association. Dolan was responsible for 51 assists while the previous mark was only 28. Needless to say, this is a still-existent Major League record, but oh, how unfair it is to ask our modern-day players to compete with an assist record that was created in a ballpark no larger than our softball field of today.

CENTER FIELD

NATIONAL LEAGUE

Most Putouts

1876	Jack Remsen, Har	177
1881	Hardy Richardson, Buf	179
1882	Ned Hanlon, Det	194
1883	Ned Hanlon, Det	216
1884	Ned Hanlon, Det	241
1886	Dick Johnston, Bos	243
1887	Dick Johnston, Bos	339
1891	Mike Griffin, Bkn	353
1892	Jim McAleer, Cle	367
1899	Jimmy Slagle, Was	407
1916	Max Carey, Pit	419
1917	Max Carey, Pit	440
1922	Max Carey, Pit	449
1923	Max Carey, Pit	450
1928	**Taylor Douthit, StL**	**547**

Most Assists

1876	Lip Pike, StL	13
1877	Bill Crowley, Lou	20
1879	Paul Hines, Pro	24
1881	**Hardy Richardson, Buf**	**45**

Most Assists after 1900

1900	**George Van Haltren, NY**	**28**

Most Errors

1876	Jim O'Rourke, Bos	27
1879	Al Hall, Tro	27
1880	Bill Crowley, Buf	33
1882	George Gore, Chi	33
1883	**Pete Hotaling, Cle**	**42**

Most Errors after 1900

1900	Jimmy Barrett, Cin	24
1901	Danny Green, Chi	24
1903	**Cy Seymour, Cin**	**36**

AMERICAN LEAGUE

Most Putouts

1901	Ollie Pickering, Cle	315
1902	Jimmy Barrett, Det	326
1904	Jimmy Barrett, Det	339
1906	Chick Stahl, Bos	344
1911	Ty Cobb, Det	376
1912	Burt Shotton, StL	381
1914	Tris Speaker, Bos	423
1917	Happy Felsch, Chi	440
1920	Sam Rice, Was	454
1924	Baby Doll Jacobson, StL	484
1948	Dom DiMaggio, Bos	503
1977	**Chet Lemon, Chi**	**512**

Most Assists

1901	Jimmy Barrett, Det	31
1907	Joe Birmingham, Cle	33
1909	**Tris Speaker, Bos**	**35**
1912	**Tris Speaker, Bos**	**35**

Most Errors

1901	Jimmy Barrett, Det	21
1901	Irv Waldron, Was	21
1909	Ray Demmitt, NY	21
1912	**Clyde Milan, Was**	**25**
1913	**Tris Speaker, Bos**	**25**

MAJOR LEAGUE

Most Putouts

1876	Jack Remsen, Har, NL	177
1881	Hardy Richardson, Buf, NL	179
1882	Ned Hanlon, Det, NL	194
1883	Ned Hanlon, Det, NL	216
1884	Ned Hanlon, Det, NL	241
1886	Curt Welsh, StL, AA	297
1887	Dick Johnston, Box, NL	339
1891	Mike Griffin, Bkn, NL	353
1892	Jim McAleer, Cle, NL	367
1899	Jimmy Slagle, Was, NL	407
1914	Tris Speaker, Bos, AL	423
1917	Max Carey, Pit, AL	440
1920	Sam Rice, Was, AL	454
1924	Baby Doll Jacobson, StL, AL	484
1928	**Taylor Douthit, StL, NL**	**547**

Most Assists

1876	Lip Pike, StL, NL	13
1877	Bill Crowley, Lou, NL	20
1879	Paul Hines, Pro, NL	24
1881	**Hardy Richardson, Buf, NL**	**45**

Most Assists after 1900

1900	George Van Haltren, NY, NL	28
1904	Jimmy Barrett, Det, AL	29
1907	Joe Birmingham, Cle, AL	33
1909	**Tris Speaker, Bos, AL**	**35**
1912	**Tris Speaker, Bos, AL**	**35**

Most Errors

1876	Jim O'Rourke, Bos, NL	27
1879	Al Hall, Tro, NL	27
1880	Bill Crowley, Buf, NL	33
1882	George Gore, Chi, NL	33
1883	Pete Hotaling, Cle, NL	42
1889	**Charlie Duffee, StL, AA**	**43**

Most Errors after 1900

1900	Jimmy Barrett, Cin, NL	24
1901	Danny Green, Chi, NL	24
1903	**Cy Seymour, Cin, NL**	**36**

DID YOU KNOW ... *That as of 1920, in order for a fielder to qualify for a fielding title he has to appear in at least 100 games? Prior to this, a player had to appear in 60 percent of a season's games.*

CENTER FIELD

NATIONAL LEAGUE	AMERICAN LEAGUE	MAJOR LEAGUE

Most Double Plays

1876	Lip Pike, StL	5	1901	Ollie Pickering, Cle	9	1876	Lip Pike, StL, NL	5
1876	Jack Remsen, Har	5	1902	Fielder Jones, Chi	11	1876	Jack Remsen, Har, NL	5
1878	Jack Remsen, Chi	5	1905	Ben Koehler, StL	11	1878	Jack Remsen, Chi, NL	5
1880	Paul Hines, Pro	7	1909	Tris Speaker, Bos	12	1880	Paul Hines, Pro, NL	7
1882	Ned Hanlon, Det	8	1914	Tris Speaker, Bos	12	1882	Ned Hanlon, Det, NL	8
1887	Dick Johnston, Bos	9	**1919**	**Happy Felsch, Chi**	**15**	1885	Henry Larkin, Phi, AA	9
1889	Jimmy Ryan, Chi	9				1887	Dick Johnston, Bos, NL	9
1889	Jim McAleer, Cle	9				1889	Curt Welch, Phi, AA	10
1890	George Davis, Cle	9				1890	Mike Griffin, Phi, PL	10
1891	Steve Brodie, Bos	9				1893	Tom Brown, Lou, NL	13
1893	**Tom Brown, Lou**	**13**				**1919**	**Happy Felsch, Chi, AL**	**15**

Most Double Plays after 1900

1900	George Van Haltren, NY	7
1901	Danny Green, Chi	7
1902	Ginger Beaumont, Pit	8
1904	Phil Geier, Bos	11
1905	**Cy Seymour, Cin**	**12**
1907	**Ginger Beaumont, Bos**	12

Most Total Chances

1876	Jack Remsen, Har	213	1901	Ollie Pickering, Cle	355	1876	Jack Remsen, Har, NL	213
1881	Hardy Richardson, Buf	245	1902	Jimmy Barrett, Det	362	1881	Hardy Richardson, Buf, NL	245
1883	Ned Hanlon, Det	259	1904	Jimmy Barrett, Det	379	1883	Ned Hanlon, Det, NL	259
1884	Ned Hanlon, Det	310	1906	Chick Stahl, Bos	383	1884	Ned Hanlon, Det, NL	310
1887	Dick Johnston, Bos	400	1911	Ty Cobb, Det	418	1886	Curt Welch, StL, AA	332
1892	Tom Brown, Lou	422	1912	Burt Shotton, StL	426	1887	Dick Johnston, Bos, NL	400
1899	Jimmy Slagle, Was	448	1913	Tris Speaker, Bos	429	1891	Mike Griffin, Bkn, AA	400
1916	Max Carey, Pit	459	1914	Tris Speaker, Bos	467	1892	Tom Brown, Lou, NL	422
1917	Max Carey, Pit	478	1917	Happy Felsch, Chi	471	1899	Jimmy Slagle, Was, NL	448
1922	Max Carey, Pit	486	1920	Sam Rice, Was	498	1914	Tris Speaker, Bos, AL	467
1923	Max Carey, Pit	497	1924	Baby Doll Jacobson, StL	498	1917	Max Carey, Pit, NL	478
1928	**Taylor Douthit, StL**	**566**	1948	Dom DiMaggio, Bos	526	1920	Sam Rice, Was, AL	498
			1977	**Chet Lemon, Chi**	**536**	1924	Baby Doll Jacobson, StL, NL	498
						1928	**Taylor Douthit, StL, NL**	**566**

DID YOU KNOW . . . *That the rule giving a batter a hit when a batted ball hits a runner was put into effect in 1888?*

CENTER FIELD

NATIONAL LEAGUE

Highest Fielding Average

1876	Paul Hines, Chi	.923
1878	Jack Remsen, Chi	.944
1889	Jim Fogarty, Phi	.961
1892	Mike Griffin, Bkn	.986
1906	Roy Thomas, Phi	.986
1913	Tommy Leach, Chi	.990
1927	Jigger Statz, Bkn	.990
1930	Wally Roettger, NY	.992
1932	Wally Berger, Bos	.993
1934	Len Koenecke, Bkn	.994
1936	Johnny Cooney, Bkn	.994
1939	Terry Moore, StL	.994
1940	Harry Craft, Cin	.997
1944	Johnny Hopp, StL	.997
1951	Lloyd Merriman, Cin	.997
1962	Tony Gonzalez, Phi	1.000
1966	Curt Flood, StL	1.000
1979	Terry Puhl, Hou	1.000
1981	Ken Landreaux, LA	1.000

AMERICAN LEAGUE

Highest Fielding Average

1901	Dummy Hoy, Chi	.958
1902	Harry Bay, Cle	.973
1903	Fielder Jones, Chi	.985
1904	Harry Bay, Cle	.987
1906	Fielder Jones, Chi	.988
1918	Amos Strunk, Bos	.988
1929	Fred Schulte, StL	.989
1931	Tommy Oliver, Bos	.993
1941	Mike Kreevich, Chi	.994
1943	Milt Byrnes, StL	.997
1947	Joe DiMaggio, NY	.997
1962	Jimmy Piersall, Was	.997
1968	**Mickey Stanley, Det**	**1.000**
1969	**Ken Berry, Chi**	**1.000**
1970	**Mickey Stanley, Det**	**1.000**
1972	**Ken Berry, Cal**	**1.000**

MAJOR LEAGUE

Highest Fielding Average

1876	Paul Hines, Chi, NL	.923
1878	Jack Remsen, Chi, NL	.944
1884	Dave Rowe, StL, AA	.947
1886	Curt Welch, StL, AA	.952
1887	Pop Corkhill, Cin, AA	.952
1889	Jim Fogarty, Phi, AA	.961
1892	Mike Griffin, Bkn, NL	.986
1904	Harry Bay, Cle, AL	.987
1906	Fielder Jones, Chi, AL	.988
1913	Tommy Leach, Chi, NL	.990
1927	Jigger Statz, Bkn, NL	.990
1930	Wally Roettger, NY, NL	.992
1931	Tommy Oliver, Bos, AL	.993
1932	Wally Berger, Bos, AL	.993
1934	Len Koenecke, Bkn, NL	.994
1936	Johnny Cooney, Bkn, NL	.994
1939	Terry Moore, StL, NL	.994
1940	Harry Craft, Cin, NL	.997
1943	Milt Byrnes, StL, AL	.997
1944	Johnny Hopp, StL, NL	.997
1947	Joe DiMaggio, NY, AL	.997
1951	Lloyd Merriman, Cin, NL	.997
1962	Tony Gonzalez, Phi, NL	1.000
1966	Curt Flood, StL, NL	1.000
1968	Mickey Stanley, Det, AL	1.000
1969	Ken Berry, Chi, AL	1.000
1970	Mickey Stanley, Det, AL	1.000
1972	Ken Berry, Cal, AL	1.000
1979	Terry Puhl, Hou, NL	1.000
1981	Ken Landreaux, LA, NL	1.000

NATIONAL LEAGUE SUMMARY

Top Record Producers

1	Max Carey, Pit	8
2	Ned Hanlon, Det	6
3	Jack Remsen, Chi	5
4	Dick Johnston, Bos	4
5	Hardy Richardson, Buf	3

Most Outstanding Record Producers

Taylor Douthit, StL	2 for	120 years
Hardy Richardson, Buf	3 for	110 years
Tom Brown, Lou	2 for	102 years
Jimmy Slagle, Was	2 for	34 years
Tony Gonzalez, Phi	1 for	26 years

AMERICAN LEAGUE SUMMARY

Top Record Producers

1	Tris Speaker	8
2	Jimmy Barrett	6
3	Ollie Pickering	3
3	Happy Felsch	3

Most Outstanding Record Producers

Tris Speaker	8 for	171 years
Happy Felsch	3 for	75 years
Dom DiMaggio	2 for	58 years
Baby Doll Jacobson	2 for	48 years
Jimmy Barrett	6 for	25 years

MAJOR LEAGUE SUMMARY

Top Record Producers

1	Ned Hanlon, Det, NL	6
2	Jack Remsen, Chi, NL	5
3	Mike Griffin, Bkn, NL	4

Most Outstanding Record Producers

Taylor Douthit, StL, NL	2 for	120 years
Hardy Richardson, Buf, NL	3 for	110 years
Happy Felsch, Chi, AL	2 for	72 years
Mickey Stanley, Det, AL	2 for	38 years
Tom Brown, Lou, NL	2 for	33 years

Ned Hanlon was the first superstar centerfielder in baseball. He set three consecutive putout records and back-to-back total chance records during the pioneer days of baseball. After 1900 it was Max Carey of the Pirates who set a bushel of records. Carey had four consecutive putout marks from 1916 through 1923, and did likewise in total chances. Taylor Douthit was another super centerfielder, and his 547 putouts and 566 total chances in the 1928 season are both National and Major League records that still stand. Willie Mays set many career records, but in his 22-year career he never set a seasonal fielding record.

In the American League, Jimmy Barrett of the Tigers had consecutive putout and total chance records in 1902 and 1904, while Ty Cobb, Tris Speaker and Happy Felsch were also outstanding. Dom DiMaggio in 1948 was the first American Leaguer to garner more than 500 putouts. Chet Lemon is the American League all-time leader in putouts with 512 and total chances with 536, both established in 1977.

Prior to 1900, the longest-lasting fielding average record was owned by Mike Griffin of the Dodgers, who fielded .986 back in 1892. This super achievement lasted 12 years before Harry Bay of Cleveland improved it by one point. Tommy Leach was the first to hit the .990 level, and his record was good for 17 years before Wally Roettger of the Giants was able to turn in a neat .992 season. This record was upped to .997 by five players, and then in 1962 Tony Gonzalez of the Phils became the first centerfielder in history to go through a season without making an error.

Since then, five others have been perfect, with Mickey Stanley and Ken Berry doing it twice.

RIGHT FIELD

NATIONAL LEAGUE		
Most Putouts		
1876	Jack Manning, Bos	73
1876	Ed Booth, NY	73
1877	Orator Shaffer, Lou	121
1879	Jake Evans, Tro	153
1883	Orator Shaffer, Buf	182
1884	Jim Lillie, Buf	190
1886	Sam Thompson, Det	194
1887	Jim Fogarty, Phi	273
1898	Dusty Miller, Cin	292
1899	Jimmy Sheckard, Bal	298
1913	Owen Wilson, Pit	301
1914	Owen Wilson, StL	312
1920	Greasy Neale, Cin	347
1925	Kiki Cuyler, Pit	362
1928	Lance Richbourg, Bos	367
1930	Kiki Cuyler, Chi	377
1932	**Babe Herman, Cin**	**392**

Most Assists
1876	Dick Higham, Har	16
1877	Orator Shaffer, Lou	21
1878	John Cassidy, Chi	30
1879	**Orator Shaffer, Chi**	**50**

Most Assists after 1900
1900	Elmer Flick, Phi	23
1901	Elmer Flick, Phi	23
1902	Patsy Donovan, StL	30
1907	**Mike Mitchell, Cin**	**39**

Most Errors
1876	Ed Booth, NY	26
1877	Orator Shaffer, Lou	28
1878	John Cassidy, Chi	28
1879	Orator Shaffer, Chi	37
1884	Jim Lillie, Buf	40
1892	**George Van Haltren, Bal**	**43**

Most Errors after 1900
1900	Elmer Flick, Phi	24
1908	**Red Murray, StL**	**28**

AMERICAN LEAGUE		
Most Putouts		
1901	Cy Seymour, Bal	271
1907	Bob Ganley, Was	276
1917	Baby Doll Jacobson, StL	292
1920	Jack Tobin, StL	293
1923	Babe Ruth, NY	378
1961	Al Kaline, Det	378
1971	**Del Unser, Was**	**394**

DID YOU KNOW... *That since 1931, when a runner is hit by a batted ball, the putout is credited to the nearest fielder?*

Most Assists
1901	Cy Seymour, Bal	23
1906	**Harry Niles, StL**	**34**
1911	**Danny Murphy, Phi**	**34**

Most Errors
1901	Bill Hallman, Mil	26

MAJOR LEAGUE		
Most Putouts		
1876	Jack Manning, Bos, NL	73
1876	Ed Booth, NY, NL	73
1877	Orator Shaffer, Lou, NL	121
1879	Jake Evans, Tro, NL	153
1883	Orator Shaffer, Buf, NL	182
1884	Jim Lillie, Buf, NL	190
1885	Hugh Nicol, StL, AA	213
1887	Jim Fogarty, Phi, NL	273
1898	Dusty Miller, Cin, NL	292
1899	Jimmy Sheckard, Bal, NL	298
1913	Owen Wilson, Pit, NL	301
1914	Owen Wilson, StL, NL	312
1920	Greasy Neale, Cin, NL	347
1923	Babe Ruth, NY, AL	378
1932	Babe Herman, Cin, NL	392
1971	**Del Unser, Was, AL**	**394**

Most Assists
1876	Dick Higham, Har, NL	16
1877	Orator Shaffer, Lou, NL	21
1878	John Cassidy, Chi, NL	30
1879	**Orator Shaffer, Chi, NL**	**50**

Most Assists after 1900
1900	Elmer Flick, Phi, NL	23
1901	Elmer Flick, Phi, NL	23
1901	Cy Seymour, Bal, AL	23
1902	Patsy Donovan, StL, NL	30
1906	Harry Niles, StL, AL	34
1907	**Mike Mitchell, Cin, NL**	**39**

Most Errors
1876	Ed Booth, NY, NL	26
1877	Orator Shaffer, Lou, NL	28
1878	John Cassidy, Chi, NL	28
1879	Orator Shaffer, Chi, NL	37
1883	Tom Brown, Col, AA	42
1892	**George Van Haltren, Bal, NL**	**43**

Most Errors after 1900
1900	Elmer Flick, Phi, NL	24
1901	Bill Hallman, Mil, AL	26
1908	**Red Murray, StL, NL**	**28**

RIGHT FIELD

NATIONAL LEAGUE	AMERICAN LEAGUE	MAJOR LEAGUE

Most Double Plays

	NATIONAL LEAGUE			AMERICAN LEAGUE			MAJOR LEAGUE	
1876	Dave Pearson, Cin	2	1901	Bill Hallman, Mil	6	1876	Dave Pearson, Cin, NL	2
1876	Joe Blong, StL	2	1902	Charley Hemphill, StL	6	1876	Joe Blong, StL, NL	2
1877	Bob Addy, Cin	5	1903	Danny Green, Chi	8	1877	Bob Addy, Cin, NL	5
1878	John Cassidy, Chi	6	1904	Sam Crawford, Det	8	1878	John Cassidy, Chi, NL	6
1881	Lon Knight, Det	6	1907	Ty Cobb, Det	12	1881	Lon Knight, Det, NL	6
1882	Curry Foley, Buf	7				1882	Curry Foley, Buf, NL	7
1885	Paul Radford, Pro	7				1885	Paul Radford, Pro, NL	7
1886	Sam Thompson, Det	11				1886	Tom Brown, Pit, AA	12
1894	Jimmy Bannon, Bos	12				1888	Tom McCarthy, StL, AA	12
1899	Jimmy Sheckard, Bal	14				1894	Jimmy Bannon, Bos, NL	12
						1899	Jimmy Sheckard, Bal, NL	14

Most Double Plays after 1900

1900	Elmer Flick, Phi	6				1900	Elmer Flick, Phi, NL	6
1901	Patsy Donovan, StL	8				1901	Patsy Donovan, StL, NL	8
1903	Jimmy Sebring, Pit	11				1903	Jimmy Sebring, Pit, NL	11
						1907	Ty Cobb, Det, AL	12

Most Total Chances

1876	Ed Booth, NY	110	1901	Cy Seymour, Bal	311	1876	Ed Booth, NY, NL	110
1877	Orator Shaffer, Lou	170	1907	Bob Ganley, Was	318	1877	Orator Shaffer, Lou, NL	170
1879	Jake Evans, Tro	207	1912	Joe Jackson, Cle	319	1879	Jake Evans, Tro, NL	207
1883	Orator Shaffer, Buf	259	1920	Jack Tobin, StL	324	1883	Orator Shaffer, Buf, NL	259
1884	Jim Lillie, Buf	271	1923	Babe Ruth, NY	409	1884	Jim Lillie, Buf, NL	271
1887	Jim Fogarty, Phi	339	1971	Del Unser, Was	412	1887	Jim Fogarty, Phi, NL	339
1898	Dusty Miller, Cin	339				1898	Dusty Miller, Cin, NL	339
1899	Jimmy Sheckard, Bal	351				1899	Jimmy Sheckard, Bal, NL	351
1914	Owen Wilson, StL	352				1914	Owen Wilson, StL, NL	352
1920	Greasy Neale, Cin	371				1920	Greasy Neale, Cin, NL	371
1925	Kiki Cuyler, Pit	396				1923	Babe Ruth, NY, AL	409
1930	Chuck Klein, Phi	423				1930	Chuck Klein, Phi, NL	423
1932	Babe Herman, Cin	424				1932	Babe Herman, Cin, NL	423
1977	Dave Parker, Pit	430				1977	Dave Parker, Pit, NL	430

Highest Fielding Average

1876	Joe Blong, StL	.895	1901	Socks Seybold, Phi	.954	1876	Joe Blong, StL, NL	.895
1880	Orator Shaffer, Cle	.901	1902	Socks Seybold, Phi	.963	1880	Orator Shaffer, Cle, NL	.901
1881	Jake Evans, Tro	.926	1903	Socks Seybold, Phi	.964	1881	Jake Evans, Tro, NL	.926
1886	Sam Thompson, Det	.945	1904	Socks Seybold, Phi	.975	1883	Pop Corkhill, Cin, AA	.930
1888	Mike Tiernan, NY	.960	1905	Sam Crawford, Det	.988	1884	Pop Corkhill, Cin, AA	.934
1894	Sam Thompson, Phi	.977	1907	Ed Hahn, Chi	.990	1885	Pop Corkhill, Cin, AA	.939
1901	Willie Keeler, Bkn	.985	1933	Dick Porter, Cle	.996	1886	Sam Thompson, Det, NL	.945
1905	Otis Clymer, Pit	.986	1965	Rocky Colavito, Cle	1.000	1888	Mike Tiernan, NY, NL	.960
1908	Wildfire Schulte, Chi	.994	1968	Ken Harrelson, Bos	1.000	1890	Jim Fogarty, Phi, PL	.963
1951	Willard Marshall, Bos	1.000	1971	Al Kaline, Det	1.000	1894	Sam Thompson, Phi, NL	.977
1968	Johnny Callison, Phi	1.000	1981	Ken Singleton, Bal	1.000	1901	Willie Keeler, Bkn, NL	.985
1981	Terry Puhl, Hou	1.000				1905	Sam Crawford, Det, Al	.988
						1907	Ed Hahn, Chi, AL	.990
						1908	Wildfire Schulte, Chi, NL	.994
						1933	Dick Porter, Cle, AL	.996
						1951	Willard Marshall, Bos, NL	1.000
						1965	Rocky Colavito, Cle, AL	1.000
						1968	Ken Harrelson, Bos, AL	1.000
						1968	Johnny Callison, Phi, NL	1.000
						1971	Al Kaline, Det, AL	1.000
						1981	Terry Puhl, Hou, NL	1.000
						1981	Ken Singleton, Bal, AL	1.000

RIGHT FIELD

NATIONAL LEAGUE SUMMARY		AMERICAN LEAGUE SUMMARY		MAJOR LEAGUE SUMMARY	

Top Record Producers

	NATIONAL LEAGUE		AMERICAN LEAGUE		MAJOR LEAGUE	

NATIONAL LEAGUE SUMMARY

Top Record Producers

1	Orator Shaffer, Cle	9
2	Sam Thompson, Det	4
3	Jimmy Sheckard, Bal	3
3	Kiki Cuyler, Pit	3
3	Owen Wilson, StL	3
3	Jake Evans, Tro	3

Most Outstanding Record Producers

Jimmy Sheckard, Bal	3 for 118 years
Orator Shaffer, Cle	9 for 117 years
Babe Herman, Cin	2 for 96 years
Wildfire Schulte, Chi	1 for 43 years
Willard Marshall, Bos	1 for 37 years

AMERICAN LEAGUE SUMMARY

Top Record Producers

| 1 | Socks Seybold, Phi | 4 |
| 2 | Cy Seymour, Bal | 3 |

Most Outstanding Record Producers

Babe Ruth, NY	2 for 86 years
Harry Niles, StL	1 for 82 years
Ty Cobb, Det	1 for 81 years
Danny Murphy, Phi	1 for 77 years
Del Unser, Was	2 for 34 years

MAJOR LEAGUE SUMMARY

Top Record Producers

1	Orator Shaffer, Cle, NL	9
2	Jimmy Sheckard, Bal, NL	3
2	Pop Corkhill, Cin, AA	3
2	Jake Evans, Tro, NL	3
2	Owen Wilson, StL, NL	3
2	Jim Fogarty, Phi, PL	3

Most Outstanding Record Producers

Jimmy Sheckard, Bal, NL	3 for 118 years
Orator Shaffer, Cle, NL	9 for 117 years
Babe Herman, Cin, NL	2 for 84 years
Willard Marshall, Bos, NL	1 for 37 years
Jim Fogarty, Phi, PL	3 for 26 years

Orator Shaffer created seven records in right field to lead the pioneer players. Jake Evans, Sam Thompson and Jimmy Sheckard followed and were also outstanding. Shaffer's 50 assists in 1879 (from a short right field) are National and Major League records that still stand. Jimmy Sheckard's 14 double plays in 1899 is another long-standing record created while playing on smaller fields.

Unless the rules committee has a change of heart, both of these records will remain National and Major League marks.

When a more modern player sets a fielding record it really is quite an achievement, which is the case with Babe Herman's 392 putouts in 1932 and Dave Parker's total chance record of 430 set in 1977. Naturally the fielding average leaders are the modern players with the high-tech gloves; in that light, Wildfire Schulte's .994 fielding average in 1908 was a remarkable feat, because the gloves and fields then were still very poor. His record was so great that it took 43 years before another National League rightfielder could do better. In 1951 Willard Marshall became the first to go through a season without committing a miscue.

In the American League, Cy Seymour was the first fine rightfielder, along with Socks Seybold, who set four consecutive fielding average marks. Seymour was the leader in putouts, assists and total chances in the very first year of American League play.

Not much is written about the fabulous defensive ability of Babe Ruth, but a look at the outfield records clearly proves that the Babe was a super outfielder in addition to being the game's greatest hitter.

He probably would have made the Hall of Fame as a pitcher, had he pitched for his entire career. In 1919, while still with the Red Sox, Ruth was placed in left field for the first time in his career and he responded by setting an American League fielding average record of .992, which lasted 24 years. That same record was also good enough to become a Major League mark that lasted four years. After he went to the Yankees, the Babe played one more year in left field and then was moved to right field. In 1923, he established an American and Major League record in putouts and total chances. His putouts mark was so outstanding that it took 38 years and Al Kaline to break that record. Ruth's total chance mark lasted 48 years, and was finally snapped, by only three chances, by Del Unser. Babe Ruth's total chance record is still second on the all-time list. Unser because the busiest rightfielder in history by three chances in 1971 and his 394 putouts are also an American and Major League record.

As in most cases, the assists record is held by an early player, this time Danny Murphy, who registered 34 assists in 1911. A great player who displayed his defensive ability in the double play department is none other than Ty Cobb, the "Georgia Peach," who possessed a fine arm and participated in 12 double plays back in 1907. This mark still stands.

One of baseball's finest fielding averages was the mark produced by Dick Porter of the Indians in 1933 when he posted a cool .996. His splendid feat stood the test of time for 22 years, when Rocky Colavito became the first American League rightfielder to get through a full season without an error. Ken "The Hawk" Harrelson duplicated this marvelous achievement in 1968, as did Al Kaline in 1971 and Ken Singleton in 1981.

Dave Parker remains the busiest rightfielder in Major League history due to his record-shattering 430 total chances in 1977.

CHAPTER 6

CAREER FIELDING RECORDS

NATIONAL LEAGUE QUIZ

1. Can you name the first first baseman who played in 2,000 games?
2. The most games record at first base has not been broken in 81 years. Name the record holder.
3. This exceptional first baseman participated in 1,733 double plays, the most ever in the NL. Can you name him?
4. This fine second baseman left the NL in 1983 with 2,427 games played, the most by any NL second baseman. Who is he?
5. Can you name the second baseman with the highest fielding average?

AMERICAN LEAGUE QUIZ

1. The Chicago White Sox had two outstanding shortstops who made over 4,000 putouts. Both are in the Hall of Fame. Name them.
2. This fabulous third baseman has all six of that position's career fielding records and all six remain unbroken. Who is he?
3. Can you name the first AL catcher to appear in 1,500 games?
4. Who is the only AL leftfielder to play in 2,000 games?
5. Can you name the centerfielder with the most games played, putouts, assists, double plays and total chances?

MAJOR LEAGUE QUIZ

1. Two centerfielders are tied with the most errors at 361. Do you know them?
2. Can you name the two centerfielders with the highest fielding average?
3. Name three rightfielders who have played in more than 2,000 games.
4. This Hall of Fame rightfielder has the most putouts. Who is he?
5. The assists record for rightfielders is 322 and has not been broken in 63 years. Do you know who holds this mark?

FIRST BASE

NATIONAL LEAGUE			AMERICAN LEAGUE			MAJOR LEAGUE		
Most Games			*Most Games*			*Most Games*		
1879–84	Bill Phillips, Cle	531	1901–05	Candy LaChance, Bos	581	1876–86	Joe Start, Pro, NL	797
1876–86	Joe Start, Pro	797	1901–09	Jiggs Donahue, Chi	745	1879–88	Bill Phillips, Cle, NL	1032
1878–89	John Morrill, Bos	915	1902–10	Tom Jones, StL	1033	1882–94	Charlie Comiskey, StL,	
1879–97	Cap Anson, Chi	2058	1905–14	Hal Chase, NY	1171		AA	1363
1888–07	**Jake Beckley, Pit**	**2256**	1901–15	Harry Davis, Phi	1392	1879–97	Cap Anson, Chi, NL	2058
			1911–22	Stuffy McInnis, Phi	1608	**1888–07**	**Jake Beckley, Pit, NL**	**2377**
			1915–34	Joe Judge, Was	2042			
			1923–39	Lou Gehrig, NY	2136			
			1939–58	**Mickey Vernon, Was**	**2227**			
Most Putouts			*Most Putouts*			*Most Putouts*		
1879–84	Bill Phillips, Cle	5261	1901–05	Candy LaChance, Bos	6048	1876–86	Joe Start, Pro, NL	8343
1876–86	Joe Start, Pro	8343	1901–09	Jiggs Donahue, Chi	7989	1879–88	Bill Phillips, Cle, NL	10,540
1879–97	Cap Anson, Chi	20,761	1902–10	Tom Jones, StL	10,420	1882–94	Charlie Comiskey,	
1888–07	**Jake Beckley, Pit**	**22,453**	1905–14	Hal Chase, NY	11,472		StL, AA	13,821
			1901–15	Harry Davis, Phi	13,535	1879–97	Cap Anson, Chi, NL	20,761
			1911–22	Stuffy McInnis, Phi	16,506	**1888–07**	**Jake Beckley, Pit,**	
			1915–34	Joe Judge, Was	18,759		**NL**	**23,709**
			1923–39	Lou Gehrig, NY	19,510			
			1939–58	**Mickey Vernon, Was**	**19,560**			
Most Assists			*Most Assists*			*Most Assists*		
1879–84	Bill Phillips, Cle	147	1901–05	Candy LaChance, Bos	220	1876–86	Joe Start, Pro, NL	177
1876–86	Joe Start, Pro	177	1901–09	Jiggs Donahue, Chi	550	1879–88	Bill Phillips, Cle, NL	305
1878–89	John Morrill, Bos	327	1902–10	Tom Jones, StL	665	1883–90	Sid Farrar, Phi, NL	358
1879–97	Cap Anson, Chi	955	1905–14	Hal Chase, NY	691	1882–94	Charlie Comiskey,	
1888–07	Jack Beckley, Pit	1257	1901–15	Harry Davis, Phi	835		StL, AA	508
1894–11	**Fred Tenney, Bos**	**1363**	1911–22	Stuffy McInnis, Phi	1013	1879–97	Cap Anson, Chi, NL	955
			1915–28	George Sisler, StL	1270	1888–07	Jake Beckley, Pit, NL	1315
			1939–58	**Mickey Vernon, Was**	**1425**	1894–11	Fred Tenney, Bos, NL	1363
						1915–30	**George Sisler, StL, AL**	**1528**
Most Errors			*Most Errors*			*Most Errors*		
1879–84	Bill Phillips, Cle	204	1901–05	Candy LaChance, Bos	96	1876–86	Joe Start, Pro, NL	283
1876–86	Joe Start, Pro	284	1901–09	Frank Isbell, Chi	99	1879–88	Bill Phillips, Cle, NL	324
1879–97	**Cap Anson, Chi**	**583**	1902–10	Tom Jones, StL	175	1882–94	Charlie Comiskey,	
			1905–14	**Hal Chase, NY**	**279**		StL, AA	403
Most Errors after 1900						**1879–97**	**Cap Anson, Chi, NL**	**583**
1900–07	Jake Beckley, Pit	178						
1900–11	**Fred Tenney, Bos**	**254**				*Most Errors after 1900*		
						1900–07	Jake Beckley, Pit, NL	178
						1900–11	Fred Tenney, Bos, NL	254
						1905–14	**Hal Chase, NY, AL**	**279**
Most Double Plays			*Most Double Plays*			*Most Double Plays*		
1879–84	Bill Phillips, Cle	267	1901–05	Candy LaChance, Bos	286	1876–86	Joe Start, Pro, NL	343
1876–86	Joe Start, Pro	343	1901–09	Frank Isbell, Chi	339	1879–88	Bill Phillips, Cle, NL	511
1878–89	John Morrill, Bos	393	1902–10	Tom Jones, StL	436	1882–94	Charlie Comiskey,	
1879–97	Cap Anson, Chi	1189	1904–13	George Stoval, Cle	538		StL, AA	740
1888–07	Jake Beckley, Pit	1265	1901–15	Harry Davis, Phi	559	1879–97	Cap Anson, Chi, NL	1189
1922–35	Jim Bottomley, StL	1441	1911–22	Stuffy McInnis, Phi	983	1888–07	Jake Beckley, Pit, NL	1326
1918–36	**Charlie Grimm, Chi**	**1733**	1915–25	Wally Pipp, NY	989	1916–34	Joe Judge, Was, AL	1500
			1915–28	George Sisler, StL	1131	1918–36	Charlie Grimm,	
			1915–34	Joe Judge, Was	1461		Chi, NL	1733
			1923–39	Lou Gehrig, NY	1574	1930–47	Joe Kuhel, Was, AL	1769
			1930–47	Joe Kuhel, Was	1757	**1939–60**	**Mickey Vernon,**	
			1939–58	**Mickey Vernon, Was**	**2008**		**Was, AL**	**2044**

FIRST BASE

NATIONAL LEAGUE		
Most Total Chances		
1879–84	Bill Phillips, Cle	5612
1876–86	Joe Start, Pro	8804
1879–97	Cap Anson, Chi	22,299
1888–07	**Jake Beckley, Pit**	**23,742**

Highest Fielding Average		
1879–84	Bill Philllips, Cle	.963
1876–86	Joe Start, Pro	.967
1883–89	Sid Farrar, Phi	.974
1881–97	Roger Connor, NY	.977
1884–99	Patsy Tebeau, Cle	.985
1898–09	Dan McGann, NY	.988
1907–21	Ed Konetchy, StL	.990
1910–24	Jake Daubert, Bkn	.991
1914–25	Walter Holke, Bos	.993
1918–36	Charlie Grimm, Chi	.993
1934–48	Frank McCormick, Cin	.995
1964–72	**Wes Parker, LA**	**.996**
1969–87	**Steve Garvey, LA**	**.996**

AMERICAN LEAGUE		
Most Total Chances		
1901–05	Candy LaChance, Bos	6364
1901–09	Jiggs Donahue, Chi	8638
1902–10	Tom Jones, StL	11,260
1905–14	Hal Chase, NY	12,442
1901–15	Harry Davis, Phi	14,644
1911–22	Stuffy McInnis, Phi	17,648
1915–34	Joe Judge, Was	20,284
1923–39	Lou Gehrig, NY	20,790
1939–58	**Mickey Vernon, Was**	**21,131**

Highest Fielding Average		
1901–05	Candy LaChance, Bos	.985
1901–09	Jiggs Donahue, Chi	.988
1911–22	Stuffy McInnis, Phi	.992
1915–34	Joe Judge, Was	.993
1956–65	Vic Power, Cle	.994
1968–81	**Jim Spencer, Cal**	**.995**
1977–88	**Eddie Murray, Bal**	**.995**

MAJOR LEAGUE		
Most Total Chances		
1876–86	Joe Start, Pro, NL	8803
1879–88	Bill Phillips, Cle, NL	11,169
1882–94	Charlie Comiskey, StL, AA	14,732
1879–97	Cap Anson, Chi, NL	22,299
1888–07	**Jake Beckley, Pit, NL**	**25,505**

Highest Fielding Average		
1876–86	Joe Start, Pro, NL	.967
1879–88	Bill Phillips, Cle, NL	.969
1883–90	Sid Farrar, Phi, NL	.974
1881–97	Roger Connor, NY, NL	.977
1894–99	Patsy Tebeau, Cle, NL	.985
1898–08	Dan McGann, NY, NL	.988
1907–21	Ed Konetchy, StL, NL	.990
1910–24	Jake Daubert, Bkn, NL	.991
1917–25	Walter Holke, Bos, NL	.993
1916–34	Joe Judge, Was, AL	.993
1934–48	Frank McCormick, Cin, NL	.995
1964–72	Wes Parker, LA, NL	.995
1969–87	**Steve Garvey, LA, NL**	**.996**

NATIONAL LEAGUE SUMMARY	
Top Record Producers	
1 Bill Phillips, Cle	6
1 Joe Start, Pro	6
3 Cap Anson, Chi	5
3 Jake Beckley, Pit	5

Most Outstanding Record Producers		
Jake Beckley, Pit	5 for	275 years
Fred Tenney, Bos	1 for	77 years
Cap Anson, Chi	5 for	52 years
Charlie Grimm, Chi	1 for	52 years

AMERICAN LEAGUE SUMMARY	
Top Record Producers	
1 Candy LaChance, Bos	6
1 Stuffy McInnis, Phi	6
2 Jiggs Donahue, Chi	5
2 Tom Jones, StL	5
2 Harry Davis, Phi	5
2 Joe Judge, Was	5
2 Mickey Vernon, Was	5

Most Outstanding Record Producers		
Mickey Vernon, Was	5 for	150 years
Lou Gehrig, NY	4 for	65 years
Stuffy McInnis, Phi	6 for	57 years
Joe Judge, Was	5 for	51 years

MAJOR LEAGUE SUMMARY	
Top Record Producers	
1 Joe Start, Pro, NL	6
1 Bill Phillips, Cle, NL	6
2 Charlie Comiskey, StL, AA	5
2 Cap Anson, Chi, NL	5
2 Jake Beckley, Pit, NL	5

Most Outstanding Record Producers		
Jake Beckley, Pit, NL	5 for	274 years
George Sisler, StL, AL	1 for	58 years
Cap Anson, Chi, NL	5 for	50 years

Bill Phillips and Joe Start were two fine pioneer first basemen of the National League. They set the original marks for others to beat.

Cap Anson was the first to have a very long career at first base, and his five records lasted ten years each before they were passed by Jake Beckley, whose records have been the most difficult of all first basemen's to break. Beckley had a remarkable 20-year career; it was good enough to land him in the Hall of Fame in 1971. In all, he created five NL marks that were also Major League records. Three of his NL and Major League records still stand. He is the current leader in games, with 2,377; putouts, 23,709; and total chances, 23,742; which makes him the most active first baseman in history. He was pretty good with the bat as well, as he batted .308 and belted 2,931 hits.

Fred Tenney of the Braves was also a sensational first sacker and has the most assists in NL history.

Charlie Grimm of the Cubs is the all-time NL leader in double plays with 1,733, which he accumulated in a fine career that lasted from 1918 through 1936.

Two of the best-fielding first basemen have been Walter Holke and Frank McCormick. Holke's record .993 lifetime average lasted 23 years before it was broken, and McCormick's .995 average stood for 24 years before being toppled.

Mickey Vernon has long been known as one of the AL's most outstanding first basemen, and he has created the most difficult records to surpass: of his five records, none have been broken.

Lou Gehrig of the New York Yankees shows that he was more than just a sensational hitter. His four marks lasted a total of 65 years and earn him the number two position.

Stuffy McInnis is one of the AL's finest-fielding first basemen. He was the first to reach the .992 range, an average record that stood for 12 years. Most remarkable

Joe Start and Bill Phillips show up as top producers in the Major League category because they were among the first players on the scene. Other fine first basemen have not been able to crack the top five list due to the difficult standards set by Comiskey, Anson and, most particularly, Beckley.

Since Beckley had 20 and Anson 19 years of play at first base, others would have to have a similar longevity to accumulate numbers that would surpass them.

The Most Outstanding Producers list shows the tre-

Two former Dodgers, Wes Parker and Steve Garvey, share the highest fielding average with .996.

about McInnis' fielding average is that it was established from 1911 through 1922, when gloves were not nearly the quality of the gloves of players who followed.

Joe Judge was another super first baseman, and he upped McInnis' record by one point. Judge has the distinction of having held the fielding average record longer than any other first baseman. His .993 mark stood for 31 years before Vic Power averaged a fine .994. Jim Spencer and Eddie Murray share the present AL title for career fielding average, with .995s.

mendous difficulty other first basemen have had in trying to match Beckley's feats, as his records have been in the books for a total of 274 years. Mickey Vernon and George Sisler are the only two players aside from Beckley who have unbroken records. Sisler's 1,528 assists has headed the list since 1930. Mickey Vernon, the all-time champion in double plays, is the only first baseman to go over the 2,000 mark.

Steve Garvey continues to hold the top spot in fielding average with .996.

SECOND BASE

NATIONAL LEAGUE			AMERICAN LEAGUE			MAJOR LEAGUE		

Most Games

	NATIONAL LEAGUE			AMERICAN LEAGUE			MAJOR LEAGUE	

Most Games

National League			American League			Major League		
1879–87	Jack Farrell, Pro	688	1901–09	Jimmy Williams, NY	921	1879–88 Jack Farrell, Pro, NL, AA		740
1880–90	Fred Dunlap, Cle	854	1901–16	Nap Lajoie, Cle	1721	1876–91 Jack Burdock, Bos, NL		956
1876–91	Jack Burdock, Bos	886	**1906–30**	**Eddie Collins, Chi**	**2650**	1882–97 Fred Pfeffer, Chi, NL		1537
1882–97	Fred Pfeffer, Chi	1413				1882–99 Bid McPhee, Cin, AA		2125
1897–09	Claude Ritchey, Pit	1478				**1906–30 Eddie Collins, Chi, AL**		**2650**
1904–16	Miller Huggins, StL	1531						
1907–20	Larry Doyle, NY	1730						
1902–29	Johnny Evers, Chi	1735						
1919–37	Frankie Frisch, StL	1775						
1931–47	Billy Herman, Chi	1829						
1945–63	Red Schoendienst, StL	1834						
1956–72	Bill Mazeroski, Pit	2094						
1963–83	**Joe Morgan, Cin**	**2427**						

Most Putouts

National League			American League			Major League		
1879–87	Jack Farrell, Pro	1559	1901–09	Jimmy Williams, NY	2769	1879–88 Jack Farrell, Pro, NL,		
1880–90	Fred Dunlap, Cle	2405	1901–16	Nap Lajoie, Cle	4599	AA		1559
1876–91	Jack Burdock, Bos	2465	**1906–30**	**Eddie Collins, Chi**	**6526**	1876–91 Jack Burdock, Bos, NL		2637
1882–97	Fred Pfeffer, Chi	4172				1882–97 Fred Pfeffer, Chi, NL		4613
1931–47	Billy Herman, Chi	4694				1882–99 Bid McPhee, Cin, AA		6300
1956–72	Bill Mazeroski, Pit	4974				**1906–30 Eddie Collins, Chi, AL**		**6526**
1963–83	**Joe Morgan, Cin**	**5541**						

Most Assists

National League			American League			Major League		
1879–87	Jack Farrell, Pro,	2055	1901–09	Jimmy Williams, NY	3509	1879–88 Jack Farrell, Pro, NL,		
1880–90	Fred Dunlap, Cle	2633	1901–16	Nap Lajoie, Cle	5239	AA		2055
1876–91	Jack Burdock, Bos	2668	**1906–30**	**Eddie Collins, Chi**	**7630**	1876–91 Jack Burdock, Bos, NL		2860
1882–97	Fred Pfeffer, Chi	4599				1882–97 Fred Pfeffer, Chi, NL		4986
1904–16	Miller Huggins, StL	4683				1882–99 Bid McPhee, Cin, AA		6593
1902–29	Johnny Evers, Chi	4998				**1906–30 Eddie Collins, Chi, AL**		**7630**
1924–35	Hughie Critz, Cin	5041						
1919–37	Frankie Frisch, StL	5671						
1956–72	Bill Mazeroski, Pit	6685						
1963–83	**Joe Morgan, Cin**	**6738**						

Most Errors

National League			American League			Major League		
1879–87	Jack Farrell, Pro	411	1901–09	Jimmy Williams, NY	292	1879–88 Jack Farrell, Pro, NL, AA		411
1876–91	Jack Burdock, Bos	488	1901–16	Nap Lajoie, Cle	350	1876–91 Jack Burdock, Bos, NL		530
1882–97	**Fred Pfeffer, Chi**	**749**	**1906–30**	**Eddie Collins, Chi**	**435**	**1882–97 Fred Pfeffer, Chi, NL**		**825**

Most Errors after 1900

National League						Major League		
1901–09	Claude Ritchey, Pit	273				1901–09 Jimmy Williams, NY, AL		292
1904–16	Miller Huggins, StL	372				1900–16 Nap Lajoie, Cle, AL		380
1907–20	**Larry Doyle, NY**	**442**				**1906–30 Eddie Collins, Chi, AL**		**435**

Most Double Plays

National League			American League			Major League		
1879–87	Jack Farrell, Pro	238	1901–09	Jimmy Williams, NY	426	1879–88 Jack Farrell, Pro, NL, AA		238
1880–90	Fred Dunlap, Cle	430	1901–16	Nap Lajoie, Cle	883	1882–97 Fred Pfeffer, Chi, NL		879
1882–97	Fred Pfeffer, Chi	806	1906–30	Eddie Collins, Chi	1215	1882–99 Bid McPhee, Cin, AA		1145
1924–35	Hughie Critz, Cin	943	1924–42	Charlie Gehringer, Det	1444	1906–30 Eddie Collins, Chi, AL		1215
1919–37	Frankie Frisch, StL	998	1937–51	Bobby Doerr, Bos	1478	1924–42 Charley Gehringer,		
1931–47	Billy Herman, Chi	1157	**1947–65**	**Nellie Fox, Chi**	**1619**	Det, AL		1444
1945–63	Red Schoendienst, StL	1280				1937–51 Bobby Doerr, Bos, AL		1478
1956–72	**Bill Mazeroski, Pit**	**1706**				1947–65 Nellie Fox, Chi, AL		1619
						1956–72 Bill Mazeroski,		
						Pit, NL		**1706**

SECOND BASE

NATIONAL LEAGUE

Most Total Chances

1879–87	Jack Farrell, Pro	4025
1880–90	Fred Dunlap, Cle	5441
1876–91	Jack Burdock, Bos	5621
1882–97	Fred Pfeffer, Chi	9520
1919–37	Frankie Frisch, StL	9968
1931–47	Billy Herman, Chi	10,565
1956–72	Bill Mazeroski, Pit	11,863
1963–83	**Joe Morgan, Cin**	**12,513**

Highest Fielding Average

1879–87	Jack Farrell, Pro	.897
1880–90	Fred Dunlap, Cle	.926
1891–98	Lou Bierbauer, Pit	.948
1890–99	Bid McPhee, Cin, AA	.955
1897–09	Claude Ritchey, Pit	.958
1924–35	Hughie Critz, Cin	.973
1919–37	Frankie Frisch, StL	.973
1945–63	Red Schoendienst, StL	.983
1956–72	Bill Mazeroski, Pit	.983
1964–77	Tommy Helms, Cin	.983
1969–80	**Dave Cash, Phi**	**.984**

AMERICAN LEAGUE

Most Total Chances

1901–09	Jimmy Williams, NY	6570
1901–16	Nap Lajoie, Cle	10,188
1906–30	**Eddie Collins, Chi**	**14,591**

Highest Fielding Average

1901–09	Jimmy Williams, NY	.956
1901–16	Nap Lajoie, Cle	.967
1906–30	Eddie Collins, Chi	.969
1924–42	Charlie Gehringer, Det	.976
1937–51	Bobby Doerr, Bos	.980
1947–65	**Nellie Fox, Chi**	**.984**
1956–67	**Jerry Lumpe, Det**	**.984**
1970–77	**Cookie Rojas, KC**	**.984**

DID YOU KNOW . . . *That the first standard baseball was composed mainly of woolen yarn, did not contain more than one ounce of vulcanized rubber in mold form and was covered with leather?*

MAJOR LEAGUE

Most Total Chances

1879–88	Jack Farrell, Pro, NL, AA	4025
1876–91	Jack Burdock, Bos, NL	6027
1882–97	Fred Pfeffer, Chi, NL	10,424
1882–99	Bid McPhee, Cin, AA	13,658
1906–30	**Eddie Collins, Chi, AL**	**14,591**

Highest Fielding Average

1879–88	Jack Farrell, Pro, NL, AA	.897
1880–91	Fred Dunlap, Cle, NL	.926
1886–98	Lou Bierbauer, Pit, NL	.948
1893–99	Heinie Reitz, Bal, NL	.953
1897–09	Claude Ritchey, Pit, NL	.958
1896–16	Nap Lajoie, Cle, AL	.963
1906–30	Eddie Collins, Chi, AL	.969
1924–35	Hughie Critz, Cin, NL	.973
1919–37	Frankie Frisch, StL, NL	.973
1924–42	Charlie Gehringer, Det, AL	.976
1937–51	Bobby Doerr, Bos, AL	.980
1947–65	**Nellie Fox, Chi, AL**	**.984**
1956–67	**Jerry Lumpe, Det, AL**	**.984**
1962–77	**Cookie Rojas, Phi, NL**	**.984**
1969–80	**Dave Cash, Phi, NL**	**.984**

NATIONAL LEAGUE SUMMARY

Top Record Producers

1	Jack Farrell, Pro	6
1	Fred Dunlap, Cle	6
1	Bill Mazeroski, Pit	6
4	Fred Pfeffer, Chi	5
4	Frankie Frisch, StL	5
6	Jack Burdock, Bos	4
6	Billy Herman, Chi	4
6	Joe Morgan, Cin	4

Most Outstanding Record Producers

Fred Pfeffer, Chi	5 for	161 years
Frankie Frisch, StL	5 for	91 years
Billy Herman, Chi	4 for	82 years
Bill Mazeroski, Pit	6 for	68 years
Red Schoendienst, StL	3 for	35 years

AMERICAN LEAGUE SUMMARY

Top Record Producers

1	Jimmy Williams, NY	6
1	Nap Lajoie, Cle	6
1	Eddie Collins, Chi	6

Most Outstanding Record Producers

Eddie Collins, Chi	6 for	258 years
Nap Lajoie, Cle	6 for	84 years
Nellie Fox, Chi	2 for	44 years
Jimmy Williams, NY	6 for	42 years
Bobby Doerr, Bos	2 for	28 years

MAJOR LEAGUE SUMMARY

Top Record Producers

1	Jack Farrell, Pro, NL, AA	6
1	Eddie Collins, Chi, AL	6
2	Fred Pfeffer, Chi, NL	5
2	Bid McPhee, Cin, AA	5
3	Jack Burdock, Bos, NL	4

Most Outstanding Record Producers

Eddie Collins, Chi, AL	6 for	251 years
Bid McPhee, Cin, AA	5 for	155 years
Bobby Doerr, Bos, AL	2 for	28 years
Nellie Fox, Chi, AL	2 for	28 years

SECOND BASE

Jack Farrell, Fred Dunlap, Jack Burdock and Fred Pfeffer were some of the pioneer second basemen who were standouts, and they were responsible for setting the original records. Of this group, Pfeffer captured the records that were the most difficult to break. He was the first to play in more than 1,000 games, and his putouts mark lasted 50 years before Billy Herman topped it. Pfeffer's other outstanding records are his double play total, which stood for 38 years, and his total chances, which was not broken for 40 years.

Hall of Famer Frankie Frisch established five marks, which rank second in number of years held. Three of Frisch's marks lasted a decade each. His assists record stood for 35 years, while his fielding average was good enough for 26 years.

Billy Herman is another Hall of Famer who ranks high in the standings. His four marks lasted a total of 82 years. Herman's games and double play marks stood for 16 years each, while his putouts and total chance records each lasted a quarter century before they were shattered.

Bill Mazeroski was the first second baseman to play in more than 2,000 games, and he broke every record in every positive category. Four of his marks lasted 11 years each. His greatest achievement was in turning the double play; his 1,706 DPs is both a National and Major League record that still stands.

The busiest of all NL second basemen was little Joe Morgan, who can boast of having the most unbroken career fielding records. Morgan played the most games, made the most putouts, assists and total chances. Since he has only been out of the NL for five years, we can expect him to rise in the rankings in coming years.

Jimmy Williams, Nap Lajoie and Eddie Collins dominated the six positive fielding categories and are rated as some of the AL's best. Of this group, Eddie Collins had the longest career and played in more games (2,650) than any second baseman in baseball history. Four of his six records remain unbroken. In addition to leading in games played, Collins is the champion in putouts, assists, and total chances, with numbers so high they may never be broken.

Jimmy Williams was the first second baseman in the AL to have a nine-year career and the records started with him. Nap Lajoie matched those nine years and continued for another seven years; when he retired in 1916, he held every career fielding record in the AL.

It would take a player with an unusually long career to pass Lajoie's achievements, and Eddie Collins did just that. Collins, however, has been passed in double plays, first by Charlie Gehringer in 1942, who was then passed by Bobby Doerr, who in turn surrendered to Nellie Fox, who is the present AL double play champion.

Nellie Fox, Jerry Lumpe and Cookie Rojas, each having had a .984 fielding average, share that top spot, with Fox having the longest reign. Most remarkable about Fox's achievements is that his small size did not prevent him from turning the most double plays, even with much bigger players trying to bust him up.

Bobby Doerr, the first second baseman to reach the 1,500 range in DPs and .980 in fielding average, was recently inducted into the Hall of Fame. His two fine records lasted 14 years before Nellie Fox improved upon them.

Lost in the shuffle between the National and American Leagues is one of baseball's most outstanding second basemen, Bid McPhee. Because he played half his career in the American Association and half in the National League, his record-setting numbers do not appear until they are combined under the Major League category.

When McPhee retired in 1899, he was the first second baseman to have played in 2,000 games, and he had recorded the most putouts, assists, double plays and total chances of any player who preceded him. So great were his achievements that each of them lasted 31 years before they were broken. Yet McPhee has not been recognized for Hall of Fame honors. It took the great Hall of Famer Eddie Collins to break McPhee's records.

It is easy to see that Jack Farrell, Jack Burdock and Fred Pfeffer were three of the early players to excel at second base. McPhee, however, doubled most of their achievements, and ranks as the greatest second baseman prior to 1900. Very few modern players have been able to post the numbers of McPhee, even though they play longer schedules and have much finer fields and gloves to use.

The four greatest second basemen at turning the double play appear to be Charlie Gehringer, Bobby Doerr, Nellie Fox and Bill Mazeroski. They raised the record from the 1400s to Maz's 1706.

It is very difficult to name the best-fielding second baseman, as the type of gloves and condition of the playing surface have a lot to do with fielding averages. It is possible for an early player who has a lower fielding average to have possessed similar or superior talents to later players with higher averages.

SHORTSTOP

NATIONAL LEAGUE	AMERICAN LEAGUE	MAJOR LEAGUE

Most Games

	NATIONAL LEAGUE			AMERICAN LEAGUE			MAJOR LEAGUE	
1876–81	Johnny Peters, Chi	370	1902–07	Monte Cross, Phi	711	1876–84	Johnny Peters, Chi, NL	456
1876–86	Dave Force, Buf	564	1902–08	George Davis, Chi	721	1876–86	Dave Force, Buf, NL	564
1881–91	Monte Ward, NY	698	1901–10	Freddy Parent, Bos	1129	1882–89	Bill Gleason, StL, AA	796
1880–94	Arthur Irwin, Phi	845	1902–16	Bobby Wallace, StL	1449	1881–91	Monte Ward, NY, NL	826
1880–95	Jack Glasscock, Cle	1590	1908–23	Donnie Bush, Det	1867	1880–94	Arthur Irwin, Phi, NL	947
1890–03	Herman Long, Bos	1595	1910–27	Roger Peckinpaugh, NY	1983	1880–95	Jack Glasscock, Cle, NL	1628
1892–06	Tommy Corcoran, Cin	1817	1930–50	Luke Appling, Chi	2218	1889–03	Herman Long, Bos, NL	1792
1891–11	Billy Dahlen, Chi	2132	**1956–73**	**Luis Aparicio, Chi**	**2581**	1890–07	Tommy Corcoran, Cin, NL	2073
1912–31	**Rabbit Maranville, Bos**	**2154**				1891–11	Billy Dahlen, Chi, NL	2132
						1912–35	Rabbit Maranville, Bos, NL	2154
						1930–50	Luke Appling, Chi, AL	2218
						1956–73	**Luis Aparicio, Chi, AL**	**2581**

Most Putouts

	NATIONAL LEAGUE			AMERICAN LEAGUE			MAJOR LEAGUE	
1876–81	Johnny Peters, Chi	526	1902–07	Monte Cross, Phi	1587	1876–84	Johnny Peters, Chi, NL	616
1876–86	Dave Force, Buf	570	1901–10	Freddy Parent, Bos	2265	1882–89	Bill Gleason, StL, AA	894
1882–89	Sam Wise, Bos	840	1902–16	Bobby Wallace, StL	3185	1884–90	Frank Fennelly, Cin, AA	995
1881–91	Monte Ward, NY	1078	1908–23	Donnie Bush, Det	4038	1881–91	Monte Ward, NY, NL	1381
1880–94	Arthur Irwin, Phi	1091	1930–50	Luke Appling, Chi	4398	1880–95	Jack Glasscock, Cle, NL	2737
1880–95	Jack Glasscock, Cle	2693	**1956–73**	**Luis Aparicio, Chi**	**4548**	1889–03	Herman Long, Bos, NL	4219
1890–03	Herman Long, Bos	3742				1890–07	Tommy Corcoran, Cin, NL	4550
1892–06	Tommy Corcoran, Cin	3979				1891–11	Billy Dahlen, Chi, NL	4850
1891–11	Billy Dahlen, Chi	4850				**1912–35**	**Rabbit Maranville, Bos, NL**	**5139**
1912–31	**Rabbit Maranville, Bos**	**5139**						

Most Assists

	NATIONAL LEAGUE			AMERICAN LEAGUE			MAJOR LEAGUE	
1876–81	Johnny Peters, Chi	1130	1902–07	Monte Cross, Phi	2118	1876–84	Johnny Peters, Chi, NL	1410
1876–86	Dave Force, Buf	1633	1902–08	George Davis, Chi	2402	1876–86	Dave Force, Buf, NL	1633
1881–91	Monte Ward, NY	2134	1901–10	Freddy Parent, Bos	3714	1882–89	Bill Gleason, StL, AA	2303
1880–94	Arthur Irwin, Phi	2579	1902–16	Bobby Wallace, StL	4825	1884–90	Frank Fennelly, Cin, AA	2571
1880–95	Jack Glasscock, Cle	5371	1908–23	Donnie Bush, Det	6119	1881–91	Monte Ward, NY, NL	2584
1890–03	Herman Long, Bos	5484	1910–27	Roger Peckinpaugh, NY	6334	1880–94	Arthur Irwin, Phi, NL	2910
1892–06	Tommy Corcoran, Cin	6121	1930–50	Luke Appling, Chi	7218	1880–95	Jack Glasscock, Cle, NL	5478
1891–11	**Billy Dahlen, Chi**	**7500**	**1956–73**	**Luis Aparicio, Chi**	**8016**	1889–03	Herman Long, Bos, NL	6130
						1890–07	Tommy Corcoran, Cin, NL	7106
						1891–11	Billy Dahlen, Chi, NL	7500
						1956–73	**Luis Aparicio, Chi, AL**	**8016**

Most Errors

	NATIONAL LEAGUE			AMERICAN LEAGUE			MAJOR LEAGUE	
1876–81	Johnny Peters, Chi	222	1902–07	Monte Cross, Phi	251	1876–84	Johnny Peters, Chi, NL	271
1882–89	Sam Wise, Bos	380	1901–10	Freddy Parent, Bos	466	1882–89	Bill Gleason, StL, AA	517
1881–91	Monte Ward, NY	405	1902–16	Bobby Wallace, StL	488	1884–90	Frank Fennelly, Cin, AA	584
1880–94	Arthur Irwin, Phi	477	**1908–23**	**Donnie Bush, Det**	**675**	1880–95	Jack Glasscock, Cle, NL	805
1880–95	Jack Glasscock, Cle	786				**1889–03**	**Herman Long, Bos, NL**	**1050**
1890–03	Herman Long, Bos	912						
1891–11	**Billy Dahlen, Chi**	**975**						

SHORTSTOP

NATIONAL LEAGUE

Most Double Plays

1876–81	Johnny Peters, Chi	96
1876–86	Dave Force, Buf	123
1881–89	Jack Rowe, Det	138
1881–91	Monte Ward, NY	230
1880–95	Jack Glasscock, Cle	600
1890–03	Herman Long, Bos	692
1892–06	Tommy Corcoran, Cin	732
1891–11	Billy Dahlen, Chi	876
1915–30	Dave Bancroft, Phi	988
1912–31	Rabbit Maranville, Bos	1183
1940–58	Pee Wee Reese, Bkn	1246
1951–66	**Roy McMillan, Cin**	**1304**

Most Total Chances

1876–81	Johnny Peters, Chi	1878
1876–86	Dave Force, Buf	2435
1882–89	Sam Wise, Bos	2772
1881–91	Monte Ward, NY	3617
1880–94	Arthur Irwin, Phi	4147
1880–95	Jack Glasscock, Cle	8850
1890–03	Herman Long, Bos	10,138
1892–06	Tommy Corcoran, Cin	10,876
1891–11	**Billy Dahlen, Chi**	**13,325**

Highest Fielding Average

1876–81	Johnny Peters, Chi	.884
1876–86	Dave Force, Buf	.906
1880–95	Jack Glasscock, Cle	.911
1890–98	Germany Smith, Cin	.915
1892–02	Hugh Jennings, Bal	.928
1890–03	George Davis, NY	.937
1905–16	Mickey Doolan, Phi	.939
1901–17	Honus Wagner, Pit	.942
1918–24	Charlie Hollocker, Chi	.955
1927–38	Woody English, Chi	.956
1930–43	Leo Durocher, StL	.962
1931–47	Billy Jurges, Chi	.964
1936–50	Eddie Miller, Cin	.972
1951–66	Roy McMillan, Cin	.972
1962–74	Dal Maxvill, StL	.973
1970–80	Roger Metzger, Hou	.976
1970–85	**Larry Bowa, Phi**	**.980**

AMERICAN LEAGUE

Most Double Plays

1902–07	Monte Cross, Phi	186
1902–08	George Davis, Chi	287
1901–10	Freddy Parent, Bos	375
1902–16	Bobby Wallace, StL	495
1908–23	Donnie Bush, Det	566
1910–27	Roger Peckinpaugh, NY	928
1928–45	Joe Cronin, Bos	1165
1930–50	Luke Appling, Chi	1424
1956–73	**Luis Aparicio, Chi**	**1553**

DID YOU KNOW... *That in baseball played before Alexander Cartwright's revisions, the shortstop and second baseman played short left field and short right field? There was no such thing as a double-play combination.*

Most Total Chances

1902–07	Monte Cross, Phi	3956
1902–08	George Davis, Chi	4075
1901–10	Freddy Parent, Bos	6445
1902–16	Bobby Wallace, StL	8498
1908–23	Donnie Bush, Det	10,846
1930–50	Luke Appling, Chi	12,259
1956–73	**Luis Aparicio, Chi**	**12,930**

Highest Fielding Average

1902–07	Monte Cross, Phi	.938
1902–08	George Davis, Chi	.946
1904–19	Terry Turner, Cle	.953
1914–26	Everett Scott, Bos	.965
1938–52	Lou Boudreau, Cle	.973
1965–81	**Mark Belanger, Bal**	**.977**

DID YOU KNOW... *That a win can be credited to only one relief pitcher in a game? If two pitchers qualify for a win, the official scorer gives the win to the most effective pitcher, according to a ruling in 1973.*

MAJOR LEAGUE

Most Double Plays

1876–84	Johnny Peters, Chi, NL	117
1876–86	Dave Force, Buf, NL	123
1882–89	Bill Gleason, StL, AA	182
1884–90	Frank Fennelly, Cin, AA	255
1881–91	Monte Ward, NY, NL	289
1880–95	Jack Glasscock, Cle, NL	604
1889–03	Herman Long, Bos, NL	759
1891–11	Billy Dahlen, Chi, NL	876
1910–27	Roger Peckinpaugh, NY, AL	928
1915–30	Dave Bancroft, Phi, NL	988
1912–35	Rabbit Maranville, Bos, NL	1183
1930–50	Luke Appling, Chi, AL	1424
1956–73	**Luis Aparicio, Chi, AL**	**1553**

Most Total Chances

1876–84	Johnny Peters, Chi, NL	2297
1876–86	Dave Force, Buf, NL	2435
1882–89	Bill Gleason, StL, AA	3714
1884–90	Frank Fennelly, Cin, AA	4150
1881–91	Monte Ward, NY, NL	4475
1880–94	Arthur Irwin, Phi, NL	4680
1880–95	Jack Glasscock, Cle, NL	9021
1889–03	Herman Long, Bos, NL	11,399
1890–07	Tommy Corcoran, Cin, NL	12,612
1891–11	**Billy Dahlen, Chi, NL**	**13,325**

Highest Fielding Average

1876–84	Johnny Peters, Chi, NL	.884
1876–86	Dave Force, Buf, NL	.906
1880–95	Jack Glasscock, Cle, NL	.911
1891–07	Hugh Jennings, Bal, NL	.928
1890–09	Hugh Davis, NY, NL	.940
1904–19	Terry Turner, Cle, AL	.953
1914–26	Everett Scott, Bos, AL	.965
1936–50	Eddie Miller, Cin, NL	.972
1938–52	Lou Boudreau, Cle, AL	.973
1962–75	Dal Maxvill, StL, NL	.973
1970–80	Roger Metzger, Hou, NL	.976
1965–82	Mark Belanger, Bal, AL	.977
1970–85	**Larry Bowa, Phi, NL**	**.980**

DID YOU KNOW... *That Lip Pike in 1876 was the first Jewish baseball player?*

SHORTSTOP

NATIONAL LEAGUE SUMMARY		AMERICAN LEAGUE SUMMARY		MAJOR LEAGUE SUMMARY	
Top Record Producers		*Top Record Producers*		*Record Producers*	
1 Johnny Peters, Chi	6	1 Monte Cross, Phi	6	1 Johnny Peters, Chi, NL	6
1 Dave Force, Buf	6	2 George Davis, Chi	5	1 Jack Glasscock, Cle, NL	6
1 Jack Glasscock, Cle	6	2 Freddy Parent, Bos	5	3 Dave Force, Buf, NL	5
4 Monte Ward, NY	5	2 Bobby Wallace, StL	5	3 Bill Gleason, StL, AA	5
4 Herman Long, Bos	5	2 Donnie Bush, Det	5	3 Monte Ward, NY, NL	5
4 Tommy Corcoran, Cin	5	2 Luke Appling, Chi	5	3 Herman Long, Bos, NL	5
4 Billy Dahlen, Chi	5	2 Luis Aparicio, Chi	5	3 Tommy Corcoran, Cin, NL	5
				3 Billy Dahlen, Chi, NL	5

Most Outstanding Record Producers		*Most Outstanding Record Producers*		*Most Outstanding Record Producers*	
Billy Dahlen, Chi	5 for 215 years	Luke Appling, Chi	5 for 115 years	Billy Dahlen, Chi, NL	5 for 203 years
Rabbit Maranville, Bos	3 for 141 years	Luis Aparicio, Chi	5 for 75 years	Rabbit Maranville, Bos	2 for 68 years
Jack Glasscock, Cle	6 for 43 years	Donnie Bush, Det	5 for 68 years	Jack Glasscock, Cle, NL	6 for 52 years
		Roger Peckinpaugh, NY	2 for 46 years	Luke Appling, Chi, AL	2 for 46 years
				Luis Aparicio, Chi, AL	3 for 45 years

Johnny Peters, Dave Force and Monte Ward were the three earliest shortstops to post records, while Jack Glasscock, Herman Long and Tommy Corcoran improved upon them with ease.

Billy Dahlen looms as the shortstop whose marks were the most difficult to break, as his five records have lasted a total of 215 years. Dahlen became the first to play 2,000 games and record 4,000 putouts and 7,000 assists. His assists and total chance records remain unbroken.

Monte Cross, George Davis and Freddy Parent set the early marks in the AL, and Bobby Wallace broke their records and proved to be the most productive shortstop during the first 16 years of AL history.

Donnie Bush was soon making strides to better Wallace's achievements, and when he retired in 1923 Bush was the best AL shortstop to date. His records were so fine that they lasted a total of 68 years, which is the second best in AL history. Bush was the first to reach the 4,000 plateau in putouts, 6,000 in assists, 500 in double plays and 10,000 in total chances.

Roger Peckinpaugh of the Yankees was also doing

The Major League records start with Johnny Peters of Chicago. His six records are matched by Jack Glasscock, the most active of all pioneer shortstops. Glasscock had the highest quality of records in the early going, and they were broken by Herman Long and Tommy Corcoran.

Billy Dahlen is the Major League leader in records that have lasted the most years. His two most impressive marks are his 13,325 total chances, the most of any shortstop in history, and his 7,500 assists, which is second best. Dahlen's 4,850 putouts are also second best, but his assists mark lasted 62 years before being broken. Dahlen's total chances record is now the oldest unbroken record by any shortstop.

Rabbit Maranville has two exciting records. He was the first to participate in more than 1,000 double plays,

Rabbit Maranville has three outstanding records which place him in the number two position. The Rabbit played more games at shortstop than any other NL player at that position, and his 5,139 putouts remain not only an NL best but also a Major League record.

Jack Glasscock is in third place with six records that have lasted a total of 43 years. Glasscock was the first to play in 1,500 games and record more than 2,000 putouts, 5,000 assists, 600 double plays and 8,000 total chances.

some exceptional things during Bush's era. When he hung up his spikes in 1927, he had passed Bush in games played, and almost doubled the total of Bush's double plays. Roger's two records land him fourth among outstanding producers.

Two of the AL's greatest shortstops come from the Chicago White Sox. Sitting alone at the top is Hall of Famer Luke Appling; each of Appling's five marks lasted 23 years before Luis Aparicio could improve upon them, and now "Little Looie" is the man to beat. Aparicio's five records remain unbroken.

and his 5,139 putouts is still number one.

Luke Appling and Luis Aparicio, both of the White Sox, are two other premier shortstops, and both are Hall of Famers. Appling was the dominant shortstop in the American League from 1930 through 1950, during which time he set two Major League records. When he retired in 1950, he had played the most games of any shortstop, 2,218, and had made more double plays, 1,424. These marks lasted 23 years before fellow White Sox great Luis Aparicio improved upon both of them.

Aparicio has the most unbroken records. He has played the most games, 2,581, has the most assists, 8,016, and the most double plays, 1,553. He is presently in the fifth position in total years, and it is likely that he will rise higher in the standings as the years go by.

THIRD BASE

NATIONAL LEAGUE		
Most Games		
1878–85	Ned Williamson, Chi	664
1876–88	Ezra Sutton, Bos	677
1876–89	Deacon White, Buf	762
1881–94	Jerry Denny, Pro	1109
1885–98	Billy Nash, Bos	1290
1898–11	Harry Steinfeldt, Cin	1386
1920–37	Pie Traynor, Pit	1864
1952–68	**Eddie Mathews, Mil**	**2181**
Most Putouts		
1878–85	Ned Williamson, Chi	825
1876–89	Deacon White, Buf	852
1880–92	Tom Burns, Chi	1016
1881–94	Jerry Denny, Pro	1759
1885–98	Billy Nash, Bos	1885
1920–37	**Pie Traynor, Pit**	**2291**
Most Assists		
1878–85	Ned Williamson, Chi	1628
1881–94	Jerry Denny, Pro	2316
1885–98	Billy Nash, Bos	2665
1920–37	Pie Traynor, Pit	3525
1952–68	Eddie Mathews, Mil	4323
1960–73	**Ron Santo, Chi**	**4581**
Most Errors		
1878–85	Ned Williamson, Chi	367
1876–89	Deacon White, Buf	414
1881–94	**Jerry Denny, Pro**	**547**
Most Errors after 1900		
1900–11	Harry Steinfeldt, Cin	289
1920–37	**Pie Traynor, Pit**	**323**

AMERICAN LEAGUE		
Most Games		
1901–07	Lave Cross, Phi	846
1901–08	Bill Coughlin, Det	978
1901–10	Bill Bradley, Cle	1191
1908–22	Frank Baker, Phi	1548
1908–24	Larry Gardner, Bos	1655
1923–35	Willie Kamm, Chi	1672
1930–46	Pinky Higgins, Det	1768
1944–62	Eddie Yost, Was	2008
1955–77	**Brooks Robinson, Bal**	**2870**
Most Putouts		
1901–07	Lave Cross	997
1901–08	Bill Coughlin, Det	1271
1901–10	Bill Bradley, Cle	1487
1908–22	Frank Baker, Phi	2142
1944–62	Eddie Yost, Was	2356
1955–77	**Brooks Robinson, Bal**	**2697**
Most Assists		
1901–07	Lave Cross, Phi	1606
1901–08	Jimmy Collins, Bos	1904
1901–10	Bill Bradley, Cle	2488
1908–22	Frank Baker, Phi	3133
1908–24	Larry Gardner, Bos	3372
1944–62	Eddie Yost, Was	3659
1955–77	**Brooks Robinson, Bal**	**6205**
Most Errors		
1901–07	Lave Cross, Phi	166
1901–08	Jimmy Collins, Bos	230
1901–10	Bill Bradley, Cle	252
1908–22	Frank Baker, Phi	322
1930–46	**Pinky Higgins, Det**	**354**

MAJOR LEAGUE		
Most Games		
1876–88	Ezra Sutton, Bos, NL	677
1878–90	Ned Williamson, Chi, NL	716
1880–91	Art Whitney, Pit, AA	802
1879–92	Hick Carpenter, Cin, AA	1059
1881–94	Jerry Denny, Pro, NL	1109
1883–96	Arlie Latham, StL, AA	1571
1887–07	Lave Cross, Phi, NL	1721
1920–37	Pie Traynor, Pit, NL	1864
1944–62	Eddie Yost, Was, AL	2008
1952–68	Eddie Mathews, Mil, NL	2181
1955–77	**Brooks Robinson, Bal, AL**	**2870**
Most Putouts		
1876–88	Ezra Sutton, Bos, NL	788
1878–90	Ned Williamson, Chi, NL	878
1880–91	Art Whitney, Pit, AA	979
1879–92	Hick Carpenter, Cin, AA	1413
1881–94	Jerry Denny, Pro, NL	1759
1883–96	Arlie Latham, StL, AA	1961
1887–07	Lave Cross, Phi, NL	2304
1895–08	Jimmy Collins, Bos, AL	2372
1955–77	**Brooks Robinson, Bal, AL**	**2697**
Most Assists		
1876–88	Ezra Sutton, Bos, NL	1177
1878–90	Ned Williamson, Chi, NL	1719
1879–92	Hick Carpenter, Cin, AA	1961
1881–94	Jerry Denny, Pro, NL	2316
1883–96	Arlie Latham, StL, AA	3530
1887–07	Lave Cross, Phi, NL	3703
1952–68	Eddie Mathews, Mil, NL	4323
1955–77	**Brooks Robinson, Bal, AL**	**6205**
Most Errors		
1876–88	Ezra Sutton, Bos, NL	271
1878–90	Ned Williamson, Chi, NL	401
1879–92	Hick Carpenter, Cin, AA	579
1883–96	**Arlie Latham, StL, AA**	**812**
Most Errors after 1900		
1901–07	Lave Cross, Phi, NL	190
1900–11	Harry Steinfeldt, Chi, NL	289
1900–15	Bill Bradley, Cle, AL	313
1909–29	**Jimmy Austin, StL, AL**	**345**

THIRD BASE

NATIONAL LEAGUE

Most Double Plays

1878–85	Ned Williamson, Chi	113
1880–92	Tom Burns, Chi	117
1881–94	Jerry Denny, Pro	145
1885–98	Billy Nash, Bos	211
1912–27	Heinie Groh, Cin	266
1920–37	Pie Traynor, Pit	308
1952–68	Eddie Mathews, Mil	369
1960–73	**Ron Santo, Chi**	**395**

Most Total Chances

1878–85	Ned Williamson, Chi	2820
1881–94	Jerry Denny, Pro	4622
1885–98	Billy Nash, Bos	5041
1920–37	Pie Traynor, Pit	6140
1952–68	Eddie Mathews, Mil	6665
1960–73	**Ron Santo, Chi**	**6853**

Highest Fielding Average

1878–85	Ned Williamson, Chi	.873
1876–88	Ezra Sutton, Bos	.878
1880–92	Tom Burns, Chi	.890
1890–96	Chippy McGarr, Cle	.903
1894–00	Lave Cross, Phi	.944
1903–17	Hans Lobert, Cin	.945
1913–21	Charlie Deal, Chi	.961
1912–27	Heinie Groh, Cin	.967
1972–92	**Ken Reitz, StL**	**.970**

DID YOU KNOW . . . *That Alexander Cartwright is the baseball genius who set the bases exactly 90 feet apart?*

AMERICAN LEAGUE

Most Double Plays

1901–07	Lave Cross, Phi	71
1901–08	Jimmy Collins, Bos	111
1901–10	Bill Bradley, Cle	160
1908–22	Frank Baker, Phi	259
1923–35	Willie Kamm, Chi	295
1934–45	Harlond Clift, StL	307
1944–62	Eddie Yost, Was	345
1955–77	**Brooks Robinson, Bal**	**618**

Most Total Chances

1901–07	Lave Cross, Phi	2769
1901–08	Bill Coughlin, Det	3359
1901–10	Bill Bradley, Cle	4227
1908–22	Frank Baker, Phi	5597
1923–35	Willie Kamm, Chi	5608
1944–62	Eddie Yost, Was	6285
1955–77	**Brooks Robinson, Bal**	**9165**

Highest Fielding Average

1901–07	Lave Cross, Phi	.944
1908–22	Frank Baker, Phi	.945
1908–24	Larry Gardner, Bos	.949
1921–31	Joe Dugan, NY	.959
1923–35	Willie Kamm, Chi	.967
1943–57	George Kell, Det	.969
1955–77	**Brooks Robinson,**	

DID YOU KNOW . . . *That Alexander Cartwright established three outs for an inning and nine innings for a game in 1845?*

MAJOR LEAGUE

Most Double Plays

1876–88	Ezra Sutton, Bos, NL	85
1878–90	Ned Williamson, Chi, NL	119
1879–92	Hick Carpenter, Cin, AA	142
1881–94	Jerry Denny, Pro, NL	145
1883–96	Arlie Latham, StL, AA	251
1908–22	Frank Baker, Phi, AL	259
1912–27	Heinie Groh, Cin, NL	266
1923–35	Willie Kamm, Chi, AL	295
1920–37	Pie Traynor, Pit, NL	308
1944–62	Eddie Yost, Was, AL	345
1952–68	Eddie Mathews, Mil, NL	369
1960–73	Ron Santo, Chi, NL	395
1955–77	**Brooks Robinson, Bal, AL**	**618**

Most Total Chances

1876–88	Ezra Sutton, Bos, NL	2236
1878–90	Ned Williamson, Chi, NL	2998
1879–92	Hick Carpenter, Cin, AA	3953
1881–94	Jerry Denny, Pro, NL	4622
1883–96	Arlie Latham, StL, AA	6303
1891–07	Lave Cross, Phi, NL	6401
1895–08	Jimmy Collins, Bos, AL	6539
1952–68	Eddie Mathews, Mil, NL	6665
1960–73	Ron Santo, Chi, NL	6853
1955–77	**Brooks Robinson, Bal, AL**	**9165**

Highest Fielding Average

1878–88	Ezra Sutton, Bos, NL	.878
1880–91	Art Whitney, Pit, AA	.881
1886–92	Tom Burns, Chi, NL	.890
1884–96	Chippy McGarr, Bos, NL	.903
1887–07	Lave Cross, Phi, NL	.942
1899–15	Bill Bradley, Cle, AL	.943
1903–17	Hans Lobert, Cin, NL	.945
1912–21	Charlie Deal, Chi, NL	.961
1912–27	Heinie Groh, Cin, NL	.967
1923–35	Willie Kamm, Chi, AL	.967
1943–57	George Kell, Det, AL	.969
1955–77	**Brooks Robinson, Bal, AL**	**.971**

THIRD BASE

NATIONAL LEAGUE SUMMARY

Top Record Producers

1	Ned Williamson, Chi	6
2	Jerry Denny, Pro	5
2	Billy Nash, Bos	5
2	Pie Traynor, Pit	5
5	Eddie Mathews, Mil	4

Most Outstanding Record Producers

Pie Traynor, Pit	5 for 176 years
Billy Nash, Bos	5 for 159 years
Heinie Groh, Cin	2 for 65 years
Ron Santo, Chi	3 for 45 years
Eddie Matthews, Mil	4 for 34 years

AMERICAN LEAGUE SUMMARY

Top Record Producers

1	Lave Cross, Phi	6
1	Frank Baker	6
1	Brooks Robinson, Bal	6
2	Bill Bradley, Cle	5
2	Eddie Yost, Was	5
6	Willie Kamm, Chi	4

Most Outstanding Record Producers

Eddie Yost, Was	5 for 75 years
Frank Baker, Phi	6 for 72 years
Brooks Robinson, Bal	6 for 66 years
Bill Bradley, Cle	6 for 60 years
Willie Kamm, Chi	4 for 60 years

MAJOR LEAGUE SUMMARY

Top Record Producers

1	Ezra Sutton, Bos, NL	6
1	Brooks Robinson, Bal, AL	6
3	Ned Williamson, Chi, NL	5
3	Hick Carpenter, Cin, AA	5
3	Jerry Denny, Pro, NL	5
3	Arlie Latham, StL, AA	5
3	Lave Cross, Phi, NL	5

Most Outstanding Record Producers

Jimmy Collins, Bos, AL	2 for 129 years
Lave Cross, Phi, NL	5 for 101 years
Arlie Latham, StL, AA	5 for 70 years
Brooks Robinson, Bal, AL	6 for 66 years
Pie Traynor, Pit, NL	2 for 50 years

PIE TRAYNOR
Many people called Pie Traynor the best third baseman ever. (Fans of Brooks Robinson will disagree.) Though Pie committed more errors than anyone else in this century (in the National League), some of his other records back up his claim to excellence.

THIRD BASE

Ned Williamson, Jerry Denny and Billy Nash were three outstanding third basemen prior to 1900. Nash was extremely effective, as his five records were quite difficult to break. His records have accumulated a total of 159 years in longevity, which is good enough to take the number two position on the all-time list.

After 1900, Hall of Famers Pie Traynor and Eddie Mathews were two of the NL's finest. Traynor is the NL's all-time leader in putouts with 2,291. He was the first to participate in 300 double plays and gather 3,000 assists and 6,000 total chances.

Mathews has played in more games than any NL third sacker, was the first to reach 4,000 in assists and is second in double plays and total chances.

Heinie Groh established two super records during his 1912–1927 career. His 266 double plays lasted 10 years, and his fine fielding average of .967 was an achievement that lasted for 55 years!

Ron Santo has the most unbroken records, and he is sure to remain on the Most Outstanding list in the years to come. Santo is the present leader in assists, with 4,581; double plays, with 395; and total chances, with 6,853.

One of the most successful of the early third basemen was "Home Run" Frank Baker. Baker starred from 1908 through 1922 and established all six positive records. His talents are apparent in the fact that only Eddie Yost has records that lasted more years.

Baker was the first to play in 1,500 games, put out 2,000 runners and make 3,000 assists. He was also the first to go over the 5,000 level in total chances.

Eddie Yost starred from 1944 through 1962 and is second in almost every category. Yost's five marks lasted longer than any AL third basemen.

It shouldn't be long, however, before Brooks Robinson takes over the top spot. Brooks owns all six positive records and it will be a long, long time before another third baseman surpasses them.

Willie Kamm and Larry Gardner deserve to be mentioned for their fine work with the glove. Kamm established four records for 60 years, while Gardner was close behind with three marks for 56 years.

The Major League category of records is important because it gives players who played a number of years in several of the various "major leagues" an opportunity to show their career achievements. Perfect examples are Jimmy Collins, Lave Cross and Arlie Latham. They do not show up well in the separate leagues, but when their achievements are combined, they prove to have been some of baseball's finest third basemen.

An oddity occurs in the case of Jimmy Collins, who has only two ML records, but they have lasted longer than all others put together. Collins, who is a Hall of Famer, put out 2,372 men and had 6,539 total chances.

His putouts record was 69 years old when Brooks Robinson passed it. His total chances mark stood for 60 years before Eddie Mathews came along.

Pie Traynor is another Hall of Famer with two Major League records of exception. Traynor's 1,864 games played was in the book for a quarter century, as was his double play mark.

Brooks Robinson is not only the most prolific AL record holder, but all six of his marks are also *unbroken* Major League records. It is easy to see what a superior third baseman he has been.

CATCHING

NATIONAL LEAGUE			AMERICAN LEAGUE			MAJOR LEAGUE		

Most Games

1876–83	John Clapp, StL, NL	323	1901–08	Ossee Schreckengost, Phi	676	1876–83	John Clapp, StL, NL	323
1879–88	Barney Gilligan, Pro, NL	458	1901–12	Lou Criger, Bos	714	1879–88	Barney Gilligan, Pro, NL	458
1878–89	Silver Flint, Chi, NL	727	1901–16	Billy Sullivan, Chi	1033	1878–89	Silver Flint, Chi, NL	727
1878–93	Charlie Bennett, Det, NL	954	1909–25	Oscar Stanage, Det	1073	1878–93	Charlie Bennett, Det, NL	954
1884–00	Jack Clements, Phi, NL	1073	1915–26	Hank Severeid, StL	1181	1884–00	Jack Clements, Phi, NL	1073
1886–02	Wilbert Robinson, Bal, NL	1316	1912–28	Ray Schalk, Chi	1721	1886–02	Wilbert Robinson, Bal, NL	1316
1884–12	Deacon McGuire, Was, NL	1611	**1929–47**	**Rick Ferrell, Was**	**1805**	1884–12	Deacon McGuire, Was, NL	1611
1912–29	Ray Schalk, Chi, AL	1726				1912–29	Ray Schalk, Chi, AL	1726
1922–41	Gabby Hartnett, Chi, NL	1790				1922–41	Gabby Hartnett, Chi, NL	1790
1928–47	Al Lopez, Bkn, NL	1918				1928–47	Al Lopez, Bkn, NL	1918
1972–88	**Bob Boone, Phi, NL**	**2056**				**1972–88**	**Bob Boone, Phi, NL**	

Most Putouts

1876–83	John Clapp, StL, NL	1519	1901–08	Ossee Schreckengost, Phi	4057	1876–83	John Clapp, StL, NL	1519
1879–88	Barney Gilligan, Pro, NL	2232	1901–16	Billy Sullivan, Chi	4409	1879–88	Barney Gilligan, Pro, NL	2232
1878–89	Silver Flint, Chi, NL	3339	1915–26	Hank Severeid, StL	5340	1878–89	Silver Flint, Chi, NL	3339
1878–93	Charlie Bennett, Det, NL	4954	1912–28	Ray Schalk, Chi	7171	1878–93	Charlie Bennett, Det, NL	4954
1886–02	Wilbert Robinson, Bal, NL	5089	1928–46	Bill Dickey, NY	7965	1886–02	Wilbert Robinson, Bal, NL	5089
1884–12	Deacon McGuire, Was, NL	6907	1946–65	Yogi Berra, NY	8711	1884–12	Deacon McGuire, Was, NL	6907
1912–29	Ray Schalk, Chi, AL	7171	**1961–76**	**Bill Freehan, Det**	**9941**	1912–29	Ray Schalk, Chi, AL	7171
1922–41	Gabby Hartnett, Chi, NL	7292				1922–41	Gabby Hartnett, Chi, NL	7292
1928–46	Bill Dickey, NY, AL	7965				1928–46	Bill Dickey, NY, AL	7965
1946–65	Yogi Berra, NY, AL	8711				1946–65	Yogi Berra, NY, AL	8711
1957–70	John Roseboro, LA, NL	9291				1957–70	John Roseboro, LA, NL	9291
1961–76	Bill Freehan, Det, AL	9941				**1961–76**	**Bill Freehan, Det, AL**	**9941**
1972–88	**Bob Boone, Phi, NL**	**10,199**						

Most Assists

1876–83	John Clapp, StL	354	1901–08	Ossee Schreckengost, Phi	852	1876–83	John Clapp, StL, NL	354
1880–87	Fatty Briody, Cle	448	1901–12	Lou Criger, Bos	968	1883–87	Charlie Reipschlager, NY, AA	484
1879–88	Barney Gilligan, Pro	583	1901–16	Billy Sullivan, Chi	1176	1879–88	Barney Gilligan, Pro, NL	583
1878–89	Silver Flint, Chi	991	1909–25	Oscar Stanage, Det	1340	1878–89	Silver Flint, Chi, NL	991
1878–93	Charlie Bennett, Det	1017	**1912–28**	**Ray Schalk, Chi**	**1811**	1886–02	Wilbert Robinson, Bal, NL	1443
1885–01	Deacon McGuire, Was	1102				1884–03	Chief Zimmer, Cle, NL	1580
1884–03	Chief Zimmer, Cle	1328				**1884–12**	**Deacon McGuire, Was, NL**	**1859**
1901–11	Bill Bergen, Bkn	1444						
1901–13	Johnny Kling, Chi	1552						
1902–16	**Red Dooin, Phi**	**1590**						

CATCHING

NATIONAL LEAGUE		AMERICAN LEAGUE		MAJOR LEAGUE	

NATIONAL LEAGUE

Most Errors

1876–83	John Clapp, StL	229
1879–88	Barney Gilligan, Pro	271
1878–89	**Silver Flint, Chi**	**416**

Most Errors after 1900

1900–09	Frank Bowerman, NY	118
1901–11	Bill Bergen, Bkn	153
1901–13	Johnny Kling, Chi	198
1902–16	**Red Dooin, Phi**	**275**

Most Double Plays

1876–83	John Clapp, StL	24
1880–87	Fatty Briody, Cle	27
1879–88	Barney Gilligan, Pro	58
1878–93	Charlie Bennett, Det	111
1884–03	Chief Zimmer, Cle	115
1901–13	Jimmy Kling, Chi	122
1911–29	Ivy Wingo, Cin	141
1923–40	Jimmie Wilson, Phi	153
1922–41	**Gabby Hartnett, Chi**	**173**

Most Total Chances

1876–83	John Clapp, StL	2102
1879–88	Barney Gilligan, Pro	3186
1878–89	Silver Flint, Chi	4746
1878–93	Charlie Bennett, Det	6339
1901–13	Johnny Kling, Chi	7047
1922–41	Gabby Hartnett, Chi	8685
1961–74	Johnny Edwards, Cin	9710
1967–83	Johnny Bench, Cin	10,207
1972–88	**Bob Boone, Phi**	**11,445**

AMERICAN LEAGUE

Most Errors

1901–08	Ossee Schreckengost, Phi	136
1909–25	Oscar Stanage, Det	223

Most Double Plays

1901–08	Ossee Schreckengost, Phi	45
1901–12	Lou Criger, Bos	78
1901–16	Billy Sullivan, Chi	98
1909–25	Oscar Stanage, Det	109
1912–28	**Ray Schalk, Chi**	**221**

Most Total Chances

1901–08	Ossee Schreckengost, Phi	5045
1901–16	Billy Sullivan, Chi	5714
1915–26	Hank Severeid, StL	6477
1912–28	Ray Schalk, Chi	9157
1946–65	Yogi Berra, NY	9619
1961–76	**Bill Freehan, Det**	**10,734**

DID YOU KNOW . . . *That Roger Bresnahan, catcher for the NY Giants, invented the shin guards—in 1906?*

MAJOR LEAGUE

Most Errors

1876–83	John Clapp, StL, NL	229
1879–88	Barney Gilligan, Pro, NL	271
1878–89	Silver Flint, Chi, NL	416
1884–12	**Deacon McGuire, Was, NL**	**525**

Most Errors after 1900

1901–08	Ossee Schreckengost, Phi, AL	136
1901–11	Bill Bergen, Bkn, NL	153
1901–13	Johnny Kling, Chi, NL	198
1902–16	**Red Dooin, Phi, NL**	**275**

Most Double Plays

1876–83	John Clapp, StL, NL	24
1883–87	Charlie Reipschlager, NY, AA	24
1879–88	Barney Gilligan, Pro, NL	58
1878–93	Charlie Bennett, Det, NL	111
1884–03	Chief Zimmer, Cle, NL	135
1884–12	Deacon McGuire, Was, NL	142
1911–28	Steve O'Neill, Cle, AL	175
1912–29	**Ray Schalk, Chi, AL**	**221**

Most Total Chances

1876–83	John Clapp, StL, NL	2102
1879–88	Barney Gilligan, Pro, NL	3186
1878–89	Silver Flint, Chi, NL	4746
1878–93	Charlie Bennett, Det, NL	6339
1886–02	Wilbert Robinson, Bal, NL	6946
1884–12	Deacon McGuire, Was, NL	9291
1946–65	Yogi Berra, NY, AL	9619
1957–70	John Roseboro, LA, NL	10,073
1961–76	Bill Freehan, Det, AL	10,734
1972–88	**Bob Boone, Phi, NL**	**11,445**

CATCHING

NATIONAL LEAGUE

Highest Fielding Average

1876–83	John Clapp, StL	.891
1879–86	Jack Rowe, Buf	.918
1883–87	Mert Hackett, Bos	.920
1878–93	Charlie Bennett, Det	.938
1892–99	John Grim, Bkn	.944
1892–00	Wilbert Robinson, Bal	.954
1893–01	Ed McFarland, Phi	.964
1902–06	Jack O'Neill, StL	.974
1906–18	George Gibson, Pit	.977
1911–21	Bill Killifer, Phi	.981
1916–25	Walter Schmidt, Pit	.982
1914–27	Frank Snyder, StL	.982
1913–28	Bubbles Hargrave, Cin	.984
1927–35	Shanty Hogan, Bos	.985
1949–65	Del Crandall, Mil	.989
1957–67	John Roseboro, LA	.989
1961–71	**Tom Haller, SF**	.992
1961–74	**Johnny Edwards, Cin**	.992

AMERICAN LEAGUE

Highest Fielding Average

1901–08	Ossee Schreckengost, Phi	.970
1904–11	Red Kleinow, NY	.970
1901–12	Lou Criger, Bos	.976
1901–16	Billy Sullivan, Chi	.976
1910–17	John Henry, Was	.979
1915–26	Hank Severeid, StL	.981
1925–37	Mickey Cochrane, Phi	.985
1926–38	Ray Hayworth, Det	.986
1928–46	Bill Dickey, NY	.988
1932–46	Frank Pytlak, Cle	.988
1939–51	**Buddy Rosar, Phi**	.993
1955–68	**Elston Howard, NY**	.993
1961–76	**Bill Freehan, Det**	.993

MAJOR LEAGUE

Highest Fielding Average

1876–83	John Clapp, StL, NL	.891
1879–86	Jack Rowe, Buf, NL	.918
1883–87	Mert Hackett, Bos, NL	.920
1882–91	Jim Keenan, Cin, AA	.934
1884–93	Jocko Milligan, Phi, AA	.936
1881–99	John Grim, Bkn, NL	.944
1886–02	Wilbert Robinson, Bal, NL	.944
1902–06	Jack O'Neill, StL, NL	.974
1910–18	John Henry, Was, AL	.979
1911–26	Hank Severeid, StL, AL	.981
1913–30	Bubbles Hargrave, Cin, NL	.984
1925–37	Shanty Hogan, Bos, NL	.985
1925–37	Mickey Cochrane, Phi, AL	.985
1928–46	Bill Dickey, NY, AL	.988
1939–51	**Buddy Rosar, Phi, AL**	.993
1955–68	**Elston Howard, NY, AL**	.993
1961–76	**Bill Freehan, Det, AL**	.993

NATIONAL LEAGUE SUMMARY

Top Record Producers

1	John Clapp, StL	6
1	Charlie Bennett, Det	6
3	Barney Gilligan, Pro	5
3	Johnny Kling, Chi	5
5	Silver Flint, Chi	4
5	Gabby Hartnett, Chi	4

Most Outstanding Record Producers

Gabby Hartnett, Chi	4 for 109 years
Johnny Kling, Chi	5 for 78 years
Charlie Bennett, Det	6 for 71 years
Red Dooin, Phi	1 for 72 years
Al Lopez, Bkn	1 for 42 years

AMERICAN LEAGUE SUMMARY

Top Record Producers

1	Ossee Schreckengost, Phi	6
1	Billy Sullivan, Chi	6
3	Ray Schalk, Chi	5
4	Lou Criger, Bos	4
4	Hank Severeid, StL	4

Most Outstanding Record Producers

Ray Schalk, Chi	5 for 194 years
Billy Sullivan, Chi	6 for 48 years
Rick Ferrell, Was	1 for 41 years
Bill Freehan, Det	3 for 36 years
Ossee Schreckengost, Phi	6 for 31 years

MAJOR LEAGUE SUMMARY

Top Record Producers

1	John Clapp, StL, NL	6
2	Barney Gilligan, Pro, NL	5
2	Wilbert Robinson, Bal, NL	5
2	Deacon McGuire, Was, NL	5
5	Silver Flint, Chi, NL	4
5	Charlie Bennett, Det, NL	4

Most Outstanding Record Producers

Deacon McGuire, Was, NL	5 for 179 years
Ray Schalk, Chi, AL	3 for 83 years
Al Lopez, Bkn, NL	1 for 41 years
Charlie Bennett, Det, NL	4 for 35 years
Wilbert Robinson, Bal, NL	4 for 35 years
Bill Freehan, Det, AL	3 for 30 years

John Clapp, Charlie Bennett, Barney Gilligan and Silver Flint were four of the finest catchers during the early years. Of these, Bennett created the records most difficult to break.

After 1900, Red Dooin, Johnny Kling, Gabby Hartnett and Al Lopez set some of the most impressive records. Lopez's 1,861 games caught is the most ever by a National League catcher. Red Dooin is the assists king with 1,590, a record that has stood since 1916. Gabby Hartnett, a Hall of Famer, is atop the double play record, while the most active of all National League catchers is Johnny Bench of the Reds. Bench claims two unbroken marks in putouts and total chances and is the only National League catcher with more than 9,000 putouts and

10,000 total chances. He will definitely move up in the standings as the years go by. Bench is a sure bet for Hall of Fame honors.

The catchers who set the standards for fewest errors and highest fielding averages were Jack O'Neill and Shanty Hogan. O'Neill's .974 average lasted 12 years. In 1935, Hogan hung up his spikes with a super .985 mark that would stay in the book for 30 years, until Del Crandall came along. Crandall came in with with a fabulous .989 career average in 1965. He was matched by John Roseboro in 1967, and these marks stood until Tom Haller became the new leader with his super .992 average in 1971. He was joined by Johnny Edwards in 1974, and the two of them are the present champions.

CATCHING

Ossee Schreckengost of the Athletics had the first American League career worthy of mention. He was the first to play in more than 500 games, and his records lasted a number of years before being broken.

Lou Criger was the next catcher to accumulate numbers that would place him in the record book during his fine career from 1901 to 1912. Criger broke Schreckengost's games, assists, and double play records, and then added the fielding average record as he passed Red Kleinow's and Schreckengost's .970 mark.

Billy Sullivan was another catcher who began his career during the first year of the American League. Sully caught from 1901 through 1916 and was the first to put on the pads for 1,000 games. He passed Schreckengost in put-outs and total chances, passed Criger in assists and double plays and tied Criger in fielding average. Sully's records have stood the second longest period of time.

The records that have been the most difficult to break are those of Hall of Famer Ray Schalk. Schalk, who starred for the White Sox from 1912 to 1928, has had five records, two of which have never been broken.

The catcher who has played the most games is Rick Ferrel. Bill Dickey and Yogi Berra have set records for most putouts, but Bill Freehan is the present champion in that category. Freehan can be proud of having the most unbroken records, as no one has passed his 10,734 total chances, and he shares the fielding average of .993 with Elston Howard and Buddy Rosar.

One of the finest catching careers was had by Deacon McGuire, who starred from 1884 to 1912. He was the first to catch more than 1,500 games and make 6,000 putouts, and his 1,859 assists are the most in history. McGuire was the first to reach the 9,000 total chances plateau and is in third place in double plays with 142. His records have lasted more years than those of any catcher in baseball.

Ray Schalk, the outstanding American League receiver, is second with his three super records, and Al Lopez is third on the strength of having caught the most games. Bill Freehan remains the most active catcher, with the most putouts and total chances.

LEFT FIELD

NATIONAL LEAGUE

Most Games

1876–83	Tom York, Pro	585
1880–86	Pete Gillespie, NY	638
1878–88	Abner Dalrymple, Chi	919
1880–89	George Wood, Det	927
1879–90	Joe Hornung, Bos	938
1892–01	Jesse Burkett, Cle	1360
1898–12	Jimmy Sheckard, Chi	1985
1894–15	Fred Clarke, Pit	2191
1909–26	**Zack Wheat, Bkn**	**2288**

Most Putouts

1876–83	Tom York, Pro	1074
1880–86	Pete Gillespie, NY	1138
1878–88	Abner Dalrymple, Chi	1612
1879–90	Joe Hornung, Bos	1642
1892–98	Elmer Smith, Pit	1850
1892–01	Jesse Burkett, Cle	2728
1898–12	Jimmy Sheckard, Chi	3763
1894–15	Fred Clarke, Pit	4788
1909–26	**Zack Wheat, Bkn**	**4837**

Most Assists

1876–83	Tom York, Pro	84
1878–88	Abner Dalrymple, Chi	140
1879–90	Joe Hornung, Bos	143
1892–01	Jesse Burkett, Cle	180
1898–12	**Jimmy Sheckard, Chi**	**264**

Most Errors

1876–83	Tom York, Pro	158
1878–88	**Abner Dalrymple, Chi**	**280**

Most Errors after 1900

1900–12	Jimmy Sheckard, Chi	127
1909–26	**Zack Wheat, Bkn**	**178**

Most Double Plays

1876–83	Tom York, Pro	15
1880–86	Pete Gillespie, NY	20
1878–88	Abner Dalrymple, Chi	25
1880–89	George Wood, Det	25
1883–92	Cliff Carroll, Pro	25
1892–98	Elmer Smith, Pit	29
1892–01	Jesse Burkett, Cle	44
1898–12	**Jimmy Sheckard, Chi**	**64**

AMERICAN LEAGUE

Most Games

1902–05	Jesse Burkett, StL	565
1902–10	Topsy Hartsel, Phi	1110
1902–11	Pat Dougherty, Chi	1117
1911–21	Duffy Lewis, Bos	1432
1912–25	Bobby Veach, Det	1742
1922–38	**Goose Goslin, Was**	**2007**

Most Putouts

1902–05	Jesse Burkett, StL	1072
1902–10	Topsy Hartsel, Phi	1744
1911–21	Duffy Lewis, Bos	2610
1912–25	Bobby Veach, Det	3653
1922–38	**Goose Goslin, Was**	**4395**

Most Assists

1902–05	Jesse Burkett, StL	62
1901–10	Matty McIntyre, Det	110
1911–21	**Duffy Lewis, Bos**	**207**

Most Errors

1902–05	Jesse Burkett, StL	81
1902–11	Pat Dougherty, Chi	118
1911–21	Duffy Lewis, Bos	122
1922–38	**Goose Goslin, Was**	**195**

Most Double Plays

1902–05	Jesse Burkett, StL	18
1901–10	Matty McIntyre, Det	25
1911–21	Duffy Lewis, Bos	40
1912–25	**Bobby Veach, Det**	**41**

MAJOR LEAGUE

Most Games

1876–85	Tom York, Pro, NL	690
1878–88	Abner Dalrymple, Chi, NL	919
1879–90	Joe Hornung, Bos, NL	1072
1880–92	George Wood, Det, NL	1232
1892–05	Jesse Burkett, Cle, NL	1925
1898–12	Jimmy Sheckard, Chi, NL	1989
1894–15	Fred Clarke, Pit, NL	2191
1909–27	**Zack Wheat, Bkn, NL**	**2350**

Most Putouts

1876–85	Tom York, Pro, NL	1174
1878–88	Abner Dalrymple, Chi, NL	1612
1879–90	Joe Hornung, Bos, NL	1892
1880–92	George Wood, Det, NL	2061
1892–05	Jesse Burkett, Cle, NL	3800
1894–15	Fred Clarke, Pit, NL	4788
1909–27	**Zack Wheat, Bkn, NL**	**4942**

Most Assists

1876–85	Tom York, Pro, NL	91
1878–88	Abner Dalrymple, Chi, NL	140
1879–90	Joe Hornung, Bos, NL	175
1880–92	George Wood, Det, NL	193
1892–05	Jesse Burkett, Cle, NL	242
1898–12	**Jimmy Sheckard, Chi, NL**	**265**

Most Errors

1876–85	Tom York, Pro, NL	178
1878–88	Abner Dalrymple, Chi, NL	280
1892–05	**Jesse Burkett, Cle, NL**	**321**

Most Errors after 1900

1902–05	Jesse Burkett, StL, AL	81
1902–11	Pat Dougherty, Chi, AL	118
1900–12	Jimmy Sheckard, Chi, NL	127
1909–26	Zack Wheat, Bkn, NL	178
1922–38	**Goose Goslin, Was, AL**	**195**

Most Double Plays

1876–85	Tom York, Pro, NL	16
1880–86	Pete Gillespie, NY, NL	20
1878–88	Abner Dalrymple, Chi, NL	25
1879–90	Joe Hornung, Bos, NL	33
1880–92	George Wood, Det, NL	44
1892–05	Jesse Burkett, Cle, NL	62
1898–12	**Jimmy Sheckard, Chi, NL**	**64**

LEFT FIELD

NATIONAL LEAGUE			AMERICAN LEAGUE			MAJOR LEAGUE		
Most Total Chances			*Most Total Chances*			*Most Total Chances*		
1876–83	Tom York, Pro	1316	1902–05	Jesse Burkett, StL	1215	1876–85	Tom York, Pro, NL	1443
1880–86	Pete Gillespie, NY	1350	1902–10	Topsy Hartsel, Phi	1909	1878–88	Abner Dalrymple, Chi, NL	2032
1878–88	Abner Dalrymple, Chi	2032	1911–21	Duffy Lewis, Bos	2939	1879–90	Joe Hornung, Bos, NL	2242
1892–98	Elmer Smith, Pit	2137	**1922–38**	**Goose Goslin, Was**	**4791**	1880–92	George Wood, Det, NL	2519
1892–01	Jesse Burkett, Cle	3175				1892–05	Jesse Burkett, Cle, NL	4363
1898–12	Jimmy Sheckard, Chi	4197				1894–15	Fred Clarke, Pit, NL	5301
1894–15	**Fred Clarke, Pit**	**5301**				**1909–27**	**Zack Wheat, Bkn, NL**	**5349**
Highest Fielding Average			*Highest Fielding Average*			*Highest Fielding Average*		
1876–83	Tom York, Pro	.884	1902–05	Jesse Burkett, StL	.934	1876–85	Tom York, Pro, NL	.879
1880–86	Pete Gillespie, NY	.900	1901–10	Matty McIntyre, Det	.961	1880–86	Pete Gillespie, NY, NL	.900
1879–90	Joe Hornung, Bos	.921	1912–16	Hank Shanks, Was	.973	1879–90	Joe Hornung, Bos, NL	.921
1893–97	Eddie Burke, NY	.927	1923–36	Heinie Manush, Was	.980	1893–97	Eddie Burke, NY, NL	.927
1893–01	Ed Delahanty, Phi	.953	1928–38	Al Simmons, Phi	.986	1888–02	Ed Delahanty, Phi, NL	.953
1894–05	Joe Kelley, Bal	.961	1949–53	Hoot Evers, Det	.986	1894–05	Joe Kelley, Bal, NL	.961
1905–16	Sherry Magee, Phi	.972	1949–58	Gene Woodling, NY	.989	1912–16	Hank Shanks, Was, AL	.973
1927–32	Chick Hafey, StL	.973	1956–60	Charlie Maxwell, Det	.990	1927–32	Chick Hafey, StL, NL	.973
1926–33	Riggs Stephenson, Chi	.975	**1968–82**	**Joe Rudi, Oak**	**.991**	1926–33	Riggs Stephenson, Chi, NL	.975
1935–47	Augie Galan, Chi	.982				1923–36	Heinie Manush, Was, AL	.980
1946–53	Sid Gordon, Bos	.984				1928–38	Al Simmons, Phi, AL	.986
1967–74	**Pete Rose, Cin**	**.991**				1949–53	Hoot Evers, Det, AL	.986
						1949–58	Gene Woodling, NY, AL	.989
						1956–60	Charlie Maxwell, Det, AL	.990
						1967–74	**Pete Rose, Cin, NL**	**.991**
						1968–82	**Joe Rudi, Oak, AL**	**.991**

NATIONAL LEAGUE SUMMARY			AMERICAN LEAGUE SUMMARY			MAJOR LEAGUE SUMMARY		
Top Record Producers			*Top Record Producers*			*Top Record Producers*		
1 Tom York, Pro		6	1 Jesse Burkett, StL		6	1 Tom York, Pro, NL		6
2 Pete Gillespie, NY		5	2 Duffy Lewis, Bos		5	1 Joe Hornung, Bos, NL		6
2 Abner Dalrymple, Chi		5	3 Topsy Hartsell, Phi		3	3 Abner Dalrymple, Chi, NL		5
2 Jesse Burkett, Cle		5	3 Bobby Veach, Det		3	3 George Wood, Det, NL		5
2 Jimmy Sheckard, Chi		5	3 Goose Goslin, Was		3	3 Jesse Burkett, Cle, NL		5
			3 Matty McIntyre, Det		3			
Most Outstanding Record Producers			*Most Outstanding Record Producers*			*Most Outstanding Record Producers*		
Jimmy Sheckard, Chi	5 for 161 years		Goose Goslin, Was	3 for 150 years		Zack Wheat, Bkn, NL	3 for 183 years	
Zack Wheat, Bkn	2 for 124 years		Duffy Lewis, Bos	5 for 96 years		Jimmy Sheckard, Chi, NL	3 for 155 years	
Fred Clarke, Pit	3 for 95 years		Bobby Veach, Det	3 for 89 years		George Wood, Det, NL	5 for 65 years	
Jesse Burkett, Cle	5 for 55 years					Jesse Burkett, Cle, NL	5 for 41 years	
Joe Hornung, Bos	4 for 37 years					Fred Clarke, Pit, NL	3 for 36 years	

LEFT FIELD

Jimmy Sheckard has the most impressive set of records, which have earned him the top position. Zack Wheat is a solid second, and he and Sheckard both have two longstanding unbroken records of which to be proud.

Fred Clarke takes the number three spot on the all-time records list as a result of being the most active leftfielder in National League history. Clarke's 5,301 total chances just edges out Zack Wheat for that honor.

Prior to 1900, the most outstanding leftfielders were Tom York, Pete Gillespie, Joe Hornung and Abner Dalrymple.

Jesse Burkett was one of the first outstanding leftfielders in the American League and was the first to appear in 500 games. Thus he has the honor of being the top record producer.

The most impressive records were created by the Hall of Famer Goose Goslin, who can boast of having three unbroken marks. The Goose leads in games, putouts and total chances.

Duffy Lewis of the Red Sox was also exceptional and has posted five records for 96 years and second place. Duffy was the first to come up with more than 2,000 putouts, and his 207 assists still stands.

Bobby Veach has the number three position with three marks lasting 89 years. He had the honor of being the first to play in more than 1,500 games and register 3,000 putouts and he is presently the double play king in the American League.

Joe Rudi is the fielding average leader at .991, but Hank Shanks has the most impressive and longest-lasting average record. Shanks averaged .973 from 1912 through 1916 with the poor gloves of his era—a remarkable achievement, which lasted 20 years before Heinie Manush became the first to reach the .980 plateau in 1936.

In the Major League category, Zack Wheat and Jimmy Sheckard are the premier leftfielders among the ranks of outstanding producers. Zack commands the number one position with three records lasting 183 years, while Sheckard's three marks have been good for 155 years. Wheat is tops in games played, putouts, and total chances, while Sheckard is king in assists and double plays.

Newcomer Pete Rose joins Joe Rudi with the highest fielding average of .991, and Hank Shanks has the distinction of having the longest reign in the fielding average category. His fine achievement of .973 lasted 17 years before it was broken by leftfielders who had much better gloves to work with.

Pete Rose is now famous for passing Ty Cobb in the hit parade, but he was a valuable player on defense as well. He did not possess the same grace, speed or strong arm as other outfielders, but he could play many positions and do an adequate job. Rose played third base, first base and the outfield and he always finished high in fielding averages.

CENTER FIELD

NATIONAL LEAGUE			AMERICAN LEAGUE			MAJOR LEAGUE		
Most Games			*Most Games*			*Most Games*		
1879–84	Pete Hotaling, Cle	507	1901–05	Jimmy Barrett, Det	591	1876–84	Jack Remsen, Chi, NL	330
1876–90	Paul Hines, Pro	1204	1901–06	Chick Stahl, Bos	776	1876–86	Jim O'Rourke, NY, NL	478
1879–92	George Gore, Chi	1204	1902–08	Fielder Jones, Chi	1158	1879–88	Pete Hotaling, Cle, NL	825
1888–02	Dummy Hoy, Was	1295	1908–19	Clyde Milan, Was	1669	1876–91	Paul Hines, Pro, NL	1251
1893–03	George Van Haltren, NY	1537	1905–26	Ty Cobb, Det	2666	1879–92	George Gore, Chi, NL	1297
1916–29	Edd Roush, Cin	1679	**1907–28**	**Tris Speaker, Cle**	**2700**	1887–98	Mike Griffin, Bkn, NL	1478
1927–45	Lloyd Waner, Pit	1704				1888–02	Dummy Hoy, Was, NL	1690
1948–62	Richie Ashburn, Phi	2007				1905–26	Ty Cobb, Det, AL	2666
1951–73	**Willie Mays, NY**	**2843**				1907–28	Tris Speaker, Cle, AL	2700
						1951–73	**Willie Mays, NY, NL**	**2843**
Most Putouts			*Most Putouts*			*Most Putouts*		
1879–84	Pete Hotaling, Cle	880	1901–05	Jimmy Barrett, Det	1268	1876–84	Jack Remsen, Chi, NL	674
1876–90	Paul Hines, Pro	2177	1901–06	Chick Stahl, Bos	1542	1876–86	Jim O'Rourke, NY, NL	927
1881–92	Ned Hanlon, Det	2207	1902–08	Fielder Jones, Chi	2216	1879–88	Pete Hotaling, Cle, NL	1476
1891–98	Mike Griffin, Bkn	2481	1908–19	Clyde Milan, Was	3590	1876–91	Paul Hines, Pro, NL	2258
1888–02	Dummy Hoy, Was	2899	1905–26	Ty Cobb, Det	5207	1879–92	George Gore, Chi, NL	2314
1899–11	Roy Thomas, Phi	3071	**1907–28**	**Tris Speaker, Cle**	**6730**	1887–98	Mike Griffin, Bkn, NL	3535
1907–21	Dode Paskert, Phi	3391				1888–02	Dummy Hoy, Was, NL	3721
1910–29	Max Carey, Pit	4415				1905–26	Ty Cobb, Det, AL	5207
1927–45	Lloyd Waner, Pit	4569				1907–28	Tris Speaker, Cle, AL	6730
1948–62	Richie Ashburn, Phi	5902				**1951–73**	**Willie Mays, NY, NL**	**7095**
1951–73	**Willie Mays, NY**	**7095**						
Most Assists			*Most Assists*			*Most Assists*		
1879–84	Pete Hotaling, Cle	113	1901–05	Jimmy Barrett, Det	101	1876–84	Jack Remsen, Chi, NL	48
1876–90	Paul Hines, Pro	203	1902–08	Fielder Jones, Chi	130	1876–85	Dave Eggler, Buf, NL	49
1879–92	George Gore, Chi	229	1908–19	Clyde Milan, Was	257	1876–86	Jim O'Rourke, NY, NL	86
1893–03	**George Van Haltren, NY**	**242**	1905–26	Ty Cobb, Det	293	1879–88	Pete Hotaling, Cle, NL	163
			1907–28	**Tris Speaker, Cle**	**438**	1876–91	Pete Hines, Pro, NL	211
						1879–92	George Gore, Chi, NL	240
						1887–98	Mike Griffin, Bkn, NL	243
						1888–02	Dummy Hoy, Was, NL	259
						1905–26	Ty Cobb, Det, AL	293
						1907–28	**Tris Speaker, Cle, AL**	**438**
Most Errors			*Most Errors*			*Most Errors*		
1879–84	Pete Hotaling, Cle	169	1901–05	Jimmy Barrett, Det	61	1876–84	Jack Remsen, Chi, NL	81
1876–90	Paul Hines, Pro	292	1901–06	Chick Stahl, Bos	64	1876–86	Jim O'Rourke, NY, NL	138
1879–92	**George Gore, Chi**	**339**	1908–19	Clyde Milan, Was	191	1879–88	Pete Hotaling, Cle, NL	246
			1905–26	Ty Cobb, Det	214	1876–91	Paul Hines, Pro, NL	307
Most Errors after 1900			**1907–28**	**Tris Speaker, Cle**	**222**	**1879–92**	**George Gore, Chi, NL**	**361**
1900–10	**Ginger Beaumont, Pit**	**118**				**1888–02**	**Dummy Hoy, Was, NL**	**361**
Most Double Plays			*Most Double Plays*			*Most Double Plays*		
1879–84	Pete Hotaling, Cle	23	1901–05	Jimmy Barrett, Det	26	1876–84	Jack Remsen, Chi, NL	14
1876–90	Paul Hines, Pro	45	1902–08	Fielder Jones, Chi	39	1879–88	Pete Hotaling, Cle, NL	38
1891–98	Mike Griffin, Bkn	53	1908–19	Clyde Milan, Was	54	1876–91	Paul Hines, Pro, NL	49
1910–29	**Max Carey, Pit**	**55**	1905–26	Ty Cobb, Det	80	1887–98	Mike Griffin, Bkn, NL	75
			1907–28	**Tris Speaker, Cle**	**135**	1905–26	Ty Cobb, Det, AL	80
						1907–28	**Tris Speaker, Cle, AL**	**135**

CENTER FIELD

NATIONAL LEAGUE	AMERICAN LEAGUE	MAJOR LEAGUE

NATIONAL LEAGUE

Most Total Chances

1879–84	Pete Hotaling, Cle	1162
1876–90	Paul Hines, Pro	2658
1879–92	George Gore, Chi	2736
1888–02	Dummy Hoy, Was	3383
1907–21	Dode Paskert, Phi	3694
1910–29	Max Carey, Pit	4788
1927–45	Lloyd Waner, Pit	4886
1948–62	Richie Ashburn, Phi	6183
1951–73	**Willie Mays, NY**	**7431**

Highest Fielding Average

1879–84	Pete Hotaling, Cle	.857
1876–90	Paul Hines, Pro	.890
1881–92	Ned Hanlon, Det	.896
1891–98	Mike Griffin, Bkn	.967
1899–11	Roy Thomas, Phi	.971
1907–14	Tommy Leach, Pit	.975
1931–37	Wally Berger, Bos	.979
1936–41	**Johnny Cooney, Bos**	**.990**

AMERICAN LEAGUE

Most Total Chances

1901–05	Jimmy Barrett, Det	1430
1901–06	Chick Stahl, Bos	1685
1902–08	Fielder Jones, Chi	2403
1908–19	Clyde Milan, Was	4038
1905–26	Ty Cobb, Det	5714
1907–28	**Tris Speaker, Cle**	**7390**

Highest Fielding Average

1901–05	Jimmy Barrett, Det	.957
1901–06	Chick Stahl, Bos	.962
1902–08	Fielder Jones, Chi	.976
1911–24	Amos Strunk, Phi	.980
1929–34	Mule Haas, Phi	.985
1951–57	Jim Busby, Chi	.988
1955–62	Jim Piersall, Bos	.990
1966–71	Ted Uhlaender, Min	.990
1968–78	**Mickey Stanley, Det**	**.991**
1967–84	**Amos Otis, KC**	**.991**

MAJOR LEAGUE

Most Total Chances

1876–84	Jack Remsen, Chi, NL	803
1876–86	Jim O'Rourke, NY, NL	1151
1879–88	Pete Hotaling, Cle, NL	1885
1876–91	Paul Hines, Pro, NL	2776
1879–92	George Gore, Chi, NL	2915
1887–98	Mike Griffin, Bkn, NL	3951
1888–02	Dummy Hoy, Was, NL	4341
1905–26	Ty Cobb, Det, AL	5714
1907–28	Tris Speaker, Cle, AL	7390
1951–73	**Willie Mays, NY, NL**	**7431**

Highest Fielding Average

1876–84	Jack Remsen, Chi, NL	.989
1884–93	Curt Welch, StL, NL	.930
1887–98	Mike Griffin, Bkn, NL	.955
1899–08	Fielder Jones, Chi, AL	.970
1899–11	Roy Thomas, Phi, NL	.971
1907–14	Tommy Leach, Pit, NL	.975
1908–24	Amos Strunk, Chi, NL	.980
1925–38	Mule Haas, Chi, AL	.985
1936–41	Johnny Cooney, Bos, NL	.990
1950–67	Jimmy Piersall, Bos, NL	.990
1966–71	Ted Uhlaender, Min, AL	.990
1968–78	**Mickey Stanley, Det, AL**	**.991**
1967–84	**Amos Otis, KC, AL**	**.991**

NATIONAL LEAGUE SUMMARY

Top Record Producers

1	Pete Hotaling, Cle	6
1	Paul Hines, Pro	6
3	George Gore, Chi	3
3	Dummy Hoy, Was	3
3	Lloyd Waner, Pit	3
3	Richie Ashburn, Phi	3
3	Willie Mays, NY	3
3	Mike Griffin, Bkn	3
3	Max Carey, Pit	3

Most Outstanding Record Producers

George Van Haltren, NY	2 for	111 years
Max Carey, Pit	3 for	91 years
Lloyd Waner, Pit	3 for	48 years
Mike Griffin, Bkn	3 for	48 years
Johnny Cooney, Chi	1 for	45 years
Willie Mays, NY	3 for	39 years
Pete Hotaling, Cle	6 for	36 years
Richie Ashburn, Phi	3 for	36 years
Dummy Hoy, Was	3 for	29 years

AMERICAN LEAGUE SUMMARY

Top Record Producers

1	Jimmy Barrett, Det	6
1	Fielder Jones, Chi	6
2	Clyde Milan, Was	5
2	Ty Cobb, Det	5
2	Tris Speaker, Cle	5

Most Outstanding Record Producers

Tris Speaker, Cle	5 for	300 years
Fielder Jones, Chi	6 for	71 years
Clyde Milan, Was	5 for	35 years

MAJOR LEAGUE SUMMARY

Top Record Producers

1	Jack Remsen, Chi, NL	6
1	Mike Griffin, Bkn, NL	6
2	Jim O'Rourke, NY, NL	5
2	Pete Hotaling, Cle, NL	5
2	Paul Hines, Pro, NL	5
2	Ty Cobb, Det, AL	5
2	Tris Speaker, Cle, AL	5

Most Outstanding Record Producers

Tris Speaker, Cle, AL	5 for	255 years
Dummy Hoy, Was, NL	4 for	96 years
Mike Griffin, Bkn, NL	6 for	54 years
Willie Mays, NY, NL	3 for	45 years

CENTER FIELD

Pete Hotaling, Paul Hines, Mike Griffin and George Gore were the pre-1900 standouts in center field, while George Van Haltren and Dummy Hoy starred at the turn of the century.

Van Haltren became the first to play in 1,500 games, and this record lasted 26 years before Hall of Famer Edd Roush took this honor away from him. However, no one could take the assists mark away from Van Haltren; his two records have lasted so long that he is in the number one position on the all-time longevity list.

Of course, Van Haltren's records are partly due to the playing conditions of his time. His assists record in particular needs some explanation. During the 1890s the ball was "dead"; it did not travel very far. Thus outfielders could play shallow, and it was much easier for them to throw runners out. As the ball became more lively and was hit farther, outfielders had to play deeper. As a result, they found it more difficult to throw runners out. But this doesn't mean that Van Haltren wasn't a fine outfielder with a strong arm. There is no way of comparing his ability with the players of today.

Max Carey was another excellent centerfielder. He possessed great speed, which allowed him to reach balls others could only catch on one bounce. As a result, he became the first to accumulate 4,000 putouts. He also had a fine throwing arm, as indicated by his unbroken double play record. Carey is second on the Most Outstanding Producers list.

Jimmy Barrett was the first American League centerfielder to set records, and Fielder Jones was the first to set records that would stand the test of time. Jones was a super fielder; his .976 fielding average lasted 16 years before it was broken. In all, his marks would last 71 years, the second best in the American League.

Mule Haas obviously was no mule in the cow pasture, as his reign in the fielding department lasted 23 years before Jim Busby could snap it. Haas posted a fine fielding average of .985 from 1929 through 1934, and Busby improved the record to .988 by 1957.

The Major League records show two fabulous centerfielders who deserve special recognition. The first is Dummy Hoy, who played with the handicap of not being able to hear or speak. Can you imagine being deaf-mute and playing the game of baseball? Certainly he had to fear colliding with fellow outfielders while racing after balls up the alley. Yet he established four records which lasted almost a quarter of a century before being broken!

Lloyd Waner and Mike Griffin are tied for third, each having three marks lasting 48 years. Griffin's 53 double plays was a fine record that lasted 31 years before Max Carey was able to break it. Griffin was the surest fielder of all the early players. He posted an unusually high fielding average of .967, which is remarkable when one considers he accomplished the feat prior to 1900.

Waner, who is a Hall of Famer, was the first to play in 1,700 games. Each of his three records stood for 16 years before Richie Ashburn could do better.

Johnny Cooney has only one record, but it indicates he was a sensation in the field and that he caught most balls he reached. His .990 fielding average represents the highest of any National League centerfielder, even though it was achieved from 1936 through 1941, when gloves still weren't at their best.

Many experts argue that Willie Mays is the greatest centerfielder of all time, and they have a lot of proof. Willie has the most unbroken records of any centerfielder and handled more balls than any centerfielder in baseball history. He is the leader in games played, putouts and total chances.

Richie Ashburn is another centerfielder who deserves mention, as he was the first to play in 2,000 games and accumulate 5,000 putouts and 6,000 total chances. Each of his three records lasted 12 years—until the "Say Hey Kid," Willie Mays, came along.

The centerfielder with the most impressive set of stats is Hall of Famer Tris Speaker, who is in first place with five records, *all* of which have remained unbroken for more than half a century. His records have a longevity factor of 300 years!

Of the modern-day players, Amos Otis and Mickey Stanley are the fielding average champions, each having .991.

Mike Griffin was a few years ahead of Hoy, and he, too, was a superb centerfielder prior to 1900. Griff's marks lasted 54 years, while Hoy's stellar achievements were good for 96 years.

The number one position belongs to the great Tris Speaker with five records, two of which remain unbroken. Speaker is far in front of all other centerfielders in terms of longevity, with marks that have lasted 255 years. He is still the assists king and double play leader.

WILLIE MAYS
No other centerfielder has played as many games or caught as many fly balls as the "Say Hey Kid." Curiously, this perhaps greatest of all centerfielders set no single-season records.

But again, in fairness to our great modern centerfielders, Speaker played most of his career with the dead ball and achieved his records partially by being able to play shallow. With this taken into consideration, the title of baseball's greatest centerfielder of all time goes to Willie Mays. Willie currently has three unbroken records: he has played more games, caught more balls, and had more total chances than any centerfielder in baseball history.

RIGHT FIELD

NATIONAL LEAGUE		
Most Games		
1879–84	Jake Evans, Tro	432
1877–85	Orator Shaffer, Cle	611
1878–93	King Kelly, Chi	991
1885–98	Sam Thompson, Phi	1400
1892–07	Patsy Donovan, Pit	1469
1926–44	Paul Waner, Pit	2279
1928–46	Mel Ott, NY	2313
1955–72	**Roberto Clemente, Pit**	**2370**
Most Putouts		
1879–84	Jake Evans, Tro	752
1877–85	Orator Shaffer, Cle	974
1878–93	King Kelly, Chi	998
1885–98	Sam Thompson, Phi	2128
1892–07	Patsy Donovan, Pit	2291
1922–29	Curt Walker, Cin	2352
1926–44	**Paul Waner, Pit**	**4806**
Most Assists		
1879–84	Jake Evans, Tro	149
1877–85	Orator Shaffer, Cle	244
1878–93	**King Kelly, Chi**	**339**
Most Assists after 1900		
1900–07	Patsy Donovan, Pit	78
1905–13	John Titus, Phi	155
1926–44	Paul Waner, Pit	238
1928–45	Mel Ott, NY	246
1955–72	**Roberto Clemente, Pit**	**266**
Most Errors		
1878–84	Jake Evans, Tro	92
1877–85	Orator Shaffer, Cle	207
1878–93	**King Kelly, Chi**	**240**
Most Errors after 1900		
1900–07	Patsy Donovan, StL	32
1901–12	George Browne, NY	91
1918–26	Ross Youngs, NY	114
1926–44	Paul Waner, Pit	130
1955–72	**Roberto Clemente, Pit**	**140**

AMERICAN LEAGUE		
Most Games		
1902–05	Danny Green, Chi	515
1901–07	Buck Freeman, Bos	556
1901–08	Socks Seybold, Phi	912
1903–17	Sam Crawford, Det	1489
1909–25	Harry Hooper, Bos	2153
1953–74	**Al Kaline, Det**	**2488**
Most Putouts		
1902–05	Danny Green, Chi	786
1901–07	Buck Freeman, Bos	865
1901–08	Socks Seybold, Phi	1324
1903–17	Sam Crawford, Det	2049
1909–25	Harry Hooper, Bos	3718
1953–74	**Al Kaline, Det**	**5035**
Most Assists		
1902–05	Danny Green, Chi	49
1901–07	Buck Freeman, Bos	55
1901–08	Socks Seybold, Phi	84
1903–09	Willie Keeler, NY	90
1902–10	Elmer Flick, Cle	91
1903–17	Sam Crawford, Det	159
1909–25	**Harry Hooper, Bos**	**322**
Most Errors		
1902–05	Danny Green, Chi	52
1901–08	Socks Seybold, Phi	53
1903–09	Willie Keeler, NY	55
1902–10	Elmer Flick, Cle	64
1909–25	**Harry Hooper, Bos**	**140**

DID YOU KNOW . . . *That prior to 1897, a pitcher was charged with an earned run even when runs were scored on errors?*

MAJOR LEAGUE		
Most Games		
1879–85	Jake Evans, Tro, NL	452
1882–88	Tom Brown, Pit, AA	661
1877–90	Orator Shaffer, Cle, NL	833
1882–92	Chicken Wolf, Lou, AA	1042
1885–06	Sam Thompson, Det, NL	1408
1890–07	Patsy Donovan, Pit, NL	1598
1899–17	Sam Crawford, Det, AL	1786
1909–25	Harry Hooper, Bos, AL	2153
1926–45	Paul Waner, Pit, NL	2288
1926–47	Mel Ott, NY, NL	2313
1955–72	Roberto Clemente, Pit, NL	2370
1953–74	**Al Kaline, Det, AL**	**2488**
Most Putouts		
1879–85	Jake Evans, Tro, NL	752
1882–88	Tom Brown, Pit, AA	975
1877–90	Orator Shaffer, Cle, NL	1227
1882–92	Chicken Wolf, Lou, AA	1641
1885–06	Sam Thompson, Det, NL	2128
1890–07	Patsy Donovan, Pit, NL	2508
1899–17	Sam Crawford, Det, AL	2522
1909–25	Harry Hooper, Bos, AL	3718
1926–45	Paul Waner, Pit, NL	4806
1953–74	**Al Kaline, Det, AL**	**5035**
Most Assists		
1879–85	Jake Evans, Tro, NL	149
1877–90	Orator Shaffer, Cle, NL	285
1878–93	**King Kelly, Chi, NL**	**339**
Most Assists after 1900		
1902–07	Patsy Donovan, Pit, NL	78
1903–08	George Browne, Bos, NL	93
1905–13	John Titus, Phi, NL	155
1903–17	Sam Crawford, Det, Al	159
1909–25	**Harry Hooper, Bos, AL**	**322**
Most Errors		
1879–85	John Cassidy, Tro, NL	111
1882–88	Tom Brown, Pit, AA	225
1877–90	Orator Shaffer, Cle, NL	234
1878–93	**King Kelly, Chi, NL**	**240**
Most Errors after 1900		
1902–05	Danny Green, Chi, AL	52
1901–08	Socks Seybold, Phi, AL	53
1900–09	Willie Keeler, NY, AL	79
1901–11	George Browne, NY, NL	91
1900–17	Sam Crawford, Det, AL	94
1909–25	**Harry Hooper, Bos, AL**	**140**
1955–72	**Roberto Clemente, Pit, NL**	**140**

RIGHT FIELD

NATIONAL LEAGUE

Most Double Plays

1879–84	Jake Evans, Tro	19
1877–85	Orator Shaffer, Cle	20
1878–93	King Kelly, Chi	22
1883–94	Paul Radford, Bos	34
1885–98	**Sam Thompson, Phi**	**61**

Most Double Plays after 1900

1900–07	Patsy Donovan, StL	23
1901–12	George Browne, NY	29
1906–13	Wildfire Schulte, Chi	33
1918–26	Ross Youngs, NY	43
1926–44	Paul Waner, Pit	53
1928–46	**Mel Ott, NY**	**58**

Most Total Chances

1879–84	Jake Evans, Tro	993
1877–85	Orator Shaffer, Cle	1425
1878–93	King Kelly, Chi	1577
1885–98	Sam Thompson, Phi	2575
1892–07	Patsy Donovan, Pit	2655
1926–44	**Paul Waner, Pit**	**5174**

Highest Fielding Average

1879–84	Jake Evans, Tro	.908
1890–95	Oyster Burns, Bkn	.936
1894–02	Willie Keeler, Bal	.965
1906–13	Wildfire Schulte, Chi	.969
1908–13	Owen Wilson, Pit	.969
1916–25	Max Flack, Chi	.974
1925–33	Kiki Cuyler, Chi	.974
1926–44	Paul Waner, Pit	.974
1928–46	Mel Ott, NY	.980
1945–52	Tommy Holmes, Bos	.988
1975–81	**Bake McBride, Phi**	**.990**

AMERICAN LEAGUE

Most Double Plays

1902–05	Danny Green, Chi	20
1901–08	Socks Seybold, Phi	29
1903–17	Sam Crawford, Det	38
1909–25	**Harry Hooper, Bos**	**79**

Most Total Chances

1902–05	Danny Green, Chi	887
1901–07	Buck Freeman, Bos	967
1901–08	Socks Seybold, Phi	1461
1903–17	Sam Crawford, Det	2268
1909–25	Harry Hooper, Bos	4180
1953–74	**Al Kaline, Det**	**5278**

Highest Fielding Average

1902–05	Danny Green, Chi	.938
1901–07	Buck Freeman, Bos	.948
1901–08	Socks Seybold, Phi	.962
1903–17	Sam Crawford, Det	.975
1937–48	Tommy Henrich, NY	.984
1958–66	Roger Maris, NY	.985
1953–74	Al Kaline, Det	.985
1973–87	**Dwight Evans, Bos**	**.987**

MAJOR LEAGUE

Most Double Plays

1879–85	Jake Evans, Tro, NL	19
1882–88	Tom Brown, Pit, AA	28
1877–90	Orator Shaffer, Cle, NL	29
1882–92	Chicken Wolf, Lou, AA	42
1885–06	Sam Thompson, Det, NL	61
1890–07	Patsy Donovan, Pit, NL	63
1909–25	**Harry Hooper, Bos, AL**	**79**

Most Total Chances

1879–85	Jake Evans, Tro, NL	993
1882–88	Tom Brown, Pit, AA	1332
1877–90	Orator Shaffer, Cle, NL	1746
1882–92	Chicken Wolf, Lou, AA	2038
1885–06	Sam Thompson, Det, NL	2575
1890–07	Patsy Donovan, Pit, NL	2896
1909–25	Harry Hooper, Bos, AL	4180
1926–45	Paul Waner, Pit, NL	5174
1953–74	**Al Kaline, Det, AL**	**5278**

Highest Fielding Average

1879–85	Jake Evans, Tro, NL	.908
1883–86	Pop Corkhill, Cin, AA	.930
1890–95	Oyster Burns, Bkn	.936
1892–10	Willie Keeler, NY, AL	.961
1908–16	Owen Wilson, Pit, NL	.969
1906–18	Wildfire Schulte, Chi, NL	.969
1914–25	Max Flack, Chi, NL	.974
1921–38	Kiki Cuyler, Chi, NL	.974
1937–48	Tommy Henrich, NY, AL	.984
1945–52	Tommy Holmes, Bos, NL	.989
1977–83	Bake McBride, Phi, NL	.989

NATIONAL LEAGUE SUMMARY

Top Record Producers

1	Jake Evans, Tro	6
2	Orator Shaffer, Cle	5
2	King Kelly, Chi	5
2	Paul Waner, Pit	4

Most Outstanding Record Producers

King Kelly, Chi	5 for	112 years
Sam Thompson, Det	3 for	108 years
Patsy Donovan, Pit	3 for	96 years
Paul Waner, Pit	4 for	92 years

AMERICAN LEAGUE SUMMARY

Top Record Producers

1	Danny Green, Chi	6
1	Socks Seybold, Phi	6
1	Sam Crawford, Det	6
4	Buck Freeman, Bos	5
4	Harry Hooper, Bos	5
6	Al Kaline, Det	4

Most Outstanding Record Producers

Harry Hooper, Bos	5 for	273 years
Sam Crawford, Det	6 for	71 years
Socks Seybold, Phi	6 for	52 years
Al Kaline, Det	4 for	52 years

MAJOR LEAGUE SUMMARY

Top Record Producers

1	Jake Evans, Tro, NL	6
2	Tom Brown, Pit, AA	5
3	Orator Shaffer, Cle, NL	4
3	Chicken Wolf, Lou, AA	4
3	Sam Thompson, Det, NL	4
3	Patsy Donovan, Pit, NL	4
3	Harry Hooper, Bos, AL	4

Most Outstanding Record Producers

Harry Hooper, Bos, AL	4 for	125 years
King Kelly, Chi, NL	1 for	95 years
Paul Waner, Pit, NL	3 for	60 years
Chicken Wolf, Lou, AA	4 for	56 years
Patsy Donovan, Pit, NL	4 for	56 years
Al Kaline, Det, AL	3 for	42 years

RIGHT FIELD

Jake Evans, Orator Shaffer and King Kelly were three of the rightfielders to shine prior to 1900. Kelly is the only Hall of Famer of the three, and he set some impressive records, which lasted more years than any rightfielder's records in National League history. The bulk of the longevity of Kelly's records is his yet-unbroken assists record.

Sam Thompson is another pre-1900 rightfielder to excel. He, too, is a Hall of Famer, and established three records that have stood the test of time for 108 years. Thompson was the first to appear in 1,000 games, make 2,000 putouts and have 2,500 total chances. His record for most double plays still stands.

Playing the first several years of his career in the 1800s and the last seven after 1900, Patsy Donovan set three fine marks that were good for 96 years and third place. His games played and total chance marks lasted 37 years, and his putouts record stood for 22 years.

Paul Waner proved that he was a Hall of Famer not only with the bat, but also with the glove. He produced four records lasting 92 years and was the busiest of all National League rightfielders, with putouts and total chances that have never been passed.

Not many know that slugger Mel Ott of the Giants was a super, strong-armed rightfielder. But the stats indicate he participated in more double plays after 1900 than any modern player.

Roberto Clemente, easily one of the best defensive rightfielders in history, set the National League record for most games at his position, and would have increased it except for his tragic death in a plane crash.

Of the four most outstanding record producers, three are in the Hall of Fame. Harry Hooper, Sam Crawford and Al Kaline were true superstars, and their records reflect their talents.

Danny Green, Buck Freeman, and Socks Seybold were the early leaders and set fine records for others to improve upon. Hooper set the marks most difficult to break, as his five records have withstood the test of time for 273 years. Hooper has two unbroken marks in assists and double plays, while Al Kaline has three unbroken records in games played, putouts and total chances. Kaline is presently in fourth place, but he is sure to rise; it will be a long time before another rightfielder betters his achievements.

Sam Crawford was the first outstanding rightfielder in the American League, starring from 1903 to 1917. Sam was the first to play in 1,000 games, record more than 2,000 putouts, and compile 100 assists. Crawford's .975 fielding average had the longest reign of any American League rightfielder. It lasted 31 years before Tommy Henrich of the Yankees could do better.

When combining the achievements of both the National and American Leagues, Harry Hooper comes out on top, with the records that rank highest in longevity. His four marks are significant, having lasted 125 years. However, in fairness to the modern players, Hooper played most of his career in the dead ball era. As a result, Hooper is the leader in assists and double plays. When the live ball came into use, modern players easily captured the putouts and total chance records because the live ball traveled farther and was easier to hit into the outfield than the dead ball. Again, it would be helpful if the rules committee would create a distinction between old records and records generated after the live ball was introduced.

King Kelly had 339 assists, an amazing number when you consider he only played right field in 998 games. But that's a reflection of how easy it was to get assists at the shorter distances. We must also realize that it takes a certain degree of accuracy to throw runners out, and apparently Kelly and Hooper were indeed accurate.

Al Kaline will go down in history as one of the greatest of all rightfielders, as he has three unbroken Major League records. Other greats at this position are Paul Waner, Mel Ott, Sam Crawford, Harry Hooper and Roberto Clemente.

CHAPTER 7

ROOKIE BATTING RECORDS

NATIONAL LEAGUE QUIZ

1. Who is the only NL rookie to play in all 162 games?
2. Can you name the only rookie to come to bat more than 700 times?
3. Who was the first rookie to get more than 200 hits?
4. The doubles record is 52 and has not been broken in 57 years. Do you know this fine rookie?
5. The triples record is 87 years old. Who holds it?

AMERICAN LEAGUE QUIZ

1. This Hall of Famer hit 20 homers when he was a rookie in 1925. Do you know him?
2. Name the rookie who has the highest home run percentage.
3. This famous Yankee scored more runs than any rookie in AL history. Name him.
4. Can you name this splendid player who has the most bases on balls and RBIs?
5. Who was the first AL rookie home run champion?

MAJOR LEAGUE QUIZ

1. Name the rookie with the highest slugging average.
2. The highest rookie batting average occurred in the very first year of baseball. Who dunnit?
3. Who is the rookie with the most hits?
4. Two fine rookie sluggers are tied with 38 home runs. Do you know them?
5. Do you know the rookie who has the most strike-outs?

NATIONAL LEAGUE	AMERICAN LEAGUE	MAJOR LEAGUE

NATIONAL LEAGUE

Most Games

1876	Jim O'Rourke, Bos	70
1876	Jack Manning, Bos	70
1876	George Wright, Bos	70
1876	Harry Schaefer, Bos	70
1879	Charlie Eden, Cle	81
1879	Buttercup Dickerson, Cin	81
1879	Pete Hotaling, Cin	81
1880	Fred Dunlap, Cle	85
1883	John Coleman, Phi	90
1884	Milt Scott, Det	110
1887	Marty Sullivan, Chi	115
1888	Dummy Hoy, Was	136
1889	Patsy Tebeau, Cle	136
1890	George Davis, Cle	136
1899	Buck Freeman, Was	155
1910	Zack Wheat, Bkn	156
1936	Buddy Hassett, Bkn	156
1953	Ray Jablonski, StL	157
1962	Ken Hubbs, Chi	160
1964	**Richie Allen, Phi**	**162**

Most At Bats

1876	George Wright, Bos	335
1879	Pete Hotaling, Cin	369
1880	Fred Dunlap, Cle	373
1884	Milt Scott, Det	438
1887	Marty Sullivan, Chi	472
1888	Dummy Hoy, Was	503
1889	Patsy Tebeau, Cle	521
1890	Jimmy Cooney, Chi	574
1899	Jimmy Williams, Pit	617
1927	Lloyd Waner, Pit	629
1936	Gene Moore, Bos	637
1938	Frank McCormick, Cin	640
1962	Ken Hubbs, Chi	661
1984	**Juan Samuel, Phi**	**701**

Most Hits

1876	Ross Barnes, Chi	138
1888	Dummy Hoy, Was	138
1889	Patsy Tebeau, Cle	147
1890	Jimmy Cooney, Chi	156
1894	Charlie Abbey, Was	164
1895	Bill Everett, Chi	197
1899	Jimmy Williams, Pit	219
1927	**Lloyd Waner, Pit**	**223**

Most Singles

1876	Ross Barnes, Chi	102
1888	Dummy Hoy, Was	118
1890	Steve Brodie, Bos	124
1895	Bill Everett, Chi	168
1927	**Lloyd Waner, Pit**	**198**

AMERICAN LEAGUE

Most Games

1901	Irv Waldron, Was	141
1904	Joe Cassidy, Was	152
1905	George Stone, StL	154
1909	Donnie Bush, Det	157
1961	**Jake Wood, Det**	**162**
1964	**Bobby Knoop, LA**	**162**
1966	**George Scott, Bos**	**162**

Most At Bats

1901	Irv Waldron, Was	598
1905	George Stone, StL	632
1928	Carl Lind, Cle	650
1953	**Harvey Kuenn, Det**	**679**

Most Hits

1901	Irv Waldron, Was	186
1905	George Stone, StL	187
1911	**Joe Jackson, Cle**	**233**

Most Singles

1901	Irv Waldron, Was	155
1911	Joe Jackson, Cle	162
1942	Johnny Pesky, Bos	165
1953	**Harvey Kuenn, Det**	**167**

MAJOR LEAGUE

Most Games

1876	Jack Manning, Bos, NL	70
1876	Jim O'Rourke, Bos, NL	70
1876	George Wright, Bos, NL	70
1876	Harry Schaefer, Bos, NL	70
1879	Charlie Eden, Cle, NL	81
1879	Buttercup Dickerson, Cin, NL	81
1879	Pete Hotaling, Cin, NL	81
1880	Fred Dunlap, Cle, NL	85
1883	Arlie Latham, StL, AA	98
1884	Harry Moore, Was, UL	111
1886	Reddy Mack, Lou, AA	137
1889	Ollie Beard, Cin, AA	141
1899	Buck Freeman, Was, NL	155
1909	Donnie Bush, Det, AL	157
1953	Ray Jablonski, StL, NL	157
1961	**Jake Wood, Det, AL**	**162**
1964	**Richie Allen, Phi, NL**	**162**
1964	**Bobby Knoop, LA, AL**	**162**
1966	**George Scott, Bos, AL**	**162**

Most At Bats

1876	George Wright, Bos, NL	335
1879	Pete Hotaling, Cin, NL	369
1880	Fred Dunlap, Cle, NL	373
1883	Arlie Latham, StL, AA	406
1884	Harry Moore, Was, UL	461
1886	Joe Werrick, Lou, AA	561
1890	Jimmy Cooney, Chi, NL	574
1899	Jimmy Williams, Pit, NL	617
1905	George Stone, StL, AL	632
1928	Carl Lind, Cle, AL	650
1953	Harvey Kuenn, Det, AL	679
1984	**Juan Samuel, Phi, NL**	**701**

Most Hits

1876	Ross Barnes, Chi, NL	138
1884	Dave Orr, NY, AA	162
1887	Hub Collins, Lou, AA	162
1889	Jim Burns, KC, AA	176
1895	Bill Everett, Chi, NL	197
1899	Jimmy Williams, Pit, NL	219
1911	**Joe Jackson, Cle, AL**	**233**

Most Singles

1876	Ross Barnes, Chi, NL	102
1884	Harry Moore, Was, UL	126
1887	Hub Collins, Lou, AA	131
1889	Jim Burns, KC, AA	137
1890	Harry Taylor, Lou, AA	155
1895	Bill Everett, Chi, NL	168
1927	**Lloyd Waner, Pit, NL**	**198**

NATIONAL LEAGUE			**AMERICAN LEAGUE**			**MAJOR LEAGUE**		
Most Doubles			*Most Doubles*			*Most Doubles*		
1876	Ross Barnes, Chi	21	1901	John Farrell, Was	32	1876	Ross Barnes, Chi, NL	21
1876	Dick Higham, Har	21	1911	Joe Jackson, Cle	45	1876	Dick Higham, Har, NL	21
1876	Paul Hines, Chi	21	1929	Roy Johnson, Det	45	1876	Paul Hines, Chi, NL	21
1879	Charlie Eden, Cle	31	1934	Hal Trosky, Cle	45	1879	Charlie Eden, Cle, NL	31
1894	Bill Hassermaer, Was	33	**1975**	**Fred Lynn, Bos**	**47**	1884	Sam Barkley, Tol, AA	39
1910	Zack Wheat, Bkn	36				1911	Joe Jackson, Cle, AL	45
1913	George Burns, NY	37				**1929**	**Johnny Frederick, Bkn, NL**	**52**
1921	Ray Grimes, Chi	38						
1929	**Johnny Frederick, Bkn**	**52**						
Most Triples			*Most Triples*			*Most Triples*		
1876	Ross Barnes, Chi	14	1901	Hobe Ferris, Bos	15	1876	Ross Barnes, Chi, NL	14
1879	Buttercup Dickerson, Cin	14	**1904**	**Joe Cassidy, Was**	**19**	1879	Buttercup Dickerson, Cin, NL	14
1880	Harry Stovey, Wor	14	**1909**	**Frank Baker, Phi**	**19**	1880	Harry Stovey, Wor, NL	14
1887	Marty Sullivan, Chi	16	**1911**	**Joe Jackson, Cle**	**19**	1886	Joe Werrick, Lou, AA	14
1893	George Treadway, Bal	17				1887	Marty Sullivan, Chi, NL	16
1894	Charlie Abbey, Was	18				1890	Perry Werden, Tol, AA	20
1896	Tom McCreery, Lou	21				1896	Tom McCreery, Lou, NL	21
1899	**Jimmy Williams, Pit**	**27**				**1899**	**Jimmy Williams, Pit, NL**	**27**
Most Triples after 1900						*Most Triples after 1900*		
1900	Piano Legs Hickman, NY	17				1900	Piano Legs Hickman, NY, NL	17
1904	Harry Lumley, Bkn	18				1904	Joe Cassidy, Was, AL	19
1915	**Tommy Long, StL**	**25**				1909	Frank Baker, Phi, AL	19
						1911	Joe Jackson, Cle, AL	19
						1915	**Tommy Long, StL, NL**	**25**
Most Home Runs			*Most Home Runs*			*Most Home Runs*		
1876	George Hall, Phi	5	1901	Socks Seybold, Phi	8	1876	George Hall, Phi, NL	5
1879	John O'Rourke, Bos	6	1910	Duffy Lewis, Bos	8	1879	John O'Rourke, Bos, NL	6
1880	Harry Stovey, Wor	6	1920	Bob Meusel, NY	11	1880	Harry Stovey, Wor, NL	6
1885	Sam Thompson, Det	7	1924	Ike Boone, Bos	13	1884	Cannon Ball Crane, Bos, UL	12
1887	Billy O'Brien, Was	19	1925	Lou Gehrig, NY	20	1887	Billy O'Brien, Was, NL	19
1899	Buck Freeman, Was	25	1929	Dale Alexander, Det	25	1899	Buck Freeman, Was, NL	25
1928	Del Bissonette, Bkn	25	1934	Hal Trosky, Cle	35	1928	Del Bissonette, Bkn, NL	25
1930	**Wally Berger, Bos**	**38**	1937	Rudy York, Det	35	1929	Dale Alexander, Det, AL	25
1956	**Frank Robinson, Cin**	**38**	1950	Al Rosen, Cle	37	1930	Wally Berger, Bos, NL	38
			1987	**Mark McGwire, Oak**	**49**	1956	Frank Robinson, Cin, NL	38
						1987	**Mark McGwire, Oak, AL**	**49**
Highest Home Run Percentage			*Highest Home Run Percentage*			*Highest Home Run Percentage*		
1876	George Hall, Phi	1.9	1901	Socks Seybold, Phi	1.8	1876	George Hall, Phi, NL	1.9
1879	Dan Brouthers, Tro	2.4	1912	John Cashion, Was	1.9	1879	Dan Brouthers, Tro, NL	2.4
1885	Sam Thompson, Det	2.8	1915	Babe Ruth, Bos	4.3	1884	Cannon Ball Crane, Bos, UL	2.8
1887	Billy O'Brien, Was	4.2	1925	Benny Paschal, NY	4.9	1885	Sam Thompson, Det, NL	2.8
1899	Ad Gumbert, Chi	4.6	1934	Hal Trosky, Cle	5.6	1887	Billy O'Brien, Was, NL	4.2
1927	Johnny Schulte, StL	5.8	**1937**	**Rudy York, Det**	**9.3**	1889	Ad Gumbert, Chi, NL	4.6
1930	**Wally Berger, Bos**	**6.8**				1925	Benny Paschal, NY, AL	4.9
1959	**Willie McCovey, SF**	**6.8**				1927	Johnny Schulte, StL, NL	5.8
						1930	Wally Berger, Bos, NL	6.8
						1937	**Rudy York, Det, AL**	**9.3**
Most Runs Scored			*Most Runs Scored*			*Most Runs Scored*		
1876	Ross Barnes, Chi	126	1901	Irv Waldron, Was	102	1876	Ross Barnes, Chi, NL	126
1894	Jimmy Bannon, Bos	130	1909	Donnie Bush, Det	114	1887	Mike Griffin, Bal, AA	142
1899	**Roy Thomas, Phi**	**137**	1911	Joe Jackson, Cle	126	**1889**	**Billy Hamilton, KC, AA**	**144**
			1929	Roy Johnson, Det	128			
Most Runs Scored after 1900			**1936**	**Joe DiMaggio, NY**	**132**	*Most Runs after 1900*		
1900	Jimmy Barrett, Cin	114				**1927**	**Lloyd Waner, Pit, NL**	**133**
1927	**Lloyd Waner, Pit**	**133**						

NATIONAL LEAGUE

Most RBIs

1876	Deacon White, Chi	60
1879	John O'Rourke, Bos	62
1887	Marty Sullivan, Chi	77
1893	Bill Lange, Chi	88
1894	Jimmy Bannon, Bos	114
1899	**Buck Freeman, Was**	**122**

Most RBIs after 1900

1900	Piano Legs Hickman, NY	95
1924	Glen Wright, Pit	111
1930	**Wally Berger, Bos**	**119**

Most Extra Base Hits

1876	Ross Barnes, Chi	36
1879	Charlie Eden, Cle	41
1880	Harry Stovey, Wor	41
1891	Billy Dahlen, Chi	42
1894	Bill Hassamaer, Was	54
1899	Buck Freeman, Was	69
1929	**Johnny Frederick, Bkn**	**82**

Most Total Bases

1876	Ross Barnes, Chi	190
1890	Eddie Burke, Phi	201
1891	Billy Dahlen, Chi	218
1894	Jimmy Bannon, Bos	254
1899	Buck Freeman, Was	331
1929	Johnny Frederick, Bkn	342
1964	**Richie Allen, Phi**	**352**

Most Bases on Balls

1876	Ross Barnes, Chi	20
1885	Charlie Bastian, Phi	35
1887	Marty Sullivan, Chi	36
1888	Dummy Hoy, Was	69
1890	Bob Allen, Phi	87
1899	**Roy Thomas, Phi**	**115**

Most Bases on Balls after 1900

1900	Jimmy Barrett, Cin	72
1945	Carden Gillenwater, Bos	73
1953	**Junior Gilliam, Bkn**	**100**

AMERICAN LEAGUE

Most RBIs

1901	Socks Seybold, Phi	90
1911	Ping Bodie, Chi	97
1924	Al Simmons, Phi	102
1926	Tony Lazzeri, NY	114
1929	Dale Alexander, Det	137
1934	Hal Trosky, Cle	142
1939	**Ted Williams, Bos**	**145**

Most Extra Base Hits

1901	Socks Seybold, Phi	46
1901	Johnny Farrell, Was	46
1909	Frank Baker, Phi	50
1911	Joe Jackson, Cle	71
1929	Dale Alexander, Det	83
1934	**Hal Trosky, Cle**	**89**

Most Total Bases

1901	Socks Seybold, Phi	226
1901	Irv Waldron, Was	226
1905	George Stone, StL	259
1911	Joe Jackson, Cle	337
1929	Dale Alexander, Det	363
1934	**Hal Trosky, Cle**	**374**
1964	**Tony Oliva, Min**	**374**

Most Bases on Balls

1901	John Farrell, Was	52
1909	Donnie Bush, Det	88
1921	Lu Blue, Det	103
1939	**Ted Williams, Bos**	**107**

MAJOR LEAGUE

Most RBIs

1876	Deacon White, Chi, NL	60
1879	John O'Rourke, Bos, NL	62
1887	Marty Sullivan, Chi, NL	77
1889	Jim Burns, KC, AA	97
1894	Jimmy Bannon, Bos, NL	114
1899	Buck Freeman, Was, NL	122
1929	Dale Alexander, Det, AL	137
1934	Hal Trosky, Cle, AL	142
1939	**Ted Williams, Bos, AL**	**145**

Most Extra Base Hits

1876	Ross Barnes, Chi, NL	36
1879	Charlie Eden, Cle, NL	41
1880	Harry Stovey, Wor, NL	41
1884	Dave Orr, NY, AA	54
1894	Bill Hassamaer, Was, NL	54
1899	Buck Freeman, Was, NL	69
1911	Joe Jackson, Cle, AL	71
1929	Dale Alexander, Det, AL	83
1934	**Hal Trosky, Cle, AL**	**89**

Most Total Bases

1876	Ross Barnes, Chi, NL	190
1884	Dave Orr, NY, AA	247
1894	Jimmy Bannon, Bos, NL	254
1899	Buck Freeman, Was, NL	331
1911	Joe Jackson, Cle, AL	337
1929	Dale Alexander, Det, AL	363
1934	**Hal Trosky, Cle, AL**	**374**
1964	**Tony Oliva, Min, AL**	**374**

Most Bases on Balls

1876	Ross Barnes, Chi, NL	20
1884	Yank Robinson, Bal, UL	37
1886	Ernie Burch, Bkn, AA	39
1887	Mike Griffin, Bal, AA	55
1888	Dummy Hoy, Was, NL	69
1889	Billy Hamilton, KC, AA	87
1889	Lefty Marr, Col, AA	87
1890	**Bill Joyce, Bkn, PL**	**123**

Most Bases on Balls after 1900

1939	Ted Williams, Bos, AL	107

NATIONAL LEAGUE

Most Strikeouts

1876	Johnny Ryan, Lou	23
1878	Russ McKelvey, Ind	38
1879	Mike Mansell, Syr	45
1880	Harry Stovey, Wor	46
1883	Mert Hackett, Bos	48
1884	Milt Scott, Det	62
1885	Charlie Bastian, Phi	82
1915	Doug Baird, Pit	88
1923	George Grantham, Chi	92
1934	Dolf Camilli, Phi	94
1937	Vince DiMaggio, Bos	111
1940	Chet Ross, Bos	127
1960	Pancho Herrera, Phi	136
1964	Richie Allen, Phi	138
1966	Byron Browne, Chi	143
1969	Larry Hisle, Phi	152
1984	**Juan Samuel, Phi**	**168**

Most Stolen Bases (modern rule)

1898	Elmer Flick, Phi	23
1899	Emmett Heidrick, StL	55
1913	Hap Myers, Bos	57
1984	Juan Samuel, Phi	72
1985	**Vince Coleman, StL**	**110**

Highest Batting Average
1876 Ross Barnes, Chi .429

Highest Batting Average after 1900

1900	Jimmy Barrett, Cin	.316
1910	Fred Snodgrass, NY	.321
1921	Ray Grimes, Chi	.321
1922	Hack Miller, Chi	.352
1924	Kiki Cuyler, Pit	.354
1927	**Lloyd Waner, Pit**	**.355**

Highest Slugging Average

1876	Ross Barnes, Chi	.590
1930	George Watkins, StL	.621
1957	Bob Hazle, Mil	.649
1959	**Willie McCovey, SF**	**.656**

Most Pinch At Bats

1876–1892	None	
1893	Jake Stenzel, Pit	6
1899	Pearce Childs, Phi	10
1902	Mike O'Neill, StL	12
1907	Fred Osborn, Phi	19
1909	Ham Hyatt, Pit	37
1915	**Dan Costello, Pit**	**46**
1927	Mel Ott, NY	46

AMERICAN LEAGUE

Most Strikeouts

1901–10	Records not kept	
1911	Joe Jackson, Cle	56
1914	John Leary, StL	71
1915	Wally Pipp, NY	81
1926	Tony Lazzeri, NY	96
1932	Bruce Campbell, StL	104
1961	Jake Wood, Det	141
1966	George Scott, Bos	152
1968	Reggie Jackson, Oak	171
1986	**Pete Incaviglia, Tex**	**185**

DID YOU KNOW . . . *That a foul bunt on a third strike was not a strikeout until 1909?*

Most Stolen Bases (modern rule)

1901	John Farrell, Was	25
1905	George Stone, StL	26
1906	Dave Altizer, Was	37
1909	**Donnie Bush, Det**	**53**

DID YOU KNOW . . . *That prior to 1909 there was no rule to cover a double steal situation? In 1909 it was decided not to credit a stolen base to a runner when either runner was thrown out on a double steal.*

Highest Batting Average

1901	Socks Seybold, Phi	.333
1902	Pat Dougherty, Bos	.342
1911	**Joe Jackson, Cle**	**.408**

Highest Slugging Average

1901	Socks Seybold, Phi	.499
1911	Joe Jackson, Cle	.590
1925	Benny Paschal, NY	.611
1937	**Rudy York, Det**	**.651**

Most Pinch At Bats

1901	Bill Friel, Mil	3
1902	Harry Gleason, Bos	8
1903	Danny Hoffman, Phi	11
1905	Ike Van Zandt, StL	18
1908	Dode Criss, StL	41
1920	Sammy Hale, Det	52
1957	**Julio Becquer, Was**	**65**

MAJOR LEAGUE

Most Strikeouts

1876	Johnny Ryan, Lou, NL	23
1878	Russ McKelvey, Ind, NL	38
1879	Mike Mansell, Syr, NL	45
1880	Harry Stovey, Wor, NL	46
1883	Mert Hackett, Bos, NL	48
1884	Milt Scott, Det, NL	62
1885	Charlie Bastian, Phi, NL	82
1915	Doug Baird, Pit, NL	88
1923	George Grantham, Chi, NL	92
1926	Tony Lazzeri, NY, AL	96
1932	Bruce Campbell, StL, AL	104
1937	Vince DiMaggio, Bos, NL	111
1940	Chet Ross, Bos, NL	127
1961	Jake Wood, Det, AL	141
1966	George Scott, Bos, AL	152
1968	Reggie Jackson, Oak, AL	171
1986	**Pete Incaviglia, Tex, AL**	**185**

Most Stolen Bases (modern rule)

1898	Elmer Flick, Phi, NL	23
1899	John Emmett Heidrick, StL, NL	55
1913	Hap Myers, Bos, NL	57
1984	Juan Samuel, Phi, NL	72
1985	**Vince Coleman, StL, NL**	**110**

Highest Batting Average
1876 Ross Barnes, Chi, NL .429

Highest Batting Average after 1900
1911 Joe Jackson, Cle, AL .408

Highest Slugging Average

1876	Ross Barnes, Chi, NL	.590
1925	Benny Paschal, NY, AL	.611
1930	George Watkins, StL, NL	.621
1937	Rudy York, Det, AL	.651
1959	**Willie McCovey, SF, NL**	**.656**

Most Pinch At Bats

1876–92	None	
1893	Jake Stenzel, Pit, NL	6
1899	Pearce Childs, Phi, NL	10
1902	Mike O'Neill, StL, NL	12
1905	Ike Van Zandt, StL, AL	18
1907	Fred Osborn, Phi, NL	19
1908	Dode Criss, StL, AL	41
1915	Dan Costello, Pit, NL	46
1920	Sammy Hale, Det, AL	52
1957	**Julio Becquer, Was, AL**	**65**

NATIONAL LEAGUE

Most Pinch Hits
1893	Jake Stenzel, Pit	1
1893	Kid Gleason, StL	1
1894	Mike Grady, Phi	2
1894	Frank Connaughton, Bos	2
1894	Tom Parrott, Cin	2
1895	Terry Turner, Phi	2
1899	Pearce Childs, Phi	2
1907	Fred Osborn, Phi	7
1909	Ham Hyatt, Pit	9
1915	**Dan Costello, Pit**	**14**
1926	**Chick Tolson, Chi**	**14**

Highest Pinch Batting Average
(min. 10 at bats)
1899	Pearce Childs, Phi	.200
1926	**Roy Spencer, Pit**	**.600**

AMERICAN LEAGUE

Most Pinch Hits
1901	Bill Friel, Mil	2
1902	Harry Gleason, Bos	3
1903	Danny Hoffman, Phi	5
1906	Howard Wakefield, Was	9
1908	Dode Criss, StL	12
1920	Sammy Hale, Det	17
1957	**Julio Becquer, Was**	**18**

DID YOU KNOW . . . *That prior to 1907, pinch hitters, pinch runners and defensive substitutes were not credited with a game played?*

Highest Pinch Batting Average
(Min. 10 at bats)
1901	Bill Friel, Mil	.200
1902	Harry Gleason, Bos	.300
1903	Danny Hoffman, Phi	.454
1906	Howard Wakefield, Was	.562
1928	Carl Reynolds, Chi	.600
1959	**John Romano, Chi**	**.615**

MAJOR LEAGUE

Most Pinch Hits
1893	Jake Stenzel, Pit, NL	1
1894	Mike Grady, Phi, NL	2
1894	Frank Connaughton, Bos, NL	2
1899	Pearce Childs, Phi, NL	2
1901	Bill Friel, Mil, AL	2
1902	Harry Gleason, Bos, AL	3
1903	Danny Hoffman, Phi, AL	5
1906	Howard Wakefield, Was, AL	9
1908	Dode Criss, StL, AL	12
1915	Dan Costello, Pit, NL	14
1920	Sammy Hale, Det, AL	17
1955	**Julio Becquer, Was, AL**	**18**

Highest Pinch Batting Average
(min. 10 at bats)
1899	Pearce Childs, Phi, NL	.200
1901	Bill Friel, Mil, AL	.200
1902	Harry Gleason, Bos, AL	.300
1903	Danny Hoffman, Phi, Al	.454
1906	Howard Wakefield, Was, AL	.562
1926	Roy Spencer, Pit, NL	.600
1928	Carl Reynolds, Chi, AL	.600
1959	**John Romano, Chi, AL**	**.615**

NATIONAL LEAGUE SUMMARY

Top Record Producers
1	Ross Barnes, Chi	10
2	Lloyd Waner, Pit	6
3	Marty Sullivan, Chi	5
3	Dummy Hoy, Was	5
3	Buck Freeman, Was	5

Most Outstanding Record Producers
Ross Barnes, Chi	10 for 248	years
Buck Freeman, Was	5 for 191	years
Roy Thomas, Phi	2 for 177	years
Johnny Frederick, Bkn	3 for 153	years
Jimmy Williams, Pit	3 for 145	years
Lloyd Waner, Pit	3 for 135	years

AMERICAN LEAGUE SUMMARY

Top Record Producers
1	Joe Jackson, Cle	9
2	Socks Seybold, Phi	7
3	Hal Trosky, Cle	6
3	Irv Waldron, Was	6
5	George Stone, StL	5
6	Donnie Bush, Det	4
6	Dale Alexander, Det	4

Most Outstanding Record Producers
Joe Jackson, Cle	9 for 348	years
Donnie Bush, Det	4 for 145	years
Hal Trosky, Cle	6 for 138	years
Rudy York, Det	3 for 115	years
Ted Williams, Bos	2 for 98	years
Harvey Kuenn, Det	2 for 68	years
Socks Seybold, Phi	7 for 53	years

MAJOR LEAGUE SUMMARY

Top Record Producers
1	Ross Barnes, Chi, NL	10
2	Buck Freeman, Was, NL	5
3	Joe Jackson, Cle, AL	4
3	Dale Alexander, Det, AL	4
5	Harry Stovey, Wor, NL	3
5	Jim Burns, KC, AA	3
5	Jimmy Williams, Pit, NL	3
5	Harry Moore, Was, UL	3
5	Charlie Eden, Cle, NL	3
5	Hal Trosky, Cle, AL	3

Most Outstanding Record Producers
Ross Barnes, Chi, NL	10 for 221	years
Joe Jackson, Cle, AL	4 for 133	years
Lloyd Waner, Pit, NL	2 for 122	years
Jimmy Williams, Pit, NL	3 for 107	years
Billy Hamilton, KC, AA	2 for 100	years
Bill Joyce, Bkn, PL	1 for 98	years
Ted Williams, Bos, AL	2 for 98	years
Buck Freeman, Was, NL	5 for 93	years
Hal Trosky, Cle, AL	3 for 89	years
Rudy York, Det, AL	2 for 73	years
Hap Myers, Bos, NL	1 for 71	years

In 1876 everyone in the league was considered a rookie. Of the 15 major categories of records, Ross Barnes led the league in ten, a feat that is sure to never be equaled. His most impressive record is his .429 batting average, one of the few records created in the first year of baseball that still stands!

But how can the rookie of today have a fair chance at breaking Ross Barnes' record when the rules were so drastically different? In Barnes' day, it took nine balls for a base on balls, four strikes for a strikeout when the first called strike was just a warning, and foul balls did not count as strikes. The rules committee needs to do

DUMMY HOY
Dummy Hoy got his nickname because he was a mute, not because he committed the most errors of any centerfielder. Still, his talent was immediately visible, as he set 5 rookie records in 1888.

some serious thinking about the inequities of records!

Other rookie sensations prior to 1900 were Buck Freeman, Roy Thomas and Jimmy Williams. Freeman's marks, set in 1899, have lasted the second-longest amount of time. He slammed an incredible 25 home runs in the dead ball era, had 122 RBIs, which is still the present National League rookie record, and had 331 total bases and 69 extra base hits.

Roy Thomas also had a super year in 1899 when he scored 137 runs and earned 115 bases on balls. Both are still National League records.

The National League was blessed with yet another super rookie in 1899 by the name of Jimmy Williams. Williams became the first rookie to come to bat 600 times and get 200 hits, and his 27 triples is still a National League record.

Of the many exceptional rookies who came along after 1900, one who easily would have won the Rookie of the Year award was Johnny Frederick of the Dodgers, who blasted 52 doubles in 1929. The Rookie of the Year award did not begin until 1947, so Frederick (and many others) never did get the recognition they deserved. Frederick's 52 doubles and 82 extra base hits are still standing. Frederick's 342 total bases was another outstanding record, which lasted 35 years before Richie Allen set a new mark in 1964. Allen is the only National League rookie ever to play in all 162 games of a 162-game schedule.

Lloyd Waner in 1927 would have been another easy winner, as he posted three new rookie records. His 223 hits is a rookie record that still stands. Other famous players who would have won the award had it been in existence when they played were: Dan Brouthers, 1879; Roger Connor, 1880; Sam Thompson, 1885; Elmer Flick, 1898; Home Run Baker, 1909; Zack Wheat, 1910; Shoeless Joe Jackson, 1911; Wally Pipp, 1915; Rogers Hornsby, 1916; Bob Meusel, 1920; Joe Sewell, 1921; Kiki Cuyler, 1924; Earle Combs, 1925; Tony Lazzeri and Paul Waner, 1926; Mel Ott, 1927; Billy Herman, 1932; Joe Medwich, 1933; Hal Trosky, 1934; Johnny Mize and Joe DiMaggio, 1936; Ted Williams, 1939; Phil Rizzuto, 1941; and Stan Musial, 1942.

In 1984, Juan Samuel of the Phillies became the first rookie to come to bat 700 times, and he also stole 72 bases. Vince Coleman smashed that record when he stole 110 in 1985.

Wally Berger of the Braves was a standout in 1930 when he set a new home run record of 38; he has since been tied by Frank Robinson. The rookie who has the highest home run percentage is Willie McCovey, with a hefty 6.8. He is also the current slugging average champion with a sizzling .656.

"Shoeless" Joe Jackson had one of the greatest years of any rookie in baseball history. He established nine records, which have had a total longevity of 348 years! He was the first and last rookie in the American League to bat over .400, and his 233 hits are the most of any rookie in baseball history.

Socks Seybold was the outstanding rookie in the very first year of the American League. He captured seven records, which lasted a total of 53 years.

In 1961 Jake Wood became the first rookie to play in all 162 games, but this was hardly noticed since Roger Maris' 61 home runs got most of the attention that year. Bobby Knoop played in 162 games in 1964, as did George Scott of the Red Sox in 1966. Harvey Kuenn can boast of two fine records: his 679 at bats and his 167 singles are marks that have stood since 1953.

Fred Lynn is the doubles champion, while the triples crown is shared by three players. The home run record began with 8 in 1901 and had risen to 49 by 1987. Hal Trosky became the first to go over the 30 plateau when he put 35 balls out of the park in 1934. He was tied by Rudy York in 1937, and Al Rosen became the new home run champion in 1950 with 37 round-trippers. Mark McGwire slugged an amazing 49 round-trippers in 1987. Rudy York's 35 home runs created the highest home run percentage, a smashing 9.3, which is both an American and Major League record that no other rookie has ever topped.

Trosky was simply marvelous in 1934, creating six new marks. His 89 extra base hits remains unbroken, and his 374 total bases has been tied by Tony Oliva of the Twins. Trosky batted a solid .330 in his super rookie year, and then he proved he was no flash in the pan by belting 204 homers in his first seven years in the big leagues. (In all, he had a splendid 11-year career with a .302 batting average. His career slugging average was a smart .522.)

Detroit can boast of its fine shortstop Donnie Bush, who has earned the number two spot on the Most Outstanding list. Bush possesses a 79-year-old stolen base record and a 52-year-old games played mark; his 114 runs scored was a tremendous feat but lasted only two years, and his 88 bases on balls was a record that stood for 12 years. In Bush's first four seasons, he led the league in bases on balls all four times. He was another of those mighty mites, standing 5'6" tall and weighing all of 140 pounds. He was one of the American League's first outstanding shortstops, and he also smacked 1,803 hits in a fine career that lasted from 1908 through 1923.

Rudy York is the all-time American League rookie slugger, as no one has ever bettered his .651 slugging average or his 9.3 home run percentage. The pinch hit trophy goes to Julio Becquer of the Senators, who had 65 at bats and 18 hits in 1957, marks that still stand.

HAL TROSKY

In 1934, Hal Trosky broke into the big leagues in style. He had 206 hits, 45 doubles, 35 homers, 142 RBIs, 117 runs, a .330 batting average, and a .598 slugging average.

The first year of baseball, 1876, was surely one of the most exciting years the game will ever know. Major League baseball was in its rookie year. Every player in the league was a rookie and so the players who came out on top set the first rookie records.

The players were, purportedly, on their best behavior as required by the new rules placed upon them by William Hulbert, the founder of the National League. There was to be no playing on Sunday, no drinking, no swearing, and absolutely no gambling. Players were signed to a contract for a set salary for the first time (they no longer would share the gate receipts), and they were forbidden to jump from one team to another when they had a better offer. Baseball was being run as a business. Team owners were businessmen who had invested a lot of money and were determined to clean up the corruption that had crept into the game.

Prior to the formation of the National League, gambling on the games was an accepted practice, even to the point where players and umpires would place bets on the very contest in which they were involved. Out of such circumstances came the famous cry: "Kill the umpire!" And this was not an idle threat. Umpires were frequently injured by furious mobs; on one occasion, Cap Anson and some of his Chicago players prevented what could have become a lynching, by intercepting an umpire on the run and sneaking him out of town before the fans got to him. The threat was so serious that umpires would often carry guns under their clothing to protect themselves. Hulbert and his associates who formed the National League did a fine job of restoring order and honesty to our national pastime.

Rookie records and season records were one and the same in 1876. As mentioned in Chapter 1, Ross Barnes had the marvelous accomplishment of capturing 10 of the 15 records that year, and no player in baseball history since has ever been so dominant. "Shoeless" Joe Jackson came the closest in the American League when he captured nine records in one year.

Jimmy Williams was another super rookie, and his three marks lasted 107 years, which is good enough for third place among outstanding producers. Williams is presently the all-time leader in triples with 27.

In fourth place is Hall of Famer and premier base stealer Billy Hamilton. Blessed with blazing speed and an exceptional sense for smart base running, Sliding Billy was baseball's first great stolen base champion. His ability to draw bases on balls, as well as his .344 lifetime batting average, resulted in his scoring an amazing total of 144 runs, a rookie record that has never been broken.

One of the early home run threats in an era (1890) when not many homers were hit was hard-slugging Bill Joyce. So feared was Joyce that he was walked 123 times, the most of any rookie in history

Hap Myers held the stolen base record for 71 years before Juan Samuel of the Phillies snapped his mark in 1984. Samuel became the only rookie to bat over 700 times. Lloyd Waner's 198 singles is a long-unbroken record. Joe Jackson has the most hits, Johnny Frederick claims the doubles crown and Mark McGwire is the new home run champion.

CHAPTER 8

ROOKIE PITCHING RECORDS

NATIONAL LEAGUE QUIZ

1. Two pitchers have started 68 games and completed 66. Who was the National League pitcher to have done this?
2. The most wins ever registered by a rookie is 47. Who is he?
3. This unbeatable pitcher was 10–0 in 1941. Do you know him?
4. This old-timer allowed less than one run per game. Name him.
5. Can you name the pitcher who presently holds the strikeout mark?

AMERICAN LEAGUE QUIZ

1. Who was the first rookie pitcher to strike out more than 200 batters?
2. Two pitchers share the shutout record at 8. Name them.

3. Who was the first pitcher to relieve in more than 70 games?
4. The most wins ever recorded by a relief pitcher is 14. Name him.
5. Who is the current wins-saves champion?

MAJOR LEAGUE QUIZ

1. One pitcher has the most games record for relief pitchers. Who is he?
2. Do you know the rookie who has lost the most games?
3. The most strikeouts ever recorded by a rookie pitcher is 513. Who is this amazing pitcher?
4. Another unbreakable record was set in the very first year of baseball when this rookie tossed 16 shutouts. Name him.
5. Can you name the first pitcher to win more than 10 games in relief?

NATIONAL LEAGUE	AMERICAN LEAGUE	MAJOR LEAGUE

NATIONAL LEAGUE

Most Total Games
1876	Jim Devlin, Lou	68
1880	Lee Richmond, Wor	74
1976	Butch Metzger, SD	77
1985	**Tim Burke, Mon**	**78**

Most Games Started
1876	Jim Devlin, Lou	68

Most Games Started after 1900
1900	Ed Scott, Cin	36
1901	Christy Mathewson, NY	38
1905	**Irv Young, Bos**	**42**
1908	**George McQuillan, Phi**	**42**

Most Games Completed
1876	Jim Devlin, Lou	66

Most Games Completed after 1900
1900	Ed Scott, Cin	32
1901	Christy Mathewson, NY	36
1905	Irv Young, Bos	41

Most Wins
1876	Al Spalding, Chi	47

Most Wins after 1900
1900	Ed Scott, Cin	17
1901	Christy Mathewson, NY	20
1908	George McQuillan, Phi	23
1911	**Grover Alexander, Phi**	**28**

Most Losses
1876	Jim Devlin, Lou	35
1883	**John Coleman, Phi**	**48**

Most Losses after 1900
1900	Ed Scott, Cin	21
1901	Long John Hughes, Chi	21
1905	**Harry McIntyre, Bkn**	**25**
1907	**Stony McGlynn, StL**	**25**

Highest Winning Percentage (min. 10 games)
1876	Al Spalding, Chi	.783
1876	Jack Manning, Bos	.783
1887	Larry Twitchell, Det	.917
1941	**Howie Krist, StL (10-0)**	**1.000**

AMERICAN LEAGUE

Most Total Games
1901	Roy Patterson, Chi	41
1908	Rube Manning, NY	41
1909	Bob Groom, Was	44
1913	Reb Russell, Chi	51
1944	Joe Berry, Phi	53
1961	Frank Funk, Cle	56
1962	Dick Radatz, Bos	62
1966	Ken Sanders, KC	62
1982	**Ed Vande Berg, Sea**	**78**

Most Starts
1901	Roscoe Miller, Det	36
1913	Reb Russell, Chi	36
1918	Scott Perry, Phi	36
1922	Herman Pillette, Det	37

Most Games Completed
1901	Roscoe Miller, Det	35

Most Wins
1901	Roscoe Miller, Det	23
1908	Ed Summers, Det	24
1910	**Russ Ford, NY**	**26**

Most Losses
1901	Bill Reidy, Mil	20
1904	Beany Jacobson, Was	23
1909	Bob Groom, Was	26

DID YOU KNOW ... *That in 1876 the pitcher could deliver the ball from anywhere within a six-foot-square box?*

Highest Winning Percentage (min. 10 games)
1901	Casey Patten, Was	.643
1908	Ed Summers, Det	.667
1909	Harry Krause, Phi	.692
1910	Russ Ford, NY	.813
1979	**Ron Davis, NY**	**.875**

MAJOR LEAGUE

Most Total Games
1876	Jim Devlin, Lou, NL	68
1880	Lee Richmond, Wor, NL	74
1976	Butch Metzger, SD, NL	77
1982	Ed Vande Berg, Sea, AL	78
1985	Tim Burke, Mon, NL	78
1986	**Mitch Williams, Tex**	**80**

Most Starts
1876	Jim Devlin, Lou, NL	68
1886	Matt Kilroy, Bal, AA	68

Most Starts after 1900
1900	Ed Scott, Cin, NL	36
1901	Christy Mathewson, NY, NL	38
1905	**Irv Young, Bos, NL**	**42**
1908	**George McQuillan, Phi, NL**	**42**

Most Games Completed
1876	Jim Devlin, Lou, NL	66
1886	Matt Kilroy, Bal, AA	66

Most Games Completed after 1900
1900	Ed Scott, Cin, NL	32
1901	Christy Mathewson, NY, NL	36
1905	Irv Young, Bos, NL	41

Most Wins
1876	Al Spalding, Chi, NL	47

Most Wins after 1900
1900	Ed Scott, Cin, NL	17
1901	Christy Mathewson, NY, NL	20
1908	George McQuillan, Phi, NL	23
1911	**Grover Alexander, Phi, NL**	**28**

Most Losses
1876	Jim Devlin, Lou, NL	35
1883	**John Coleman, Phi, NL**	**48**

Most Losses after 1900
1900	Ed Scott, Cin, NL	21
1901	Long John Hughes, Chi, NL	21
1904	Beany Jacobson, Was, AL	23
1905	Harry McIntyre, Bkn, NL	25
1907	Stony McGlynn, StL, NL	25
1909	**Bob Groom, Was, AL**	**26**

Highest Winning Percentage
1876	Al Spalding, Chi, NL	.783
1876	Jack Manning, Bos, NL	.783
1887	Larry Twitchell, Det, NL	.917
1941	**Howie Krist, StL, NL**	**1.000**

NATIONAL LEAGUE

Lowest ERA
1876	George Bradley, StL	1.23
1880	**Tim Keefe, Tro**	**0.86**

Lowest ERA after 1900
1900	Ed Scott, Cin	3.82
1901	Christy Mathewson, NY	2.41
1908	George McQuillan, Phi	1.53
1909	**Babe Adams, Pit**	**1.11**

Most Innings Pitched
1876	Jim Devlin, Lou	622

Most Innings Pitched after 1900
1900	Ed Scott, Cin	323
1901	Christy Mathewson, NY	336
1905	**Irv Young, Bos**	**378**

Most Hits Allowed
1876	Bobby Mathews, NY	693
1883	**John Coleman, Phi**	**772**

Most Hits Allowed after 1900
1900	Ed Scott, Cin	380

Most Bases on Balls Allowed
1876	Joe Borden, Bos	51
1877	Tricky Nichols, StL	53
1878	The Only Nolan, Ind	56
1880	Larry Corcoran, Chi	99
1884	Ed Begley, NY	99
1887	Mark Baldwin, StL	122
1891	Chick Fraser, Lou	166
1955	**Sam Jones, Chi**	**185**

Most Strikeouts
1876	Jim Devlin, Lou	122
1878	Will White, Cin	169
1880	Larry Corcoran, Chi	268
1984	**Dwight Gooden, NY**	**276**

DID YOU KNOW . . . *That from 1876 to 1881, the pitcher's box was located 45 feet from home plate? And that from 1882 to 1892 the distance was 50 feet? It was moved to 60'6" in 1893.*

Most Shutouts
1876	George Bradley, StL	16

Most Shutouts after 1900
1901	Christy Mathewson, NY	5
1907	**Irv Young, Bos**	**7**
1908	**George McQuillan, Phi**	**7**
1911	**Grover Alexander, Phi**	**7**
1968	**Jerry Koosman, NY**	**7**

AMERICAN LEAGUE

Lowest ERA
1901	George Winter, Bos	2.80
1902	Highball Wilson, Phi	2.43
1904	Otto Hess, Cle	1.67
1908	Ed Summers, Det	1.64
1909	**Harry Krause, Phi**	**1.39**

Most Innings Pitched
1901	Roscoe Miller, Det	332.0
1918	**Scott Perry, Phi**	**332.1**

Most Hits Allowed
1901	Bill Reidy, Mil	364

Most Bases on Balls Allowed
1901	Earl Moore, Cle	107
1911	Gene Krapp, Cle	136
1914	Jim Shaw, Was	137
1916	**Elmer Myers, Phi**	**168**

Most Strikeouts
1901	Roy Patterson, Chi	127
1903	Chief Bender, Phi	127
1904	Fred Glade, StL	156
1910	Russ Ford, NY	209
1955	**Herb Score, Cle**	**245**

Most Shutouts
1901	Roy Patterson, Chi	4
1901	Casey Patten, Was	4
1901	Earl Moore, Cle	4
1902	Addie Joss, Cle	5
1904	Fred Glade, StL	6
1909	Harry Krause, Phi	7
1910	**Russ Ford, NY**	**8**
1913	**Reb Russell, Chi**	**8**

MAJOR LEAGUE

Lowest ERA
1876	George Bradley, StL, NL	1.23
1880	**Tim Keefe, Tro, NL**	**0.86**

Lowest ERA after 1900
1900	Ed Scott, Cin, NL	3.82
1901	Christy Mathewson, NY, NL	2.41
1904	Otto Hess, Cle, AL	1.67
1908	George McQuillan, Phi, NL	1.53
1909	**Babe Adams, Pit, NL**	**1.11**

Most Innings Pitched
1876	Jim Devlin, Lou, NL	622

Most Innings Pitched after 1900
1900	Ed Scott, Cin, NL	323
1901	Christy Mathewson, NY, NL	336
1905	**Irv Young, Bos, NL**	**378**

Most Hits Allowed
1876	Bob Mathews, NY, NL	693
1883	**John Coleman, Phi, NL**	**772**

Most Hits Allowed after 1900
1900	Ed Scott, Cin, NL	380

Most Bases on Balls Allowed
1876	Joe Borden, Bos, NL	51
1877	Tricky Nichols, StL, NL	53
1877	Terry Larkin, Har, NL	53
1878	The Only Nolan, Ind, NL	56
1880	Larry Corcoran, Chi, NL	99
1884	Ed Begley, NY, NL	99
1886	Matt Kilroy, Bal. AA	182
1955	**Sam Jones, Chi, NL**	**185**

Most Strikeouts
1876	Jim Devlin, Lou, NL	122
1878	Will White, Cin, NL	169
1880	Larry Corcoran, Chi, NL	268
1884	Larry McKeon, Ind, AA	308
1886	**Matt Kilroy, Bal, AA**	**513**

Most Strikeouts after 1900
1900	Ed Scott, Cin, NL	92
1901	John Hughes, Chi, NL	225
1911	Grover Alexander, Phi, NL	227
1955	Herb Score, Cle, AL	245
1984	**Dwight Gooden, NY, NL**	**276**

Most Shutouts
1876	George Bradley, StL, NL	16

Most Shutouts after 1900
1900	None	
1901	Christy Mathewson, NY, NL	5
1907	Irv Young, Bos, NL	7
1908	George McQuillan, Phi, NL	7
1909	Harry Krause, Phi, AL	7
1910	**Russ Ford, NY, AL**	**8**
1913	**Reb Russell, Chi, AL**	**8**

NATIONAL LEAGUE			AMERICAN LEAGUE			MAJOR LEAGUE		
Most Relief Appearances			*Most Relief Appearances*			*Most Relief Appearances*		
1876	Jack Manning, Bos	14	1901	Bert Husting, Mil	8	1876	Jack Manning, Bos, NL	14
1906	George Ferguson, NY	21	1902	Charlie Shields, Bal	8	1906	George Ferguson, NY, NL	21
1920	Huck Betts, Phi	23	1904	Ed Walsh, Chi	10	1913	Joe Bush, Phi, AL	24
1922	Claude Jonnard, NY	33	1905	Bill Hogg, NY	17	1915	Carl Mays, Bos, AL	32
1930	Joe Heving, NY	39	1907	Tex Pruiett, Bos	18	1924	Firpo Marberry, Was, AL	35
1948	Bobby Hogue, Bos	39	1913	Joe Bush, Phi	24	1926	Joe Pate, Phi, AL	45
1951	George Spencer, NY	53	1915	Carl Mays, Bos	32	1944	Joe Berry, Phi, AL	53
1952	Hoyt Wilhelm, NY	71	1924	Firpo Marberry, Was	35	1952	Hoyt Wilhelm, NY, NL	71
1976	Butch Metzger, SD	77	1926	Joe Pate, Phi	45	1976	Butch Metzger, SD, NL	77
1985	**Tim Burke, Mon**	**78**	1944	Joe Berry, Phi	53	1982	Ed Vande Berg, Sea, AL	78
			1961	Frank Funk, Cle	56	1985	Tim Burke, Mon, NL	78
			1962	Dick Radatz, Bos	62	**1986**	**Mitch Williams, Tex, AL**	**80**
			1982	Ed Vande Berg, Sea	78			
			1986	**Mitch Williams, Tex**	**80**			
Most Relief Wins			*Most Relief Wins*			*Most Relief Wins*		
1876	Jack Manning, Bos	4	1901	Roy Patterson, Chi	2	1876	Jack Manning, Bos, NL	4
1909	Babe Adams, Pit	6	1901	Erwin Harvey, Chi	2	1891	Clark Griffith, StL, AA	7
1922	Claude Jonnard, NY	6	1901	Bill Reidy, Mil	2	1913	Joe Bush, Phi, AL	7
1928	Jim Faulkner, NY	7	1902	Ed Walsh, Chi	2	1926	Joe Pate, Phi, AL	9
1930	Joe Heving, NY	7	1903	Rube Kisenger, Det	2	1927	Wilcy Moore, NY, AL	13
1939	Junior Thompson, Cin	8	1904	Frank Smith, Chi	2	**1952**	**Hoyt Wilhelm, NY, NL**	**15**
1946	Emil Kush, Chi	8	1904	Barney Pelty, StL	2			
1948	Bobby Hogue, Bos	8	1905	Bill Hogg, NY	4			
1951	George Spencer, NY	8	1908	Ed Summers, Det	5			
1952	**Hoyt Wilhelm, NY**	**15**	1911	Vean Gregg, Cle	5			
			1912	Hugh Bedient, Bos	6			
			1913	Joe Bush, Phi	7			
			1926	Joe Pate, Phi	9			
			1927	Wilcy Moore, NY	13			
			1979	**Ron Davis, NY**	**14**			
Most Relief Losses			*Most Relief Losses*			*Most Relief Losses*		
1876–1898	Twenty have one loss		1901	Roy Patterson, Chi	2	1876–1884	Many tied with one	
1899	Sam Leever, Pit	5	1901	Bill Reidy, Mil	2	1885	Pop Corkhill, Cin, AA	3
1909	Forrest More, StL	5	1905	Bill Hogg, NY	3	1899	Sam Leever, Pit, NL	5
1922	Tony Kaufmann, Chi	6	1908	Burt Keeley, Was	3	1909	Forrest More, Bos, NL	5
1928	Jim Faulkner, NY	6	1910	Elmer Koestner, Cle	4	1916	Jim Bagby, Cle, AL	6
1936	Claude Passeau, Phi	7	1916	Jim Bagby, Cle	6	1920	Ben Karr, Bos, AL	6
1952	**Lew Burdette, Bos**	**8**	1920	Ben Karr, Bos	6	1921	Jim Middleton, Det, AL	8
			1921	Jim Middleton, Det	8	1944	Joe Berry, Phi, AL	8
			1944	Joe Berry, Phi	8	1952	Lew Burdette, Bos, NL	8
			1961	**Frank Funk, Cle**	**11**	**1961**	**Frank Funk, Cle, AL**	**11**

NATIONAL LEAGUE

Most Saves

1876	Jack Manning, Bos	5
1906	George Ferguson, NY	6
1930	Joe Heving, NY	6
1937	Cliff Melton, NY	7
1939	Bob Bowman, StL	9
1952	Joe Black, Bkn	15
1955	Jack Meyer, Phi	16
1965	Frank Linzy, SF	21
1975	Rawley Eastwick, Cin	22
1986	**Todd Worrell, StL**	**36**

DID YOU KNOW . . . *That in 1876, four teams had one-man pitching staffs? Chicago had Al Spalding (47–13), St. Louis had George Bradley (45–19), Louisville had Jim Devlin (30–35) and New York had Bobby Mathews (21–34).*

Most Relief Wins and Saves

1876	Jack Manning, Bos	9
1922	Claude Jonnard, NY	11
1930	Joe Heving, NY	13
1939	Bob Bowman, StL	16
1952	Joe Black, Bkn	29
1965	Frank Linzy, SF	30
1986	**Todd Worrell, StL**	**45**

AMERICAN LEAGUE

Most Saves

1901	Erwin Harvey, Chi	1
1901	Roscoe Miller, Det	1
1901	Bert Husting, Mil	1
1902	Clarence Wright, Cle	1
1904	Ed Walsh, Chi	1
1905	Jim Buchanan, StL	2
1906	John Eubank, Det	2
1907	Tex Pruiett, Bos	3
1913	Joe Boehling, Was	4
1913	Reb Russell, Chi	4
1914	Jack Bentley, Was	4
1914	Red Faber, Chi	4
1915	Carl Mays, Bos	7
1921	Jim Middleton, Det	7
1922	Hub Pruett, StL	7
1924	Firpo Marberry, Was	15
1958	Ryne Duren, NY	20
1962	**Dick Radatz, Bos**	**24**

Most Relief Wins and Saves

1901	Erwin Harvey, Chi	3
1904	Ed Walsh, Chi	3
1905	Bill Hogg, NY	5
1908	Ed Summers, Det	6
1909	Jack Warhop, NY	6
1911	Fred Blanding, Cle	6
1912	Hugh Bedient, Bos	8
1913	Joe Bush, Phi	10
1915	Carl Mays, Bos	12
1924	Firpo Marberry, Was	21
1927	Wilcy Moore, NY	26
1958	Ryne Duren, NY	26
1962	**Dick Radatz, Bos**	**33**

MAJOR LEAGUE

Most Saves

1876	Jack Manning, Bos, NL	5
1906	George Ferguson, NY, NL	6
1915	Carl Mays, Bos, AL	7
1921	Jim Middleton, Det, AL	7
1922	Hub Pruett, StL, AL	7
1924	Firpo Marberry, Was, AL	15
1958	Ryne Duren, NY, AL	20
1962	Dick Radatz, Bos, AL	24
1986	**Todd Worrell, StL, NL**	**36**

Most Relief Wins and Saves

1876	Jack Manning, Bos, NL	9
1913	Joe Bush, Phi, AL	10
1915	Carl Mays, Bos, AL	12
1924	Firpo Marberry, Was, AL	21
1927	Wilcy Moore, NY, AL	26
1952	Joe Black, Bkn, NL	29
1962	Dick Radatz, Bos, AL	33
1986	**Todd Worrell, Cin, NL**	**45**

NATIONAL LEAGUE SUMMARY

Top Record Producers

1	Jim Devlin, Lou	5
2	Jack Manning, Bos	4
3	Joe Heving, NY	3
3	Claude Jonnard, NY	3

Most Outstanding Record Producers

Jim Devlin, Lou	5 for 338 years
Grover Alexander, Phi	2 for 154 years
Al Spalding, Chi	2 for 123 years
Jack Manning, Bos	4 for 120 years
George Bradley, StL	2 for 116 years
Tim Keefe, Tro	1 for 108 years

AMERICAN LEAGUE SUMMARY

Top Record Producers

1	Ed Summers, Det	5
2	Roy Patterson, Chi	4
2	Roscoe Miller, Det	4
2	Russ Ford, NY	4

Most Outstanding Record Producers

Russ Ford, NY	4 for 268 years
Roscoe Miller, Det	4 for 123 years
Reb Russell, Chi	3 for 111 years
Harry Krause, Phi	3 for 81 years

MAJOR LEAGUE SUMMARY

Top Record Producers

1	Jim Devlin, Lou, NL	5
2	Jack Manning, Bos, NL	4
3	Matt Kilroy, Bal, AA	3
3	Joe Bush, Phi, AL	3

Most Outstanding Record Producers

Jim Devlin, Lou, NL	5 for 342 years
Matt Kilroy, Bal, AA	3 for 306 years
Al Spalding, Chi, NL	2 for 123 years
George Bradley, StL, NL	2 for 116 years
Tim Keefe, Tro, NL	1 for 108 years

In 1876, Jim Devlin established five of the original rookie pitching records, and three of them have never been broken. Of course they never will be broken if the rules committee continues to disregard the extreme differences in pitching conditions prior to 1900.

The initial practice was that each team had a one-man pitching staff, with no thought of relief pitchers. Pitchers were replaced by strong-armed infielders or outfielders only if injured, and thus Devlin has started, completed and pitched more innings than any rookie in baseball history.

Al Spalding and George Bradley were two other outstanding pitchers in baseball's first year. Spalding was the manager and ace pitcher for the Chicago White

Stockings, and he led them to the first pennant by winning 47 games. Bradley was just as spectacular, winning 45 games including 16 shutouts. His ERA was a splendid 1.23.

Bradley's shutouts and ERA point up some interesting facts. During this first year of baseball, it was a completely bare-handed game. Baseball gloves had not yet been invented, nor had the telephone or electric lights. Travel was by train, or by horse and buggy, and General Custer was fighting the Battle of Little Bighorn against the Indians just a few states away in the Montana Territory.

The playing fields were very rough and bumpy and yet George Bradley was able to toss 16 shutouts! And

CHRISTY MATHEWSON
The famous screwballer set many records when he broke in with the New York Giants in 1901. His greatest achievement was in the 1905 World Series, when he spun three consecutive shutouts. He tallied 373 career wins.

FIRPO MARBERRY
Firpo Marberry was one of the first star relief pitchers. He also set many league-leading records.

for a full season, hold the opposing teams to 1.23 runs per game! And even with all that, his St. Louis team still did not win the pennant!

The top "emergency" pitcher of 1876 was Jack Manning, ordinarily an outfielder, who was beckoned to help out in 14 games of which he won four and saved five, though the concept of a "save" was more than a half-century away. In fact, it took 30 years for another relief pitcher to break his appearance mark, 39 years to break his wins records and 46 years to over take his wins-saves production.

Tim Keefe posted a remarkable league-leading 0.86 ERA in 1880 to set a rookie record that will most likely never be broken; however, he appeared in only 12 games and pitched 105 innings. This is another area in which the rules committee should reconsider the qualifications of pioneer rookies versus modern-day rookies.

Russ Ford of the Yankees was one of the American League's greatest rookies. His four records have been the most difficult to break and have now lasted 268 years in total. His .813 winning percentage stood the test of time for 69 years, his 209 strikeouts lasted 45 years, his eight shutouts has only been tied and his 26 wins is still the most of any American League pitcher.

The first superstar rookie pitcher was Roscoe Miller in 1901. He started 36 games, completed 35, won 23 and pitched 332 innings. Reb Russell and Harry Krause stood out as well. Russell was the first to appear in 50 games, and he tied Russ Ford with eight shutouts.

Krause won 18 and lost 8 for a record .692 winning percentage, and his 1.39 ERA is a long-standing record.

Baseball was cheated out of seeing the development of a gifted rookie pitcher when Herb Score was hit in the eye by a batted ball. Score, who set a rookie record by striking out 245 batters in 1955, never recovered from his injury, and baseball lost a pitcher with unlimited potential.

In the relief pitching department, Wilcy Moore of the Yankees was the first to win more than ten games. His 13 victories in 1927 was a record that would last 52 years before Ron Davis, also of the Yankees, would turn in a sensational season with 14 wins against only two losses. This remarkable feat by Davis likewise gave him the present winning percentage record of .875. Davis also added nine saves in 1979 when he appeared in 44 games.

Dick Radatz of the Red Sox was the first to appear in more than 60 games, and this fine mark stood for 20 years before Ed Vande Berg of the Mariners trotted in from the bullpen 78 times in 1982 and Mitch Williams relieved 80 times in 1986. Radatz is still in the driver's seat in the wins-saves category.

Matt Kilroy was born in 1866, just about the time Candy Cummings was throwing the first curve ball. At the age of 20, Kilroy was a Major League rookie pitcher with Baltimore of the American Association. Baltimore was a last-place team, so Kilroy could win only 29 games while dropping 34. He started an astounding 68 games, completed 66 and worked a whopping 583 innings, with a 3.37 ERA. But that was only the tip of the iceberg. Kilroy spun five shutouts and struck out an unbelievable 513 batters! The best veteran pitchers were able to get was about 300 strikeouts, and this 20-year-old phenom almost doubled that. How great was Matt Kilroy?

It is understandable that pioneer pitchers could start and complete almost all of the games they appeared in, because they used an underhand, submarine-style pitching delivery, which was much easier on the arm than the overhand pitching of today. It also had to be a little easier pitching just 50 feet from home plate, as was the rule of the day, rather than today's 60′ 6″. But Kilroy created his amazing strikeout total under the rule that allowed the batters to call for a high or low pitch, with which the pitcher had to comply. If the pitcher did not throw the ball in the batter's desired range the umpire would call "bad ball," and seven bad balls would result in a base on balls. Batters also had the advantage of using a flat surface on one side of the bat, a rule that was put into effect the year before. But the most amazing rule of all was the one that dictated that foul balls were not counted as strikes. This meant that in order for Kilroy to be credited with a strikeout the batter had to completely miss three pitches or be called out on strikes.

In 1941, Howie Krist became the first rookie pitcher in baseball history to go through a season undefeated. With the minimum qualification of ten decisions, Krist won ten games and lost none. Joe Pate held the prior record with a 9–0 mark set in 1926, and there are several who had 7–0 records.

Hoyt Wilhelm and Joe Black were two modern relief pitchers who established records worthy of mention. Wilhelm was the first rookie to appear in more than 70 games and his 15 wins is the most ever. In the same year, Joe Black was equally amazing, winning 14 and saving 15 for a record 29 wins-saves mark. Dick Radatz became the new wins-saves champion in 1962 when he recorded nine wins and 24 saves for a win-save record of 33 that still stands today.

CHAPTER 9

ROOKIE FIELDING RECORDS

NATIONAL LEAGUE QUIZ

1. Name the first first baseman to register 1,500 putouts.
2. This first baseman was the first to record 100 assists, and his mark lasted 30 years before it was broken. Who was he?
3. Can you name the rookie first baseman who has the highest fielding average?
4. This outstanding second baseman was the first to reach the 400 level in putouts, and his record still stands after 61 years. Name him.
5. This Hall of Fame second baseman is the rookie leader in assists with 527. Who is he?

AMERICAN LEAGUE QUIZ

1. Who is the only second baseman with more than 400 putouts?
2. Name the present double play champion at second base.
3. Who is the shortstop with the most errors?
4. This fine shortstop has 946 total chances, a mark that still stands after 79 years. Name him.
5. One of the oldest AL records is the 232 putouts set at third base in 1901. Who set it?

MAJOR LEAGUE QUIZ

1. The Major League record for putouts at third base is 101 years old. Name the baseman who holds it.
2. This rookie catcher registered 170 assists, a mark that still stands after 75 years. Do you know him?
3. Only one catcher has ever recorded more than 1,000 total chances. Who is he?
4. Who is the only outfielder not to make an error?
5. Who was the rookie Astro rightfielder who set a fielding record in 1974?

FIRST BASE

NATIONAL LEAGUE		

Most Putouts

1876	Harry Dehlman, StL	750
1879	Oscar Walker, Buf	828
1883	Sid Farrar, Phi	1038
1884	Milt Scott, Det	1120
1887	Billy O'Brien, Was	1159
1901	Kitty Bransfield, Pit	1374
1906	Jim Nealon, Pit	1592
1917	**Walt Holke, NY**	**1635**

Most Assists

1876	Joe Gerhardt, Lou	13
1877	Juice Latham, Lou	24
1879	Oscar Walker, Buf	30
1883	Sid Farrar, Phi	31
1884	Alex McKinnon, NY	31
1890	Peek-A-Boo Veach, Cle	40
1895	Scoops Carey, Bal	43
1901	Kitty Bransfield, Pit	52
1906	Jim Nealon, Pit	102
1936	Buddy Hassett, Bkn	121
1957	**Ed Bouchee, Phi**	**125**

Most Errors

1876	Tim Murnane, Bos	55

Most Errors after 1900

1900	John Ganzel, Chi	17
1901	Kitty Bransfield, Pit	18
1906	Jim Nealon, Pit	23
1936	**Buddy Hassett, Bkn**	**26**

Most Double Plays

1876	Tim Murnane, Bos	30
1878	Chub Sullivan, Cin	33
1879	Oscar Walker, Buf	52
1884	Alex McKinnon, NY	57
1895	Scoops Carey, Bal	73
1906	Jim Nealon, Pit	90
1914	Butch Schmidt, Bos	109
1922	Roy Leslie, Phi	110
1930	Gus Suhr, Pit	142
1947	**Jackie Robinson, Bkn**	**144**

Most Total Chances

1876	Harry Dehlman, StL	791
1879	Oscar Walker, Buf	907
1883	Sid Farrar, Phi	1108
1884	Milt Scott, Det	1184
1887	Billy O'Brien, Was	1217
1901	Kitty Bransfield, Pit	1454
1906	Jim Nealon, Pit	1717
1917	**Walt Holke, NY**	**1724**

AMERICAN LEAGUE		

Most Putouts

1903	Charlie Carr, Det	1276
1908	Jerry Freeman, Was	1548
1914	George Burns, Det	1576
1921	**Earl Sheely, Chi**	**1637**

Most Assists

1903	Charlie Carr, Det	111
1921	Earl Sheely, Chi	119
1931	**Jack Burns, StL**	**125**

Most Errors

1903	Charlie Carr, Det	25
1904	Jake Stahl, Was	29
1905	Hal Chase, NY	31
1908	**Jerry Freeman, Was**	**41**

Most Double Plays

1903	Charlie Carr, Det	60
1905	Hal Chase, NY	63
1908	Jerry Freeman, Was	69
1914	George Burns, Det	72
1915	Wally Pipp, NY	85
1921	Earl Sheely, Chi	121
1929	Dale Alexander, Det	129
1931	Jack Burns, StL	131
1934	Hal Trosky, Cle	145
1942	**Les Fleming, Cle**	**152**

Most Total Chances

1903	Charlie Carr, Det	1412
1908	Jerry Freeman, Was	1655
1914	George Burns, Det	1685
1921	**Earl Sheely, Chi**	**1778**

MAJOR LEAGUE		

Most Putouts

1876	Harry Dehlman, StL, NL	750
1879	Oscar Walker, Buf, NL	828
1882	Charlie Comiskey, StL, AA	860
1883	Sid Farrar, Phi, NL	1038
1884	Dave Orr, NY, AA	1161
1887	Tom Tucker, Bal, AA	1346
1890	Mike Lehane, Col, AA	1430
1906	Jim Nealon, Pit, NL	1592
1917	Walt Holke, NY, NL	1635
1921	**Earl Sheely, Chi, AL**	**1637**

Most Assists

1876	Joe Gerhardt, Lou, NL	13
1877	Juice Latham, Lou, NL	24
1879	Oscar Walker, Buf, NL	30
1883	Sid Farrar, Phi, NL	31
1884	John Kerins, Ind, AA	41
1887	Tom Tucker, Bal, AA	50
1890	Mike Lehane, Col, AA	73
1903	Charlie Carr, Det, AL	111
1921	Earl Sheely, Chi, AL	119
1931	**Jack Burns, StL, AL**	**125**
1957	**Ed Bouchee, Phi, NL**	**125**

Most Errors

1876	**Tim Murnane, Bos, NL**	**55**

Most Errors after 1900

1900	John Ganzel, Chi, NL	17
1901	Kitty Bransfield, Pit, NL	18
1903	Charlie Carr, Det, AL	25
1904	Jake Stahl, Was, AL	29
1905	Hal Chase, NY, AL	31
1908	**Jerry Freeman, Was, AL**	**41**

Most Double Plays

1876	Tim Murnane, Bos, NL	30
1878	Chub Sullivan, Cin, NL	33
1879	Oscar Walker, Buf, NL	52
1884	Alex McKinnon, NY, NL	57
1890	Mike Lehane, Col, AA	80
1906	Jim Nealon, Pit, NL	90
1914	Butch Schmidt, Bos, NL	109
1921	Earl Sheely, Chi, AL	121
1929	Dale Alexander, Det, AL	129
1930	Gus Suhr, Pit, NL	142
1934	Hal Trosky, Cle, AL	145
1942	**Les Fleming, Cle, AL**	**152**

Most Total Chances

1876	Harry Dehlman, StL, NL	791
1879	Oscar Walker, Buf, NL	907
1883	Sid Farrar, Phi, NL	1108
1884	Dave Orr, NY, AA	1234
1887	Tom Tucker, Bal, AA	1431
1890	Mike Lehane, Col, AA	1530
1906	Jim Nealon, Pit, NL	1717
1917	Walt Holke, NY, NL	1724
1921	**Earl Sheely, Chi, AL**	**1778**

FIRST BASE

NATIONAL LEAGUE

Highest Fielding Average

1876	Joe Start, NY	.964
1878	Chub Sullivan, Cin	.975
1895	Scoops Carey, Bal	.987
1906	Jim Nealon, Pit	.987
1910	Jake Daubert, Bkn	.989
1914	Butch Schmidt, Bos	.990
1917	Gene Paulette, StL	.993
1936	Johnny Mize, StL	.994
1938	Frank McCormick, Cin	.995
1946	**Eddie Waitkus, Chi**	**.996**

AMERICAN LEAGUE

Highest Fielding Average

1903	Charlie Carr, Det	.982
1906	Claude Rossman, Cle	.984
1915	Wally Pipp, NY	.992
1931	Jack Burns, StL	.993
1934	**Zeke Bonura, Chi**	**.996**

MAJOR LEAGUE

Highest Fielding Average

1876	Joe Start, NY, NL	.964
1878	Chub Sullivan, Cin, NL	.975
1887	Tom Tucker, Bal, AA	.976
1888	Jay Faatz, Cle, AA	.989
1910	Jake Daubert, Bkn, NL	.989
1914	Butch Schmidt, Bos, NL	.990
1915	Wally Pipp, NY, AL	.992
1917	Gene Paulette, StL, NL	.993
1931	Jack Burns, StL, AL	.993
1936	Johnny Mize, StL, NL	.994
1938	Frank McCormick, Cin, NL	.995
1934	**Zeke Bonura, Chi, AL**	**.996**
1946	**Eddie Waitkus, Chi, NL**	**.996**

NATIONAL LEAGUE SUMMARY

Top Record Producers

1	Jim Nealon, Pit	5
2	Oscar Walker, Buf	4
3	Sid Farrar, Phi	3
3	Kitty Bransfield, Pitt	3
3	Scoops Carey, Bal	3

Most Outstanding Record Producers

Walt Holke, NY	2 for	142 years
Jim Nealon, Pit	5 for	66 years
Eddie Waitkus, Chi	1 for	42 years
Jackie Robinson, Bkn	1 for	41 years
Ed Bouchee, Phi	1 for	31 years

AMERICAN LEAGUE SUMMARY

Top Record Producers

1	Charlie Carr, Det	5
2	Earl Sheely, Chi	4
3	Jack Burns, StL	3
3	George Burns, Det	3
3	Jerry Freeman, Was	3

Most Outstanding Record Producers

Earl Sheely, Chi	4 for	152 years
Jack Burns, StL	3 for	63 years
Zeke Bonura, Chi	1 for	54 years
Les Fleming, Cle	1 for	46 years
Charlie Carr, Det	5 for	33 years

MAJOR LEAGUE SUMMARY

Top Record Producers

1	Oscar Walker, Buf, NL	4
1	Tom Tucker, Bal, AA	4
1	Mike Lehane, Col, AA	4
1	Earl Sheely, Chi, AL	4
5	Sid Farrar, Phi, NL	3
5	Jim Nealon, Pit, NL	3

Most Outstanding Record Producers

Earl Sheely, Chi, AL	4 for	152 years
Mike Lehane, Col, AA	2 for	61 years
Zeke Bonura, Chi, AL	1 for	54 years
Les Fleming, Cle, AL	1 for	46 years
Eddie Waitkus, Chi, NL	1 for	42 years
Jim Nealon, Pit, NL	3 for	30 years

SECOND BASE

NATIONAL LEAGUE

Most Putouts

1876	Jack Burdock, Har	211
1878	Joe Quest, Ind	228
1880	Pop Smith, Cin	282
1893	Heinie Reitz, Bal	315
1903	Ed Abbaticchio, Bos	316
1904	Miller Huggins, Cin	337
1923	George Grantham, Chi	374
1927	**Fresco Thompson, Phi**	**424**

Most Assists·

1876	Ed Somerville, Lou	251
1879	Thorny Hawkes, Tro	264
1880	Fred Dunlap, Cle	290
1884	Ed Andrews, Phi	326
1893	Heinie Reitz, Bal	421
1904	Miller Huggins, Cin	448
1923	George Grantham, Chi	518
1932	**Billy Herman, Chi**	**527**

Most Errors

1876	Ed Somerville, Lou	69
1880	**Pop Smith, Cin**	**89**

Most Errors after 1900

1900	No rookies	
1901	Ray Nelson, NY	22
1902	Tim Flood, Bkn	41
1903	Ed Abbaticchio, Bos	45
1904	**Miller Huggins, Cin**	**46**

Most Double Plays

1876	Charlie Sweasy, Cin	30
1880	Fred Dunlap, Cle	44
1893	Heinie Reitz, Bal	62
1923	George Grantham, Chi	90
1927	Fresco Thompson, Phi	97
1932	Billy Herman, Chi	102
1944	Emil Verban, StL	105
1983	**Bill Doran, Hou**	**109**

Most Total Chances

1876	Ed Somerville, Lou	530
1879	Thorny Hawkes, Tro	540
1880	Pop Smith, Cin	614
1884	Ed Andrews, Phi	634
1893	Heinie Reitz, Bal	784
1904	Miller Huggins, Cin	831
1923	George Grantham, Chi	947
1932	**Billy Herman, Chi**	**966**

AMERICAN LEAGUE

Most Putouts

1901	Hobe Ferris, Bos	359
1928	Carl Lind, Cle	390
1961	Chuck Schilling, Bos	397
1973	**Pedro Garcia, Mil**	**405**

Most Assists

1901	Hobe Ferris, Bos	450
1926	Tony Lazzeri, NY	461
1928	Carl Lind, Cle	505
1964	**Bobby Knoop, LA**	**522**

Most Errors

1901	Hobe Ferris, Bos	61

Most Double Plays

1901	Hobe Ferris, Bos	68
1926	Tony Lazzeri, NY	72
1928	Carl Lind, Cle	116
1951	Bobby Young, StL	118
1961	Chuck Schilling, Bos	121
1964	Bobby Knoop, LA	123
1976	**Bob Randall, Min**	**124**

Most Total Chances

1901	Hobe Ferris, Bos	870
1928	**Carl Lind, Cle**	**932**

MAJOR LEAGUE

Most Putouts

1876	Jack Burdock, Har, NL	211
1878	Joe Quest, Ind, NL	228
1880	Pop Smith, Cin, NL	282
1883	Sam Crane, NY, AA	283
1884	Sam Barkley, Tol, AA	318
1886	Lou Bierbauer, Phi, AA	380
1927	**Fresco Thompson, Phi, NL**	**424**

Most Assists

1876	Ed Somerville, Lou, NL	251
1879	Thorny Hawkes, Tro, NL	264
1880	Fred Dunlap, Cle, NL	290
1884	Sam Barkley, Tol, AA	358
1886	Reddy Mack, Lou, AA	446
1923	George Grantham, Chi, NL	518
1932	**Billy Herman, Chi, NL**	**527**

Most Errors

1876	Ed Somerville, Lou, NL	69
1880	**Pop Smith, Cin, NL**	**89**

Most Errors after 1900

1900	No Rookies	
1901	Hobe Ferris, Bos, AL	61

Most Double Plays

1876	Charlie Sweasy, Cin, NL	30
1880	Fred Dunlap, Cle, NL	44
1884	Sam Barkley, Tol, AA	46
1886	Reddy Mack, Lou, AA	60
1901	Hobe Ferris, Bos, AL	68
1923	George Grantham, Chi, NL	90
1927	Fresco Thompson, Phi, NL	97
1928	Carl Lind, Cle, AL	116
1951	Bobby Young, StL, AL	118
1961	Chuck Schilling, Bos, AL	121
1964	Bobby Knoop, LA, AL	123
1976	**Bob Randall, Min, AL**	**124**

Most Total Chances

1876	Ed Somerville, Lou, NL	530
1879	Thorny Hawkes, Tro, NL	540
1880	Pop Smith, Cin, NL	614
1883	Sam Crane, NY, AA	619
1884	Sam Barkley, Tol, AA	727
1886	Lou Bierbauer, Phi, AA	889
1923	George Grantham, Chi, NL	947
1932	**Billy Herman, Chi, NL**	**966**

SECOND BASE

NATIONAL LEAGUE		
Highest Fielding Average		
1876	Ross Barnes, Chi	.910
1879	Jack Glasscock, Cle	.919
1893	Heinie Reitz, Bal	.939
1902	Tim Flood, Bkn	.942
1904	Miller Huggins, Cin	.945
1906	Pug Bennett, StL	.948
1907	Otto Knabe, Phi	.960
1913	Heinie Groh, Cin	.963
1917	Jake Pitler, Pit	.966
1921	Sammy Bohne, Cin	.973
1940	Ham Schulte, Phi	.980
1956	**Don Blasingame, StL**	**.986**

AMERICAN LEAGUE		
Highest Fielding Average		
1901	Billy Gilbert, Mil	.936
1904	Gus Dundon, Chi	.973
1951	Bobby Young, StL	.980
1961	**Chuck Schilling, Bos**	**.991**

MAJOR LEAGUE		
Highest Fielding Average		
1876	Ross Barnes, Chi, NL	.910
1879	Jack Glasscock, Cle, NL	.919
1882	Bid McPhee, Cin, AA	.920
1884	Sam Barkley, Tol, AA	.930
1890	Bill Higgins, StL, AA	.951
1904	Gus Dundon, Chi, AL	.973
1940	Ham Schulte, Phi, NL	.980
1956	Don Blasingame, StL, NL	.986
1961	**Chuck Schilling, Bos, AL**	**.991**

NATIONAL LEAGUE SUMMARY

Top Record Producers

1	Heinie Reitz, Bal	5
2	Miller Huggins, Cin	4
2	George Grantham, Chi	4
4	Billy Herman, Chi	3

Most Outstanding Record Producers

Billy Herman, Chi	3 for	124 years
Heinie Reitz, Bal	5 for	74 years
Fresco Thompson, Phi	2 for	66 years
Miller Huggins, Cin	4 for	59 years

AMERICAN LEAGUE SUMMARY

Top Record Producers

1	Hobe Ferris, Bos	4
1	Carl Lind, Cle	4
3	Chuck Schilling, Bos	3

Most Outstanding Record Producers

Carl Lind, Cle	4 for	154 years
Hobe Ferris, Bos	4 for	104 years
Chuck Schilling, Bos	3 for	42 years

MAJOR LEAGUE SUMMARY

Top Record Producers

1	Sam Barkley, Tol, AA	5
2	George Grantham, Chi, NL	3

Most Outstanding Record Producers

Billy Herman, Chi, NL	2 for	112 years
Lou Bierbauer, Phi, AA	2 for	78 years
Fresco Thompson, Phi, NL	2 for	62 years
Reddy Mack, Lou, AA	2 for	52 years

SHORTSTOP

NATIONAL LEAGUE	AMERICAN LEAGUE	MAJOR LEAGUE

Most Putouts

	NATIONAL LEAGUE			AMERICAN LEAGUE			MAJOR LEAGUE	
1876	Dave Force, Phi	108	1901	Wid Conroy, Mil	285	1876	Dave Force, Phi, NL	108
1882	Fred Pfeffer, Tro	161	1903	Lee Tannehill, Chi	291	1882	Fred Pfeffer, Tro, NL	161
1885	Charlie Bastian, Phi	164	1904	Charley O'Leary, Det	308	1885	Charlie Bastian, Phi, NL	164
1889	Bill Hallman, Phi	237	1909	Donnie Bush, Det	308	1887	Ed McKeon, Cle, AA	195
1890	Bob Allen, Phi	337	**1912**	**Buck Weaver, Chi**	**342**	1889	Herman Long, KC, AA	335
1929	**Charley Gelbert, StL**	**338**				1890	Bob Allen, Phi, NL	337
						1912	**Buck Weaver, Chi**	**342**

Most Assists

	NATIONAL LEAGUE			AMERICAN LEAGUE			MAJOR LEAGUE	
1876	George Wright, Bos	251	1901	Freddy Parent, Bos	446	1876	George Wright, Bos, NL	251
1880	Arthur Irwin, Wor	339	1902	John Gochnaur, Cle	447	1880	Arthur Irwin, Wor, NL	339
1890	Bob Allen, Phi	500	1903	Lee Tannehill, Chi	457	1887	Ed McKeon, Cle, AA	351
1924	**Glen Wright, Pit**	**601**	1909	Donnie Bush, Det	567	1888	Henry Easterday, KC, AA	459
						1889	Ollie Beard, Cin, AA	537
						1909	Donnie Bush, Det, Al	567
						1924	**Glen Wright, Pit, NL**	**601**

Most Errors

	NATIONAL LEAGUE			AMERICAN LEAGUE			MAJOR LEAGUE	
1876	Jimmy Hallihan, NY	67	1901	Freddy Parent, Bos	63	1876	Jimmy Hallihan, NY, NL	67
1882	Fred Pfeffer, Tro	73	1903	Lee Tannehill, Chi	76	1882	Bill Gleason, StL, AA	85
1893	**Joe Sullivan, Was**	**102**	**1908**	**Neal Ball, NY**	**80**	1887	Ed McKeon, Cle, AA	99
						1889	**Herman Long, KC, AA**	**117**

Most Errors after 1900

	NATIONAL LEAGUE						MAJOR LEAGUE	
1902	Joe Tinker, Chi	72				1901	Freddy Parent, Bos, AL	63
1903	**Harvey Aubrey, Bos**	**74**				1902	Joe Tinker, Chi, NL	72
						1903	Lee Tannehill, Chi, AL	76
						1908	**Neal Ball, NY, AL**	**80**

Most Double Plays

	NATIONAL LEAGUE			AMERICAN LEAGUE			MAJOR LEAGUE	
1876	George Wright, Bos	16	1901	Freddy Parent, Bos	52	1876	George Wright, Bos, NL	16
1876	Johnny Peters, Chi	16	1902	John Gochnaur, Cle	59	1876	Johnny Peters, Chi, NL	16
1880	Arthur Irwin, Tro	27	1916	Whitey Witt, Phi	59	1880	Arthur Irwin, Wor, NL	27
1882	Fred Pfeffer, Tro	35	1921	Joe Sewell, Cle	75	1882	Fred Pfeffer, Tro, NL	35
1889	Bill Hallman, Phi	39	1925	Ike Davis, Chi	97	1889	Ollie Beard, Cin, AA	63
1890	Bob Allen, Phi	68	1928	Red Kress, StL	99	1890	Bob Allen, Phi, NL	68
1923	Heinie Sand, Phi	91	1941	Phil Rizzuto, NY	109	1921	Joe Sewell, Cle, AL	75
1924	Glen Wright, Pit	102	1950	Chico Carrasquel, Chi	112	1923	Heinie Sand, Phi, NL	91
1954	**Ernie Banks, Chi**	**105**	**1979**	**Alfredo Griffin, Tor**	**124**	1924	Glen Wright, Pit, NL	102
						1941	Phil Rizzuto, NY, AL	109
						1950	Chico Carrasquel, Chi, AL	113
						1979	**Alfredo Griffin, Tor, AL**	**124**

Most Total Chances

	NATIONAL LEAGUE			AMERICAN LEAGUE			MAJOR LEAGUE	
1876	Dave Force, Phi	384	1901	Freddy Parent, Bos	769	1876	Dave Force, Phi, NL	384
1880	Arthur Irwin, Wor	485	1903	Lee Tannehill, Chi	824	1882	Fred Pfeffer, Tro, NL	510
1882	Fred Pfeffer, Tro	510	**1909**	**Donnie Bush, Det**	**946**	1882	Bill Gleason, StL, AA	510
1885	Charlie Bastian, Phi	563				1885	Charlie Bastian, Phi, NL	563
1889	Bill Hallman, Phi	641				1887	Ed McKeon, Cle, AA	645
1890	Bob Allen, Phi	906				1889	Herman Long, KC, AA	931
1924	**Glen Wright, Pit**	**963**				1909	Donnie Bush, Det, AL	946
						1924	**Glen Wright, Pit, NL**	**963**

SHORTSTOP

NATIONAL LEAGUE

Highest Fielding Average

1876	Johnny Peters, Chi	.932
1890	Jimmy Cooney, Chi	.936
1913	Rabbit Maranville, Bos	.949
1926	Johnny Butler, Bkn	.949
1933	Blondy Ryan, NY	.950
1954	Ernie Banks, Chi	.959
1970	**Larry Bowa, Phi**	**.979**

AMERICAN LEAGUE

Highest Fielding Average

1901	Wid Conroy, Mil	.922
1902	John Gochnaur, Cle	.933
1903	Charlie Moran, Was	.943
1914	Everett Scott, Bos	.949
1925	Jackie Tavener, Det	.963
1953	Harvey Kuenn, Det	.973
1978	**Alan Trammell, Det**	**.979**

MAJOR LEAGUE

Highest Fielding Average

1876	Johnny Peters, Chi, NL	.932
1890	Jimmy Cooney, Chi, NL	.936
1913	Rabbit Maranville, Bos, NL	.949
1914	Everett Scott, Bos, AL	.949
1925	Jackie Tavener, Det, AL	.963
1953	Harvey Kuenn, Det, AL	.973
1970	**Larry Bowa, Phi, NL**	**.979**
1978	Alan Trammell, Det, AL	.979

NATIONAL LEAGUE SUMMARY

Top Record Producers

1	Bob Allen, Phi	4
2	Fred Pfeffer, Tro	3
2	Bill Hallman, Phi	3
2	Arthur Irwin, Wor	3
2	Glen Wright, Pit	3

Most Outstanding Record Producers

Glen Wright, Pit	3 for 158 years
Bob Allen, Phi	4 for 140 years
Charley Gelbert, StL	1 for 59 years
Ernie Banks, Chi	2 for 50 years

AMERICAN LEAGUE SUMMARY

Top Record Producers

1	Lee Tannehill, Chi	3
1	Donnie Bush, Det	3
1	Freddy Parent, Bos	3
1	John Gochnaur, Cle	3

Most Outstanding Record Producers

Donnie Bush, Det	3 for 161 years
Buck Weaver, Chi	1 for 76 years
Chico Carrasquel, Chi	1 for 29 years
Harvey Kuenn, Det	1 for 25 years

MAJOR LEAGUE SUMMARY

Top Record Producers

1	Fred Pfeffer, Tro, NL	3
1	Ed McKeon, Cle, AA	3
1	Glen Wright, Pit, NL	3

Most Outstanding Record Producers

Glen Wright, Pit, NL	3 for 145 years
Buck Weaver, Chi, AL	1 for 76 years
Bob Allen, Phi, NL	2 for 53 years

THIRD BASE

NATIONAL LEAGUE	AMERICAN LEAGUE	MAJOR LEAGUE

Most Putouts

NATIONAL LEAGUE		AMERICAN LEAGUE		MAJOR LEAGUE	
1876 Cap Anson, Chi	135	1901 Bill Coughlin, Was	232	1876 Cap Anson, Chi, NL	135
1881 Jerry Denny, Pro	144			1881 Jerry Denny, Pro, NL	144
1884 Joe Mulvey, Phi	151			1884 Joe Mulvey, Phi, NL	151
1889 Patsy Tebeau, Cle	185			1886 Joe Werrick, Lou, AA	162
1890 Will Smalley, Cle	221			**1887 Denny Lyons, Phi, AA**	**255**
1899 Jimmy Williams, Pit	**251**				

Most Putouts after 1900

1900 Piano Legs Hickman, NY, NL	183
1901 Bill Coughlin, Was, AL	**232**

Most Assists

NATIONAL LEAGUE		AMERICAN LEAGUE		MAJOR LEAGUE	
1876 Cap Anson, Chi	147	1901 Bill Coughlin, Was	275	1876 Cap Anson, Chi, NL	147
1879 Hardy Richardson, Buf	153	1909 Frank Baker, Phi	277	1879 Hardy Richardson, Buf, NL	153
1880 Art Whitney, Wor	162	1912 Eddie Foster, Was	348	1880 Art Whitney, Wor, NL	162
1881 Jerry Denny, Pro	181	**1923 Rube Lutzke, Cle**	**358**	1881 Jerry Denny, Pro, NL	181
1884 Joe Mulvey, Phi	216			1883 Arlie Latham, StL, AA	256
1889 Patsy Tebeau, Cle	287			1886 Joe Werrick, Lou, AA	257
1890 Will Smalley, Cle	327			1888 Bill Shindle, Bal, AA	340
1899 Jimmy Williams, Pit	**354**			1890 Charlie Reilly, Col, AA	354
				1899 Jimmy Williams, Pit, NL	354
				1923 Rube Lutzke, Cle, AL	**358**

Most Errors

NATIONAL LEAGUE		AMERICAN LEAGUE		MAJOR LEAGUE	
1876 Al Nichols, NY	73	1901 Bill Coughlin, Was	43	1876 Al Nichols, NY, NL	73
1884 Joe Mulvey, Phi	73	**1912 Eddie Foster, Was**	**45**	1882 Bill Gleason, StL, AA	83
1895 Bill Everett, Chi	75			1883 Jerry McCormick, Bal, AA	84
1900 Piano Legs Hickman, NY	**86**			1891 Pete Gilbert, Bal, AA	84
				1900 Piano Legs Hickman, NY, NL	**86**

Most Double Plays

NATIONAL LEAGUE		AMERICAN LEAGUE		MAJOR LEAGUE	
1876 Cap Anson, Chi	8	1901 Bill Coughlin, Was	16	1876 Cap Anson, Chi, NL	8
1878 Frank Hankinson, Chi	9	1909 Jimmy Austin, NY	19	1878 Frank Hankinson, Chi, NL	9
1879 Hardy Richardson, Buf	13	1912 Eddie Foster, Was	22	1879 Hardy Richardson, Buf, NL	13
1884 Joe Mulvey, Cle	20	1916 Charlie Pick, Phi	25	1883 Arlie Latham, StL, AA	14
1889 Patsy Tebeau, Cle	26	1923 Ossie Bluege, Was	30	1884 Joe Mulvey, Phi, NL	20
1890 Will Smalley, Cle	27	1939 Jim Tabor, Bos	32	1887 Denny Lyons, Phi, AA	29
1925 Les Bell, StL	**39**	1943 Billy Johnson, NY	32	1891 Pete Gilbert, Bal, AA	34
1973 Ron Cey, LA	**39**	1954 Jim Finigan, Phi	34	**1925 Les Bell, StL, NL**	**39**
		1969 Bill Melton, Chi	**36**	**1973 Ron Cey, LA, NL**	**39**

Most Total Chances

NATIONAL LEAGUE		AMERICAN LEAGUE		MAJOR LEAGUE	
1876 Cap Anson, Chi	332	1901 Bill Coughlin, Was	550	1876 Cap Anson, Chi, NL	332
1881 Jerry Denny, Pro	387	1912 Eddie Foster, Was	561	1881 Jerry Denny, Pro, NL	387
1884 Joe Mulvey, Phi	440	**1923 Rube Lutzke, Cle**	**579**	1883 Arlie Latham, StL, AA	434
1889 Patsy Tebeau, Cle	526			1884 Joe Mulvey, Phi, NL	440
1890 Will Smalley, Cle	612			1886 Joe Werrick, Lou, AA	491
1899 Jimmy Williams, Pit	**671**			1887 Denny Lyons, Phi, AA	543
				1888 Bill Shindle, Bal, AA	605
				1890 Charlie Reilly, Col, AA	626
				1899 Jimmy Williams, Pit, NL	**671**

Most Total Chances after 1900

NATIONAL LEAGUE			MAJOR LEAGUE	
1900 Bill Bradley, Chi	516		1900 Piano Legs Hickman, NY, NL	545
1949 Willie Jones, Phi	516		**1901 Bill Coughlin, Was, AL**	**550**
1951 Randy Jackson, Chi	**545**			

THIRD BASE

NATIONAL LEAGUE

Highest Fielding Average
1876	Joe Battin, StL	.867
1878	Frank Hankinson, Chi	.875
1882	Mike Muldoon, Cle	.880
1889	Patsy Tebeau, Cle	.897
1895	Jimmy Collins, Lou	.926
1902	Ed Gremminger, Bos	.951
1909	Ed Lennox, Bkn	.959
1911	Eddie Zimmerman, Bkn	.961
1924	Ernie Padgett, Bos	.967
1937	**Don Gutteridge, StL**	**.978**

AMERICAN LEAGUE

Highest Fielding Average
1901	Bill Coughlin, Was	.922
1909	Jimmy Austin, NY	.928
1923	Rube Lutzke, Cle	.940
1943	**Billy Johnson, NY**	**.966**

MAJOR LEAGUE

Highest Fielding Average
1876	Joe Battin, StL, NL	.867
1878	Frank Hankinson, Chi, NL	.875
1882	Mike Muldoon, Cle, NL	.880
1888	Bill Shindle, Bal, AA	.922
1895	Jimmy Collins, Lou, NL	.926
1902	Ed Gremminger, Bos, NL	.951
1909	Ed Lennox, Bkn, NL	.959
1911	Eddie Zimmerman, Bkn, NL	.961
1924	Ernie Padgett, Bos, NL	.967
1937	**Don Gutteridge, StL, NL**	**.978**

NATIONAL LEAGUE SUMMARY

Top Record Producers
1	Patsy Tebeau, Cle	5
2	Cap Anson, Chi	4
2	Joe Mulvey, Phi	4
2	Will Smalley, Cle	4
5	Jerry Denny, Pro	3
5	Jimmy Williams, Pit	3

Most Outstanding Record Producers
Jimmy Williams, Pit	3 for	267 years
Will Smalley, Cle	4 for	62 years
Les Bell, StL	1 for	58 years
Don Gutteridge, StL	1 for	51 years

AMERICAN LEAGUE SUMMARY

Top Record Producers
1	Bill Coughlin, Was	5
2	Eddie Foster, Was	3
2	Rube Lutzke, Cle	3
4	Billy Johnson, NY	2

Most Outstanding Record Producers
Rube Lutzke, Cle	3 for	150 years
Bill Coughlin, Was	5 for	122 years
Billy Johnson, NY	2 for	56 years

MAJOR LEAGUE SUMMARY

Top Record Producers
1	Cap Anson, Chi, NL	4
2	Jerry Denny, Pro, NL	3
2	Joe Mulvey, Phi, NL	3
2	Joe Werrick, Lou, AA	3
2	Denny Lyons, Phi, AA	3
2	Arlie Latham, StL, AA	3
2	Bill Shindle, Bal, AA	3

Most Outstanding Record Producers
Jimmy Williams, Pit, NL	2 for	113 years
Denny Lyons, Phi, AA	3 for	106 years
Rube Lutzke, Cle, AL	1 for	65 years
Les Bell, StL, NL	1 for	58 years
Don Gutteridge, StL, NL	1 for	51 years
Pete Gilbert, Bal, AA	1 for	34 years

CATCHING

NATIONAL LEAGUE		
Most Putouts		
1876	John Clapp, StL	333
1883	Mike Hines, Bos	382
1887	Connie Mack, Was	391
1890	Malachi Kitteridge, Chi	458
1930	Al Lopez, Bkn	465
1941	Clyde McCullough, Chi	481
1954	Bill Sarni, StL	486
1957	Cal Neeman, Chi	703
1966	Randy Hundley, Chi	871
1968	**Johnny Bench, Cin**	**942**
Most Assists		
1876	Pop Snyder, Lou	86
1878	Silver Flint, Ind	102
1883	Mike Hines, Bos	103
1887	**Tom Daly, Chi**	**148**
1912	**Ivy Wingo, StL**	**148**
Most Errors		
1876	**Nat Hicks, NY**	**94**
Most Errors after 1900		
1900	Mike Kahoe, Cin	11
1902	**Red Dooin, Phi**	**29**
Most Double Plays		
1876	John Clapp, StL	5
1878	Silver Flint, Ind	7
1881	Buck Ewing, Tro	9
1887	**Connie Mack, Was**	**15**
Most Total Chances		
1876	John Clapp, StL	445
1883	Mike Hines, Bos	547
1887	Connie Mack, Was	563
1890	Malachi Kitteridge, Chi	605
1957	Cal Neeman, Chi	767
1966	Randy Hundley, Chi	970
1968	**Johnny Bench, Cin**	**1053**
Highest Fielding Average		
1876	Doug Allison, Har	.881
1877	Bill Harbidge, Har	.881
1878	Silver Flint, Ind	.908
1881	Buck Ewing, Tro	.915
1887	Tom Daly, Chi	.935
1890	Jerry Harrington, Cin	.957
1896	Ed McFarland, StL	.961
1901	Bill Bergen, Cin	.970
1903	Ed Phelps, Pit	.980
1913	Bert Whaling, Bos	.990
1954	**Bill Sarni, StL**	**.996**

AMERICAN LEAGUE		
Most Putouts		
1901	Bill Maloney, Mil	284
1902	Harry Bemis, Cle	333
1903	Fred Abbott, Cle	337
1905	Mike Heydon, Was	368
1913	Ray Schalk, Chi	599
1962	Buck Rodgers, LA	826
1972	**Carlton Fisk, Bos**	**846**
Most Assists		
1901	Bill Maloney, Mil	111
1902	Harry Bemis, Cle	120
1905	Mike Heydon, Was	125
1913	**Sam Agnew, StL**	**170**
Most Errors		
1901	Roger Bresnahan, Bal	23
1905	Mike Heydon, Was	23
1910	**Bill Killifer, StL**	**29**
Most Double Plays		
1901	Bill Maloney, Mil	6
1903	Fred Abbott, Cle	9
1909	Oscar Stanage, Det	12
1910	Bill Killifer, StL	16
1913	**Ray Schalk, Chi**	**18**
Most Total Chances		
1901	Bill Maloney, Mil	415
1902	Harry Bemis, Cle	470
1905	Mike Heydon, Was	516
1913	Ray Schalk, Chi	768
1962	Buck Rodgers, LA	909
1972	**Carlton Fisk, Bos**	**933**
Highest Fielding Average		
1901	Fritz Buelow, Det	.967
1913	Ray Schalk, Chi	.980
1925	Benny Bengough, NY	.993
1952	**Clint Courtney, StL**	**.996**

DID YOU KNOW . . . *That the first catcher to wear a mask was Deacon White of Chicago in 1876? (Some sources say it was in 1877.)*

MAJOR LEAGUE		
Most Putouts		
1876	John Clapp, StL, NL	333
1883	Rudy Kemmler, Col, AA	388
1884	Jocko Milligan, Phi, AA	474
1913	Ray Schalk, Chi, AL	599
1957	Cal Neeman, Chi, NL	703
1962	Buck Rodgers, LA, AL	826
1966	Randy Hundley, Chi, NL	871
1968	**Johnny Bench, Cin, NL**	**942**
Most Assists		
1876	Pop Snyder, Lou, NL	86
1878	Silver Flint, Ind, NL	102
1882	Ed Whiting, Bal, AA	108
1887	Tom Daly, Chi, NL	148
1890	Harry Sage, Tol, AA	153
1913	**Sam Agnew, StL, AL**	**170**
Most Errors		
1876	**Nat Hicks, NY, NL**	**94**
Most Errors after 1900		
1900	Mike Kahoe, Cin, NL	11
1901	Roger Bresnahan, Bal, AL	23
1902	**Red Dooin, Phi, NL**	**29**
1910	**Bill Killifer, StL, AL**	**29**
Most Double Plays		
1876	John Clapp, StL, NL	5
1878	Sliver Flint, Ind, NL	7
1881	Buck Ewing, Tro, NL	9
1883	Rudy Kemmler, Col, AA	10
1887	Connie Mack, Was, NL	15
1910	Bill Killifer, StL, AL	16
1913	**Ray Schalk, Chi, AL**	**18**
Most Total Chances		
1876	John Clapp, StL, NL	445
1882	Ed Whiting, Bal, AA	488
1883	Rudy Kemmler, Col, AA	556
1884	Jocko Milligan, Phi, AA	611
1913	Ray Schalk, Chi, AL	768
1962	Buck Rodgers, LA, AL	909
1968	**Johnny Bench, Cin, NL**	**1053**
Highest Fielding Average		
1876	Doug Allison, Har, NL	.881
1877	Bill Harbidge, Har, NL	.881
1878	Sliver Flint, Ind, NL	.908
1881	Buck Ewing, Tro, NL	.915
1882	Jack O'Brien, Phi, AA	.925
1884	Jocko Milligan, Phi, AA	.939
1890	Jerry Harrington, Cin, NL	.957
1896	Ed McFarland, StL, NL	.961
1903	Ed Phelps, Pit, NL	.980
1913	Bert Whaling, Bos, NL	.990
1925	Benny Bengough, NY, AL	.993
1952	**Clint Courtney, StL, AL**	**.996**

CATCHING

NATIONAL LEAGUE SUMMARY

Top Record Producers

1	John Clapp, StL, NL	3
1	Mike Hines, Bos, NL	3
1	Connie Mack, Was, NL	3
1	Silver Flint, Ind, NL	3

Most Outstanding Record Producers

Connie Mack, Was, NL	3 for	117 years
Malachi Kitteridge, Chi, NL	2 for	107 years
Ivy Wingo, StL, NL	1 for	76 years
Bert Whaling, Bos, NL	1 for	41 years
Johnny Bench, Cin, NL	2 for	40 years

AMERICAN LEAGUE SUMMARY

Top Record Producers

1	Bill Maloney, Mil	4
1	Ray Schalk, Chi	4
3	Harry Bemis, Cle	3
3	Mike Heydon, Was	3

Most Outstanding Record Producers

Ray Schalk, Chi	4 for	185 years
Sam Agnew, StL	1 for	75 years
Mike Heydon, Was	3 for	73 years
Clint Courtney, StL	1 for	36 years
Carlton Fisk, Bos	2 for	32 years

MAJOR LEAGUE SUMMARY

Top Record Producers

1	Ray Schalk, Chi, AL	4
2	John Clapp, StL, NL	3
2	Rudy Kemmler, Col, AA	3
2	Jocko Milligan, Phi, AA	3
2	Silver Flint, Ind, NL	3

Most Outstanding Record Producers

Ray Schalk, Chi, AL	4 for	185 years
Sam Agnew, StL, AL	1 for	75 years
Jocko Milligan, Phi, AA	3 for	64 years
Johnny Bench, Cin, NL	2 for	40 years
Clint Courtney, StL, AL	1 for	36 years

LEFT FIELD

NATIONAL LEAGUE

Most Putouts

1876	Fred Treacey, NY	202
1879	Mike Mansell, Syr	204
1888	Walt Wilmot, Was	260
1899	Jack O'Brien, Was	266
1904	Fred Odwell, Cin	284
1909	Rube Ellis, StL	332
1910	**Bill Collins, Bos**	**355**

Most Assists

1876	Fred Treacey, NY	9
1878	Abner Dalrymple, Mil	11
1879	Joe Hornung, Buf	12
1879	Billy Riley, Cle	12
1880	Pete Gillespie, Tro	14
1888	Walk Wilmot, Was	19
1899	Jack O'Brien, Was	21
1909	**Rube Ellis, StL**	**28**

Most Errors

1876	George Hall, Phi	39
1876	Fred Treacey, NY	39
1888	**Walt Wilmot, Was**	**41**

Most Errors after 1900

1900	Sam Crawford, Cin	14
1902	**George Barkley, StL**	**28**

Most Double Plays

1876	George Hall, Phi	3
1877	Mike Dorgan, StL	3
1878	Abner Dalrymple, Mil	3
1880	Pete Gillespie, Tro	5
1899	Jack O'Brien, Was	5
1904	Fred Odwell, Cin	6
1909	Rube Ellis, StL	9
1932	**Joe Moore, NY**	**10**

Most Total Chances

1876	Fred Treacey, NY	250
1888	Walt Wilmot, Was	320
1909	Rube Ellis, StL	377
1910	**Bill Collins, Bos**	**387**

AMERICAN LEAGUE

Most Putouts

1901	Matty McIntyre, Phi	155
1902	Pat Dougherty, Bos	170
1905	George Stone, StL	278
1909	Clyde Engle, NY	299
1929	**Roy Johnson, Det**	**377**

Most Assists

1901	Matty McIntyre, Phi	8
1902	Pat Dougherty, Bos	8
1905	George Stone, StL	15
1909	Clyde Engle, NY	17
1910	**Duffy Lewis, Bos**	**28**

Most Errors

1901	Matty McIntyre, Phi	14
1902	Pat Dougherty, Bos	20
1911	Harry Hogan, StL	22
1913	Bobby Veach, Det	24
1929	Roy Johnson, Det	31

Most Double Plays

1902	Pat Dougherty, Bos	1
1904	Frank Huelsman, Was	2
1905	George Stone, StL	5
1909	Clyde Engle, NY	5
1910	**Duffy Lewis, Bos**	**9**

Most Total Chances

1901	Matty McIntyre, Phi	177
1902	Pat Dougherty, Bos	198
1905	George Stone, StL	307
1909	Clyde Engle, NY	334
1929	**Roy Johnson, Det**	**433**

MAJOR LEAGUE

Most Putouts

1876	Fred Treacey, NY, NL	202
1879	Mike Mansell, Syr, NL	204
1883	Tom Dolan, StL, AA	214
1887	Darby O'Brien, NY, AA	244
1888	Walt Wilmot, Was, NL	260
1899	Jack O'Brien, Was, NL	266
1904	Fred Odwell, Cin, NL	284
1909	Rube Ellis, StL, NL	332
1910	Bill Collins, Bos, NL	355
1929	**Roy Johnson, Det, AL**	**377**

Most Assists

1876	Fred Treacey, NY, NL	9
1878	Abner Dalrymple, Mil, NL	11
1879	Joe Hornung, Buf, NL	12
1879	Billy Riley, Cle, NL	12
1880	Pete Gillespie, Tro, NL	14
1882	Jud Birchall, Phi, AA	14
1883	**Tom Dolan, StL, AA**	**51**

Most Assists after 1900

1900	Sam Crawford, Cin, NL	18
1904	Fred Odwell, Cin, NL	18
1909	Rube Ellis, StL, NL	28
1910	Duffy Lewis, Bos, AL	28
1914	**Chet Chadbourne, KC, FL**	**34**

Most Errors

1876	George Hall, Phi, NL	39
1876	Fred Treacey, NY, NL	39
1888	**Walt Wilmot, Was, NL**	**41**

Most Errors after 1900

1900	Sam Crawford, Cin, NL	14
1901	Matty McIntyre, Phi, AL	14
1902	George Barclay, StL, NL	28
1929	**Roy Johnson, Det, AL**	**31**

Most Double Plays

1876	George Hall, Phi, NL	3
1877	Mike Dorgan, StL, NL	3
1878	Abner Dalrymple, Mil, NL	3
1880	Pete Gillespie, Tro, NL	5
1887	Myron Allen, Cle, AA	6
1909	Rube Ellis, StL, NL	9
1910	Duffy Lewis, Bos, AL	9
1932	**Joe Moore, NY, NL**	**10**

Most Total Chances

1876	Fred Treacey, NY, NL	250
1883	Tom Dolan, StL, AA	277
1887	Darby O'Brien, NY, AA	289
1888	Walt Wilmot, Was, NL	320
1909	Rube Ellis, StL, NL	377
1929	**Roy Johnson, Det, AL**	**433**

LEFT FIELD

NATIONAL LEAGUE

Highest Fielding Average

1876	Andy Leonard, Bos	.925
1890	Joe Knight, Cin	.925
1898	Jimmy Sheckard, Bkn	.926
1899	Jack O'Brien, Was	.926
1904	Fred Odwell, Cin	.956
1905	Wildfire Schulte, Chi	.981
1927	**Dick Spalding, Phi**	**.992**

NATIONAL LEAGUE SUMMARY

Top Record Producers

1	Jack O'Brien, Was	4
1	Rube Ellis, StL	4
1	Walt Wilmot, Was	3
2	Fred Odwell, Cin	3
2	Fred Treacey, NY	3

Most Outstanding Record Producers

Bill Collins, Bos	2 for 156 years
Rube Ellis, StL	4 for 104 years
Dick Spalding, Phi	1 for 61 years
Joe Moore, NY	1 for 56 years
Walt Wilmot, Was	3 for 33 years

AMERICAN LEAGUE

Highest Fielding Average

1901	Matty McIntyre, Phi	.921
1904	Frank Huelsman, Was	.960
1912	Howard Shanks, Was	.962
1913	Johnny Johnston, StL	.965
1918	Merlin Kopp, Phi	.972
1936	Joe DiMaggio, NY	.978
1979	**Billy Sample, Tex**	**1.000**

AMERICAN LEAGUE SUMMARY

Top Record Producers

1	Matty McIntyre, Phi	4
1	Pat Dougherty, Bos	4
1	George Stone, StL	4
1	Clyde Engle, NY	4

Most Outstanding Record Producers

Duffy Lewis, Bos	2 for 156 years
Roy Johnson, Det	2 for 118 years
Clyde Engle, NY	4 for 51 years
Joe DiMaggio, NY	1 for 43 years

MAJOR LEAGUE

Highest Fielding Average

1876	Andy Leonard, Bos, NL	.925
1882	Joe Sommer, Cin, AA	.925
1883	Tom Dolan, StL, AA	.957
1905	Wildfire Schulte, Chi, NL	.981
1927	Dick Spalding, Phi, NL	.992
1979	**Billy Sample, Tex, AL**	**1.000**

MAJOR LEAGUE SUMMARY

Top Record Producers

1	Tom Dolan, StL, AA	4
2	Fred Treacey, NY, NL	3
2	Rube Ellis, StL, NL	3

Most Outstanding Record Producers

Tom Dolan, StL, AA	4 for 137 years
Roy Johnson, Det, AL	2 for 118 years
Joe Moore, NY, NL	1 for 56 years
Dick Spalding, Phi, NL	1 for 52 years

CENTER FIELD

NATIONAL LEAGUE		AMERICAN LEAGUE		MAJOR LEAGUE	
Most Putouts		*Most Putouts*		*Most Putouts*	
1876 Jack Remsen, Har	177	1901 Irv Waldron, Was	237	1876 Jack Remsen, StL, NL	177
1884 Jim Fogarty, Phi	193	1905 Charlie Jones, Was	240	1884 Curt Welch, Tol, AA	206
1888 Dummy Hoy, Was	296	1907 Denny Sullivan, Bos	296	1887 Mike Griffin, Bal, AA	256
1899 Jimmy Slagle, Was	407	1911 Bert Shotton, StL	356	1888 Dummy Hoy, Was, NL	296
1929 Johnny Frederick, Bkn	410	1924 Al Simmons, Phi	390	1889 Jim Burns, KC, AA	323
1932 Kiddo Davis, Phi	411	1925 Earle Combs, NY	401	1899 Jimmy Slagle, Was, NL	407
1938 Harry Craft, Cin	436	1930 Tommy Oliver, Bos	477	1930 Tommy Oliver, Bos, AL	477
1945 Carden Gillenwater, Bos	**451**				
Most Assists		*Most Assists*		*Most Assists*	
1876 Lip Pike, StL	13	1901 Irv Waldron, Was	16	1876 Lip Pike, StL, NL	13
1877 Bill Crowley, Lou	20	1905 Charlie Jones, Was	24	1877 Bill Crowley, Lou, NL	20
1888 Dummy Hoy, Was	26	1905 Ben Koehler, StL	24	1884 Curt Welch, Tol, AA	24
1889 Jim McAleer, Cle	29	1907 Joe Birmingham, Cle	33	1888 Harry Lyons, StL, AA	32
1890 George Davis, Cle	**35**			**1889 Charlie Duffee, StL, AA**	**43**
Most Assists after 1900				*Most Assists after 1900*	
1900 Jimmy Barrett, Cin, NL	**25**			1900 Jimmy Barrett, Cin, NL	25
				1907 Joe Birmingham, Cle, AL	**33**
Most Errors		*Most Errors*		*Most Errors*	
1876 Charley Jones, Cin	27	1901 Irv Waldron, Was	21	1876 Charley Jones, Cin, NL	27
1876 Jim O'Rourke, Bos	27	1909 Ray Demmitt, NY	21	1876 Jim O'Rourke, Bos, NL	27
1879 Andy Hall, Tro	27			1879 Andy Hall, Tro, NL	27
1888 Dummy Hoy, Was	**37**			1884 Curt Welch, Tol, AA	29
				1888 Dummy Hoy, Was, NL	**37**
Most Errors after 1900				*Most Errors after 1900*	
1900 Jimmy Barrett, Cin	**24**			1900 Jimmy Barrett, Cin, NL	24
Most Double Plays		*Most Double Plays*		*Most Double Plays*	
1876 Jack Remsen, Har	5	1901–04 None		1876 Jack Remsen, Har, NL	5
1876 Lip Pike, StL	5	1905 Ben Koehler, StL	11	1876 Lip Pike, StL, NL	5
1888 Dummy Hoy, Was	7			1888 Dummy Hoy, Was, NL	7
1889 Jim McAleer, Cle	9			1889 Jimmy McAleer, Cle, NL	9
1890 George Davis, Cle	**9**			1890 George Davis, Cle, NL	9
				1905 Ben Koehler, StL, AL	**11**
Most Double Plays after 1900					
1900 Jimmy Barrett, Cin	6				
1908 Al Shaw, StL	7				
1928 Denny Sothern, Phi	7				
1943 Buster Adams, Phi	**8**				
Most Total Chances		*Most Total Chances*		*Most Total Chances*	
1876 Jack Remsen, Har	213	1901 Irv Waldron, Was	274	1876 Jack Remsen, Har, NL	213
1884 Jim Fogarty, Phi	224	1905 Charlie Jones, Was	275	1884 Curt Welch, Tol, AA	259
1888 Dummy Hoy, Was	359	1907 Joe Birmingham, Cle	323	1887 Mike Griffin, Bal, AA	291
1899 Jimmy Slagle, Was	448	1911 Bert Shotton, StL	397	1888 Dummy Hoy, Was, NL	359
1938 Harry Craft, Cin	459	1924 Al Simmons, Phi	417	1889 Jim Burns, KC, AA	366
1945 Carden Gillenwater, Bos	**485**	1925 Earle Combs, NY	422	.1930 Tommy Oliver, Bos, AL	495
		1927 Alex Metzler, Chi	428		
		1930 Tommy Oliver, Bos	.495		

DID YOU KNOW . . . *That prior to 1920, a fair or foul ball was judged by where it landed rather than by where it went over the fence?*

CENTER FIELD

NATIONAL LEAGUE

Highest Fielding Average

1876	Paul Hines, Chi	.923
1889	Jim McAleer, Cle	.955
1898	Algie McBride, Cin	.959
1907	Art Krueger, Cin	.972
1909	Rebel Oakes, Cin	.979
1935	Terry Moore, StL	.984
1938	Ernie Koy, Bkn	.984
1942	Tommy Holmes, Bos	.990
1959	George Altman, Chi	.990
1974	Rowland Office, Atl	.994

NATIONAL LEAGUE SUMMARY

Top Record Producers

1	Dummy Hoy, Was	4
2	Jack Remsen, Har	3
2	Jimmy McAleer, Cle	3

Most Outstanding Record Producers

George Davis, Cle	2 for 196 years
Jimmy McAleer, Cle	3 for 107 years
Carden Gillenwater, Bos	2 for 86 years
Jimmy Slagle, Was	2 for 69 years

AMERICAN LEAGUE

Highest Fielding Average

1901	Irv Waldron, Was	.919
1905	Ben Koehler, StL	.969
1907	Denny Sullivan, Bos	.975
1924	Al Simmons, Phi	.976
1925	Earle Combs, NY	.979
1930	Tommy Oliver, Bos	.982
1939	Barney McCoskey, Det	.986
1940	Walt Judnich, StL	.989
1943	**Milt Byrnes, StL**	.997

AMERICAN LEAGUE SUMMARY

Top Record Producers

1	Irv Waldron, Was	4
2	Charlie Jones, Was	3
2	Al Simmons, Phi	3
2	Earle Combs, NY	3
2	Tommy Oliver, Bos	3
2	Ben Koehler, StL	3

Most Outstanding Record Producers

Tommy Oliver, Bos	3 for 125 years
Joe Birmingham, Cle	2 for 85 years
Ben Koehler, StL	3 for 77 years
Milt Byrnes, StL	1 for 45 years

MAJOR LEAGUE

Highest Fielding Average

1876	Paul Hines, Chi, NL	.923
1887	Mike Griffin, Bal, AA	.924
1889	Jimmy McAleer, Cle, NL	.955
1898	Algie McBride, Cin, NL	.959
1907	Denny Sullivan, Bos, AL	.975
1940	Walt Judnich, StL, AL	.989
1942	Tommy Holmes, Bos, NL	.990
1943	**Milt Byrnes, StL, AL**	.997

MAJOR LEAGUE SUMMARY

Top Record Producers

1	Jack Remsen, StL, NL	3
1	Curt Welch, Tol, AA	3
1	Mike Griffin, Bal, AA	3
1	Dummy Hoy, Was, NL	3

Most Outstanding Record Producers

Tommy Oliver, Bos, AL	2 for 116 years
Charlie Duffee, StL, AA	1 for 99 years
Ben Koehler, StL, AL	1 for 83 years
Jim Burns, KC, AA	2 for 51 years
Milt Byrnes, StL, AL	1 for 45 years

RIGHT FIELD

NATIONAL LEAGUE			AMERICAN LEAGUE			MAJOR LEAGUE		
Most Putouts			*Most Putouts*			*Most Putouts*		
1876	Jack Manning, Bos	73	1901	Bill Hallman, Mil	226	1876	Jack Manning, Bos, NL	73
1876	Eddie Booth, NY	73	1911	Joe Jackson, Cle	242	1876	Eddie Booth, NY, NL	73
1877	Orator Shaffer, Lou	121	1928	Doug Taitt, Bos	251	1877	Orator Shaffer, Lou, NL	121
1879	Jake Evans, Tro	153	1932	Bruce Campbell, StL	297	1879	Jake Evans, Tro, NL	153
1890	Steve Brodie, Bos	225	1939	Ted Williams, Bos	318	1883	Pop Corkhill, Cin, AA	162
1894	Jimmy Bannon, Bos	240	**1977**	**Jim Norris, Cle**	**320**	1894	Jimmy Bannon, Bos, NL	240
1904	Spike Shannon, StL	246				1904	Spike Shannon, StL, NL	246
1907	Mike Mitchell, Cin	265				1907	Mike Mitchell, Cin, NL	265
1926	Paul Waner, Pit	307				1914	Benny Kauf, Ind, FL	310
1935	**Ival Goodman, Cin**	**322**				**1935**	**Ival Goodman, Cin, NL**	**322**
Most Assists			*Most Assists*			*Most Assists*		
1876	Dick Higham, Har	16	1901	Bill Hallman, Mil	22	1876	Dick Higham, Har, NL	16
1877	Orator Shaffer, Lou	21	**1906**	**Harry Niles, StL**	**34**	1877	Orator Shaffer, Lou, NL	21
1878	King Kelly, Cin	24				1878	King Kelly, Cin, NL	24
1879	Jake Evans, Tro	30				1879	Jake Evans, Tro, NL	30
1894	**Jimmy Bannon, Bos**	**43**				**1894**	**Jimmy Bannon, Bos, NL**	**43**
Most Assists after 1900						*Most Assists after 1900*		
1901	Lefty Davis, Pit	18				1901	Bill Hallman, Mil, AL	22
1902	Pat Carney, Bos	19				1904	Harry Lumley, Bkn, NL	26
1903	Jimmy Sebring, Pit	20				1906	Harry Niles, StL, AL	34
1904	Harry Lumley, Bkn	26				**1907**	**Mike Mitchell, Cin, NL**	**39**
1907	**Mike Mitchell, Cin**	**39**						
Most Errors			*Most Errors*			*Most Errors*		
1876	Eddie Booth, NY	26	**1901**	**Bill Hallman, Mil**	**26**	1876	Eddie Booth, NY, NL	26
1877	Orator Shaffer, Lou	28				1877	Orator Shaffer, Lou, NL	28
1879	Charlie Eden, Cle	29				1879	Charlie Eden, Cle, NL	29
1894	**Jimmy Bannon, Bos**	**41**				1882	Ed Swartwood, Pit, AA	29
						1894	**Jimmy Bannon, Bos, NL**	**41**
Most Errors after 1900								
1901	Lefty Davis, Pit	4				*Most Errors after 1900*		
1902	Pat Carney, Bos	13				**1901**	**Bill Hallman, Mil, AL**	**26**
1903	Jimmy Sebring, Pit	18						
1915	**Tom Long, StL, NL**	**20**						
Most Double Plays			*Most Double Plays*			*Most Double Plays*		
1876	Dave Pearson, Cin	2	1901	Bill Hallman, Mil	6	1876	Dave Pearson, Cin, NL	2
1876	Joe Blong, StL	2	1911	Joe Jackson, Cle	8	1876	Joe Blong, StL, NL	2
1877	John Cassidy, Har	2	**1928**	**Doug Taitt, Bos**	**8**	1877	John Cassidy, Har, NL	2
1878	King Kelly, Cin	2				1878	King Kelly, Cin, NL	2
1879	Jake Evans, Tro	4				1879	Jake Evans, Tro, NL	4
1882	Chief Roseman, Tro	6				1882	Chief Roseman, Tro, NL	6
1890	Steve Brodie, Bos	6				**1894**	**Jimmy Bannon, Bos, NL**	**12**
1894	**Jimmy Bannon, Bos**	**12**						
						Most Double Plays after 1900		
Most Double Plays after 1900						1901	Lefty Davis, Pit, NL	7
1901	Lefty Davis, Pit	7				1902	Pat Carney, Bos, NL	7
1902	Pat Carney, Bos	7				**1903**	**Jimmy Sebring, Pit, NL**	**11**
1903	**Jimmy Sebring, Pit**	**11**						

DID YOU KNOW . . . *That because of the dead ball used in the early days, many outfield fences were less than 250 feet?*

RIGHT FIELD

NATIONAL LEAGUE		AMERICAN LEAGUE		MAJOR LEAGUE	

NATIONAL LEAGUE

Most Total Chances

1876	Eddie Booth, NY	110
1877	Orator Shaffer, Lou	170
1879	Jake Evans, Tro	207
1890	Steve Brodie, Bos	256
1894	Jimmy Bannon, Bos	324
1926	Paul Waner, Pit	336
1935	**Ival Goodman, Cin**	**353**

Highest Fielding Average

1876	Joe Blong, StL	.895
1888	Count Campau, Det	.933
1890	Steve Brodie, Bos	.953
1901	Lefty Davis, Pit	.975
1904	Spike Shannon, StL	.978
1916	Joe Wilhoit, Bos	.979
1938	Goody Rosen, Bkn	.989
1974	**Greg Gross, Hou**	**.994**

AMERICAN LEAGUE

Most Total Chances

1901	Bill Hallman, Mil	274
1911	Joe Jackson, Cle	286
1932	Bruce Campbell, StL	329
1939	**Ted Williams, Bos**	**348**

Highest Fielding Average

1901	Socks Seybold, Phi	.954
1906	Harry Niles, StL	.967
1924	Ike Boone, Bos	.976
1947	**Sam Mele, Bos**	**.992**
1973	**Bob Coluccio, Mil**	**.992**

MAJOR LEAGUE

Most Total Chances

1876	Eddie Booth, NY, NL	110
1877	Orator Shaffer, Lou, NL	170
1879	Jake Evans, Tro, NL	207
1894	Jimmy Bannon, Bos, NL	324
1914	**Benny Kauff, Ind, FL**	**358**

Highest Fielding Average

1876	Joe Blong, StL, NL	.895
1882	Chicken Wolf, Lou, AA	.902
1883	Pop Corkhill, Cin AA	.930
1888	Count Campau, Det, NL	.933
1890	Steve Brodie, Bos, NL	.953
1901	Lefty Davis, Pit, NL	.975
1904	Spike Shannon, StL, NL	.978
1947	**Sam Mele, Bos, AL**	**.992**
1973	**Bob Coluccio, Mil, AL**	**.992**

NATIONAL LEAGUE SUMMARY

Top Record Producers

1	Jake Evans, Tro	4
1	Steve Brodie, Bos	4
1	Jimmy Bannon, Bos	4
4	Orator Shaffer, Lou	3

Most Outstanding Record Producers

Jimmy Bannon, Bos	4 for 230 years
Ival Goodman, Cin	2 for 106 years
Jake Evans, Tro	4 for 40 years
Goody Rosen, Bkn	1 for 36 years

AMERICAN LEAGUE SUMMARY

Top Record Producers

1	Bill Hallman, Mil	4
2	Joe Jackson, Cle	3

Most Outstanding Record Producers

Joe Jackson, Cle	3 for 115 years
Harry Niles, StL	2 for 100 years
Ted Williams, Bos	2 for 87 years
Doug Taitt, Bos	2 for 62 years

MAJOR LEAGUE SUMMARY

Top Record Producers

1	Jake Evans, Tro, NL	4
1	Jimmy Bannon, Bos, NL	4
3	Orator Shaffer, Lou, NL	3

Most Outstanding Record Producers

Jimmy Bannon, Bos, NL	4 for 218 years
Benny Kauff, Ind, FL	2 for 93 years
Ival Goodman, Cin, NL	1 for 53 years
Spike Shannon, StL, NL	1 for 43 years

If the longevity of records is the measuring tool that tells us who the greatest fielders were, this is a brief summary of the Major League results at each position.

At first base, Earl Sheely of the White Sox ranks number one with four records lasting 152 years. Billy Herman of the Cubs is the premier second baseman with two marks good for 112 years. Old-Timer Glen Wright of the Pirates is the top shortstop with three records for 145 years. At third base, Jimmy Williams's achievements have been in the books for 113 years as a result of his two outstanding records. Ray Schalk of the White Sox leads all catchers with four fabulous marks for 185 years. Tom Dolan from St. Louis in the old American Association is the leading leftfielder with four marks for 137 years. In center field it is Tommy Oliver of the Red Sox who tallied 2 super records lasting 116 years, and in right field Jimmy Bannon of the Braves tops them all with four records lasting a total of 218 years.

Jimmy Bannon, Ray Schalk and Earl Sheely have the three longest sets of records, with Bannon the only member of this entire group to have three unbroken records. Players with two unbroken marks are Earl Sheely, Billy Herman, Glen Wright and Tommy Oliver. Jimmy Williams, Ray Schalk and Tom Dolan each have one record intact.

JOE DiMAGGIO

Joe DiMaggio had a tremendous year as a rookie. He rapped 206 hits, 44 doubles, 15 triples, 29 homers, and 125 RBIs, scored 132 runs, batted .323, and slugged .576. He also set a rookie major league fielding record— as a leftfielder.

JACKIE ROBINSON

In 1947, Jackie Robinson served notice about his personal talent and integrity—and the rightness of blacks to play in the major league. Did you know he started his career playing first base—and he set a National League record for double plays that still stands?

CHAPTER 10

LEAGUE LEADERS CAREER BATTING TITLE RECORDS

NATIONAL LEAGUE QUIZ

1. This hustling player is not yet in the Hall of Fame, but he is the only National Leaguer ever to lead the league in hits seven times. Do you know him?
2. Can you name the outstanding contact hitter whose seven singles crowns are the most in National League history?
3. This Hall of Famer set five records in the doubles category and is presently tied for top honors with eight doubles titles. Name him.
4. This smooth-hitting lefthander established three consecutive triples title records and is the only player to win five triples crowns. Who is he?
5. Only one slugger has won seven home run titles. He played for the Pittsburgh Pirates and is presently a sportscaster. Name him.

AMERICAN LEAGUE QUIZ

1. This marvelous hitter tied Nap Lajoie for the most hits titles and went on to establish four records. He is the only player to lead the league in hits eight times. Name him.
2. This scrappy little hitter also is not in the Hall of Fame, but he has the distinction of leading the league in singles an unprecedented nine times. Who is he?
3. The player who has hit more doubles than any other has been the doubles champion eight times. Do you know him?
4. Can you name the slugger who led the league in home runs 12 times and home run percentage 13 times?
5. Three Hall of Famers are tied for the most total bases crowns. How many can you name?

MAJOR LEAGUE QUIZ

1. This remarkable hitter led the majors in various batting categories 69 times, eight of which were in runs scored and six in runs batted in. Do you know him?
2. Only one player has led the major league in bases on balls 11 times. Who was he?
3. Billy Hamilton was one of the greatest base stealers of all time. He won seven titles but was tied by a speedster who went on to win more stolen base titles than any other. Name him.
4. Can you name the sensational hitter who has won the most batting average titles?
5. Who was the first player to win seven slugging average crowns?

NATIONAL LEAGUE		AMERICAN LEAGUE		MAJOR LEAGUE	
Most Hits Titles		*Most Hits Titles*		*Most Hits Titles*	
1876 Ross Barnes, Chi	1	1901 Nap Lajoie, Phi	1	1876 Ross Barnes, Chi, NL	1
1877 Deacon White, Bos	1	1902 Piano Legs Hickman, Cle	1	1877 Deacon White, Bos, NL	1
1878 Joe Start, Chi	1	1903 Pat Dougherty, Bos	1	1878 Joe Start, Chi, NL	1
1879 Paul Hines, Pro	1	1904 Nap Lajoie, Cle	2	1879 Paul Hines, Pro, NL	1
1880 Abner Dalrymple, Chi	1	1906 Nap Lajoie, Cle	3	1880 Abner Dalrymple, Chi, NL	1
1881 Cap Anson, Chi	1	1909 Ty Cobb, Det	3	1881 Cap Anson, Chi, NL	1
1882 Dan Brouthers, Buf	1	1910 Nap Lajoie, Cle	4	1882 Dan Brouthers, Buf, NL	1
1883 Dan Brouthers, Buf	2	1911 Ty Cobb, Det	4	1883 Dan Brouthers, Buf, NL	2
1890 Jack Glasscock, NY	2	1912 Ty Cobb, Det	5	1890 Jack Glasscock, NY, NL	2
1890 Sam Thompson, Phi	2	1915 Ty Cobb, Det	6	1890 Sam Thompson, Phi, NL	2
1892 Dan Brouthers, Bkn	3	1917 Ty Cobb, Det	7	1892 Dan Brouthers, Bkn, NL	3
1893 Sam Thompson, Phi	3	**1919 Ty Cobb, Det**	**8**	1893 Sam Thompson, Phi, NL	3
1898 Jesse Burkett, Cle	3			1904 Ginger Beaumont, Pit, NL	3
1901 Jesse Burkett, StL	4	**DID YOU KNOW**...*That a batter was*		1906 Nap Lajoie, Cle, AL	3
1907 Ginger Beaumont, Bos	4	*not charged with a strike for hitting a*		1907 Ginger Beaumont, Pit, NL	4
1924 Rogers Hornsby, StL	4	*foul bunt until 1894?*		1910 Nap Lajoie, Cle, Al	4
1948 Stan Musial, StL	4			1911 Ty Cobb, Det, AL	4
1949 Stan Musial, StL	5	**DID YOU KNOW**...*That the sacrifice*		1912 Ty Cobb, Det, AL	5
1952 Stan Musial, StL	6	*bunt was first recognized in 1889, but*		1915 Ty Cobb, Det, AL	6
1976 Pete Rose, Cin	6	*the batter was charged with a time at*		1917 Ty Cobb, Det, AL	7
1981 Pete Rose, Phi	**7**	*bat?*		**1919 Ty Cobb, Det, AL**	**8**
Most Singles Titles		*Most Singles Titles*		*Most Singles Titles*	
1876 Ross Barnes, Chi	1	1901 Nap Lajoie, Phi	1	1876 Ross Barnes, Chi, NL	1
1877 Cal McVey, Chi	1	1902 Lave Cross, Phi	1	1877 Cal McVey, Chi, NL	1
1878 Joe Start, Chi	1	1903 Pat Dougherty, Bos	1	1878 Joe Start, Chi, NL	1
1878 Abner Dalrymple, Mil	1	1904 Willie Keeler, NY	1	1878 Abner Dalrymple, Mil, NL	1
1879 Paul Hines, Pro	1	1905 Willie Keeler, NY	2	1879 Paul Hines, Pro, NL	1
1880 Cap Anson, Chi	1	1906 Willie Keeler, NY	3	1880 Cap Anson, Chi, NL	1
1881 Cap Anson, Chi	2	1911 Ty Cobb, Det	3	1881 Cap Anson, Chi, NL	2
1888 Cap Anson, Chi	3	1912 Ty Cobb, Det	4	1888 Cap Anson, Chi, NL	3
1892 Billy Hamilton, Phi	3	1915 Ty Cobb, Det	5	1892 Billy Hamilton, Phi, NL	3
1894 Billy Hamilton, Phi	4	1917 Ty Cobb, Det	6	1894 Billy Hamilton, Phi, NL	4
1907 Ginger Beaumont, Bos	4	1919 Ty Cobb, Det	7	1907 Ginger Beaumont, Bos, NL	4
1931 Lloyd Waner, Pit	4	1958 Nellie Fox, Chi	7	1912 Ty Cobb, Det, AL	4
1935 Bill Terry, NY	4	1959 Nellie Fox, Chi	8	1915 Ty Cobb, Det, AL	5
1945 Stan Hack, Chi	4	**1960 Nellie Fox, Chi**	**9**	1917 Ty Cobb, Det, AL	6
1956 Richie Ashburn, Phi	4			1919 Ty Cobb, Det, AL	7
1957 Richie Ashburn, Phi	5			1958 Nellie Fox, Chi, AL	7
1958 Richie Ashburn, Phi	6			1959 Nellie Fox, Chi, AL	8
1959 Richie Ashburn, Phi	**7**			**1960 Nellie Fox, Chi, AL**	**9**
Most Doubles Titles		*Most Doubles Titles*		*Most Doubles Titles*	
1876 Paul Hines, Chi	1	1901 Nap Lajoie, Phi	1	1876 Ross Barnes, Chi, NL	1
1876 Dick Higham, Har	1	1902 Ed Delahanty, Was	1	1876 Paul Hines, Chi, NL	1
1876 Ross Barnes, Chi	1	1903 Socks Seybold, Phi	1	1876 Dick Higham, Har, NL	1
1877 Cap Anson, Chi	1	1904 Nap Lajoie, Cle	2	1877 Cap Anson, Chi, NL	1
1878 Dick Higham, Pro	2	1906 Nap Lajoie, Cle	3	1878 Dick Higham, Pro, NL	2
1881 Paul Hines, Pro	2	1910 Nap Lajoie, Cle	4	1881 Paul Hines, Pro, NL	2
1882 King Kelly, Chi	2	1918 Tris Speaker, Cle	4	1882 King Kelly, Chi, NL	2
1884 Paul Hines, Pro	3	1920 Tris Speaker, Cle	5	1884 Paul Hines, Pro, NL	3
1888 Dan Brouthers, Det	3	1921 Tris Speaker, Cle	6	1888 Dan Brouthers, Det, NL	3
1889 Ed Delahanty, Phi	3	1922 Tris Speaker, Cle	7	1889 King Kelly, Bos, NL	3
1901 Ed Delahanty, Phi	4	**1923 Tris Speaker, Cle**	**8**	1899 Ed Delahanty, Phi, NL	3
1904 Honus Wagner, Pit	4			1901 Ed Delahanty, Phi, NL	4
1905 Honus Wagner, Pit	5			1902 Ed Delahanty, Was, AL	5
1906 Honus Wagner, Pit	6			1906 Honus Wagner, Pit, NL	5
1907 Honus Wagner, Pit	7			1907 Honus Wagner, Pit, NL	6
1908 Honus Wagner, Pit	**8**			1908 Honus Wagner, Pit, NL	7
1954 Stan Musial, Stl	**8**			**1909 Honus Wagner, Pit, NL**	**8**
				1923 Tris Speaker, Cle, AL	**8**
				1954 Stan Musial, StL, NL	**8**

NATIONAL LEAGUE		AMERICAN LEAGUE		MAJOR LEAGUE	

Most Triples Titles

NATIONAL LEAGUE		AMERICAN LEAGUE		MAJOR LEAGUE	
1876 Ross Barnes, Chi	1	1901 Bill Keister, Bal	1	1876 Ross Barnes, Chi, NL	1
1877 Deacon White, Bos	1	1901 Jimmy Williams, Bal	1	1877 Deacon White, Bos, NL	1
1878 Tom York, Pro	1	1902 Jimmy Williams, Bal	2	1878 Tom York, Pro, NL	1
1879 Buttercup Dickerson, Cin	1	1906 Elmer Flick, Cle	2	1879 Buttercup Dickerson, Cin, NL	1
1880 Harry Stovey, Wor	1	1907 Elmer Flick, Cle	3	1880 Harry Stovey, Wor, NL	1
1881 Jack Rowe, Buf	1	1913 Sam Crawford, Det	3	1881 Jack Rowe, Buf, NL	1
1882 Roger Connor, Tro	1	1914 Sam Crawford, Det	4	1882 Roger Connor, Tro, NL	1
1883 Dan Brouthers, Buf	1	**1915 Sam Crawford, Det**	**5**	1883 Dan Brouthers, Buf, NL	1
1884 Buck Ewing, NY	1			1884 Harry Stovey, Phi, AA	2
1885 Jim O'Rourke, NY	1			1886 Harry Stovey, Phi, AA	3
1886 Roger Connor, NY	2			1891 Harry Stovey, Phi, AA	4
1891 Harry Stovey, Bos	2			1914 Sam Crawford, Det, AL	4
1903 Honus Wagner, Pit	2			**1915 Sam Crawford, Det, AL**	**5**
1908 Honus Wagner, Pit	3			**1951 Stan Musial, StL, NL**	**5**
1940 Arky Vaughn, Pit	3				
1948 Stan Musial, StL	3				
1949 Stan Musial, StL	4				
1951 Stan Musial, StL	**5**				

Most Home Run Titles

NATIONAL LEAGUE		AMERICAN LEAGUE		MAJOR LEAGUE	
1876 George Hall, Phi	1	1901 Nap Lajoie, Phi	1	1876 George Hall, Phi, NL	1
1877 Lip Pike, Cin	1	1902 Socks Seybold, Phi	1	1877 Lip Pike, Cin, NL	1
1878 Paul Hines, Pro	1	1903 Buck Freeman, Bos	1	1878 Paul Hines, Pro, NL	1
1879 Charley Jones, Bos	1	1904 Harry Davis, Phi	1	1879 Charley Jones, Bos, NL	1
1880 Harry Stovey, Wor	1	1905 Harry Davis, Phi	2	1880 Harry Stovey, Wor, NL	1
1880 John O'Rourke, Bos	1	1906 Harry Davis, Phi	3	1881 Dan Brouthers, Buf, NL	1
1881 Dan Brouthers, Buf	1	1907 Harry Davis, Phi	4	1882 George Wood, Det, NL	1
1882 George Wood, Det	1	1914 Frank Baker, Phi	4	1883 Harry Stovey, Phi, AA	2
1883 Buck Ewing, NY	1	1921 Babe Ruth, NY	4	1884 Harry Stovey, Phi, AA	3
1884 Ned Williamson, Chi	1	1923 Babe Ruth, NY	5	1885 Harry Stovey, Phi, AA	4
1885 Abner Dalrymple, Chi	1	1924 Babe Ruth, NY	6	1886 Harry Stovey, Phi, AA	5
1886 Dan Brouthers, Det	2	1926 Babe Ruth, NY	7	1889 Harry Stovey, Phi, AA	6
1895 Sam Thompson, Phi	2	1927 Babe Ruth, NY	8	1919 Gavvy Cravath, Phi, NL	6
1897 Hugh Duffy, Bos	2	1928 Babe Ruth, NY	9	1924 Babe Ruth, NY, AL	6
1908 Tim Jordan, Bkn	2	1929 Babe Ruth, NY	10	1926 Babe Ruth, NY, AL	7
1911 Wildfire Schulte, Chi	2	1930 Babe Ruth, NY	11	1927 Babe Ruth, NY, AL	8
1914 Gavvy Cravath, Phi	2	**1931 Babe Ruth, NY**	**12**	1928 Babe Ruth, NY, AL	9
1915 Gavvy Cravath, Phi	3			1929 Babe Ruth, NY, AL	10
1917 Gavvy Cravath, Phi	4			1930 Babe Ruth, NY, AL	11
1918 Gavvy Cravath, Phi	5			**1931 Babe Ruth, NY, AL**	**12**
1919 Gavvy Cravath, Phi	6				
1942 Mel Ott, NY	6				
1951 Ralph Kiner, Pit	6				
1952 Ralph Kiner, Pit	**7**				

NATIONAL LEAGUE

Most Home Run Percentage Titles

1876	George Hall, Phi	1
1877	Lip Pike, Cin	1
1878	Paul Hines, Pro	1
1879	Charley Jones, Bos	1
1880	Charley Jones, Bos	2
1886	Dan Brouthers, Det	2
1895	Jack Clements, Phi	2
1908	Tim Jordan, Bkn	2
1911	Wildfire Schulte, Chi	2
1913	Gavvy Cravath, Phi	2
1914	Gavvy Cravath, Phi	3
1915	Gavvy Cravath, Phi	4
1917	Gavvy Cravath, Phi	5
1918	Gavvy Cravath, Phi	6
1937	Mel Ott, NY	6
1938	Mel Ott, NY	7
1939	Mel Ott, NY	8
1942	Mel Ott, NY	9
1944	**Mel Ott, NY**	**10**

Most Total Bases Titles

1876	Ross Barnes, Chi	1
1877	Deacon White, Bos	1
1878	Paul Hines, Pro	1
1878	Tom York, Pro	1
1878	Joe Start, Chi	1
1879	Paul Hines, Pro	2
1883	Dan Brouthers, Buf	2
1884	Abner Dalrymple, Chi	2
1886	Dan Brouthers, Det	3
1892	Dan Brouthers, Bkn	4
1908	Honus Wagner, Pit	4
1909	Honus Wagner, Pit	5
1924	Rogers Hornsby, StL	5
1925	Rogers Hornsby, StL	6
1929	Rogers Hornsby, Chi	7
1967	Hank Aaron, Atl	7
1969	**Hank Aaron, Atl**	**8**

Most Runs Scored Titles

1876	Ross Barnes, Chi	1
1877	Jim O'Rourke, Bos	1
1878	Dick Higham, Pro	1
1879	Charley Jones, Bos	1
1880	Abner Dalrymple, Chi	1
1881	George Gore, Chi	1
1882	George Gore, Chi	2
1885	King Kelly, Chi	2
1886	King Kelly, Chi	3
1895	Billy Hamilton, Phi	3
1897	Billy Hamilton, Bos	4
1919	George Burns, NY	4
1920	**George Burns, NY**	**5**
1929	**Rogers Hornsby, Chi**	**5**
1954	**Stan Musial, StL**	**5**

AMERICAN LEAGUE

Most Home Run Percentage Titles

1901	Mike Grady, Was	1
1902	Socks Seybold, Phi	1
1903	Piano Legs Hickman, Cle	1
1903	Buck Freeman, Bos	1
1904	Harry Davis, Phi	1
1905	Harry Davis, Phi	2
1906	Harry Davis, Phi	3
1907	Harry Davis, Phi	4
1921	Babe Ruth, NY	4
1922	Babe Ruth, NY	5
1923	Babe Ruth, NY	6
1924	Babe Ruth, NY	7
1926	Babe Ruth, NY	8
1927	Babe Ruth, NY	9
1928	Babe Ruth, NY	10
1929	Babe Ruth, NY	11
1930	Babe Ruth, NY	12
1931	**Babe Ruth, NY**	**13**

Most Total Bases Titles

1901	Nap Lajoie, Phi	1
1902	Piano Legs Hickman, Cle	1
1903	Buck Freeman, Bos	1
1904	Nap Lajoie, Cle	2
1906	George Stone, StL	2
1908	Ty Cobb, Det	2
1909	Ty Cobb, Det	3
1910	Nap Lajoie, Cle	3
1911	Ty Cobb, Det	4
1915	Ty Cobb, Det	5
1917	**Ty Cobb, Det**	**6**
1928	**Babe Ruth, NY**	**6**
1951	**Ted Williams, Bos**	**6**

Most Runs Scored Titles

1901	Nap Lajoie, Phi	1
1902	Dave Fultz, Phi	1
1903	Pat Dougherty, Bos	1
1904	Pat Dougherty, NY	2
1910	Ty Cobb, Det	2
1911	Ty Cobb, Det	3
1915	Ty Cobb, Det	4
1916	Ty Cobb, Det	5
1924	Babe Ruth, NY	5
1926	Babe Ruth, NY	6
1927	Babe Ruth, NY	7
1928	**Babe Ruth, NY**	**8**

MAJOR LEAGUE

Most Home Run Percentage Titles

1876	George Hall, Phi, NL	1
1877	Lip Pike, Cin, NL	1
1878	Paul Hines, Pro, NL	1
1879	Charley Jones, Bos, NL	1
1880	Charley Jones, Bos, NL	2
1884	Harry Stovey, Phi, AA	2
1885	Harry Stovey, Phi, AA	3
1886	Harry Stovey, Phi, AA	4
1889	Harry Stovey, Phi, AA	5
1917	Gavvy Cravath, Phi, NL	5
1918	Gavvy Cravath, Phi, NL	6
1923	Babe Ruth, NY, AL	6
1924	Babe Ruth, NY, AL	7
1926	Babe Ruth, NY, AL	8
1927	Babe Ruth, NY, AL	9
1928	Babe Ruth, NY, AL	10
1929	Babe Ruth, NY, AL	11
1930	Babe Ruth, NY, AL	12
1931	**Babe Ruth, NY, AL**	**13**

Most Total Bases Titles

1876	Ross Barnes, Chi, NL	1
1877	Deacon White, Bos, NL	1
1878	Paul Hines, Pro, NL	1
1878	Joe Start, Chi, NL	1
1879	Paul Hines, Pro, NL	2
1883	Dan Brouthers, Buf, NL	2
1884	Abner Dalrymple, Chi, NL	3
1886	Dan Brouthers, Det, NL	3
1892	Dan Brouthers, Bkn, NL	4
1908	Honus Wagner, Pit, NL	4
1909	Honus Wagner, Pit, NL	5
1915	Ty Cobb, Det, AL	5
1917	Ty Cobb, Det, AL	6
1925	Rogers Hornsby, StL, NL	6
1929	Rogers Hornsby, Chi, NL	7
1967	Hank Aaron, AtL, NL	7
1969	**Hank Aaron, AtL, NL**	**8**

Most Runs Scored Titles

1876	Ross Barnes, Chi, NL	1
1877	Jim O'Rourke, Bos, NL	1
1878	Dick Higham, Pro, NL	1
1879	Charley Jones, Bos, NL	1
1880	Abner Dalrymple, Chi, NL	1
1881	George Gore, Chi, NL	1
1882	George Gore, Chi, NL	2
1885	King Kelly, Chi, NL	2
1886	King Kelly, Chi, NL	3
1895	Billy Hamilton, Phi, NL	3
1897	Billy Hamilton, Bos, NL	4
1915	Ty Cobb, Det, AL	4
1916	Ty Cobb, Det, AL	5
1924	Babe Ruth, NY, AL	5
1926	Babe Ruth, NY, AL	6
1927	Babe Ruth, NY, AL	7
1928	**Babe Ruth, NY, AL**	**8**

NATIONAL LEAGUE

Most RBI Titles

1876	Deacon White, Chi	1
1877	Deacon White, Bos	2
1886	Cap Anson, Chi	2
1888	Cap Anson, Chi	3
1891	**Cap Anson, Chi**	4
1909	Honus Wagner, Pit	4
1918	Sherry Magee, Cin	4
1925	Rogers Hornsby, StL	4
1966	Hank Aaron, Atl	4
1986	Mike Schmidt, Phi	4

Most Bases on Balls Titles

1876	Ross Barnes, Chi	1
1877	Jim O'Rourke, Bos	1
1878	Jack Remsen, Chi	1
1878	Terry Larkin, Chi	1
1879	Charley Jones, Bos	1
1880	Bill Ferguson, Tro	1
1881	John Clapp, Cle	1
1882	George Gore, Chi	1
1883	Tom York, Cle	1
1884	George Gore, Chi	2
1886	George Gore, Chi	3
1895	Billy Hamilton, Phi	3
1896	Billy Hamilton, Bos	4
1897	Billy Hamilton, Bos	5
1904	Roy Thomas, Phi	5
1906	Roy Thomas, Phi	6
1907	**Roy Thomas, Phi**	7

Most Stolen Base Titles

1876–86	Records not kept	
1887	Monte Ward, NY	1
1888	Dummy Hoy, Was	1
1889	Jim Fogarty, Phi	1
1890	Billy Hamilton, Phi	1
1891	Billy Hamilton, Phi	2
1892	Monte Ward, Bkn	2
1894	Billy Hamilton, Phi	3
1895	Billy Hamilton, Phi	4
1896	Billy Hamilton, Bos	5
1898	Billy Hamilton, Bos	6
1920	Max Carey, Pit	6
1922	Max Carey, Pit	7
1923	Max Carey, Pit	8
1924	**Max Carey, Pit**	9

AMERICAN LEAGUE

Most RBI Titles

1901	Nap Lajoie, Phi	1
1902	Buck Freeman, Bos	1
1903	Buck Freeman, Bos	2
1904	Nap Lajoie, Cle	2
1906	Harry Davis, Phi	2
1908	Ty Cobb, Det	2
1909	Ty Cobb, Det	3
1911	Ty Cobb, Det	4
1923	Babe Ruth, NY	4
1926	Babe Ruth, NY	5
1928	**Babe Ruth, NY**	6

Most Bases on Balls Titles

1901	Dummy Hoy, Chi	1
1902	Topsy Hartsel, Phi	1
1903	Jimmy Barrett, Det	1
1904	Jimmy Barrett, Det	2
1905	Topsy Hartsel, Phi	2
1906	Topsy Hartsel, Phi	3
1907	Topsy Hartsel, Phi	4
1908	Topsy Hartsel, Phi	5
1914	Donnie Bush, Det	5
1926	Babe Ruth, NY	5
1927	Babe Ruth, NY	6
1928	Babe Ruth, NY	7
1930	Babe Ruth, NY	8
1931	Babe Ruth, NY	9
1932	Babe Ruth, NY	10
1933	**Babe Ruth, NY**	11

Most Stolen Base Titles

1901	Frank Isbell, Chi	1
1902	Topsy Hartsel, Phi	1
1903	Harry Bay, Cle	1
1904	Harry Bay, Cle	2
1906	Elmer Flick, Cle	2
1909	Ty Cobb, Det	2
1911	Ty Cobb, Det	3
1915	Ty Cobb, Det	4
1916	Ty Cobb, Det	5
1917	Ty Cobb, Det	6
1945	George Case, Was	6
1961	Luis Aparicio, Chi	6
1962	Luis Aparicio, Chi	7
1963	Luis Aparicio, Chi	8
1964	**Luis Aparicio, Chi**	9

MAJOR LEAGUE

Most RBI Titles

1876	Deacon White, Chi, NL	1
1877	Deacon White, Bos, NL	2
1886	Cap Anson, Chi, NL	2
1888	Cap Anson, Chi, NL	3
1891	Cap Anson, Chi, NL	4
1909	Honus Wagner, Pit, NL	4
1911	Ty Cobb, Det, AL	4
1918	Sherry Magee, Cin, NL	4
1923	Babe Ruth, NY, AL	4
1925	Rogers Hornsby, StL, NL	4
1926	Babe Ruth, NY, AL	5
1928	**Babe Ruth, NY, AL**	6

Most Bases on Balls Titles

1876	Ross Barnes, Chi, NL	1
1877	Jim O'Rourke, Bos, NL	1
1878	Jack Remsen, Chi, NL	1
1879	Charley Jones, Bos, NL	1
1880	Bob Ferguson, Tro, NL	1
1881	John Clapp, Cle, NL	1
1882	George Gore, Chi, NL	1
1883	Tom York, Cle, NL	1
1884	George Gore, Chi, NL	2
1886	George Gore, Chi, NL	3
1895	Billy Hamilton, Phi, NL	3
1896	Billy Hamilton, Bos, NL	4
1897	Billy Hamilton, Bos, NL	5
1904	Roy Thomas, Phi, NL	5
1906	Roy Thomas, Phi, NL	6
1907	Roy Thomas, Phi, NL	7
1928	Babe Ruth, NY, AL	7
1930	Babe Ruth, NY, AL	8
1931	Babe Ruth, NY, AL	9
1932	Babe Ruth, NY, AL	10
1933	**Babe Ruth, NY, AL**	11

Most Stolen Base Titles

1876–86	Records not kept	
1887	Monte Ward, NY, NL	1
1888	Dummy Hoy, Was, NL	1
1889	Billy Hamilton, KC, AA	1
1890	Billy Hamilton, Phi, NL	2
1891	Billy Hamilton, Phi, NL	3
1894	Billy Hamilton, Phi, NL	4
1895	Billy Hamilton, Phi, NL	5
1896	Billy Hamilton, Bos, NL	6
1898	Billy Hamilton, Bos, NL	7
1922	Max Carey, Pit, NL	7
1923	Max Carey, Pit, NL	8
1924	Max Carey, Pit, NL	9
1925	**Max Carey, Pit, NL**	10

NATIONAL LEAGUE

Most Batting Average Titles

1876	Ross Barnes, Chi	1
1877	Deacon White, Bos	1
1878	Paul Hines, Pro	1
1879	Cap Anson, Chi	1
1880	George Gore, Chi	1
1881	Cap Anson, Chi	2
1883	Dan Brouthers, Buf	2
1886	King Kelly, Chi	2
1888	Cap Anson, Chi	3
1889	Dan Brouthers, Bos	3
1892	Dan Brouthers, Bkn	4
1906	Honus Wagner, Pit	4
1907	Honus Wagner, Pit	5
1908	Honus Wagner, Pit	6
1909	Honus Wagner, Pit	7
1911	**Honus Wagner, Pit**	**8**

Most Slugging Average Titles

1876	Ross Barnes, Chi	1
1877	Deacon White, Bos	1
1878	Paul Hines, Pro	1
1880	George Gore, Chi	1
1881	Dan Brouthers, Buf	1
1882	Dan Brouthers, Buf	2
1883	Dan Brouthers, Buf	3
1884	Dan Brouthers, Buf	4
1885	Dan Brouthers, Buf	5
1886	Dan Brouthers, Det	6
1909	Honus Wagner, Pit	6
1924	Rogers Hornsby, StL	6
1925	Rogers Hornsby, StL	7
1928	Rogers Hornsby, Bos	8
1929	**Rogers Hornsby, Chi**	**9**

NATIONAL LEAGUE SUMMARY

Top Record Producers

1	Dan Brouthers, Buf	20
2	Honus Wagner, Pit	15
3	Billy Hamilton, Phi	11
4	Gavvy Cravath, Phi	10
4	Rogers Hornsby, StL	10

Most Outstanding Record Producers

Honus Wagner, Pit	15 for 290 years
Rogers Hornsby, StL	10 for 253 years

AMERICAN LEAGUE

Most Batting Average Titles

1901	Nap Lajoie, Phi	1
1902	Ed Delahanty, Was	1
1903	Nap Lajoie, Cle	2
1904	Nap Lajoie, Cle	3
1909	Ty Cobb, Det	3
1910	Ty Cobb, Det	4
1911	Ty Cobb, Det	5
1912	Ty Cobb, Det	6
1913	Ty Cobb, Det	7
1914	Ty Cobb, Det	8
1915	Ty Cobb, Det	9
1917	Ty Cobb, Det	10
1918	Ty Cobb, Det	11
1919	**Ty Cobb, Det**	**12**

DID YOU KNOW ... *That since 1967, in order to qualify for a batting or slugging title, a batter must have a total of 3.1 plate appearances for every scheduled game?*

Most Slugging Average Titles

1901	Nap Lajoie, Phi	1
1902	Ed Delahanty, Was	1
1903	Nap Lajoie, Cle	2
1904	Nap Lajoie, Cle	3
1909	Ty Cobb, Det	3
1910	Ty Cobb, Det	4
1911	Ty Cobb, Det	5
1912	Ty Cobb, Det	6
1914	Ty Cobb, Det	7
1917	Ty Cobb, Det	8
1926	Babe Ruth, NY	8
1927	Babe Ruth, NY	9
1928	Babe Ruth, NY	10
1929	Babe Ruth, NY	11
1930	Babe Ruth, NY	12
1931	**Babe Ruth, NY**	**13**

AMERICAN LEAGUE SUMMARY

Top Record Producers

1	Ty Cobb, Det	44
2	Babe Ruth, NY	40
3	Nap Lajoie, Cle	22

Most Outstanding Record Producers

Babe Ruth, NY	40 for 432 years
Ty Cobb, Det	44 for 389 years
Sam Crawford, Det	3 for 75 years
Nap Lajoie, Cle	22 for 72 years
Tris Speaker, Cle	5 for 70 years

MAJOR LEAGUE

Most Batting Average Titles

1876	Ross Barnes, Chi, NL	1
1877	Deacon White, Bos, NL	1
1878	Paul Hines, Pro, NL	1
1879	Cap Anson, Chi, NL	1
1880	George Gore, Chi, NL	1
1881	Cap Anson, Chi, NL	2
1883	Dan Brouthers, Buf, NL	2
1886	King Kelly, Chi, NL	2
1888	Cap Anson, Chi, NL	3
1889	Dan Brouthers, Bos, NL	3
1891	Dan Brouthers, Bos, AA	4
1892	Dan Brouthers, Bkn, NL	5
1907	Honus Wagner, Pit, NL	5
1908	Honus Wagner, Pit, NL	6
1909	Honus Wagner, Pit, NL	7
1911	Honus Wagner, Pit, NL	8
1914	Ty Cobb, Det, AL	8
1915	Ty Cobb, Det, AL	9
1917	Ty Cobb, Det, AL	10
1918	Ty Cobb, Det, AL	11
1919	**Ty Cobb, Det, AL**	**12**

Most Slugging Average Titles

1876	Ross Barnes, Chi, NL	1
1877	Deacon White, Bos, NL	1
1878	Paul Hines, Pro, NL	1
1880	George Gore, Chi, NL	1
1881	Dan Brouthers, Buf, NL	1
1882	Dan Brouthers, Buf, NL	2
1883	Dan Brouthers, Buf, NL	3
1884	Dan Brouthers, Buf, NL	4
1885	Dan Brouthers, Buf, NL	5
1886	Dan Brouthers, Det, NL	6
1891	Dan Brouthers, Bos, AA	7
1914	Ty Cobb, Det, AL	7
1917	Ty Cobb, Det, AL	8
1926	Babe Ruth, NY, AL	8
1927	Babe Ruth, NY, AL	9
1928	Babe Ruth, NY, AL	10
1929	Babe Ruth, NY, AL	11
1930	Babe Ruth, NY, AL	12
1931	**Babe Ruth, NY, AL**	**13**

MAJOR LEAGUE SUMMARY

Top Record Producers

1	Babe Ruth, NY, AL	33
2	Ty Cobb, Det, AL	21
3	Dan Brouthers, Buf, NL	20
4	Harry Stovey, Phi, AA	14
5	Honus Wagner, Pit, NL	12
5	Billy Hamilton, Phi, NL	12

Most Outstanding Record Producers

Babe Ruth, NY, AL	33 for 380 years
Ty Cobb, Det, AL	21 for 250 years
Honus Wagner, Pit, NL	12 for 116 years
Dan Brouthers, Buf, NL	20 for 116 years
Harry Stovey, Phi, AA	14 for 114 years

The following is a list of the top 11 offensive players in baseball history.

Top Record Producers	Total Records	Records Never Broken
1 Babe Ruth, NY, AL	130	34
2 Ty Cobb, Det, AL	115	15
3 Cap Anson, Chi, NL	104	3
4 Harry Stovey, Phi, AA	88	1
5 Nap Lajoie, Cle, AL	73	2
6 Dan Brouthers, Buf, NL	68	0
7 Honus Wagner, Pit, NL	52	5
8 Tris Speaker, Cle, AL	36	15
9 Rogers Hornsby, StL, NL	32	7
10 Stan Musial, StL, NL	24	7
11 Hank Aaron, Atl, NL	19	11

DAN BROUTHERS
One of the great early players was Dan Brouthers. He was the first Major Leaguer to win four batting titles. He ended his 19-year career with a .343 batting average.

Dan Brouthers produced more title records than any National Leaguer and was one of the greatest players prior to 1900. His talents have not gone unnoticed, as he was inducted into the Hall of Fame in 1945.

Honus Wagner produced the records that have lasted the greatest number of years, and this is a major factor toward his consideration as one of the top five of the National League's all-time greatest players.

Ty Cobb is the leader in title records, with Babe Ruth second. However, this is because Cobb earned five title records for most singles and, as we all know, the Babe was no singles hitter. A truer test of their greatness is

As expected, Babe Ruth is again at the top of the list, and that is exactly where he belongs. No other player has ever dominated the game the way he has, and perhaps no one ever will.

Ty Cobb ranks second again, but there are twice as many years between his records and the Babe's. But to rank anywhere near Babe Ruth in the standings is quite an achievement in itself. If you doubt this statement, just check the list for great players like Ted Williams, Joe DiMaggio, Willie Mays, Mickey Mantle, Stan Musial, and so on—none of them are anywhere in sight!

Dan Brouthers' records show that he is one of the greatest pre-1900 players, and Honus Wagner will always be considered the greatest all-around shortstop.

What a thrill it would have been to see Cap Anson play! It is easy to understand why most of his records have been broken, as the playing schedule of today is more than twice the number of games per season as in his day. Modern players also have the advantage of the live ball. Anson set most of his records during the 19 years that he was a player-manager for Chicago. He is a true Hall of Famer.

The most underrated and overlooked superstar seems to be Harry Stovey, another player of the pre-1900 era. Along with Dan Brouthers, Stovey was the greatest of the early home run hitters. He also was blessed with outstanding speed, as is indicated by his many triples records. Stovey was an excellent base stealer and a lifetime .300 hitter. He played half of his career in the American Association, which is another reason he has been overlooked.

Rogers Hornsby also belongs in the top five, with ten records that have lasted the second longest of any NL player.

As the years go by, Stan Musial will rise in the standings, as no player seems yet in a position to challenge his doubles, triples and runs scored titles.

seen in the longevity list. Babe Ruth is number one here, with Ty Cobb second. From there the field thins out rapidly, even though Sam Crawford, Tris Speaker, and Nap Lajoie are all superstars.

Stan Musial and Hank Aaron show their greatness by being title leaders in the major categories. Musial has tied Wagner and Speaker for the most doubles titles and has tied Crawford for the most triples crowns. Hank Aaron surpassed Wagner, Cobb and Hornsby in the total bases titles and that was a major achievement. Remember, too, that these marvelous achievements by modern players were accomplished under much tougher pitching conditions.

Not many fans are aware of the base stealing abilities of Max Carey, but clearly he was the most explosive base thief of his time. His record of ten stolen base titles will probably stand for a long time.

Tris Speaker was one of baseball's most outstanding centerfielders. Notice that 15 of his 36 records remain unbroken, and that is one of the highest ratios of unbroken records in the game.

Rogers Hornsby shows 32 records, but had he played before Babe Ruth, he would have had a lot more. Hornsby is considered by many to be the greatest right-handed hitter in baseball, and his lifetime batting average of .358 is second only to Ty Cobb's .367.

This records list cannot conclusively rank these players in order of their greatness. Fans have various criteria for judging players, and records are only one measure of greatness. Still, you cannot deny that the great players tend to leave great records. It is part of their legacy to us, almost as enjoyable as the pleasure they gave us daily when they batted in the field of glory.

NAP LAJOIE
*His .422 batting average of 1901 is still an American League record, and
he set 22 records in 8 league-leading categories.*

CHAPTER 11

LEAGUE LEADERS CAREER PITCHING TITLE RECORDS

NATIONAL LEAGUE QUIZ

1. Can you name the two pitchers who have set four complete game title records? One of them led the league six times, while the other is the present king with nine crowns.
2. This Hall of Famer led the league in wins eight times to claim the top position in this category. Who is he?
3. Only one pitcher has won four winning percentage titles, and he is not yet in the Hall of Fame. Name him.
4. Three outstanding pitchers are tied with five ERA titles. How many of them can you name?
5. A Brooklyn hurler has led the league in strikeouts more times than any other National Leaguer. Do you know him?

AMERICAN LEAGUE QUIZ

1. Rube Waddell was one of the first American League strikeout pitchers, and he won six titles. But he was tied in 1916 by a flame thrower who went on to win an amazing 12 titles and set seven records while doing it. Name this great pitcher.
2. Only one pitcher has ever led the league in shutouts seven times. Do you know him?

3. Cy Young led the league in allowing the fewest hits five times. He is tied for this honor by a modern pitcher. Do you have any idea who this could be?
4. One of the greatest relief pitchers also is not well known, but he has more saves titles than any other. Who was he?
5. Two Hall of Famers share the crown for most innings pitched titles at five. Do you know them?

MAJOR LEAGUE QUIZ

1. His nickname was "Iron Man," and he was one of the hardest-working pitchers in baseball. He is the only man who led the league for most games pitched seven times. Name this iron man.
2. Can you name the hurler who has won the most complete game titles?
3. Only one pitcher in baseball history has won five winning percentage titles. Name him.
4. This great lefthander tied Bob Feller for the most wins titles and then broke his own record twice while on his way to racking up the most wins titles in baseball. Who is he?
5. Who is the only pitcher to lead the league in ERA titles nine times?

NATIONAL LEAGUE		AMERICAN LEAGUE		MAJOR LEAGUE	
Most Games Titles		*Most Games Titles*		*Most Games Titles*	
1876 Jim Devlin, Lou	1	1901 Joe McGinnity, Bal	1	1876 Jim Devlin, Lou, NL	1
1877 Jim Devlin, Lou	2	1902 Cy Young, Bos	1	1877 Jim Devlin, Lou, NL	2
1882 Jim McCormick, Cle	2	1903 Eddie Plank, Phi	1	1882 Jim McCormick, Cle, NL	2
1884 Hoss Radbourn, Pro	2	1904 Jack Chesbro, NY	1	1884 Hoss Radbourn, Pro, NL	2
1887 John Clarkson, Chi	2	1905 Rube Waddell, Phi	1	1886 Tim Keefe, NY, NL	2
1889 John Clarkson, Bos	3	1906 Jack Chesbro, NY	2	1887 John Clarkson, Chi, NL	2
1892 Bill Hutchinson, Chi	3	1908 Ed Walsh, Chi	2	1889 John Clarkson, Chi, NL	3
1904 Joe McGinnity, NY	3	1910 Ed Walsh, Chi	3	1892 Bill Hutchinson, Chi, NL	3
1905 Joe McGinnity, NY	4	1911 Ed Walsh, Chi	4	1903 Joe McGinnity, NY, NL	3
1906 Joe McGinnity, NY	5	1912 Ed Walsh, Chi	5	1904 Joe McGinnity, NY, NL	4
1907 Joe McGinnity, NY	6	1929 Firpo Marberry, Was	5	1905 Joe McGinnity, NY, NL	5
		1932 Firpo Marberry, Was	6	1906 Joe McGinnity, NY, NL	6
				1907 Joe McGinnity, NY, NL	7
Most Games Completed Titles		*Most Games Completed Titles*		*Most Games Completed Titles*	
1876 Jim Devlin, Lou	1	1901 Joe McGinnity, Bal	1	1876 Jim Devlin, Lou, NL	1
1877 Jim Devlin, Lou	2	1902 Cy Young, Bos	1	1877 Jim Devlin, Lou, NL	1
1881 Jim McCormick, Cle	2	1903 Cy Young, Bos	2	1881 Jim McCormick, Cle, NL	2
1882 Jim McCormick, Cle	3	1908 Ed Walsh, Chi	2	1882 Jim McCormick, Cle, NL	3
1889 John Clarkson, Bos	3	1911 Walter Johnson, Was	2	1889 John Clarkson, Bos, NL	3
1892 Bill Hutchinson, Chi	3	1913 Walter Johnson, Was	3	1892 Bill Hutchinson, Chi, NL	3
1915 Grover Alexander, Phi	3	1914 Walter Johnson, Was	4	1903 Cy Young, Bos, AL	3
1916 Grover Alexander, Phi	4	1915 Walter Johnson, Was	5	1913 Walter Johnson, Was, AL	3
1917 Grover Alexander, Phi	5	**1916 Walter Johnson, Was**	6	1914 Walter Johnson, Was, AL	4
1920 Grover Alexander, Chi	6			1915 Walter Johnson, Was, AL	5
1960 Warren Spahn, Mil	6			1916 Walter Johnson, Was, AL	6
1961 Warren Spahn, Mil	7			1920 Grover Alexander, Chi, NL	6
1962 Warren Spahn, Mil	8			1960 Warren Spahn, Mil, NL	6
1963 Warren Spahn, Mil	9			1961 Warren Spahn, Mil, NL	7
				1962 Warren Spahn, Mil, NL	8
				1963 Warren Spahn, Mil, NL	9
Most Wins Titles		*Most Wins Titles*		*Most Wins Titles*	
1876 Al Spalding, Chi	1	1901 Cy Young, Bos	1	1876 Al Spalding, Chi, NL	1
1877 Tommy Bond, Bos	1	1902 Cy Young, Bos	2	1877 Tommy Bond, Bos, NL	1
1878 Tommy Bond, Bos	2	1903 Cy Young, Bos	3	1878 Tommy Bond, Bos, NL	2
1884 Hoss Radbourn, Pro	2	1915 Walter Johnson, Was	3	1884 Hoss Radbourn, Bos, PL	2
1887 John Clarkson, Chi	2	1916 Walter Johnson, Was	4	1887 John Clarkson, Chi, NL	2
1888 Tim Keefe, NY	2	1918 Walter Johnson, Was	5	1888 Tim Keefe, NY, NL	2
1889 John Clarkson, Bos	3	**1924 Walter Johnson, Was**	6	1889 John Clarkson, Bos, NL	3
1892 Bill Hutchinson, Chi	3	**1951 Bob Feller, Cle**	6	1892 Bill Hutchinson, Chi, NL	3
1898 Kid Nichols, Bos	3			1898 Kid Nichols, Bos, NL	3
1903 Joe McGinnity, NY	3			1902 Cy Young, Bos, AL	3
1904 Joe McGinnity, NY	4			1903 Cy Young, Bos, AL	4
1906 Joe McGinnity, NY	5			1904 Joe McGinnity, NY, NL	4
1917 Grover Alexander, Phi	5			1906 Joe McGinnity, NY, NL	5
1920 Grover Alexander, Chi	6			1917 Grover Alexander, Phi, NL	5
1959 Warren Spahn, Mil	6			1920 Grover Alexander, Phi, NL	6
1960 Warren Spahn, Mil	7			1951 Bob Feller, Cle, AL	6
1961 Warren Spahn, Mil	8			1959 Warren Spahn, Mil, NL	6
				1960 Warren Spahn, Mil, NL	7
				1961 Warren Spahn, Mil, NL	8

NATIONAL LEAGUE

Most Winning Percentage Titles

1876	Al Spalding, Chi	1
1876	Jack Manning, Bos	1
1877	Tommy Bond, Bos	1
1878	Tommy Bond, Bos	2
1884	Hoss Radbourn, Pro	2
1896	Bill Hoffer, Bal	2
1902	Jack Chesbro, Pit	2
1905	Sam Leever, Pit	2
1907	Ed Reulbach, Chi	2
1908	Ed Reulbach, Chi	3
1979	Tom Seaver, Cin	3
1981	**Tom Seaver, Cin**	**4**

Most ERA Titles

1876	George Bradley, StL	1
1877	Tommy Bond, Bos	1
1878	Monte Ward, Pro	1
1879	Tommy Bond, Bos	2
1885	Tim Keefe, NY	2
1888	Tim Keefe, NY	3
1909	Christy Mathewson, NY	3
1911	Christy Mathewson, NY	4
1913	**Christy Mathewson, NY**	**5**
1920	**Grover Alexander, Chi**	**5**
1966	**Sandy Koufax, LA**	**5**

DID YOU KNOW ... *That (as of 1951) a pitcher must pitch at least one inning for every game scheduled in order to qualify for an ERA title?*

Most Innings Pitched Titles

1876	Jim Devlin, Lou	1
1877	Jim Devlin, Lou	2
1882	Jim McCormick, Cle	2
1887	John Clarkson, Chi	2
1888	John Clarkson, Bos	3
1889	John Clarkson, Bos	4
1904	Joe McGinnity, NY	4
1915	Grover Alexander, Phi	4
1916	Grover Alexander, Phi	5
1917	Grover Alexander, Phi	6
1920	**Grover Alexander, Chi**	**7**

AMERICAN LEAGUE

Most Winning Percentage Titles

1901	Clark Griffith, Chi	1
1902	Bill Bernhard, Cle	1
1903	Cy Young, Bos	1
1904	Jack Chesbro, NY	1
1905	Andy Coakley, Phi	1
1906	Eddie Plank, Phi	1
1907	Wild Bill Donovan, Det	1
1908	Ed Walsh, Chi	1
1909	George Mullin, Det	1
1910	Chief Bender, Phi	1
1911	Chief Bender, Phi	2
1914	Chief Bender, Phi	3
1931	Lefty Grove, Phi	3
1933	Lefty Grove, Phi	4
1939	**Lefty Grove, Phi**	**5**

Most ERA Titles

1901	Cy Young, Bos	1
1902	Ed Siever, Det	1
1903	Earl Moore, Cle	1
1904	Addie Joss, Cle	1
1905	Rube Waddell, Phi	1
1906	Doc White, Chi	1
1907	Ed Walsh, Chi	1
1908	Addie Joss, Cle	2
1910	Ed Walsh, Chi	2
1913	Walter Johnson, Was	2
1918	Walter Johnson, Was	3
1919	Walter Johnson, Was	4
1924	Walter Johnson, Was	5
1932	Lefty Grove, Phi	5
1935	Lefty Grove, Bos	6
1936	Lefty Grove, Bos	7
1938	Lefty Grove, Bos	8
1939	**Lefty Grove, Bos**	**9**

Most Innings Pitched Titles

1901	Joe McGinnity, Bal	1
1902	Cy Young, Bos	1
1903	Cy Young, Bos	2
1908	Ed Walsh, Chi	2
1911	Ed Walsh, Chi	3
1912	Ed Walsh, Chi	4
1915	Walter Johnson, Was	4
1916	**Walter Johnson, Was**	**5**
1947	**Bob Feller, Cle**	**5**

MAJOR LEAGUE

Most Winning Percentage Titles

1876	Al Spalding, Chi, NL	1
1876	Jack Manning, Bos, NL	1
1877	Tommy Bond, Bos, NL	1
1878	Tommy Bond, Bos, NL	2
1884	Hoss Radbourn, Pro, NL	2
1890	Hoss Radbourn, Pro, NL	3
1908	Ed Reulbach, Chi, NL	3
1931	Lefty Grove, Phi, AL	3
1933	Lefty Grove, Phi, AL	4
1939	**Lefty Grove, Phi, AL**	**5**

Most ERA Titles

1876	George Bradley, StL, NL	1
1877	Tommy Bond, Bos, NL	1
1878	Monte Ward, Pro, NL	1
1879	Tommy Bond, Bos, NL	2
1885	Tim Keefe, NY, NL	2
1888	Tim Keefe, NY, NL	3
1909	Christy Mathewson, NY, NL	3
1911	Christy Mathewson, NY, NL	4
1913	Christy Mathewson, NY, NL	5
1920	Grover Alexander, Chi, NL	5
1924	Walter Johnson, Was, AL	5
1932	Lefty Grove, Phi, AL	5
1935	Lefty Grove, Phi, AL	6
1936	Lefty Grove, Phi, AL	7
1938	Lefty Grove, Phi, AL	8
1939	**Lefty Grove, Phi, AL**	**9**

Most Innings Pitched Titles

1876	Jim Devlin, Lou, NL	1
1877	Jim Devlin, Lou, NL	2
1882	Jim McCormick, Cle, NL	2
1886	Tim Keefe, NY, NL	2
1887	John Clarkson, Chi, NL	2
1888	John Clarkson, Bos, NL	3
1889	John Clarkson, Bos, NL	4
1903	Joe McGinnity, NY, NL	4
1904	Joe McGinnity, NY, NL	5
1916	Walter Johnson, Was, AL	5
1916	Grover Alexander, Phi, NL	5
1917	Grover Alexander, Phi, NL	6
1920	**Grover Alexander, Chi, NL**	**7**

DID YOU KNOW ... *That the height of the mound has been raised and lowered many times? The 1969 rule lowered it from 15" to 10".*

NATIONAL LEAGUE

Most Strikeout Titles

Year	Player	
1876	Jim Devlin, Lou	1
1877	Tommy Bond, Bos	1
1878	Tommy Bond, Bos	2
1884	Hoss Radbourn, Pro	2
1886	John Clarkson, Chi	2
1887	John Clarkson, Chi	3
1889	John Clarkson, Bos	4
1894	Amos Rusie, NY	4
1895	Amos Rusie, NY	5
1908	Christy Mathewson, NY	5
1917	Grover Alexander, Phi	5
1920	Grover Alexander, Chi	6
1927	Dazzy Vance, Bkn	6
1928	**Dazzy Vance, Bkn**	**7**

Most Shutout Titles

Year	Player	
1876	George Bradley, StL	1
1877	Tommy Bond, Bos	1
1878	Tommy Bond, Bos	2
1879	Tommy Bond, Bos	3
1894	Amos Rusie, NY	3
1895	Amos Rusie, NY	4
1900	Cy Young, StL	4
1916	Grover Alexander, Phi	4
1917	Grover Alexander, Phi	5
1919	**Grover Alexander, Chi**	**6**

Least Hits Allowed Titles

Year	Player	
1876	George Bradley, StL	1
1877	Tommy Bond, Bos	1
1877	Terry Larkin, Har	1
1878	Monte Ward, Pro	1
1879	Bill McGunnigle, Buf	1
1880	Tim Keefe, Tro	1
1881	Jim McCormick, Cle	1
1882	Larry Corcoran, Chi	1
1883	Will Sawyer, Cle	1
1884	Charlie Sweeney, Pro	1
1885	Tim Keefe, NY	2
1888	Tim Keefe, NY	3
1889	Tim Keefe, NY	4
1895	Amos Rusie, NY	4
1930	Dazzy Vance, Bkn	4
1963	Sandy Koufax, LA	4
1964	Sandy Koufax, LA	5
1965	**Sandy Koufax, LA**	**6**

DID YOU KNOW . . . *That for the first 17 years of baseball, pitchers did not have a rubber slab to push off from? The first rubber slab appeared in 1893.*

AMERICAN LEAGUE

Most Strikeout Titles

Year	Player	
1901	Cy Young, Bos	1
1902	Rube Waddell, Phi	1
1903	Rube Waddell, Phi	2
1904	Rube Waddell, Phi	3
1905	Rube Waddell, Phi	4
1906	Rube Waddell, Phi	5
1907	Rube Waddell, Phi	6
1916	Walter Johnson, Was	6
1917	Walter Johnson, Was	7
1918	Walter Johnson, Was	8
1919	Walter Johnson, Was	9
1921	Walter Johnson, Was	10
1923	Walter Johnson, Was	11
1924	**Walter Johnson, Was**	**12**

Most Shutout Titles

Year	Player	
1901	Clark Griffith, Chi	1
1901	Cy Young, Bos	1
1902	Addie Joss, Cle	1
1903	Cy Young, Bos	2
1904	Cy Young, Bos	3
1909	Ed Walsh, Chi	3
1914	Walter Johnson, Was	3
1915	Walter Johnson, Was	4
1918	Walter Johnson, Was	5
1919	Walter Johnson, Was	6
1924	**Walter Johnson, Was**	**7**

Least Hits Allowed Titles

Year	Player	
1901	Cy Young, Bos	1
1902	Bill Bernard, Cle	1
1903	Earl Moore, Cle	1
1904	Jack Chesbro, NY	1
1905	Rube Waddell, Phi	1
1906	Bob Pelty, StL	1
1907	Jim Dygert, Phi	1
1908	Addie Joss, Cle	1
1909	Cy Morgan, Phi	1
1910	Russ Ford, NY	1
1911	Vern Gregg, Cle	1
1912	Walter Johnson, Was	1
1913	Walter Johnson, Was	2
1919	Walter Johnson, Was	3
1924	Walter Johnson, Was	4
1925	**Walter Johnson, Was**	**5**
1979	**Nolan Ryan, Cal**	**5**

MAJOR LEAGUE

Most Strikeout Titles

Year	Player	
1876	Jim Devlin, Lou, NL	1
1877	Tommy Bond, Bos, NL	1
1878	Tommy Bond, Bos, NY	2
1884	Hoss Radbourn, Pro, NL	2
1886	John Clarkson, Chi, NL	2
1887	John Clarkson, Chi, NL	3
1889	John Clarkson, Bos, NL	4
1894	Amos Rusie, NY, NL	4
1895	Amos Rusie, NY, NL	5
1906	Rube Waddell, Phi, AL	5
1907	Rube Waddell, Phi, AL	6
1916	Walter Johnson, Was, AL	6
1917	Walter Johnson, Was, AL	7
1918	Walter Johnson, Was, AL	8
1919	Walter Johnson, Was, AL	9
1921	Walter Johnson, Was, AL	10
1923	Walter Johnson, Was, AL	11
1924	**Walter Johnson, Was, AL**	**12**

Most Shutout Titles

Year	Player	
1876	George Bradley, StL, NL	1
1877	Tommy Bond, Bos, NL	1
1878	Tommy Bond, Bos, NL	2
1879	Tommy Bond, Bos, NL	3
1894	Amos Rusie, NY, NL	3
1900	Cy Young, Cle, NL	4
1901	Cy Young, Bos, AL	5
1903	Cy Young, Bos, AL	6
1904	**Cy Young, Bos, AL**	**7**

Least Hits Allowed Titles

Year	Player	
1876	George Bradley, StL, NL	1
1877	Tommy Bond, Bos, NL	1
1877	Terry Larkin, Har, NL	1
1878	Monte Ward, Pro, NL	1
1879	Bill McGunnigle, Buf, NL	1
1880	Tim Keefe, NY, NL	1
1881	Jim McCormick, Cle, NL	1
1882	Larry Corcoran, Chi, NL	1
1883	Will Sawyer, Cle, NL	1
1884	Charlie Sweeney, Pro, NL	1
1885	Tim Keefe, NY, NL	2
1888	Tim Keefe, NY, NL	3
1889	Tim Keefe, NY, NL	4
1894	Amos Rusie, NY, NL	4
1924	Walter Johnson, Was, AL	4
1925	Walter Johnson, Was, Al	5
1964	Sandy Koufax, LA, NL	5
1965	Sandy Koufax, LA, NL	6
1981	Nolan Ryan, Hou, NL	6
1982	Nolan Ryan, Hou, NL	7
1983	**Nolan Ryan, Hou, NL**	**8**

NATIONAL LEAGUE

Least Bases on Balls Allowed Titles

1876	George Zettlein, Phi	1
1877	Tommy Bond, Bos	1
1878	Sam Weaver, Mil	1
1879	Tommy Bond, Bos	2
1884	Jim Whitney, Bos	2
1885	Jim Whitney, Bos	3
1886	Jim Whitney, KC	4
1887	Jim Whitney, Was	5
1896	Cy Young, Cle	5
1897	Cy Young, Cle	6
1898	Cy Young, Cle	7
1899	Cy Young, StL	8
1900	**Cy Young, StL**	**9**

AMERICAN LEAGUE

Least Bases on Balls Allowed Titles

1901	Cy Young, Bos	1
1902	Al Orth, Was	1
1903	Cy Young, Bos	2
1904	Cy Young, Bos	3
1905	Cy Young, Bos	4
1906	**Cy Young, Bos**	**5**
1972	Fritz Peterson, NY	5

MAJOR LEAGUE

Least Bases on Balls Allowed Titles

1876	George Zettlein, Phi, NL	1
1877	Tommy Bond, Bos, NL	1
1878	Sam Weaver, Mil, NL	1
1879	Tommy Bond, Bos, NL	2
1884	Jim Whitney, Bos, NL	2
1885	Jim Whitney, Bos, NL	3
1886	Jim Whitney, KC, NL	4
1887	Jim Whitney, Was, NL	5
1896	Cy Young, Cle, NL	5
1897	Cy Young, Cle, NL	6
1898	Cy Young, Cle, NL	7
1899	Cy Young, StL, NL	8
1901	Cy Young, Bos, AL	10
1903	Cy Young, Bos, AL	11
1904	Cy Young, Bos, AL	12
1905	Cy Young, Bos, AL	13
1906	**Cy Young, Bos, AL**	**14**

Most Saves Titles (National League)

1876	Jack Manning, Bos	1
1877	Cal McVey, Chi	1
1878	Egyptian Healy, Ind	1
1879	Monte Ward, Pro	1
1879	Curry Foley, Bos	1
1879	Bob Mathews, Pro	1
1880	Lee Richmond, Wor	1
1881	Bob Mathews, Pro	2
1882	Monte Ward, Pro	2
1894	Tony Mullane, Bal	2
1895	Kid Nichols, Bos	2
1897	Kid Nichols, Bos	3
1898	Kid Nichols, Bos	4
1911	Three Finger Brown, Chi	4
1982	Bruce Sutter, StL	4
1984	**Bruce Sutter, StL**	**5**

Most Saves Titles (American League)

1901	Bill Hoffer, Cle	1
1901	Joe McGinnity, Bal	1
1902	Jack Powell, StL	1
1903	George Mullin, Det	1
1904	Casey Patten, Was	1
1905	Rube Waddell, Phi	1
1906	Chief Bender, Phi	1
1906	Otto Hess, Cle	1
1907	Bill Dinneen, Bos	1
1907	Ed Walsh, Chi	1
1908	Ed Walsh, Chi	2
1910	Ed Walsh, Chi	3
1912	Ed Walsh, Chi	4
1929	Firpo Marberry, Was	4
1932	**Firpo Marberry, Was**	**5**

Most Saves Titles (Major League)

1876	Jack Manning, Bos, NL	1
1877	Cal McVey, Chi, NL	1
1878	Egyptian Healy, Ind, NL	1
1879	Monte Ward, Pro, NL	1
1879	Curry Foley, Bos, NL	1
1880	Lee Richmond, Wor, NL	1
1881	Bob Mathews, Pro, NL	1
1882	Monte Ward, Pro, NL	2
1888	Tony Mullane, Cin, AA	2
1889	Tony Mullane, Cin, AA	3
1893	Tony Mullane, Bal, NL	4
1894	**Tony Mullane, Bal, NL**	**5**
1932	**Firpo Marberry, Was, AL**	**5**
1984	**Bruce Sutter, StL, NL**	**5**

NATIONAL LEAGUE SUMMARY

Top Record Producers

1	Grover Alexander, Phi	16
2	Tommy Bond, Bos	14
3	John Clarkson, Chi	11
4	Joe McGinnity, NY	8

Most Outstanding Record Producers

Grover Alexander, Phi	16 for	311 years
Joe McGinnity, NY	8 for	113 years
Dazzy Vance, Bkn	3 for	94 years
Christy Mathewson, NY	4 for	89 years
Cy Young, Cle, NL	4 for	89 years

AMERICAN LEAGUE SUMMARY

Top Record Producers

1	Walter Johnson, Was	32
2	Cy Young, Bos	20
3	Ed Walsh, Chi	16
4	Rube Waddell, Phi	10

Most Outstanding Record Producers

Walter Johnson, Was	32 for	463 years
Cy Young, Bos	20 for	169 years
Firpo Marberry, Was	4 for	118 years
Lefty Grove, Phi	8 for	113 years

MAJOR LEAGUE SUMMARY

Top Record Producers

1	Cy Young, Bos, AL	17
2	Walter Johnson, Was, AL	15
3	Tommy Bond, Bos, NL	14
4	John Clarkson, Bos, NL	11
5	Tim Keefe, NY, NL	9
5	Joe McGinnity, NY, NL	9

Most Outstanding Record Producers

Cy Young, Bos, AL	17 for	199 years
Walter Johnson, Was, AL	15 for	173 years
Grover Alexander, Phi, NL	7 for	171 years
Joe McGinnity, NY, NL	9 for	115 years
Lefty Grove, Phi, AL	8 for	113 years

Grover Alexander has long been considered one of the greatest pitchers of all time. The above results are further proof that he indeed deserves this reputation.

Joe McGinnity was one of the hardest-working pitchers in baseball, and has earned the nickname "Iron Man." His records have proven just as durable.

On the strength of his marvelous strikeout ability, Dazzy Vance finds himself in the third position. He won the strikeout crown seven times, and this has never been matched by any National Leaguer.

The great Cy Young split his career between both leagues and did well everywhere he performed. His nine titles for least bases on balls allowed show that he was the greatest control pitcher of them all.

Rounding out the top five is Christy Mathewson of the Giants. Matty was one of the most difficult pitchers to score on. His five league-leading ERA titles has been tied by Grover Alexander and Sandy Koufax.

Warren Spahn shows why he has been voted into the Hall of Fame. No other National League hurler has won as many games completed titles or wins titles.

Two other modern-day pitchers have held their own against the giants of the pitching world: Tom Seaver and Sandy Koufax. Tom Terrific has won the most winning percentage crowns, while Koufax is tied with Grover Alexander in ERA titles and has won the least hits allowed title more times than any pitcher in baseball history.

SANDY KOUFAX
Sandy Koufax was the first pitcher to win the Cy Young Award 3 times. In his last 5 years he led the league in ERA with marks of 2.54, 1.88, 1.74, 2.04, and 1.73. During these 5 years, he averaged 288 strikeouts per season. His overall winning percentage was a sparkling .655. (Photo courtesy of the Los Angeles Dodgers)

WARREN SPAHN
Warren Spahn led the league in wins 8 times and complete games 9 times—both records that still stand today.

Walter Johnson compiled some amazing records during his years in the American League, as his impressive number of titles clearly demonstrates. Cy Young's American League records are even more amazing when we consider he spent most of his career in the National League and pitched only 11 years in the American League, and at the end of his career.

One of the stingiest pitchers the American League had was Lefty Grove. No other pitcher has won more winning percentage or ERA titles.

The most recent pitcher to rank highly in title records is "Rapid" Robert Feller of the Cleveland Indians. Feller possessed one of the game's liveliest fastballs,

and his confrontations with Joe DiMaggio were simply magnificent. He has the distinction of tying Walter Johnson for the most wins and most innings titles. That is great company to share.

The still-active Nolan Ryan has tied Walter Johnson in crowns for allowing the least hits per season. When Ryan finally hangs up his spikes, he too will go down in history as one of the game's most splendid pitchers.

Reliever Hoyt Wilhelm has received Hall of Fame honors and now it is time that another relief pitcher, Firpo Marberry, receives a little recognition. He certainly was one of the first superstar relief pitchers, and to this date no one has won as many saves titles.

Joe McGinnity truly deserves his "Iron Man" label, having registered a greater number of most games titles

than any other pitcher in baseball. Warren Spahn is the leader in two categories. He shows his tremendous durability by winning the most complete game crowns and his superior pitching talents by accumulating the most wins titles as well.

Lefty Grove has allowed the fewest runs to score, and is in the number one position in winning percentage titles also.

Grover Alexander overtook Walter Johnson in the most innings pitched department, but Johnson is far in front of any other pitcher in strikeout crowns.

The great Cy Young is on top in two major categories. No pitcher has won as many shutout titles, and one of the reasons for this is that Cy has an unbelievable total of 14 least bases on balls allowed titles. That, of course, is a record no other pitcher has even approached.

Tony Mullane was the first pioneer pitcher to show relief pitching talent, and he has been tied for the most saves lead by Firpo Marberry and Bruce Sutter.

When the longevity factor is considered, Cy Young is again at the top of the list with Walter Johnson and Grover Alexander close behind. Are these the three greatest pitchers of all time? Should they rank exactly in that order? Many experts would also list Lefty Grove, Christy Mathewson, Sandy Koufax and Warren Spahn among this elite group. What do you think?

CHAPTER 12

MANAGERS SEASON RECORDS

NATIONAL LEAGUE QUIZ

1. Can you name the first manager to lead his team to 100 wins in one season?
2. Do you know the manager who has suffered the most losses?
3. The highest winning percentage ever established by a manager for one season is .798. Name this manager.
4. Which manager won the pennant by the most games?
5. The most wins ever recorded for one season is 116. It happened in 1906. Can you name the manager?

AMERICAN LEAGUE QUIZ

1. This fine manager guided his team to 111 victories in 1954. Name him.
2. Connie Mack was the first American League manager to win 100 or more games in one season. Exactly how many did he win?

3. Who was the New York Yankee manager in 1927 when the team won 110 games?
4. This famous manager won the pennant by 23 games, the most in American League history. Do you know him?
5. Can you name the manager with the most losses?

MAJOR LEAGUE QUIZ

1. Can you name the manager of the first team to win the pennant?
2. John McGraw had his best season in 1904. How many games did his Giants win?
3. The highest winning percentage in Major League history is .832. Do you know this manager?
4. Who was the first manager to lose 100 or more games in one season?
5. Which manager won the pennant by the most games after 1900?

NATIONAL LEAGUE

Most Wins

1876	Al Spalding, Chi	52
1879	George Wright, Bos	59
1880	Cap Anson, Chi	67
1885	Cap Anson, Chi	87
1886	Cap Anson, Chi	90
1892	Frank Selee, Bos	102
1898	Frank Selee, Bos	103
1902	Fred Clarke, Pit	103
1904	John McGraw, NY	106
1906	**Frank Chance, Chi**	**116**

Most Losses

1876	Charlie Gould, Cin	56
1880	John Clapp, Cin	59
1883	Blondie Purcell, Phi	68
1884	Jack Chapman, Det	84
1890	Guy Hecker, Pit	113
1962	**Casey Stengel, NY**	**120**

Highest Winning Percentage

1876	Al Spalding, Chi	.788
1880	**Cap Anson, Chi**	**.798**

Highest Winning Percentage after 1900

1906	**Frank Chance, Chi**	**.763**

DID YOU KNOW . . . *That in 1876, after rain had fallen for five minutes, the game could be called at the request of either team captain?*

Most Games Won Pennant By

1876	Al Spalding, Chi	6
1877	Harry Wright, Bos	7
1880	Cap Anson, Chi	15
1902	**Fred Clarke, Pit**	**27.5**

DID YOU KNOW . . . *That the first NL season started on March 15, and extended until November 15? There were eight teams; they played each other ten times, five at home and five away, for a 70-game schedule.*

NATIONAL LEAGUE SUMMARY

Top Record Producers

1	Cap Anson, Chi	5
2	Al Spalding, Chi	3
3	Fred Clarke, Pit	2
3	Frank Selee, Bos	2

Most Outstanding Record Producers

Cap Anson, Chi	5 for 142 years
Fred Clarke, Pit	2 for 88 years
Frank Chance, Chi	1 for 82 years

AMERICAN LEAGUE

Most Wins

1901	Clark Griffith, Chi	83
1902	Connie Mack, Phi	83
1903	Jimmy Collins, Bos	91
1904	Jimmy Collins, Bos	95
1909	Hugh Jennings, Det	98
1910	Connie Mack, Phi	102
1912	Jake Stahl, Bos	105
1927	Miller Huggins, NY	110
1954	**Al Lopez, Cle**	**111**

Most Losses

1901	Hugh Duffy, Mil	89
1903	Tom Loftus, Was	94
1904	Patsy Donovan, Was	97
1905	Jimmy McAleer, StL	99
1907	Joe Cantillon, Was	102
1909	Joe Cantillon, Was	110
1916	**Connie Mack, Phi**	**117**

Highest Winning Percentage

1901	Clark Griffith, Chi	.610
1902	Connie Mack, Phi	.610
1903	Jimmy Collins, Bos	.659
1910	Connie Mack, Phi	.680
1912	Jake Stahl, Bos	.691
1927	Miller Huggins, NY	.714
1954	**Al Lopez, Cle**	**.721**

Most Games Won Pennant By

1901	Clark Griffith, Chi	4
1902	Connie Mack, Phi	5
1903	Jimmy Collins, Bos	14.5
1910	Connie Mack, Phi	14.5
1923	**Miller Huggins, NY**	**23**

DID YOU KNOW . . . *That in 1876, if a ball became lost during a game, a new ball was put into play by the umpire only after both teams looked for the ball for five minutes?*

AMERICAN LEAGUE SUMMARY

Top Record Producers

1	Jimmy Collins, Bos	4
1	Connie Mack, Phi	4
3	Clark Griffith, Chi	3
3	Miller Huggins, NY	3

Most Outstanding Record Producers

Miller Huggins, NY	3 for 119 years
Al Lopez, Cle	2 for 68 years
Jake Stahl, Bos	2 for 30 years

MAJOR LEAGUE

Most Wins

1876	Al Spalding, Chi, NL	52
1879	George Wright, Pro, NL	59
1880	Cap Anson, Chi, NL	67
1884	Henry Lucas, StL, UL	94
1887	Charlie Comiskey, StL, AA	95
1892	Frank Selee, Bos, NL	102
1898	Frank Selee, Bos, NL	102
1902	Fred Clarke, Pit, NL	103
1904	John McGraw, NY, NL	106
1906	**Frank Chance, Chi, NL**	**116**

Most Losses

1876	Charlie Gould, Cin, NL	56
1880	John Clapp, Cin, NL	59
1883	Billy Barnie, Bal, AA	68
1884	Jack Chapman, Det, NL	84
1887	Jimmy Williams, Cle, AA	92
1890	Guy Hecker, Pit, NL	113
1916	Connie Mack, Phi, AL	117
1962	**Casey Stengel, NY, NL**	**120**

Highest Winning Percentage

1876	Al Spalding, Chi, NL	.788
1880	Cap Anson, Chi, NL	.798
1884	**Henry Lucas, StL, UL**	**.832**

Highest Winning Percentage after 1900

1900	Ned Hanlon, Bkn, NL	.603
1901	Fred Clarke, Pit, NL	.647
1902	Fred Clarke, Pit, NL	.741
1906	**Frank Chance, Chi, NL**	**.763**

Most Games Won Pennant By

1876	Al Spalding, Chi, NL	6
1877	Harry Wright, Bos, NL	7
1880	Cap Anson, Chi, NL	15
1884	**Henry Lucas, StL, UL**	**35.5**

Most Games Won Pennant By after 1900

1900	Ned Hanlon, Bkn, NL	4.5
1901	Fred Clarke, Pit, NL	7.5
1902	**Fred Clarke, Pit, NL**	**27.5**

MAJOR LEAGUE SUMMARY

Top Record Producers

1	Henry Lucas, StL, UL	3
1	Cap Anson, Chi, NL	3
1	Al Spalding, Chi, NL	3

Most Outstanding Record Producers

Henry Lucas, StL, UL	3 for 211 years
Frank Chance, Chi, NL	1 for 82 years
Cap Anson, Chi, NL	3 for 12 years

Clark Griffith of the White Sox won the first AL pennant in 1901, and he was followed by the great Connie Mack in 1902. Mack became the first AL manager to win 100 games when he won the pennant for a second time in 1910. Jake Stahl and Miller Huggins also topped 100 wins and Al Lopez of the 1954 Indians won 111 games to capture the all-time AL mark. This also gives him the highest winning percentage mark at .721.

Miller Huggins has the distinction of winning the pennant by the most games, as he led the 1923 Yankees to victory by 23 games.

It has long been said that a manager is only as good as the teams he has to work with. Connie Mack managed to set records for both team wins and team losses.

Al Spalding was the first manager to win the pennant, while also serving as his own star pitcher. In 1876 he was a one-man pitching staff, who won 47 and lost 13. Spalding had been lured away from the Boston team of the National Association in 1875 by William Hulbert, the founder of the National League. Spalding later went on to form the Spalding Sporting Goods Company that we know today.

Cap Anson was also a playing manager, and his .798 winning percentage in 1880 remains the NL high.

FRED CLARKE

This Hall of Famer had a sensational 21-year career, in 19 of those years he also was a player-manager. This didn't stop him from having a lifetime batting average of .315. He also set records for assists and total chances as a leftfielder.

JOHN McGRAW
The feisty manager of the New York Giants owns many managerial records. He brought his team to the World Series a record 10 times, though he escaped with only a 3–7 record there.

Fred Clarke was another playing manager (they were common in the early days), and he won the pennant by more games than any NL manager.

In 1892, Frank Selee of Boston became baseball's first manager to win 100 games. Selee did it again in 1898, and Fred Clarke matched his 103 wins in 1902 when he won the pennant by 27½ games.

Frank Chance continues to hold the most wins crown, with 116 in 1906, while Casey Stengel's expansion-team Mets take the cake for most losses, with 120 in 1962. This prompted the mighty Casey to ask in despair, "Can't anybody here play this game?" However, it seems unfair to pin this record on an expansion team. This is just another one of the many reasons why some records should be separated into special categories.

John McGraw added his name to the 100 wins club by leading the Giants to the pennant in 1904 with 106 wins. This record was short-lived, however; Frank Chance set the all-time high, with 116 wins, in 1906.

In 1884, in the Union League (which is also considered a "major league"), Henry Lucas led a St. Louis team with 94 wins and only 19 losses, to set the all-time winning percentage record at .832. This also resulted in the record for most games by which any team has ever won a pennant, a whopping 35½ games.

CHAPTER 13

MANAGERS CAREER RECORDS

NATIONAL LEAGUE QUIZ

1. Can you name the first manager to have a 20-year career?
2. This outstanding manager lasted an amazing 33 years as a manager. Do you know him?
3. Who was the first manager to win and lose 1000 games?
4. Name the first manager to win 1500 games.
5. The highest winning percentage is .608. Name this manager.

AMERICAN LEAGUE QUIZ

1. This exceptional gentleman devoted 50 years of his life to managing in the American League. Who was he?
2. Can you name the first manager to lose 2000 games?
3. Two New York Yankee managers have compiled agers and the one who has the highest winning percentage.
4. Do you know the manager who has won the most pennants?
5. Two outstanding managers have participated in eight World Series. Do you remember them?

MAJOR LEAGUE QUIZ

1. These Hall of Famers each managed for 20 years. Name them.
2. Who was the first manager to manage 4000 games?
3. This longlasting manager has won 3776 games, the most in baseball history. Who is he?
4. Two great managers are tied for the most pennants won with ten. Do you know them?
5. Name the manager who has won the most World Series games.

NATIONAL LEAGUE	AMERICAN LEAGUE	MAJOR LEAGUE

Most Years

1876–83	Bob Ferguson, Tro	8
1876–93	Harry Wright, Phi	18
1879–98	Cap Anson, Chi	20
1899–32	**John McGraw, NY**	**33**

Most Years (American League)

1901–06	Jimmy Collins, Bos	6
1901–11	Jimmy McAleer, StL	11
1901–20	Clark Griffith, Was	17
1901–50	**Connie Mack, Phi**	**50**

Most Years (Major League)

1878–83	John Clapp, NY, NL	4
1876–87	Bob Ferguson, Tro, NL	11
1876–93	Harry Wright, Phi, NL	18
1879–98	Cap Anson, Chi, NL	20
1901–20	Clark Griffith, Was, AL	20
1899–32	John McGraw, NY, NL	33
1894–50	**Connie Mack, Phi, AL**	**53**

Most Games

1876–83	Bob Ferguson, Tro	478
1885–91	Jim Mutrie, NY	904
1876–93	Harry Wright, Phi	1917
1879–98	Cap Anson, Chi	2296
1889–07	Ned Hanlon, Bkn	2402
1897–15	Fred Clarke, Pit	2822
1899–32	**John McGraw, NY**	**4681**

Most Games (American League)

1901–06	Jimmy Collins, Bos	864
1901–11	Jimmy McAleer, StL	1658
1901–20	Clark Griffith, Was	2444
1901–50	**Connie Mack, Phi**	**7590**

Most Games (Major League)

1878–83	John Clapp, NY, NL	323
1876–87	Bob Ferguson, Tro, NL	653
1879–89	Horace Phillips, Pit, NL	782
1883–91	Jim Mutrie, NY, NL	1113
1876–93	Harry Wright, Phi, NL	1917
1879–98	Cap Anson, Chi, NL	2296
1889–07	Ned Hanlon, Bkn, NL	2530
1897–15	Fred Clarke, Pit, NL	2822
1901–20	Clark Griffith, Was, AL	2916
1899–32	John McGraw, NY, NL	4879
1894–50	**Connie Mack, Phi, AL**	**7878**

DID YOU KNOW... *That when the NL was formed in 1876, the entry fee for each team was $100?*

Most Wins

1876–83	Bob Ferguson, Tro	234
1885–91	Jim Mutrie, NY	529
1876–93	Harry Wright, Phi	1042
1879–98	Cap Anson, Chi	1297
1897–15	Fred Clarke, Pit	1602
1899–32	**John McGraw, NY**	**2744**

Most Wins (American League)

1901–06	Jimmy Collins, Bos	464
1901–11	Jimmy McAleer, StL	736
1901–20	Clark Griffith, Was	1269
1901–50	**Connie Mack, Phi**	**3627**

Most Wins (Major League)

1878–83	John Clapp, NY, NL	137
1876–87	Bob Ferguson, Tro, NL	292
1879–89	Horace Phillips, Pit, NL	339
1883–91	Jim Mutrie, NY, NL	658
1876–93	Harry Wright, Phi, NL	1042
1879–98	Cap Anson, Chi, NL	1297
1889–07	Ned Hanlon, Bkn, NL	1315
1897–15	Fred Clarke, Pit, NL	1602
1899–32	John McGraw, NY, NL	2840
1894–50	**Connie Mack, Phi, AL**	**3776**

DID YOU KNOW... *That in 1876 the winning team was rewarded by being able to keep the game balls?*

Most Losses

1876–83	Bob Ferguson, Tro	236
1885–91	Jim Mutrie, NY	345
1876–93	Harry Wright, Phi	848
1879–98	Cap Anson, Chi	957
1889–07	Ned Hanlon, Bkn	1097
1897–15	Fred Clarke, Pit	1179
1899–32	**John McGraw, NY**	**1885**

Most Losses (American League)

1901–06	Jimmy Collins, Bos	389
1901–11	Jimmy McAleer, StL	889
1901–20	Clark Griffith, StL	1129
1901–50	**Connie Mack, Phi**	**3891**

Most Losses (Major League)

1878–83	John Clapp, NY, NL	177
1876–87	Bob Ferguson, Tro, NL	351
1879–90	Horace Phillips, Pit, NL	433
1876–93	Harry Wright, Phi, NL	848
1879–98	Cap Anson, Chi, NL	957
1889–07	Ned Hanlon, Bkn, NL	1165
1897–15	Fred Clarke, Pit, NL	1179
1901–20	Clark Griffith, Was, AL	1367
1899–32	John McGraw, NY, NL	1984
1894–50	**Connie Mack, Phi, AL**	**4025**

Highest Winning Percentage

1876–83	Bob Ferguson, Tro	.490
1885–91	**Jim Mutrie, NY**	**.608**

Highest Winning Percentage (American League)

1901–06	Jimmy Collins, Bos	.544
1905–09	Nap Lajoie, Cle	.546
1915–18	Pants Rowland, Chi	.578
1918–29	Miller Huggins, NY	.595
1931–50	Joe McCarthy, NY	.621
1949–60	**Casey Stengel, NY**	**.623**

Highest Winning Percentage (Major League)

1878–83	John Clapp, NY, NL	.436
1876–87	Bob Ferguson, Tro, NL	.454
1884–91	Bill Sharsig, Phi, AA	.529
1883–91	Jim Mutrie, NY, NL	.611
1926–50	**Joe McCarthy, NY, AL**	**.614**

Most Pennants Won

1885–91	Jim Mutrie, NY	3
1879–98	Cap Anson, Chi	5
1890–05	Frank Selee, Bos	5
1889–07	Ned Hanlon, Bkn	5
1899–32	**John McGraw, NY**	**10**

Most Pennants Won (American League)

1901–06	Jimmy Collins, Bos	2
1907–20	Hugh Jennings, Det	3
1918–29	Miller Huggins, NY	6
1901–50	Connie Mack, Phi	9
1949–60	**Casey Stengel, NY**	**10**

Most Pennants Won (Major League)

1883–91	Jim Mutrie, NY, NL	3
1883–94	Charlie Comiskey, StL, AA	4
1879–98	Cap Anson, Chi, NL	5
1890–05	Frank Selee, Bos, NL	5
1889–07	Ned Hanlon, Bkn, NL	5
1913–29	Miller Huggins, NY, AL	6
1899–32	**John McGraw, NY, NL**	**10**
1934–65	**Casey Stengel, NY, AL**	**10**

NATIONAL LEAGUE

Most Consecutive Pennants Won

1877–78	Harry Wright, Bos	2
1880–82	Cap Anson, Chi	3
1921–24	**John McGraw, NY**	**4**

Most World Series Games Managed

1905–12	Frank Chance, Chi	21
1899–32	**John McGraw, NY**	**55**

Most World Series Managed

1905–12	Frank Chance, Chi	4
1899–32	**John McGraw, NY**	**10**

Most World Series Won

1905–12	Frank Chance, Chi	2
1899–32	John McGraw, NY	3
1954–76	**Walt Alston, LA**	**4**

Most World Series Games Won

1905–12	Frank Chance, Chi	11
1899–32	**John McGraw, NY**	**26**

Most World Series Games Lost

1905–12	Frank Chance, Chi	9
1899–32	**John McGraw, NY**	**28**

Most Consecutive World Series Won

1907–08	Frank Chance	2
1959–65	**Walter Alston, LA**	**3**

DID YOU KNOW...*That in 1876 a damaged ball could not be replaced unless agreed upon by both team captains?*

AMERICAN LEAGUE

Most Consecutive Pennants Won

1903–04	Jimmy Collins, Bos	2
1907–09	Hugh Jennings, Det	3
1921–23	Miller Huggins, NY	3
1926–28	Miller Huggins, NY	3
1929–31	Connie Mack, Phi	3
1936–39	Joe McCarthy, NY	4
1949–53	**Casey Stengel, NY**	**5**

Most World Series Games Managed

1901–06	Jimmy Collins, Bos	8
1905–13	Jake Stahl, Bos	8
1907–20	Hugh Jennings, Det	16
1918–29	Miller Huggins, NY	34
1901–50	Connie Mack, Phi	43
1949–60	**Casey Stengel, NY**	**63**

Most World Series Managed

1901–06	Jimmy Collins, Bos	1
1905–13	Jake Stahl, Bos	1
1904–18	Fielder Jones, Chi	1
1907–20	Hugh Jennings, Det	3
1918–29	Miller Huggins, NY	6
1901–50	Connie Mack, Phi	8
1931–50	Joe McCarthy, NY	8
1949–60	**Casey Stengel, NY**	**10**

Most World Series Won

1901–06	Jimmy Collins, Bos	1
1905–13	Jake Stahl, Bos	1
1904–18	Fielder Jones, Chi	1
1918–29	Miller Huggins, NY	3
1931–50	**Joe McCarthy, NY**	**7**
1949–60	**Casey Stengel, NY**	**7**

Most World Series Games Won

1901–06	Jimmy Collins, Bos	5
1918–29	Miller Huggins, NY	18
1931–50	Joe McCarthy, NY	29
1949–60	**Casey Stengel, NY**	**37**

Most World Series Games Lost

1901–06	Jimmy Collins, Bos	3
1905–13	Jake Stahl, Bos	3
1907–20	Hugh Jennings, Det	12
1918–29	Miller Huggins, NY	15
1901–50	Connie Mack, Phi	19
1949–60	**Casey Stengel, NY**	**26**

Most Consecutive World Series Won

1910–13	Connie Mack, Phi	2
1915–16	Bill Carrigan, Bos	2
1927–28	Miller Huggins, NY	2
1932–41	**Joe McCarthy, NY**	**6**

MAJOR LEAGUE

Most Consecutive Pennants Won

1877–78	Harry Wright, Bos, NL	2
1880–82	Cap Anson, Chi, NL	3
1885–88	Charlie Comiskey, StL, AA	4
1921–24	John McGraw, NY, NL	4
1936–39	Joe McCarthy, NY, AL	4
1949–53	**Casey Stengel, NY, AL**	**5**

Most World Series Games Managed

1897–15	Fred Clarke, Pit, NL	15
1907–20	Hugh Jennings, Det, AL	16
1905–23	Frank Chance, Chi, NL	21
1913–29	Miller Huggins, NY, AL	34
1899–32	John McGraw, NY, NL	55
1934–65	**Casey Stengel, NY, AL**	**63**

Most World Series Managed

1897–15	Fred Clarke, Pit, NL	2
1907–20	Hugh Jennings, Det, AL	3
1905–23	Frank Chance, Chi, NL	4
1899–32	**John McGraw, NY, NL**	**10**
1934–65	**Casey Stengel, NY, AL**	**10**

Most World Series Won

1901–06	Jimmy Collins, Bos, AL	1
1897–15	Fred Clarke, Pit, NL	1
1905–23	Frank Chance, Chi, NL	2
1913–29	Miller Huggins, NY, AL	3
1899–32	John McGraw, NY, NL	3
1926–50	**Joe McCarthy, NY, AL**	**7**
1934–65	**Casey Stengel, NY, AL**	**7**

Most World Series Games Won

1901–06	Jimmy Collins, Bos, AL	5
1897–15	Fred Clarke, Pit, NL	7
1905–23	Frank Chance, Chi, NL	11
1913–29	Miller Huggins, NY, AL	18
1899–32	John McGraw, NY, NL	26
1926–50	Joe McCarthy, NY, AL	29
1934–65	**Casey Stengel, NY, AL**	**37**

Most World Series Games Lost

1901–06	Jimmy Collins, Bos, AL	3
1897–15	Fred Clarke, Pit, NL	8
1907–20	Hugh Jennings, Det, AL	12
1913–29	Miller Huggins, NY, AL	15
1899–32	**John McGraw, NY, NL**	**28**

Most Consecutive World Series Won

1907–08	Frank Chance, Chi, NL	2
1910–13	Connie Mack, Phi, AL	3
1932–41	**Joe McCarthy, NY, AL**	**6**

DID YOU KNOW...*That William Hulbert founded the National League in February 1876?*

NATIONAL LEAGUE		AMERICAN LEAGUE		MAJOR LEAGUE	

Highest Winning Percentage
(minimum 3 series)

1905–12 Frank Chance, Chi   .550

Highest Winning Percentage
(min. 3 series)

1907–20	Hugh Jennings, Det	.250
1918–29	Miller Huggins, NY	.545
1932–43	Joe McCarthy, NY	.783

Highest Winning Percentage
(min. 3 series)

1905–23	Frank Chance, Chi, NL	.550
1926–50	Joe McCarthy, NY, AL	.698

NATIONAL LEAGUE SUMMARY

Top Record Producers

1	John McGraw, NY	9
2	Frank Chance, Chi	6
3	Cap Anson, Chi	5
4	Jim Mutrie, NY	4
4	Bob Ferguson, Tro	4
4	Harry Wright, Bos	4

Most Outstanding Record Producers

John McGraw, NY	9 for 500 years
Frank Chance, Chi	6 for 137 years
Jim Mutrie, NY	4 for 108 years
Cap Anson, Chi	5 for 102 years
Bob Ferguson, Tro	4 for 34 years
Fred Clarke, Pit	4 for 34 years

AMERICAN LEAGUE SUMMARY

Top Record Producers

1	Jimmy Collins, Bos	10
1	Miller Huggins, NY	10
2	Connie Mack, Phi	8
3	Joe McCarthy, NY	7
3	Casey Stengel, NY	7

Most Outstanding Record Producers

Casey Stengel, NY	7 for 203 years
Miller Huggins, NY	10 for 176 years
Connie Mack, Phi	8 for 155 years
Joe McCarthy, NY	7 for 146 years
Jimmy Collins, Bos	10 for 82 years

MAJOR LEAGUE SUMMARY

Top Record Producers

1	John McGraw, NY, NL	9
2	Joe McCarthy, NY, AL	6
2	Casey Stengel, NY, AL	6
2	Fred Clarke, Pit, NL	6
5	Connie Mack, Phi, AL	5
5	Cap Anson, Chi, NL	5

Most Outstanding Record Producers

John McGraw, NY, NL	9 for 212 years
Joe McCarthy, NY, AL	6 for 190 years
Connie Mack, Phi, AL	5 for 180 years
Casey Stengel, NY, AL	6 for 150 years
Jim Mutrie, NY, NL	4 for 65 years

The statistics in this and the previous chapter give an excellent accounting of the greatness of John McGraw. His 11 unbroken records are more than any manager. He is certainly the most dominant manager in National League history.

Frank Chance was also an exceptional manager, and his 13 records land him in second place.

Cap Anson was the first manager to complete a 20-year career, and he holds the third position, with 19 marks for 323 years.

Henry Lucas established only two records, but each of them remains unbroken after 104 years for a 208-year total. No other manager ever won the pennant by more games or finished a season with a higher winning percentage than Lucas.

There are many who say the game of baseball has not changed since Alexander Cartwright first placed the bases 90 feet apart. But that has been the only thing that has not changed. There have been drastic changes in every aspect of the game, and changes have also taken place in managing.

At first there were many player-managers; now it is rare to see this. In the early years, managers were not fired as quickly as they are today, and as a result modern-day managers will never break the longevity records of John McGraw's 33 years in the National League and Connie Mack's 50 years in the American League. One reason why Connie Mack lasted all those years was because he owned the team, and he was reluctant to leave even after all those years. He is quoted as saying, "I am not leaving because I want to, but because a lot of people around here want me to leave." There will most likely never again be a manager to break Mack's records in games managed, won and lost.

Although Connie Mack was a fine gentleman and contributed a lot to the game of baseball, he was not the greatest manager of all time. He never had the record for highest winning percentage even though his nine pennants rank second in American League history. Top honors in that department go to the "Old Perfessor," Casey Stengel of the Yankees.

Stengel can also boast of having won five consecutive pennants, the only manager ever to accomplish this feat. In all, Casey won ten pennants and managed in a record 63 games, of which he won 37 en route to winning seven World Series.

Miller Huggins and Joe McCarthy certainly deserve to be mentioned as two of the premier managers. McCarthy is tied with Stengel for World Series won with seven, and his six consecutive World Series wins and .783 winning percentage have never been bettered.

CONNIE MACK

Before Connie Mack became a manager, he put in 11 years as a player. In fact, he set a double play record for catchers in 1887. Still, it's as a manager that Cornelius MacGillicuddy is best remembered. He led the Philadelphia Athletics through thick and thin for 53 years.

Connie Mack is the senior citizen of Major League managers. No one has ever, or will ever, come close to his 53 years on the job.

Mack began his managing career while still a player with the Pirates in the National League. He took over the team near the end of the 1894 season and posted 12 wins and 10 losses. As a player that year, he batted .250 while catching in 69 games. He managed the Pirates for two more years, at which time he retired as a player to devote full time to managing. Four years went by, however, before a managerial offer came, in 1901, when he started his 50-year reign as the manager of the

Philadelphia Athletics. (It helped that he also owned the team.) He won pennants in 1902, 1905, 1910, 1911, 1913 and 1914, and then hit a long dry spell that resulted in seven consecutive last place finishes. Certainly he hadn't all of a sudden become a poor manager; he simply did not have the players who could get the job done. And it was to be yet another long spell before he could put winning teams together. There were no pennants from 1912 to 1928, but in 1929, 1930 and 1931 he won three consecutive pennants. They proved to be his last titles, as there were no more during the last 18 years of his career.

CASEY STENGEL

"The Old Perfesser" set many managing records, although he enjoyed more success leading the Bronx Bombers than he did when he tried to jumpstart the terrible 1962 Mets.

Miller Huggins can be proud of winning the pennant by more games than any American League manager. His winning three pennants in a row twice has never been equalled.

Perhaps the two greatest managers in American League history are Joe McCarthy and Casey Stengel, both of the Yankees. McCarthy was the first American League manager to retire with a winning percentage over .600. His .614 average is the highest in Major League history. "Marse Joe," as he was called, was also the first to win four consecutive pennants and manage in eight World Series, and he is tied with Stengel for most World Series wins with seven.

McCarthy is second to Stengel in World Series games won, 29 to 37, but Joe has the highest World Series winning percentage of any manager in the Major Leagues.

Many fans would say that Casey Stengel was the best manager in the game, in light of the fact that the "Old Perfessor" has 13 records that no other managers have been able to break. Casey is tied with John "Muggsy" McGraw for most pennants won; they are the only two who have won ten pennants. But no one can match Casey in consecutive pennants won, World Series games managed, and World Series games won.

Now the question is, who is the greatest manager of all time? McCarthy, Stengel and McGraw would certainly be in the top five. Who would be your choices?

BIBLIOGRAPHY

Carter, Craig, ed.
The Complete Baseball Record Book
St. Louis, Missouri: The Sporting News, 1987

Murray, Tom
SPORT Magazine's All-Time All-Stars
New York: Atheneum, 1977

Reichler, Joseph L., ed.
*The Baseball Encyclopedia: The Complete & Official Record of
Major League Baseball*
New York: Macmillan, 1987

Seymour, Harold
Baseball: The Early Years
Toronto: Oxford University Press, 1960

Siwoff, Seymour
The Book of Baseball Records
New York: Sterling, 1981

Smith Robert
The Pioneers of Baseball
Boston: Little, Brown & Co., 1978

Turkin, Hy, and S.C. Thompson
The Official Encyclopedia of Baseball, 10th edition
South Brunswick, N.J.: A.S. Barnes, 1979